CULTURAL HERITAGE LAW AND POLICY

Series Editors

The Concept of Cultural Genocide

CULTURAL HERITAGE LAW AND POLICY

The aim of this series is to publish significant and original research on, and scholarly analysis of, all aspects of cultural heritage law through the lens of international law, private international law, and comparative law. The series is wide in scope, traversing disciplines, regions, and viewpoints. Topics given particular prominence are those which, while of interest to academic lawyers, have significant bearing on policymaking and current public discourse on the interaction between art, heritage, and the law.

The Concept of Cultural Genocide

An International Law Perspective

ELISA NOVIC

OXFORD
UNIVERSITY PRESS

OXFORD
UNIVERSITY PRESS

Great Clarendon Street, Oxford, OX2 6DP,
United Kingdom

Oxford University Press is a department of the University of Oxford.
It furthers the University's objective of excellence in research, scholarship,
and education by publishing worldwide. Oxford is a registered trade mark of
Oxford University Press in the UK and in certain other countries

First Edition published in 2016

Impression: 1

Published in the United States of America by Oxford University Press
198 Madison Avenue, New York, NY 10016, United States of America

British Library Cataloguing in Publication Data
Data available

Library of Congress Control Number: 2016953199

ISBN 978–0–19–878716–7

Printed and bound by
CPI Group (UK) Ltd, Croydon, CR0 4YY

Series Editors' Preface

The conceptualization of genocide has been contested in international law since the adoption of the Genocide Convention in 1948. The parameters of the definition of genocide were especially tested before the International Criminal Tribunal for the Former Yugoslavia (ICTY) and the International Criminal Court (ICC) since the 1990s. The deliberate and immeasurable damage inflicted upon cultural heritage during the Yugoslav wars was the focal point of this drive to revisit the definition of genocide in international law.

Elisa Novic's book addresses an old problem in a new, refreshing, and multidisciplinary perspective. For decades the question of the cultural elements of genocide has occupied the literature in many fields of research, from law to historiography to anthropology and cultural studies. The legal scholarship on the subject has been predominantly concentrated within the domain of treaty law and criminal law, due to the overwhelming influence of the 1948 United Nations Convention on the Prevention and Punishment of the Crime of Genocide. This has led to conceptualizing the issue of genocide and the related hypothesis of 'cultural genocide' within the perspective of individual criminal responsibility under international law. The great merit of this book is that the author has placed the issue of cultural genocide within the broader perspective of customary international law, going beyond the limits of the treaty law deriving from the Genocide Convention, taking into account the important developments that in this broader context have taken place in the area of human rights, cultural heritage law, and state responsibility for wrongful acts. This permits the author to break out of the sterile dilemma whether the specific crime of genocide includes also cultural genocide and has led to the convincing conclusion: that the various manifestations of what has been until now labelled as 'cultural genocide' cannot be re-conducted to a fixed criminal figure of genocide, but are part of an evolutionary concept to be subsumed in the more general category of crimes against humanity and more precisely that of 'persecution'. Novic engages in thorough research of the various strands of international and national judicial practice and thoughtfully engages relevant literature from the field of history, anthropology, and social science. She deploys this to promote the dynamic evolution of international law from the original, treaty-based notion of genocide as a crime entailing individual responsibility under international law, to a collective crime of the state involving state responsibility and entailing the obligation to make reparation to victims.

It is an important contribution not only to the development of international cultural heritage law but also to international criminal law as it relates to the protection of cultural heritage and human rights.

Francesco Francioni and Ana Filipa Vrdoljak

Preface

This book offers a contemporary and exhaustive analysis of the long-lasting debate on cultural genocide in international law. Cultural genocide is both a persistent claim from alleged victim groups—predominantly minorities and indigenous peoples—as well as a persistent legal issue, evidenced by the regular resurgence of the question in the international legal discourse. This book therefore covers the evolution of international law in relation to the concept of cultural genocide since its original coining by Raphael Lemkin in his 1944 *Axis Rule in Occupied Europe*, through its rejection from the 1948 Convention on the Prevention and Punishment of the Crime of Genocide, until the most recent occurrences of the concept in international law. In light of these developments, it argues that the codification of cultural genocide, not to mention its criminalization, is unlikely to happen. Not only has the concept of cultural genocide itself evolved, so as to become difficult to be encapsulated in one single legal concept, but international norms have also proliferated in relation to the three underlying elements of cultural genocide: group, culture, and genocide.

Against this background, the text advances several ways to strengthen the international legal approach to intentional attacks against group cultures, and to ultimately settle the issue of cultural genocide. This tailored and multifaceted response relies on the identification of synergies between the various existing international legal norms and categories. Confronting an inherently international legal issue, which is located at the crossroads of several disciplines of international law, this book both reconstructs the various elements of cultural genocide within international law and provides an integrated approach of international law in respect of the concept of cultural genocide. It addresses and connects various topics such as the protection of groups, communities, and individuals, the criminalization of attacks against group cultures, state responsibility for failing to protect human rights, prevention of cultural crimes and unlawful acts, and reparation. The analysis is enriched with findings made in other academic disciplines, such as anthropology, sociology, history, and the field of 'genocide studies'.

As such, this book intends to bridge the gap between legal and non-legal scholarship on the topic of cultural genocide, by both showing the limits and promises of an international law-based approach to the complex topic of cultural genocide.

Elisa Novic

Acknowledgements

The (happy) outcome of a journey, which started in 2010 at the European University Institute, the person to be acknowledged first and foremost in respect of this book is my supervisor, Professor Francioni, for his precious guidance and support throughout the years of Ph.D. and up until the point of this publication. I am also incredibly grateful to my co-supervisor, Professor Dirk Moses, for having so kindly introduced me to new frontiers of academic scholarship, as well as to Ana Vrdoljak and Yvonne Donders for their comments at the thesis defence and their warm encouragement to transform the thesis into a book.

This work would not have been possible without the financial and material support provided by the French *Ministère de l'Enseignement Supérieur et de la Recherche* and the European University Institute.

I would also like to thank Oxford University Press for offering me this opportunity to publish, as well as the three anonymous reviewers for helping me to improve the quality of the manuscript. Special thanks go to Nicole Leyland, for having made the publication process a smooth one.

While the final result of these years is a written production, the process has involved more talking and travelling than I would have previously anticipated. Amongst the numerous people who have devoted some of their time to provide me with feedback, encouraged me in the difficult moments and challenged my ideas in a stimulated way, I wish to address special thanks to Morten Bergsmo, Martin Scheinin, Payam Akhavan, Menachem Rosensaft, Elsa Stamatopoulou, Loïc Azoulai, and Mario Buil-Merce. Furthermore, I would like to thank all of the people who patiently answered my numerous questions in Bosnia and Herzegovina in July 2013. I am also extremely grateful to Professor Sarah Cleveland for having sponsored me as a visiting fellow at Columbia University, as well as to Bernard Duhaime and Mirja Trilsch for having so kindly welcomed me at L'Université du Québec à Montréal (UQÀM) and integrated me into the Human Rights Clinique team.

One person in particular should receive the greatest amount of thanks: Stephanie Law, 'sparring partner', language corrector, and, above all, friend. Warm thanks further go to Priya Urs for the great language and friendly support during the last steps. These friendly thanks need to be extended to all those who remained available and understanding throughout these years: Antoine, Marion, Camille, Inés, Jorge, Romain, Anjela, Emma, Caroline, Clara, Juliette, Dženeta, Elise, Astrid, and Špela as well as those who I may have unfortunately omitted.

Finally, I thank my family for being such a great one and for having supported me *et supportée*: Michael and Andreea, who accompanied me so nicely in the last steps of the Ph.D. and entertained me throughout the endless Montreal winter;

Grand Mère, who honoured and surprised me with her presence throughout these years, whether in New York or Florence; and my parents, in respect of whom words hardly describe the extent of support they have provided to me. I take this occasion to remember my grandparents, Léon and Renée, unconditional supporters of their granddaughter.

Table of Contents

Table of Cases

INTERNATIONAL CASES

African Commission of Human and Peoples' Rights

Eritrea Ethiopia Claims Commission

European Committee on Social Rights

European Court of Human Rights

Extraordinary Chambers in the Courts of Cambodia

Inter-American Court of Human Rights

International Court of Justice

International Criminal Court

International Criminal Tribunal for Former Yugoslavia

International Criminal Tribunal for Rwanda

International Military Tribunals of Nuremberg

Canada

Colombia

Germany

Israel

Spain

Table of Instruments

INTERNATIONAL INSTRUMENTS

NATIONAL INSTRUMENTS

Cambodia

Canada

Guatemala

Israel

Paraguay

List of Abbreviations

AAA	American Anthropological Association
ACHR	American Convention on Human Rights
AComHPR	African Commission on Human and Peoples' Rights
ACHPR	African Charter on Human and Peoples' Rights
CERD	Convention on the Elimination of Racial Discrimination
CPK	Communist Party of Kampuchea
CPNM	Commission for the Protection of National Monuments
CRC	Convention on the Rights of the Child
ECCC	Extraordinary Chambers in the Courts of Cambodia
ECHR	European Convention on Human Rights
ECtHR	European Court of Human Rights
ECOSOC	United Nations Economic and Social Council
ECRML	European Charter for Regional or Minority Languages
EUCFR	European Union Charter of Fundamental Rights
HVO	Croatian Defence Council
IACHR	Inter-American Court of Human Rights
ICC	International Criminal Court
ICCPR	International Covenant on Civil and Political Rights
ICESCR	International Covenant on Economic, Social and Cultural Rights
ICJ	International Court of Justice
ICSPCA	International Convention on the Suppression and Prevention of the Crime of Apartheid
ICTJ	International Center for Transitional Justice
ICTR	International Criminal Tribunal for Rwanda
ICTY	International Criminal Tribunal for the Former Yugoslavia
ILA	International Law Association
ILC	International Law Commission
ILO	International Labour Organisation
OSAPG	Office of the UN Special Adviser on the Prevention of Genocide
OSCE	Organization for Security and Co-operation in Europe
OTP	ICC Office of the Prosecutor
PCIJ	Permanent Court of International Justice
TFV	Trust Fund for Victims of the ICC
UDHR	Universal Declaration of Human Rights
UNDRIP	United Nations Declaration on the Rights of Indigenous Peoples
UNESCO	United Nations Educational, Scientific, and Cultural Organisation
UNGA	United Nations General Assembly
UNPFII	United Nations Permanent Forum on Indigenous Issues
UNSAPG	United Nations Special Adviser on the Prevention of Genocide
UNSG	United Nations Secretary General
USSR	Union of the Soviet Socialist Republics
VCLT	Vienna Convention on the Law of Treaties

1
Introduction

Cultural genocide has emerged as a powerful rhetorical and political tool, which has been engaged in order to call forth the international community's attention and elicit a reaction to serious violations of cultural rights. The most famous example might be that of Tibet, with the Dalai Lama's repeated uses of the term 'cultural genocide' to describe the series of policies imposed on the Tibetans from 1950,[1] including the destruction of monasteries during the cultural revolution, restrictions to religious freedom, the imposition of the Chinese model of development and the massive colonization of Han Chinese people, which all threaten the future of the Tibetan language and culture.[2] The Taliban regime, which prohibited the practice of any culture outside their strict interpretation of Islam, also provoked strong reaction from the international community, in particular following the destruction of major pieces of cultural heritage such as the Buddhas of Bamiyan and the pre-Islamic collection of the Kabul Museum in March 2001. Observers and the official delegation of the Afghan State to the United Nations used the 'cultural genocide' rhetoric to denounce the attack against these aspects of Afghan cultural heritage.[3] The debate on 'cultural genocide' was also revived in the context of the truth and reconciliation processes in Canada and Australia, in relation to the forced transfers of Aboriginal children from their families and communities to foster families and residential schools throughout the nineteenth and twentieth centuries.[4]

[1] See e.g. Reuters, 'Dalai Lama blames Tibetan burning protests on "cultural genocide"', *The Telegraph*, 7 November 2011, available at: http://www.telegraph.co.uk/news/worldnews/asia/china/8874374/Dalai-Lama-blames-suicide-protests-on-Chinese-cultural-genocide.html (last accessed 1 February 2015).

[2] Jean-Christophe Victor, Virginie Raisson, and Franck Tétart, *Le Dessous des Cartes: Atlas Géopolitique* (Paris: Arte Editions; Taillandier, 2005) pp. 132–3; Barry Sautman, '"Cultural Genocide" and Tibet' (2003) 38 *Tex. Int'l L.J.* 173, p. 174: this piece is however biased at the outset by the author's qualification of the Tibetan leadership's claims over Tibet as 'ideology'.

[3] Christina Lamb, *The Sewing Circles of Herat* (New York: Perennial, 2004) p. 233; UNGA 'Agenda Item 46: The Situation in Afghanistan and its Implications for International Peace and Security' (9 March 2001), UNGAOR 55th Session, 94th Plenary Meeting, UN Doc. A/55/PV.94 (Intervention of the Afghan Delegation). The international community did not recognize the Taliban regime as the official government of Afghanistan, so that the state was represented at the UN by the opposition to the Taliban.

[4] Australian Human Rights Commission, *Bringing Them Home, Report of the National Inquiry into the Separation of Aboriginal and Torres Strait Islander Children from Their Families* (April 1997); Truth and Reconciliation Commission of Canada (TRC), *Honouring the Truth, Reconciling for the Future—Summary of the Final Report of the Truth and Reconciliation of Canada* (2015).

From this short account, cultural genocide emerges as potentially applicable to a wide range of experiences; it also already provides a sense of the semantic tension inherent to the concept. On the one hand, it relies on a broad definition of culture and, on the other, it sticks to the concept of genocide, which is defined very narrowly in international law. This introduction will thus seek to draw the contours of the concept of cultural genocide, before addressing the possibilities for international law to address this concept.

1.1 The Concept of Cultural Genocide

The difficulty to define cultural genocide flows from its main core element—culture—which has itself greatly evolved throughout the centuries. For a long time, culture meant 'being cultured' and hence rather focused on cultural products, such as 'the visual arts, music and literature'.[5] This 'humanistic' conception was progressively substituted with an 'anthropological' one, which is 'plural and relativistic':

> The world is divided into different cultures, each worthwhile in its way. Any particular person is a product of the particular culture in which he or she has lived, and differences between human beings are to be explained (but not judged) by differences in their culture (rather than their race).[6]

As such, culture shapes individual and collective identities and existences, which are quintessential to humanity.[7] This anthropological meaning is often assimilated with the description of a 'way of life', so that a wide range of collective and individual features are therefore likely to be qualified as 'cultural'. As such, if any aspect of life can be considered to be cultural, it follows that any attack against one such feature could potentially trigger the use of the 'cultural genocide' rhetoric. This idea ends up essentializing the importance of one given culture for the viability of one group, and the importance of a specific group for the identity of its individual members. In contrast, the prevailing anthropological discourse rather tends to underline the multiplicity of individual identities and the fluid and dynamic character of culture.[8] In other words, if one group reflects one culture, members of this group will necessarily identify themselves with more than one cultural group. Rogers Brubaker

[5] Alan Barnard and Jonathan Spencer, 'Culture' in Alan Barnard and Jonathan Spencer (eds.), *The Routledge Encyclopedia of Social and Cultural Anthropology* (2nd edn., London, New York: Routledge, 2010) pp. 168–9.

[6] Ibid.

[7] Clifford Geertz, *The Interpretation of Cultures, Selected Essays* (New York: Basic Books, 1973) p. 46.

[8] See e.g. Elsa Stamatopoulou, *Cultural Rights in International Law: Article 27 of the Universal Declaration of Human Rights and Beyond* (Leiden; Boston: Martinus Nijhoff Publishers, 2007) p. 5; Francesco Francioni, 'Beyond State Sovereignty: The Protection of Cultural Heritage as a Shared Interest of Humanity' (2004) 25 *Mich. J. Int'l L.* 1209, p. 1221; Lucas Lixinski, *Intangible Cultural Heritage in International Law* (Oxford: Oxford University Press, 2013) p. 184; Larry May, *Genocide: A Normative Account* (Cambridge; New York: Cambridge University Press, 2010) pp. 64; 85–6; Marco Odello, 'Indigenous Peoples' Rights and Cultural Identity in the Inter-American Context' (2012) 16 *I.J.H.R.* 25, p. 27.

has criticized this formulation by using the concept of 'groupism', which he defines as 'the tendency to take bounded groups as fundamental units of analysis'[9] and 'to reify [ethnic] groups (...) as if they were internally homogeneous, externally bounded groups, even unitary collective actors with common purposes'.[10] Cultural genocide is therefore likely to be subjected to potential abuse and misuse, the scope for which contributes to the scepticism surrounding the legitimacy of the concept.

Cultural genocide thus raises the question of where to draw the line in order to avoid the stubborn defence of any cultural practice for the mere sake that it is deemed cultural. This question intuitively rings the bell of the 'cultural relativist' criticism, which can itself be criticized. Cultural relativism actually constitutes a 'methodological principle' of anthropology, which consists in looking at cultures in and for themselves, without prejudice.[11] If there is indeed a risk to defend 'every practice and every belief at all costs'[12] through the cultural genocide claim, the concept also calls upon a cultural relativist approach according to its anthropological meaning, that is thinking of what a culture is and its meaning for both given communities and their individual members.

While these criticisms should be acknowledged, they cannot constitute in and of themselves an argument advocating the rejection of the concept as a whole, especially in light of a growing consensus as to the idea that 'the disappearance of peoples and cultures is a reality, not a theoretical construct of paradigm'.[13] A large number of experts consider cultural genocide to be the adequate term to reflect the experiences of some indigenous communities.[14] The issue rather consists in the establishment of criteria in order to distinguish between 'legitimate' and 'illegitimate' claims. Clearly, this is not an easy task, especially in the absence of any legal definition; the draft provision on cultural genocide was rejected from the final 1948

[9] Rogers Brubaker, *Ethnicity without Groups* (Cambridge, Mass.: Harvard University Press, 2004) pp. 2–3.

[10] Ibid., p. 8.

[11] Denys Cuche, *La Notion de Culture dans les Sciences Sociales* (4ème éd., Paris: La Découverte, 2010) pp. 145–7.

[12] Sally Engle Merry, 'Human Rights Law and the Demonization of Culture (and Anthropology along the Way)' (2003) 26 *A.A.A* 55, p. 58. For similar criticisms, see also Marie-Bénédicte Dembour, 'Following the Movement of a Pendulum: Between Universalism and Relativism' in Jane K. Cowan, Marie-Bénédicte Dembour, and Richard A. Wilson (eds.), *Culture and Rights: Anthropological Perspectives* (Cambridge, UK; New York, NY, USA: Cambridge University Press, 2001) p. 59; Cuche (n 11) pp. 144–5.

[13] Elazar Barkan, 'Genocide of Indigenous Peoples' in Robert Gellately and Ben Kiernan (eds.), *The Specter of Genocide: Mass Murder in Historical Perspective* (Cambridge: Cambridge University Press, 2003) p. 121. This opinion is shared with, inter alia, Israel W. Charny (ed.), *Encyclopedia of Genocide*, vol. 1 (Toulouse; Santa Barbara: ABC-Clio, 1999) p. 7; Daphne Anayiotos, 'The Cultural Genocide Debate: Should the UN Genocide Convention Include a Provision on Cultural Genocide, or Should the Phenomenon be Encompassed in a Separate International Treaty?' (2009) 22 *N.Y. Int'l L. Rev.* 99, p. 129; Damien Short, 'Cultural Genocide and Indigenous Peoples: A Sociological Approach' (2010) 14 *I.J.H.R.* 833.

[14] Shamiran Mako, 'Cultural Genocide and Key International Instruments: Framing the Indigenous Experience' (2012) 19 *I.J.M.G.R.* 175; David B. MacDonald and Gordon Hudson, 'The Genocide Question and Indian Residential Schools in Canada' (2012) 45 *Can.J.Pol.Sc.* 427, pp. 430–1.

Convention on the Prevention and Punishment of the Crime of Genocide (hereinafter the Genocide Convention).

The discourse surrounding cultural genocide has nonetheless persisted, especially in academic debate, with some scholars attempting to formulate definitions of cultural genocide. Raphael Lemkin, a Polish lawyer, initially coined the term 'cultural genocide' at the same time as he conceptualized genocide, conceiving the former as a technique of implementation of the latter, which would consist of the destruction of either tangible or intangible manifestations of a group culture.[15] The term is used particularly to refer to the intentional destruction of assets of cultural heritage, such as cultural or religious monuments, in contrast to the idea of 'collateral damage'.[16]

Contemporary definitions of the concept have rather used cultural genocide to describe a process of its own, which would result in the extinction of some ethnic groups' culture, either through its targeted destruction or its forced assimilation into the dominant culture.[17] Cultural genocide has thus been defined as the idea 'that a group could be suppressed by extinguishing their specific traits'[18] or as 'the total destruction of a culture, so that the identity of a people ceases to exist'.[19] Yvonne Donders provides a more thorough definition of cultural genocide:

> the destruction by the State or State organs of the culture of a community in its broad sense of the term, including the 'distinctive spiritual material, intellectual and emotional features of society or a social group', encompassing 'in addition to art and literature, lifestyles, ways of living together, value systems, traditions and beliefs'.[20]

Both the narrow and broad meanings of cultural genocide overlap to the extent that cultural genocide, understood as a technique of genocide, might itself constitute a technique of ethnocide. Hence, the understanding that '[d]enying that a group can speak its native language or practice its traditional religion will destroy the group just as readily as killing some of the members'.[21] The difference rather

[15] Raphael Lemkin, *Axis Rule in Occupied Europe: Laws of Occupation—Analysis of Government—Proposals for Redress* (2nd edn., first published 1944, Clark, N.J.: Lawbook Exchange, Ltd., 2008) pp. 79, 83–5. Lemkin's legacy is discussed in further detail in Section 2.1.

[16] Robert Bevan, *The Destruction of Memory: Architecture at War* (London: Reaktion Books, 2006) p. 7; Federico Lenzerini, 'The Role of International and Mixed Criminal Courts in the Enforcement of International Norms Concerning the Protection of Cultural Heritage' in Francesco Francioni and James Gordley (eds.), *Enforcing International Cultural Heritage Law* (Oxford: Oxford University Press, 2013) p. 45.

[17] Stefania Negri, 'Cultural Genocide in International Law: Is the Time Ripe for a Change?' (2013) 10 *T.D.M.*, p. 2.

[18] Sub-Commission on Prevention of Discrimination and Protection of Minorities (38th Session), 'Revised and updated report on the question of the prevention and punishment of the crime of genocide prepared by Mr. Benjamin Whitaker' (2 July 1985), UN Doc. E/CN.4/Sub.2/1985/6 (Whitaker Report) para. 32.

[19] Anayiotos (n 13) p. 100.

[20] Yvonne Donders, 'Old Cultures Never Die? Cultural Genocide in International Law' in Ineke Boerefijn et al. (eds.), *Human Rights and Conflict, Essays in Honour of Bas de Gaay Fortman* (Cambridge: Intersentia Publishing, 2012) pp. 290–1. The author refers to the definition of culture that is contained in the Preamble of the UNESCO Universal Declaration on Cultural Diversity (2 November 2001).

[21] May, *Genocide: A Normative Account* (n 8) p. 104.

exists at the level of the analysis, as the first definition focuses on the means of genocide and the latter on its results.

A few common characteristics emerge from the various scholarly definitions. Cultural genocide is often described as a 'subtle' genocide,[22] referring to a rather long-term process which, in spite of not being bloody, engenders the same result as genocide: the destruction of a human group, mainly through assimilationist and dispersionist policies. The effects of this 'destruction' are also described as intergenerational,[23] precluding the transmission of the group culture to the next generations, so that its effects can be considered as ongoing even long after the process took place.[24] The harm is therefore multiple: to the individual, their communities, and humanity as a whole. Finally, cultural genocide is also referred to as a 'state practice' or policy,[25] although the criminal rhetoric that accompanies the term 'genocide' implies some form of individual criminality.

In the course of this study, we refer to cultural genocide as a generic term that describes both the narrow and the broad meaning. Nevertheless, where it becomes necessary to draw a distinction, we will refer to the narrow meaning as a 'technique of cultural genocide', to use Lemkin's terminology, and the broad meaning as a 'process of genocide of its own' or 'ethnocide'.

1.2 Cultural Genocide and Genocide

Both genocide and cultural genocide have been developed as legal concepts, in the sense that they have been firstly defined and tentatively tackled in the international legal sphere. While cultural genocide has evolved on the contingency of claims, genocide has remained a fixed legal concept since its 1948 definition as articulated, enshrined in Article II of the Genocide Convention:

In the present Convention, genocide means any of the following acts committed with intent to destroy, in whole or in part, a national, ethnical, racial or religious group, as such:
(a) Killing members of the group;
(b) Causing serious bodily or mental harm to members of the group;
(c) Deliberately inflicting on the group conditions of life calculated to bring about its physical destruction in whole or in part;

[22] Barbara Perry, 'From Ethnocide to Ethnoviolence: Layers of Native American Victimization' (2002) 5 *Contemp. Just. Rev.* 231, p. 234; Robert van Krieken, 'Rethinking Cultural Genocide: Aboriginal Child Removal and Settler-Colonial State Formation' (2004) 75 *Oceania* 125, p. 138.

[23] Ana F. Vrdoljak, 'Reparations for Cultural Loss' in Federico Lenzerini (ed.), *Reparations for Indigenous Peoples: International and Comparative Perspectives* (Oxford: Oxford University Press, 2008) p. 197.

[24] Lorie M. Graham, 'Reparations, Self-Determination, and the Seventh Generation' (2008) 21 *Harv.Hum.Rts.J.* 47, pp. 68–70.

[25] Donders, 'Old Cultures Never Die?' (n 20) p. 290; Lyndel V. Prott, 'Ethnocide' in Dinah L. Shelton (ed.), *Encyclopedia of Genocide and Crimes Against Humanity*, vol. 1 (New York: Macmillan Reference USA; Thomson Gale, 2004) p. 310.

(d) Imposing measures intended to prevent births within the group;
(e) Forcibly transferring children of the group to another group.[26]

Since its codification, the legal definition of genocide has attracted a considerable amount of attention and criticism, both from inside and outside the legal sphere, so as to be qualified as an 'essentially contested concept'.[27] It has been much criticized for its alleged overly restrictive scope. These criticisms have focused on the two main elements of the definition: the *mens rea*, which contains a restrictive list of potential victim groups, on the one hand and the *actus reus*, which provides a restrictive list of potential genocidal acts, mainly focused on acts of physical and biological destruction, on the other.[28] This has given rise to a proliferation of proposals for new definitions of genocide[29] as well as the creation of alternative concepts, modelled on the '-cide' root of genocide, in order to identify and highlight some missing element of the definition,[30] some of which intersect with the concept of cultural genocide. 'Indigenocide' thus describes the specific experience of indigenous peoples, although they might legally fall into the 'ethnic group' category[31] while 'eliticide' has been used to emphasize one particular aspect of the partial destruction of a group, namely 'the killing of the leadership, the educated, and the clergy of a group', a recurring pattern of mass atrocities.[32] Other terms focus

[26] Convention on the Prevention and Punishment of the Crime of Genocide (adopted 9 December 1948, entered into force 12 January 1951) 78 UNTS 277 (Genocide Convention).

[27] Term coined by W.B. Gallie, 'Essentially Contest Concepts' (1955–1956) 56 *Proceedings of the Aristotelian Society* 167, p. 169: 'concepts the proper use of which inevitably involves endless disputes about their proper uses on the part of their users'. Applied to 'genocide' by Christopher Powell, *Barbaric Civilization: A Critical Sociology of Genocide* (Montreal: McGill-Queen's University Press, 2011) pp. 67–70.

[28] See e.g. Alexander L. Hinton, 'Towards an Anthropology of Genocide' in Alexander L. Hinton (ed.), *Annihilating Difference: The Anthropology of Genocide* (Berkeley, CT; London: University of California Press, 2002) p. 4.

[29] See e.g. Frank Chalk and Kurt Jonassohn, *The History and Sociology of Genocide: Analyses and Case Studies* (3rd edn., New Haven, CT; London: Yale University Press, 1990) p. 23; Israel W. Charny, 'A Proposed Definitional Matrix for Crimes of Genocide' in Charny (n 13) pp. 7–9. For a list of these definitions, see Wardatul Akman, 'Atrocities Against Humanity during the Liberation War in Bangladesh: A Case of Genocide' (2002) 4 *J.G.R.* 543, pp. 551–7.

[30] For instance, the word 'politicide' has gained particular resonance and emphasizes the absence of focus on political groups, while the word 'gendercide' has been developed to draw the focus on 'the gender-selective mass killing and "disappearance" of males, especially "battle-age" males, (. . .) a pervasive feature of contemporary conflict' in Adam Jones, 'Gendercide and Genocide' (2000) 2 *J.G.R.* 185, p. 189. For a list of these '-cide terms', see Bartolomé Clavero, *Genocide or Ethnocide, 1933–2007* (Milano: Giuffré Editore, 2008) p. 8; William A. Schabas, *Genocide in International Law: The Crime of Crimes* (2nd edn., Cambridge: Cambridge University Press, 2009) p. 236.

[31] Raymond Evans, '"Crime without a Name": Colonialism and the Case for "Indigenocide"' in A. Dirk Moses (ed.), *Empire, Colony, Genocide: Conquest, Occupation, and Subaltern Resistance in World History* (1st pbk. edn., New York: Berghahn Books, 2010) pp. 133–47.

[32] Samuel Totten and Paul R. Bartrop, *Dictionary of Genocide*, vol. 1. (Westport, Conn.: Greenwood Press, 2008) p. 128. Raphael Lemkin had already described similar situations under its technique of 'social genocide' in Lemkin, *Axis Rule in Occupied Europe* (n 15) p. 83. This feature has for instance been underlined in the contexts of Cambodia and of the 1971 Liberation War. See respectively Jean-Louis Margolin, 'Le "Génocide" Cambodgien: Des Particularités Irréductibles?' in Katia Boustany and Daniel Dormoy (eds.), *Génocide(s)* (Bruxelles: Bruylant; Editions de l'Université de Bruxelles, 1999)

on specific cultural features rather than the victim groups, such as 'libricide' for the destruction of books and libraries,[33] 'linguicide' or 'linguistic genocide' for the 'concerted elimination of one or several languages through explicit policies',[34] especially in contexts of 'submersion education'.[35] While coining new terms may seem counterproductive, as a means of (over) emphasizing the specific features of broader processes and therefore dissociating them from the very concept of genocide,[36] they all contribute to challenge the definition of genocide. In this regard, cultural genocide is more than another '–cide' word, not only for historical reasons—as it shares its common origins with genocide—but also because it has increasingly been accepted as part of the 'genocidal process'.

The idea of 'process' has itself recently been conceptualized, placed in contrast with the long-prevailing idea of a series of episodic events.[37] This conceptual move has very much been linked to new trends in Holocaust studies, due to increasing efforts to understand the long-term origins and consequences of the Holocaust, which is often considered as a 'prototypical' genocide.[38] A renewal has thus been observed within the scholarship of genocide, to conceptualize, in the wake of Hannah Arendt, the imperialistic roots of modern genocide.[39] In this context, Patrick Wolfe has identified a 'logic of elimination'[40] underlying every process of settlers' colonialism, which could, above a certain line, be deemed to become genocidal. This has in turn shed new light on the types of societies likely to be involved in such processes. Genocide was originally commonly thought of as the product of 'monsters' or 'dictators', that is, of an extreme and obvious form of social deviance.[41] The focus on settler colonialism has illustrated that genocide might also be the fruit

p. 200; International Commission of Jurists, 'The Events in Pakistan', Part II: Outline of Events in East Pakistan 25 March–18 December 1971.

33 Rebecca Knuth, *Libricide: The Regime-Sponsored Destruction of Books and Libraries in the Twentieth Century* (Westport, Conn.; Praeger, 2003) pp. 49–73. This feature has become an emblem of the Nazi Kristallnacht and can also be found in the Cambodian process.

34 Claude Hagège, *Halte à la Mort des Langues* (Paris: Odile Jacob, 2000) pp. 141–7.

35 Tove Skutnabb-Kangas and Robert Dunbar, 'Indigenous Children's Education as Linguistic Genocide and a Crime Against Humanity? A Global View' (2010) 1 *Gáldu Čála: Journal of Indigenous Peoples Rights*.

36 Permanent Forum on Indigenous Issues, 'Study on International Criminal Law and the Judicial Defence of Indigenous Peoples' Rights (submitted by the Special Rapporteur Bartlomé Clavero)' (8 February 2011) UN Doc. E/C.19/2011/4, para. 11.

37 A. Dirk Moses, 'Conceptual Blockages and Definitional Dilemmas in the "Racial Century": Genocides of Indigenous Peoples and the Holocaust' (2002) 36 *Patterns of Prejudice* 7, p. 34; Sheri P. Rosenberg, 'Genocide is a Process, not an Event' (2012) 7 *G.S.P.* 16, pp. 16–23.

38 Moses, 'Conceptual Blockages' (n 37) p. 17.

39 Hannah Arendt, *Origins of Totalitarianism* (New York: Schoken Books, 2004) p. 174.

40 Patrick Wolfe, 'Settler Colonialism and the Elimination of the Native' (2006) 8 *J.G.R.* 387, pp. 387–409.

41 It is sufficient to make note of the polemic created by Arendt's 'banality of evil' to describe the Nazi genocide, as the product of an ordinary administration typically embodied in Eichmann. See Hannah Arendt, *Eichmann in Jerusalem: A Report on the Banality of Evil* (first published 1951, New York: Penguin Books, 1994); for a commentary on the controversy, see David Luban, 'Hannah Arendt as a Theorist of International Criminal Law' (2011) 11 *I.C.L.R.* 621.

of so-called 'Western liberal democracies',[42] that is, of those very states which took part in the negotiations of the Genocide Convention.[43]

From this perspective of process, the relationship between cultural destruction and genocide has become tighter. Cultural genocide is thus presented as an intrinsic characteristic of every process of genocide, which can be empirically observed.[44] As a technique, it may occur concomitantly to other genocidal acts[45] or constitute a step towards genocide.[46] The latter idea tends to attribute a function to the concept in relation to genocide prevention, one of the two stated goals of the Genocide Convention. However, international law has been challenged more than once for its inability to efficiently prevent genocides.[47] In this respect, genocide prevention emerges as a field of study in which cultural genocide might find some ground for its legal revival.

The debate is much more intense in respect of the concept of ethnocide, as it opens the 'genocide without murder' debate, that is whether genocide could be said to exist without the perpetration of any physical or biological attacks against the group members, roughly summed up as 'murders'. The issue is reflected in Larry May's statement that '[t]he destruction of a group, in which individuals are not killed, is more difficult to see as a great crime'.[48] Doctrinal opinions can be split into two categories: those who advocate for a broader understanding of the crime, as Larry May does, and those who consider, on the basis of the 1948 Genocide Convention, that genocide should be thought of exclusively in physical and biological terms while cultural genocide should rather be addressed as a human rights issue, per William A. Schabas.[49]

The debate has been especially acute in relation to acts of 'forcibly transferring children from one group to another', acts that are listed as potential acts of genocide in Article II of the Genocide Convention.[50] While the insertion of

[42] See also van Krieken (n 22) pp. 125–51; A. Dirk Moses, 'Empire, Colony, Genocide: Keywords and the Philosophy of History' in Moses (ed.), *Empire, Colony, Genocide* (n 31) pp. 3–54; Powell, *Barbaric Civilization* (n 27).

[43] Johannes Morsink, 'Cultural Genocide, the Universal Declaration and Minority Rights' (1999) 21 *H.R.Q.* 1009.

[44] Ana F. Vrdoljak, *International Law, Museums and the Return of Cultural Objects* (Cambridge, UK; New York: Cambridge University Press, 2006) p. 162.

[45] Schabas, *Genocide in International Law* (n 30) p. 216.

[46] Jean-Michel Chaumont, 'Génocide et Ethnocide' in Katia Boustany and Daniel Dormoy (eds.), *Génocide(s)* (Bruxelles: Bruylant; Editions de l'Université de Bruxelles, 1999) p. 252.

[47] Leo Kuper, *The Prevention of Genocide* (New Haven, CT: Yale University Press, 1985) pp. 8–12; Vrdoljak, *International Law, Museums and the Return of Cultural Objects* (n 44) p. 168; Rosenberg (n 37) p. 17; Payam Akhavan, 'Preventing Genocide: Measuring Success by What Does Not Happen' (2011) 22 *Crim.L.F.* 1.: While the results of prevention are quite difficult to assess, the mere perpetration of genocide in Rwanda and Srebrenica, to refer to those that have been legally qualified as genocide, has fuelled this criticism.

[48] Larry May, 'How is Humanity Harmed by Genocide?' (2004) 10 *Int'L. Legal Theory* 1, p. 24.

[49] Schabas, *Genocide in International Law* (n 30) p. 10. See also Issiaka P. Lalèyê, 'Comment Meurent les Cultures? Interrogations Philosophico–Anthropologiques sur le Concept de Génocide Culturel' in Katia Boustany and Daniel Dormoy (eds.), *Génocide(s)* (Bruxelles: Bruylant; Editions de l'Université de Bruxelles, 1999) p. 292. The author coins the concept of 'culturicide' so as to replace the concept of cultural genocide outside of the genocide framework, by removing its explicit reference to 'genocide'.

[50] For two different opinions, see e.g. Raimond Gaita, 'Refocusing Genocide: A Philosophical Responsibility' in John K. Roth (ed.), *Genocide and Human Rights: A Philosophical Guide* (Houndmills, Basingstoke, Hampshire; New York: Palgrave Macmillan, 2005) p. 155; and Ward Churchill, 'Defining

this provision was not subject to major debate during the negotiations of the Genocide Convention, it seems that the delegates did not anticipate the claims that would later be brought by Aboriginal Australians, Native Americans and Canadian First Nations, Métis, and Inuit group members, namely their forced removal from their families and transfer to the above-mentioned residential schools where they endured harsh living conditions and complete isolation from their families, communities, and overall culture.

Finally, the cultural dimension is also apparent at the level of the consequences of genocide, in respect of the idea that the destruction of a group implies the destruction of a related culture. As such, the destruction of the socio-cultural fabric has been often quoted as one of the harms of genocide, beyond the death of the group members.[51]

The conceptual intertwinement of culture and genocide is evident but the question of the relevance of its legal intertwinement remains. As Robert Bevan notes, 'the fatally intertwined experience of genocide and cultural genocide has yet to find its proper place in international law'.[52] As has been outlined in this section, the persistence of the 'cultural genocide–genocide' debate is very much due to their temporary cohabitation in the draft Genocide Convention. The negotiations of this Convention occurred in the general context of the construction of the international legal order and *a fortiori* in a context of 'legal vacuum' in the sense that, at the time, the whole order was yet to be constructed. Thus, if the rejection of cultural genocide in the Genocide Convention of 1948 meant its rejection from international law as a whole, the development of international law since that time needs to be re-introduced into the framework of the analysis.

1.3 Cultural Genocide as a Persistent International Legal Issue

Twice in the story of contemporary international law has cultural genocide almost walked through its door. The first time was in 1948, when the draft provision on cultural genocide was finally rejected from the final definition of genocide, enshrined in Article II of the Genocide Convention. The second was in 2007, when a draft provision on cultural genocide and genocide was eventually substituted

the Unthinkable: Towards a Viable Understanding of Genocide' (2000) 2 *O.R.I.L.* 3, pp. 3–36. The former argues for a narrow understanding of genocide as a process of physical group destruction, unlike the latter, who argues for a broader understanding of genocide, one which would take into account various degrees of intent, so as to encompass the acts of forcible transfers of children in North America and Australia.

[51] See inter alia Lemkin, *Axis Rule in Occupied Europe* (n 15) p. 79; Claudia Card, 'Genocide and Social Death' in John K. Roth (ed.), *Genocide and Human Rights: A Philosophical Guide* (Houndmills, Basingstoke, Hampshire; New York: Palgrave Macmillan, 2005) pp. 238–54; Mohammed Abed, 'Clarifying the Concept of Genocide' (2006) 37 *Metaphilosophy* 308, p. 313; May, *Genocide: A Normative Account* (n 21) pp. 61–91; Short 'Cultural Genocide and Indigenous Peoples' (n 13) p. 836.

[52] Bevan (n 16) p. 22.

with another related to the 'elimination of cultures', during the negotiations of the United Nations Declaration on the Right of Indigenous Peoples (UNDRIP).[53] These two draft provisions are noteworthy for their completely different definitions of the same notion. While the 1948 definition was intended to criminalize attacks against cultural monuments and religious institutions, as well as the prohibition imposed on a group to practise the group language,[54] the 2007 text adopted a much broader language, that of the elimination of a group culture as a whole, as a 'collective and individual right not to be subjected to *ethnocide and cultural genocide*'.[55] Furthermore, while the draft cultural genocide provision of the Genocide Convention aimed predominantly at protecting national minorities, in the wake of the inter-war minority treaties,[56] the UNDRIP draft provision clearly came to embody the indigenization of the issue. Beyond the seemingly imperviousness of international law in dealing with the concept of cultural genocide, the two episodes display two shifts: a conceptual shift from cultural genocide to ethnocide, and a legal shift from criminal law to human rights law.

The context of the evolution of the two specific fields of genocide and cultural studies has constituted a favourable ground for renewing the debate on the place of 'cultural genocide' in international law. From the perspective of cultural genocide, the conceptual evolutions and common characteristics underlined in the previous sections reflect many facets of the discourse to be addressed in international law. A first element deals with the focus of the attack, namely culture, which covers both tangible and intangible features. A second element relates to the victims of the attack, the individuals and communities that might be harmed by attacks against the first element. The harm is manifold and concerns the viability of the community, the intergenerational transmission of the culture, the individual members' identities, and human diversity as a whole. A third element concerns the authors of these attacks, which might be committed either by individuals and/or states, especially in the case of ethnocide. The fourth and final element relates to the context of the attack, in respect of which it might happen concomitantly or preventively in a wider process of genocide, either in times of armed conflict or in peacetime.

From the perspective of international law, the terms of the debate—culture, genocide, and group—have radically evolved since its emergence in the 1940s such that both the question and answers must now be rethought in a contemporary context. Thus, when trying to derive a legal taxonomy of the material elements of

[53] Declaration on the Rights of Indigenous Peoples (adopted 13 September 2007) UNGA Res. 61/295 (UNDRIP). Discussed in Section 4.1.2.2.

[54] ECOSOC 'Ad Hoc Committee on Genocide: Summary Record of the Fourteenth Meeting' UN Doc. E/AC.25/SR.14 (27 April 1948) in Hirad Abtahi and Philippa Webb, *The Genocide Convention—The Travaux Préparatoires*, 2 vols. (Leiden; Boston: Martinus Nijhoff Publishers, 2008) p. 892.

[55] UNCHR, 'Report of the Sub-Commission on Prevention of Discrimination and Protection of Minorities on the Work of its Forty-Sixth Session' E/CN.4/Sub.2/1994/56 (26 August 1994) p. 107 (emphasis added).

[56] Mark Mazower, *No Enchanted Palace: The End of Empire and the Ideological Origins of the United Nations* (Princeton: Princeton University Press, 2009) p. 130. The system of inter-war minority treaties is described in Section 2.2.2.

'cultural genocide', one has to look into at least five different branches of international law: public international law itself,[57] international criminal law,[58] international humanitarian law, international human rights law, and international cultural heritage law.

Since most of these categories overlap with each other, these branches should be addressed in a complementary rather than dissociated perspective, while keeping in mind their respective rationales. Indeed, each category encompasses different scopes, protects different interests and contemplates different mechanisms of responsibility. Among the five categories, only international criminal law entails individual criminal responsibility. Hence, if the 'cultural genocide-genocide' debate has tended to be enclosed in criminal terms, following the appropriation of genocide by the field of international criminal law, the focus on groups and culture induces a broader approach to international law. While the criminalization of cultural genocide clearly constitutes an important objective in the international legal debate, it only partially reflects the contemporary state of international law, which now views culture almost exclusively as a matter of state responsibility. As emphasized by the various scholars' definitions, state involvement seems to be crucial in the contemporary understanding of cultural genocide. In this regard, the recent recognition of the principle of state responsibility for genocide is worth underlining as a potential point of convergence between the two international legal frameworks related to culture and genocide.[59]

1.4 Approach and Methodology

The supporters of the introduction of cultural genocide in international law have predominantly adopted two distinct approaches to the matter. The first approach consists of amending international law by virtue of the codification of

[57] The nature of the Genocide Convention as an international treaty implies a focus on its interpretation and its ability to entail state responsibility for directly perpetrating or failing to prevent and punish genocide. See *Application of the Convention on the Prevention and Punishment of the Crime of Genocide (Bosnia and Herzegovina v. Serbia and Montenegro)* (Judgment) [2007] ICJ Rep. 43.

[58] The legal definition of genocide has been transposed as such from the Genocide Convention to the various Statutes of International Criminal Tribunals, including the Rome Statute of the International Criminal Court (ICC). See Rome Statute of the International Criminal Court (adopted 17 July 1998, entered into force 1 July 2002) 2187 UNTS 3 (ICC Rome Statute) art. 6. See also Statute of the International Tribunal for the Former Yugoslavia (adopted 25 May 1993) UNSC Res. 827 (ICTY Statute) art. 4; Statute of the International Criminal Tribunal for Rwanda (adopted 8 November 1994) UNSC Res. 955 (1994) (ICTR Statute) art. 2. In addition to genocide, other international crimes have also developed, including crimes against humanity and war crimes, mostly inspired by international humanitarian law and international human rights law. See Steven R. Ratner, Jason S. Abrams, and James L. Bischoff, *Accountability for Human Rights Atrocities in International Law: Beyond the Nuremberg Legacy* (3rd edn., Oxford; New York: Oxford University Press, 2009) p. 13; Thomas Margueritte, 'International Criminal Law and Human Rights' in William A. Schabas and Nadia B. Bernaz (eds.), *Routledge Handbook of International Criminal Law* (Abingdon: Routledge, 2011) p. 436.

[59] *Application of the Genocide Convention (Bosnia and Herzegovina v. Serbia and Montenegro)* (Judgment) (n 57).

'cultural genocide'. The most developed idea is that of a Protocol to the Genocide Convention, which would tackle the crime of cultural genocide.[60] Some authors otherwise argue for a new treaty that would specifically be dedicated to cultural genocide.[61] Suggestions have also been advanced as to the scope for the inclusion of cultural genocide within the category of crimes against humanity, although it remains unclear whether cultural genocide would then constitute a crime of its own or rather part of a sub-crime against humanity.[62] The second approach consists of relying on existing mechanisms of international law and, if possible, in proceeding to a progressive interpretation of these norms in such a way as to address all of the facets listed above while remaining within the limits of the rules of interpretation established in international law. This second approach nevertheless has a cost: the potential loss of the cultural genocide label within the international legal sphere.

It should be noted at the outset that it seems very unlikely, although theoretically possible, to either revise the Genocide Convention or complete it with a Protocol.[63] Hence, William A. Schabas considers that 'among international law-makers [cultural genocide] is a dead issue'.[64] The idea of a new treaty is also utopian; particularly if one takes into consideration the rejection of the cultural genocide rhetoric from the final UNDRIP. The second approach, which looks at the matter in the wider context of international law, is thus adopted as a hypothesis to frame the research, although it shall not preclude the possibility of concluding in favour of the first approach.

This research therefore seeks to rethink the terms of the debate. Rather than just acknowledging that 'cultural genocide' is not currently addressed as such by international law, it proposes to reverse the approach in order to determine whether contemporary international law possesses the tools to address the so-called concept of 'cultural genocide'. In other words, it will address the question of whether the 'cultural genocide' gap, resulting from the rejection of the draft 'cultural genocide' provision in 1948, has been filled.

This book is thus based on both a pragmatic and progressive approach to international law. On the one hand, it argues that the codification of cultural genocide, not to mention its criminalization, is unlikely to happen in light of the evolution,

[60] Whitaker Report (n 18) para. 33; Anayiotos (n 13); Samuel Totten, William S. Parsons, and Robert K. Hitchcock, 'Genocide against Indigenous Peoples' in Alexander L. Hinton (ed.), *Annihilating Difference: The Anthropology of Genocide* (Berkeley, CT; London: University of California Press, 2002) p. 80.

[61] Sub-Commission on Prevention of Discrimination and Protection of Minorities (31st Session), 'Study on the Question of the Prevention and Punishment of the Crime of Genocide Submitted by the Special Rapporteur Nicodème Rushashyankiko' (4 July 1978) E/CN.4/Sub.2/416, para. 461; David Nersessian, 'Rethinking Cultural Genocide Under International Law', *Human Rights Dialogue: "Cultural Rights"* (Spring 2005), available at: http://www.carnegiecouncil.org/publications/archive/dialogue/2_12/section_1/5139.html (last accessed 1 February 2015).

[62] 'Study on the Question of the Prevention and Punishment of the Crime of Genocide Submitted by the Special Rapporteur Nicodème Rushashyankiko' (n 61) para. 461.

[63] William A. Schabas, 'Judicial Activism and the Crime of Genocide' in Shane Darcy and Joseph Powderly (eds.), *Judicial Creativity at the International Criminal Tribunals* (Oxford: Oxford University Press, 2010) p. 78; Skutnabb-Kangas and Dunbar (n 35) p. 85.

[64] Schabas, *Genocide in International Law* (n 30) p. 220.

since 1948, of international law. On the other hand, it also acknowledges the gravity of the acts and processes associated with the idea of cultural genocide. As such, it relies on a progressive interpretation of existing international legal norms in order to optimize their capacity to respond to intentional attacks against culture. Its ultimate goal is to contribute to the debate of cultural genocide by providing a tailored and multifaceted answer to the various dimensions and implications of a matter that is as complex as it is serious. As an inherently international legal issue, which is located at the crossroads of several disciplines of international law, the research not only aims to reconstruct the various elements of cultural genocide within international law, but also to provide an integrated international legal approach in respect of cultural genocide, which therefore covers the various relevant topics, including the protection of groups, communities, and individuals, the criminalization of attacks against group cultures, state responsibility for failing to protect human rights, the prevention of cultural crimes, and reparation.

To fulfil these objectives, the analysis therefore relies on both a traditional examination of international legal sources[65] in the above-described international legal categories and a confrontation between these sources and scholarly developments in non-legal disciplines. The reference to the sources will be modulated according to the branch of law at stake, since judicial practice may be especially relevant in the case of international criminal justice. In this respect, domestic practice will also be addressed, where relevant either in respect of the implementation of international legal norms, such as the definition of genocide, or for the purposes of clarifying the concept of cultural genocide. When reviewing international legal sources, particular attention will be dedicated to legal cases that refer in one way or another to the concept of cultural genocide or to the idea of group cultural destruction. A few case studies then emerge: the case law of the International Criminal Tribunal for the Former Yugoslavia (ICTY); cases related to claims of forcibly transferred children in Canada and Australia, as well as to truth and reconciliation processes in these countries; the case law of the Inter-American Court of Human Rights (IACHR) in relation to either cases involving genocide or group cultural destruction arising from the forcible removal of the group from its ancestral land. Domestic judicial practice will also be analysed as state practice for the purposes of identifying customary international law.

When analysing these documents, reference will be made to relevant findings of other disciplines, especially in order to shed light on conflicting understandings of some core concepts, such as the notions of group, culture, and genocide. The methodologies and objectives associated with other disciplines, such as anthropology, sociology, political science, global history, and more broadly genocide studies, can contribute to better understanding and shaping the empirical and theoretical underpinnings of such core concepts. This book thus intends to contribute to the dialogue between international law, which possesses the monopoly of the definition

[65] Statute of the International Court of Justice (adopted 26 June 1945) 993 UNTS 25 (ICJ Statute) art. 38.

of genocide and other disciplines, the perspectives of which render them equally legitimate for the purposes of refining the analysis on cultural genocide. However, it should be made clear at the outset that the findings made in these fields may not be transposable into international law, which functions according to a logic of 'legal fiction'.[66] This means that it may distort these concepts and render them legal, so as to answer its own 'special needs'.[67] As such, these 'non-legal sources' are mostly used in a heuristic way, as a tool to guide and better inform potential legal interpretations, in relation to their degree of internal and external coherence.

1.5 Structure

This introduction has underlined the lack of a uniform understanding of the concept of cultural genocide and, consequently, of the role that international law is expected to fulfil in this regard. This book therefore intends to present an exhaustive analytical review of how international law approaches the core idea underlying the concept of cultural genocide, that is the intentional destruction of group cultures, and how this framework can be strengthened and fostered.

The next three chapters undertake the mapping of international law in order to identify how the underlying elements of cultural genocide are addressed and to assess the state of the international legal prohibition of cultural genocide. The approach is both historical and legal, as one of the objectives of this part is to put the current norms in the context of their formation. Thus, Chapter 2 focuses on the legal origins of the concept of cultural genocide, as coined by Raphael Lemkin and as drafted during the negotiations of the Genocide Convention, as well as the later conceptual evolutions it has endured and its persistence in the legal sphere.

The two chapters that follow focus respectively on the two main elements of the concept of cultural genocide, namely the international legal evolution of its genocidal dimension on the one hand and of its cultural dimension on the other. Chapter 3 analyses the way in which the legal definition of genocide has been interpreted in relation to cultural considerations, especially the meaning of 'group destruction', which is pivotal in the conceptualization of both genocide and cultural genocide. This chapter also sheds light on the methodological foundations of the various possible interpretations: either a process of physical-biological group destruction or a process of socio-cultural group destruction. It critically assesses the possibilities for the definition to meet an evolutionary interpretation depending on the legal framework in which it is implemented—international criminal law or general international law—and the potential modulation of existing principles of interpretation.

[66] Guillaume Wicker, 'Fiction' in Denis Alland and Stéphane Rials (eds.), *Dictionnaire de la Culture Juridique* (Paris: Presses Universitaires de France, 2003) pp. 716–20.

[67] Ralph Poscher, 'The Hand of Midas: When Concepts Turn Legal or Deflating the Hart-Dworkin Debate' in Jaap C. Hage and Dietmar von der Pfordten (eds.), *Concepts in Law* (Oxford: Hart Publishing, 2009) p. 101.

Chapter 4 is dedicated to the broader evolution of international law in relation to the protection of group cultures, with the aim of providing a complete picture of current positive law. More specifically, it focuses on the two branches of international human rights law and international cultural heritage law and weighs these two international legal approaches to culture, in order to assess their ability to cover the material element of cultural genocide, predominantly the international prohibition of group cultural destruction. It also searches for synergies between these frameworks and those of genocide and international criminal law.[68] Once this mapping exercise is undertaken, it is then possible to draw some preliminary conclusions in relation to the state of the issue, and in particular the relevance of maintaining the focus of the analysis on the legal concept of genocide.

Considering the limited possibilities to address all facets of cultural genocide through the lens of genocide, the analysis thus opens the perspective on the basis of developments that have been identified in Chapter 4 on the international protection of group cultures.

The following chapters thus adopt a more prospective stance and strive to address the various facets that have been identified in the present introduction in a more systematic way, by relying on both emerging and well-established principles of international law. Chapter 5 therefore assesses the possibility of consolidating a crime against humanity of cultural persecution, drawing from the process of the criminalization of attacks against groups' tangible cultural heritage in front of the ICTY under the crime of persecution. The different facets of the concept of cultural genocide are tested in order to determine whether they can all be covered under the material scope of this crime against humanity.

Once the international criminal dimension induced by the concept of cultural genocide has been consolidated, Chapter 6 goes on to reflect on the ways to enhance state responsibility, beyond responsibility for breaches of either international human rights law or international cultural heritage law. More specifically, it reflects on the impact of the potential criminalization of acts of cultural genocide on the framework of state responsibility, as well as the legal and conceptual establishment of a link between cultural destruction and genocide prevention.

Chapter 7 finally addresses the question of redressing the intended cultural harm that has been discussed throughout the previous chapters. It looks at the inclusion of the cultural dimension into processes of redress that have been implemented in relevant cases, often in contexts of transitional justice. This dimension has been relatively overlooked in the context of academic discussions on cultural genocide. This chapter is therefore deemed necessary to complete the current portrait of cultural genocide in international law, and the way in which the latter addresses the harm induced by the former. It also reflects upon an approach which strives to push as far as possible the boundaries of international law in order to get as close as possible

[68] These two frameworks partly overlap since genocide is an international crime, but the framework of genocide also involves state obligations, such as the obligation to prevent genocide.

to the original justification for addressing the matter in international law: namely, victims' claims for justice.

Chapter 8 completes this book with some conclusions which critically assess the possibility for international law to effectively address cultural genocide, and reflect on the potential relevance of the concept of cultural genocide in an international legal context.

2

The Concept of Cultural Genocide

A Historical–Legal Perspective

Tracing back the history of the concept of cultural genocide aids understanding the current legal debates in relation to both its meaning, which evolved between the hands of lawyers, anthropologists, and other scholars, and the legal disciplines that have been solicited for its inclusion. As this chapter will discuss, the origins of the concept of cultural genocide are to be found in the writings of one lawyer, Raphael Lemkin, who turned out to be highly influential in the decision to draft a Genocide Convention and in the drafting itself. Lemkin managed to have a 'cultural genocide' provision included in the draft Genocide Convention. As always during diplomatic negotiations, the search for a compromise resulted in several distortions of the concept of cultural genocide. The final outcome turned out to be highly disappointing for Lemkin and his supporters since the delegates decided to reject the cultural genocide provision from the final text of the Genocide Convention. At the same time, a minority rights provision, which was considered as a human rights counterpart to the criminal provision of cultural genocide, was also rejected from the final text of the Universal Declaration of Human Rights (UDHR).

These two sets of negotiations and their final outcomes somehow sealed the fate of the concept of cultural genocide, which was doomed to evolve outside the legal sphere. Indigenous peoples throughout the world, supported by anthropologists and sociologists, were particularly active in the resurgence of the concept in order to highlight processes of cultural destruction that were affecting their communities and members. Underlying these claims was the general idea that the concept of genocide, and more generally the international legal framework established in the late 1940s, could hardly be considered as representative of the 'reality' of group destruction, and therefore, of genocide. The concept of cultural genocide just became progressively detached from the concept of genocide, to become an alternative form of genocide of its own: 'ethnocide'. Such subsequent evolutions of the concept may have contributed to the blurring of conceptual borders, which are reflected in several legal cases in which judges were confronted with instances of cultural destruction. Unravelling such conceptual tensions will enable the underlining of some legal challenges that might be expected to arise in the attempt to legally address cultural genocide.

The Concept of Cultural Genocide: An International Law Perspective. First Edition. Elisa Novic.
Published 2016 by Oxford University Press.

2.1 Raphael Lemkin's Legacy

During the Second World War, Raphael Lemkin compiled, in a book entitled *Axis Rule in Occupied Europe* published in 1944, the entire range of German legislation imposed with reference to 'captive nations'. As Ana Vrdoljak explains, '[t]he content and organization of *Axis Rule* were designed to convey how the discrimination, segregation, and eventual elimination of groups were systematically implemented through laws and decrees'.[1] He dedicated one chapter to a new concept of 'genocide', encompassing what was until then considered as a 'crime without a name', with reference to Winston Churchill's words used to describe the Nazi campaign of extermination and mass executions.[2] This new word was coined from the Greek root *genos*, which he translated as 'race' or 'kind' and the Latin root, *cide*, which relates to the idea of 'killing'. Lemkin defined this new crime broadly, as 'a coordinated plan of different actions aiming at the destruction of essential foundations of the life of national groups, with the aim of annihilating the groups themselves'.[3] As he himself admitted, while the expression was new, the crime was not. As of 1933, at the Fifth International Conference for the Unification of Penal Law, he had already proposed the criminalization of two specific '[a]cts Constituting a General (Transnational) Danger Considered as Offences Against the Law of Nations', mainly inspired by the Armenian (subsequently deemed) genocide. The first crime, the 'crime of barbarity', covered, 'first and foremost, acts of extermination directed against the ethnic, religious or social collectivities whatever the motive (political, religious, etc)'.[4] For Lemkin, '[o]ffenses of this type bring harm not only to human rights, but also and most especially they undermine the fundamental basis of the social order'.[5] The second crime, the 'crime of vandalism', rather took the 'form of systematic and organized destruction of the art and cultural heritage in which the unique genius and achievement of a collectivity are revealed in fields of science, arts and literature'.[6]

This dichotomy can be traced back to Lemkin's writing on genocide, albeit through other wording: the 'techniques of genocide'.[7] In *Axis Rule*, Lemkin provided a list of eight techniques, namely political, social, cultural, economic, biological, physical, religious, and moral genocide. He did not give exhaustive definitions of each of these techniques but rather detailed the Nazi legislation adopted in relation to each of them. Among these eight techniques, only one was directly murderous, physical

[1] Ana F. Vrdoljak, 'Human Rights and Genocide: The Work of Lauterpacht and Lemkin in Modern International Law' (2009) 20 *E.J.I.L.* 1163, p. 1184.

[2] Broadcast Speech of Prime Minister Winston Churchill (24 August 1941). Transcription available at: http://www.ibiblio.org/pha/timeline/410824awp.html (last accessed 1 February 2015).

[3] Raphael Lemkin, *Axis Rule in Occupied Europe: Laws of Occupation—Analysis of Government—Proposals for Redress* (2nd edn., first published 1944, Clark, N.J.: Lawbook Exchange, Ltd., 2008) p. 79.

[4] Raphael Lemkin, 'Les Actes Constituant un Danger Général (Interétatique) Considérés Comme Délits des Droit des Gens', *Explications Additionnelles au Rapport Spécial Présenté à la Vème Conférence pour l'Unification du Droit Pénal à Madrid* (Paris: Pédone, 1933), English version available at: http://www.preventgenocide.org/lemkin/madrid1933-english.htm (last accessed 1 February 2015).

[5] Ibid. [6] Ibid. [7] Lemkin, *Axis Rule in Occupied Europe* (n 3) pp. 82–90.

genocide. The seven other were aimed at destroying the common patterns of some specific and targeted groups. As for the specific 'cultural field', the attacks could consist in 'prohibiting or destroying cultural institutions and cultural activities; (...) substituting vocational education for education in the liberal arts, in order to prevent humanist thinking, which the occupant considers dangerous because it promotes national thinking'.[8] Lemkin illustrated this definition with reference to the prohibition of a 'local population (...) to use its own language in schools' in Luxembourg, the 'rigid control of all cultural activities' in Poland '[i]n order to prevent the expression of the national spirit through artistic media' as well as the destruction of 'national monuments [...] and libraries, archives, museums and galleries'.[9] Yet, the limits between the techniques such as cultural, religious, social, and moral genocide were quite blurred.[10] The three former sets of acts included amongst others the targeting of so-called 'intelligentsia' or respective elites, both through persecution and murder; the attempt to irremediably alter the main characteristics of the group, through the inoculation of values traditionally perceived as immoral or the special focus on children; and the imposition of a foreign language in all institutions representing the group, such as education, justice, administration. All of these examples presented cultural features.

It is unclear whether Lemkin understood genocide as necessarily involving killings (that is not to say mass killings) or not. It is actually possible to identify these two different meanings across Lemkin's work. In his chapter on 'genocide', before introducing the eight techniques, he started to present genocide as a process involving 'two phases: one, destruction of the national pattern of the oppressed group; the other, the imposition of the national pattern of the oppressor'. He considered that the similar notions of:

> 'Germanization', 'Magyarization', 'Italianization' were 'inadequate because they [did] not convey the common elements of one generic notion and moreover they treat mainly the cultural, economic, and social aspects of genocide, *leaving out the biological aspect*, such as the physical decline and even destruction of the population involved.[11]

Beyond the ambiguous character of this quote, it is nevertheless certain that mass killings alone did not constitute genocide. Lemkin summarized this dilemma in an article in 1946: 'mass murder (...) does not connote the motivation of the crime (...) [The term] denationalization (...) seems to be inadequate, since it does not connote biological destruction'.[12] The concept of 'denationalization' refers here to the German Jewish people's deprivation of nationality, which subsequently deprived them of any state protection. In the aftermath of the Second World War, the word 'denationalization' would retain some resonance, both in respect of the work of the United Nations War Crimes Commission (UNWCC)[13] and the writings of Hannah Arendt. In the *Origins of*

[8] Ibid., p. xii. [9] Ibid., p. 84. [10] Ibid., pp. 83–4, 89–90.

[11] Ibid., p. 80 (emphasis added).

[12] Raphael Lemkin, 'Genocide' (1946) 15 *The American Scholar* 227, p. 227.

[13] Ana F. Vrdoljak, *International Law, Museums and the Return of Cultural Objects* (Cambridge, UK; New York: Cambridge University Press, 2006) pp. 164–5.

Imperialism, she strove to describe the same historical process as Lemkin by rather using the terms 'denationalisation' and 'crimes against humanity'[14] to emphasize that 'Hitler's solution to the Jewish problem (...) was an eloquent demonstration to the rest of the world how really to "liquidate" all problems concerning minorities and the stateless'.[15] The line between these '-ization' words and the '-ide' word was therefore already very thin at the time.

These uncertainties can somehow be explained by re-contextualizing the conceptual innovation in relation to Lemkin's practical observations as a witness. Of the 674 pages of his book, almost 600 were dedicated to the strict observation of the 'Axis rule' in the 'occupied territories', which corresponded to seven occupying powers[16] over around sixteen occupied countries[17] and even more administrative entities. The techniques therefore varied from one context to another; the ones implemented in Poland differed from those implemented in Yugoslavia. The reasons for genocide would differ from one entity to another, though the final aim was the same: the 'destruction' of specific groups. It is for this reason that he coined a new word, based on a 'holistic conception' of the phenomenon, partly inspired by the Nazi crimes but at the same time, deemed to encompass other past and future crimes.[18] From this perspective, he subsequently became engaged in a project entitled 'Genocide in world history' in which he attempted to draw a list of all genocides that had occurred throughout history.[19] However, while the issue of 'genocide without murders' can be understood in light of the context in which he drafted *Axis Rule over Occupied Europe*, his position became even less clear in his later writings, in which his conception of 'cultural genocide' shifted to become a crime of its own.

It is not the same, however, to talk about the destruction of a culture or about the destruction of a group through an attack against its culture. Lemkin tended to talk about the two: cultural genocide was a technique of genocide while the final harm of genocide was the destruction of a group, which equated to the destruction of a culture. Groups were above all national minorities, which were mainly identified in terms of their 'culture'. As illustrated by Dirk Moses through Lemkin's unpublished archives,[20] his vision of culture was not only inspired by his own experience—the fate of his family during the Second World War[21] and his strong concerns about the

[14] David Luban, 'Hannah Arendt as a Theorist of International Criminal Law' (2011) 11 *I.C.L.R.* 621, pp. 631–5.

[15] Hannah Arendt, *Origins of Totalitarianism* (New York: Schoken Books, 2004) p. 368.

[16] Germany, Italy, Russia, Hungary, Bulgaria, Albania, and Romania.

[17] Albania, Austria, Lithuania, Latvia, Estonia, Belgium, Czechoslovakia, Denmark, France, Greece, Luxemburg, The Netherlands, Norway, Poland, part of the USSR, and Yugoslavia.

[18] A. Dirk Moses, 'Lemkin, Culture and the Concept of Genocide' in Donald Bloxham and A. Dirk Moses (eds.), *The Oxford Handbook of Genocide Studies* (Oxford: Oxford University Press, 2010) p. 34.

[19] A. Dirk Moses, 'Empire, Colony, Genocide: Keywords and the Philosophy of History' in A. Dirk Moses (ed.), *Empire, Colony, Genocide: Conquest, Occupation, and Subaltern Resistance in World History* (1st pbk. edn., New York: Berghahn Books, 2010) p. 9.

[20] Ibid., p. 8.

[21] Lemkin's family was Jewish and while he managed to flee, '[f]orty-nine of his own relatives were murdered'. William A. Schabas, 'Preface to the Second Edition' in Lemkin, *Axis Rule in Occupied Europe* (n 3) p. xii.

European minority context—but also by a certain school of anthropology. From his writings, culture emerges in its narrow understanding, mainly as a product of spiritual education, as the following statement shows:

Cultural considerations speak for international protection of national, religious and cultural groups. Our whole heritage is a product of the contributions of all nations. We can best understand this when we realize how impoverished our culture would be if the peoples doomed by Germany, such as the Jews, had not been permitted to create the Bible, or to give birth to an Einstein, a Spinoza; if the Poles had not had the opportunity to give to the world a Copernicus, a Chopin, a Curie; the Czechs, a Huss, a Dvorak; the Greeks, a Plato and a Socrates; the Russians, a Tolstoy and a Shostakovich.[22]

For Lemkin, culture seemed to result from the sum of tangible cultural heritage and outputs of an intellectual and scientific elite, a concept therefore more likely to apply to Western European societies in the wake of early conceptions of culture as 'civilisation' by the French philosophers of the Enlightenment.[23] The concept of civilization was later dismissed, rightly because of its inability to take into account 'primitive societies' as it focused mainly on material achievements.[24] This is not to say that Lemkin did not care about non-European peoples' fate, and in particular that of colonized and indigenous peoples. It is not by chance that his concept of genocide—in particular his sub-concept of cultural genocide—has received such a strong echo among various indigenous communities.[25] As illustrated by his draft 'Genocide in world history', he himself was very sensitive to the extermination and forced religious conversion of indigenous communities in Latin America.[26]

However, in spite of his statement on 'Magyarization' and 'Italianization', Lemkin was not so straightforward in condemning assimilation. Although he considered that 'the destruction of cultural symbols is genocide',[27] assimilation was not cultural genocide as long as it was 'legal'.[28] It is not clear what he meant by 'legal assimilation', especially in the colonial and post-colonial contexts of forced assimilation. This position on assimilation actually tended to reflect his faith in what could be named the 'Western civilisation of international law', in which 'humanitarian feelings have gradually been crystallized'[29] and which could therefore justify its 'diffusion'.

[22] Lemkin, 'Genocide' (n 12) p. 228.

[23] Denys Cuche, *La Notion de Culture dans les Sciences Sociales* (4ème éd., Paris: La Découverte, 2010) pp. 11–12.

[24] Ibid., p. 19; this idea was formulated by Edward Burnett Tylor in 1871.

[25] Damien Short, 'Cultural Genocide and Indigenous Peoples: A Sociological Approach' (2010) 14 *I.J.H.R.* 833. See Section 2.3.1.

[26] Raphael Lemkin 'Description of the Project', LCNYPL, Reel 3, Box 2, Folder 1' quoted in Moses 'Empire, Colony, Genocide' (n 19) p. 9.

[27] Raphael Lemkin, 'The Concept of Genocide in Anthropology', LCNYPL, Box 2, Folder 2', quoted in Moses 'Empire, Colony, Genocide' (n 19) p. 12.

[28] Raphael Lemkin, 'Memorandum on the Genocide Convention', AHJS, P-154, Box 6, Folder 5', quoted in Moses 'Empire, Colony, Genocide' (n 19) p. 15.

[29] Raphael Lemkin, 'Proposal for Introduction to the Study of Genocide', LCNYPL, Reel 3, Box 2, Folder 1, quoted in Moses 'Empire, Colony, Genocide' (n 19) p. 27.

This notion was actually based on a 'functional idea' of culture, as formulated by Bronislaw Malinowski, an anthropologist working in the first half of the twentieth century. For the latter, culture would necessarily evolve under external influence: cultural contact. On this basis, Malinowski elaborated a theory of 'needs', according to which a culture is deemed to answer individuals' basic needs through the setting up of 'institutions'.[30] As a result, 'weaker societies adopt the institutions of more efficient ones or become absorbed by them because they better fulfil basic needs'.[31] He would still recognize that '[i]f the culture of a group is violently undermined, the group itself disintegrates and its members must either become absorbed in other cultures, which is a wasteful and painful process or succumb to personal disorganization and, perhaps, physical destruction'.[32] This theory would provide the basis for Lemkin's distinction between cultural genocide and cultural diffusion or adaptation. However, Malinowski's theory of 'needs' attracted strong criticism, notably in its 'biological conception'.[33] The distinction between voluntary and non-voluntary change on the one hand and non-voluntary and forcible change on the other is still an issue today. As highlighted by Moses, 'Lemkin [did] not seem to have considered the possibility that genocide could be attempted, that much destruction could take place, and that cultural adaptation occurred nonetheless'[34] as this doctrine tended to focus more on the result of cultural adaptation than the process of potential cultural destruction.

In addition to these conceptual ambiguities and anthropological biases, Lemkin's conception of genocide underwent severe distortion during the drafting process of the Genocide Convention, as it passed through the diplomatic filter.

2.2 Cultural Genocide Through the Diplomatic Filter

The end of the Second World War provided the momentum to strengthen the international community through the establishment of the United Nations (UN), and develop legal instruments to prevent the repetition of such atrocities. Efforts were made in different directions. Lemkin's lobbying campaign triggered the opening of negotiations on a draft convention on the crime of genocide, the initial scope of which covered cultural genocide. At the same time, the UN hosted negotiations on a draft bill of rights, which initially included a provision on minority rights. These negotiations were very much intertwined, especially in relation to the two provisions on cultural genocide and minority rights. The analysis of their *travaux préparatoires* thus allows us to unfold further distortions of these concepts, through

[30] Cuche (n 23) p. 37. [31] Moses 'Empire, Colony, Genocide' (n 19) p. 27.

[32] Raphael Lemkin, 'The Concept of Genocide in Anthropology', LCNYPL, Box 2, Folder 2, quoted in Moses 'Empire, Colony, Genocide' (n 19) p. 12.

[33] Cuche (n 23) p. 37. See also Clifford Geertz, *The Interpretation of Cultures, Selected Essays* (New York: Basic Books, 1973) pp. 39–40.

[34] Moses, 'Lemkin, Culture and the Concept of Genocide' (n 18) p. 30.

amendments and revisions to the initial definitions, as well as to better understand the root causes of the persistent debate related to cultural genocide.

2.2.1 The fate of the 'cultural genocide' provision in the draft genocide convention

The fate of the concept of genocide was quite uncertain after the war, as the term did not appear as such either in the Charter of the International Military Tribunal (Nuremberg Charter),[35] nor in the judgment. Still, it was invoked several times by the Prosecutor in his indictments.[36] The genocidal acts—as they would now be categorized—were then addressed under the category of crimes against humanity. This seemingly 'new' criminal category[37] was included in order to address the crimes perpetrated by a state against its own civilian populations—in particular the Jews—whereas other criminal categories, especially war crimes, would only make possible the conviction of criminal perpetrators for crimes perpetrated against combatants and occupied populations.[38]

Ultimately, it was genocide, rather than crimes against humanity, which received codification. It is hard to explain this fact by any reason other than Lemkin's involvement; he relied upon the post-war momentum of a new international order to lobby the international community to adopt quickly an international instrument dedicated to genocide. His dedication to the task quickly turned fruitful and, as of November 1946, the then newly established UN Organisation started to work on the issue, without waiting for the outcomes of the Nuremberg and Tokyo Tribunals. Following the initiative of a few states,[39] the United Nations General Assembly (UNGA) was the first organ to engage in the process, with the unanimous adoption of Resolution 96(1) related to 'The crime of genocide' on 11 December 1946; its preamble was drawn up as follows:

> Genocide is a denial of the right of existence of entire human groups, as homicide is the denial of the right to live of individual human beings; such denial of the right of existence

[35] Charter of the International Military Tribunal (adopted 8 August 1945) 82 UNTS 280 (IMT Charter) art. 6.

[36] *Hermann Goering* et al., 'Indictment' (6 October 1945) Count 3, on war crimes: 'They conducted deliberate and systematic genocide, viz., the extermination of racial and national groups, against the civilian populations of certain occupied territories in order to destroy particular races and classes of people and national, racial, or religious groups, particularly Jews, Poles, and Gypsies and others.'

[37] Some references could be found in earlier instruments, such as the mention of the 'laws of humanity' in the preamble of the 1899 Hague Conventions. See M.C. Bassiouni, *Crimes Against Humanity: Historical Evolution and Contemporary Application* (Cambridge; New York: Cambridge University Press, 2011) pp. 86 et seq.

[38] Ana F. Vrdoljak, 'Cultural Heritage in Human Rights and Humanitarian Law' in Orna Ben-Naftali (ed.), *International Humanitarian Law and International Human Rights Law* (Oxford; New York: Oxford University Press, 2011) p. 286.

[39] 'Draft Resolution Relating to the Crime of Genocide, Proposed by the Delegations of Cuba, India and Panama' UN Doc. A/BUR/50; 'Draft Resolution Relating to the Crime of Genocide, Proposed by the Delegation of Saudi-Arabia' UN Doc. A/C.6/86, in Hirad Abtahi and Philippa Webb, *The Genocide Convention—The Travaux Préparatoires*, 2 vols. (Leiden; Boston: Martinus Nijhoff Publishers, 2008) pp. 3–7.

shocks the conscience of mankind, results in great losses to humanity in the form of cultural and other contributions represented by these human groups, and is contrary to moral law and to the spirit and aims of the United Nations.[40]

This single sentence contains a great number of fundamental principles: the right of existence granted to entire human groups; the idea according to which if the human groups are to be harmed, humanity is consequently deemed to be harmed too; and the emphasis on the cultural contribution of these groups. It also contained an ambiguity that would continue to stick to the concept even after the adoption of the Genocide Convention, as to whether the analogy with 'homicide' involved murder, or not necessarily.[41] The core of the resolution already included some of the main features of the upcoming convention: the criminal nature of acts of genocide and the emphasis on both the prevention and punishment of the crime, notably through international cooperation. It further entitled the UN Economic and Social Council (ECOSOC) to undertake a study on the topic in view of the drafting of an international instrument, which in return entrusted the Secretariat General with the same task.

From that moment, the preparatory works were arranged in three main phases: (i) the submission of the Secretariat draft and its discussion by Member States; (ii) the elaboration of a second draft by an *Ad Hoc* Committee; and (iii) its discussion within the UNGA Sixth Committee, which led to the finalization and the adoption of the Convention on the Prevention and Punishment of the Crime of Genocide. During each of these phases the cultural genocide provision encountered a different fate.

Firstly, three legal experts were appointed by the United Nations Secretary General (UNSG) to help draft the Convention: Professor Henri Donnedieu de Vabres from France, Professor Vespasian V. Pella from Romania, and Raphael Lemkin from Poland. Lemkin devoted an important part of his advocating efforts to persuading his colleagues to include a provision criminalizing cultural genocide. A Draft Convention on the Crime of Genocide was presented to the Member States of ECOSOC on 26 June 1947.[42] It contained a rather exhaustive definition of the crime of genocide, in line with Lemkin's eight techniques. The latter were reduced to three main categories, biological, physical, and cultural genocide, which were addressed in three paragraphs of draft Article II as follows:

In this Convention, the word 'genocide' means a criminal act directed against any one of the aforesaid groups of human beings, with the purpose of destroying it in whole or in part or of preventing its preservation or development.

Such acts consist of:

I. [Physical genocide] Causing the death of members of a group or injuring their health or physical integrity (. . .) [list of four acts]

[40] UNGA Res. 96(1) (11 December 1948) 'The Crime of Genocide'.

[41] See Section 3.2.1.1.

[42] ECOSOC 'Draft Convention on the Crime of Genocide' E/447 (26 June 1947) in Abtahi and Webb (n 39) pp. 209–81.

II. [Biological genocide] Restricting births (. . .) [list of three acts]
III. [Cultural genocide] Destroying the specific characteristics of the group by:
  (a) forcible transfer of children to another human group; or
  (b) forced and systematic exile of individuals representing the culture of a group; or
  (c) prohibition of the use of the national language even in private intercourse; or
  (d) systematic destruction of books printed in the national language or of religious works or prohibition of new publications; or
  (e) systematic destruction of historical or religious monuments or their diversion to alien uses, destruction or dispersion of documents and objects of historical, artistic, or religious value and of objects used in religious worship.

The document accompanying the draft mentioned 'divergent views among the experts'[43] as to the relevance of the provision on 'cultural genocide' and Lemkin's stance in favour of strong language already appeared to be isolated. The first subparagraph related to the 'forcible transfer of children' was the only one to gather unanimous support among the experts. These divisions were faithfully reflected at the states' and civil society levels during the debates. A few delegations immediately expressed their disagreement about including acts other than those related to 'physical violence' in the Convention. The United States, joined by France, argued that it would 'invite [. . .] the risk of political interference in the domestic affairs of States, and in respect of questions, which, in fact are connected with the protection of minorities'.[44] Egypt considered that it did not constitute an 'international crime'.[45] In a communication entitled '[a] Call for International Action Against Genocide', the World Federation of United Nations Association went in the same direction, warning against the possibility that the Convention 'may become a Magna Charta [sic] for life and culture'.[46] Other states strongly supported the criminalization of cultural genocide. Poland and Lebanon were in favour of a broad definition of genocide, as advocated by the UNGA in its Resolution 96(1). Many other issues also created controversy: the inclusion of political and linguistic groups within the protected groups, state responsibility, or the creation of an international jurisdiction to review acts of genocide, to name but a few.

In order to deal with these sensitive issues, it was decided that a restricted *Ad Hoc Committee* composed of seven Member States would be created to provide a new draft in light of these particular issues.[47] Within this Committee, Poland's position somehow became diminished, as it considered that cultural genocide would

[43] Ibid., p. 234.
[44] ECOSOC, 'Prevention and Punishment of Genocide, Historical Summary (2 November 1946–20 January 1948) UN Doc. E/621 (26 January 1948), in Abtahi and Webb (n 39) p. 527 (Observations of Governments on the Secretariat's Draft Convention).
[45] Ibid., p. 504.
[46] ECOSOC, 'List of Communications Received from Non-Governmental Organizations Granted Category (b) or (c) Consultative Status' UN Doc. E/C.2/64 (8 August 1947), in Abtahi and Webb (n 39) p. 472.
[47] China, France, Lebanon, Poland, USA, USSR, Venezuela.

be better enclosed in a 'convention aimed at the protection of minority groups'.[48] Despite its strong concerns about such acts, Poland claimed that they should be distinguished from 'the physical extermination of the group. The destruction of the cultural heritage of a group should be suppressed as a preparatory act to physical extermination'.[49] The Union of Soviet Socialist Republics (USSR), along with Lebanon, Pakistan, and Venezuela, became the main defenders of such a provision. The representative of the latter made an emblematic statement to emphasize the importance of the cultural genocide provision:

> [t]he cultural bond was one of the most important factors among those which united a national group, and that was so true that it was possible to wipe out a human group, as such, by destroying its cultural heritage, while allowing the individual members of the group to survive. The physical destruction of individuals was not the only possible form of genocide; it was not the indispensable condition of that crime.[50]

As the debate was becoming increasingly polarized between those focusing on the physical 'barbarity' of the act and those including once-called crimes of 'vandalism', the delegations agreed, as a compromise, to isolate the provision on cultural genocide in a separate article.[51] The underlying goal was to facilitate reservations—and perhaps its later deletion—for those countries that would have otherwise been reluctant to ratify the convention. The provision became the draft Article III and was presented as follows:

> In this Convention genocide also means any deliberate act committed with the intent to destroy the language, religion, or culture of a national, racial or religious group on grounds of the national or racial origin or the religious belief of its members such as:
> 1. Prohibiting the use of the language of the group in daily intercourse or in schools, or the printing and circulation of publications in the language of the group;
> 2. Destroying, or preventing the use of, libraries, museums, schools, historical monuments, places of worship or other cultural institutions and objects of the groups.[52]

The provision on 'forcible transfer of children' temporarily disappeared, with draft Article II mentioning solely acts of physical and biological genocide such as 'imposing measures intended to prevent births within the group'.[53]

A new draft text was submitted to the UNGA Sixth Committee and reviewed during a third and last stage. States debated each provision successively so that the

[48] ECOSOC 'Ad Hoc Committee on Genocide: Summary Record of the Third Meeting' UN Doc. E/AC.25/SR.3, (13 April 1948), in Abtahi and Webb (n 39) p. 701.

[49] ECOSOC 'Ad Hoc Committee on Genocide: Summary Record of the Fifth Meeting' UN Doc. E/AC.25/SR.5 (16 April 1948), in Abtahi and Webb (n 39) p. 728.

[50] Ibid., p. 727.

[51] ECOSOC 'Ad Hoc Committee on Genocide: Summary Record of the Tenth Meeting' UN Doc. E/AC.25/SR.10 (16 April 1948), in Abtahi and Webb (n 39) p, 842: 'The committee decided by three votes to one with two abstentions to insert the notion of cultural genocide in a separate article.'

[52] ECOSOC 'Ad Hoc Committee on Genocide: Summary Record of the Fourteenth Meeting' UN Doc. E/AC.25/SR.14 (27 April 1948), in Abtahi and Webb (n 39) p. 892.

[53] ECOSOC 'Ad Hoc Committee on Genocide (5 April–10 May 1958) Draft Convention on Prevention and Punishment of the Crime of Genocide', UN Doc. E/AC.25/12 (19 May 1948), in Abtahi and Webb (n 39) p. 1162.

draft provision on physical and biological genocide, Article II, was discussed before that of cultural genocide. It soon became foreseeable, throughout the debates, that cultural genocide would be rejected from inclusion in the Convention. In this context, the Greek delegate proposed the reintroduction of the paragraph on 'forced transfer of children' within the physical-biological genocide provision.[54] He justified the amendment by pointing out the 'physical and biological effects' of such acts, and especially the 'conditions of life (. . .) likely to cause [the children] serious harm or even death'.[55] Surprisingly, very few states expressly opposed the amendment during the debates. The United States, one of the states most concerned by the practice, even added its voice in praising the initiative.[56] Only Belgium and the Netherlands expressed their reluctance to include this provision, which 'did not necessarily mean the physical destruction of a group'.[57] By openly admitting that the nature of such acts was cultural, it was feared that a legitimate limit between those cultural acts considered odious enough to be included in the convention and those that were not would be hard to draw. On the contrary, Venezuela clearly assumed the cultural dimension of the harm, with its representative calling upon his peers not to overlook 'acts less terrible in themselves but resulting in "great losses to humanity in the form of cultural and other contributions", for which it was indebted to destroy human groups'.[58]

When the time came to review draft Article III, references to the ongoing negotiations of the forthcoming UDHR, in front of the UNGA Third Committee, gradually multiplied. It became the most efficient argument to delete the cultural genocide provision from the Genocide Convention. France, for instance, had already warned the other delegations that it would vote 'against the inclusion of [this] article [. . .]: not on principle but because it feared that the aim would not be achieved and that its wider and more comprehensive conception of cultural genocide would thus be compromised'.[59] Draft Article III was finally deleted despite a last minute attempt of the USSR to reintroduce it through an amendment; the legal definition of genocide was definitively written down in Article II, as quoted in the general introduction of the book.

The final definition of genocide thus juxtaposes two main elements. The first paragraph refers to the *mens rea* of the crime of genocide, the intent to destroy a group as such. It also contains the second element of genocide, a limited list of four potential victim groups. The second part of Article II contains the *actus reus*. It is a limited list of five potential acts, amongst which the 'forcible transfer of children'

[54] UNGA Sixth Committee (3rd Session) 'Eighty-Second Meeting' UN Doc. A/C.6/SR.82 (23 October 1948), in Abtahi and Webb (n 39) 1492.

[55] Ibid.

[56] UNGA Sixth Committee (3rd Session) 'Eighty-Second Meeting' UN Doc. A/C.6/SR.82 (23 October 1948), in Abtahi and Webb (n 39) p. 1493.

[57] Ibid., p. 1495.

[58] UNGA Sixth Committee (3rd Session) 'Eighty-Third Meeting' UN Doc. A/C.6/SR.83 (25 October 1948), in Abtahi and Webb (n 39) p. 1504.

[59] ECOSOC 'Ad Hoc Committee on Genocide: Summary Record of the Fourteenth Meeting' E/AC.25/SR.14 (27 April 1948), in Abtahi and Webb (n 39) p. 892.

encompasses the sole remaining idea of cultural genocide. This definition appears as a fragile equilibrium, as this compromise was achieved through hard and long-lasting negotiations, highly marked by the post-war historical context.

Against this background, the rejection of the cultural genocide provision can clearly be attributed to the historical crossroads at which the two-year diplomatic process took place. The post-Second World War context comprised a unique moment in which the codification of human rights and international crimes could be fostered. Yet, the outcome of the negotiations was undeniably influenced by the already-emerging ideological dissension between the United States and the USSR. These dissensions were particularly visible in relation to the discussions on 'cultural genocide'; they were also relevant in respect of other issues, and in particular, the inclusion—ultimately rejected—of 'political groups' in the list of victim groups. 'Colonialism was beginning to be challenged'[60] but still constituted a paradigm of international relations, which involved slightly more than fifty countries, as reflected by the membership to the United Nations, of which only four were African.[61] Above all, the memory of both the war and the Holocaust was fresh and the victims of this genocide were directly involved in the negotiations, either through their states or through observing organizations. It is in light of this particular context that the following arguments, which were exchanged during the negotiations, should be read.

From the debates, one can acknowledge that it was not the concept of cultural genocide itself that was questioned, even if it might have been considered to be a somewhat 'nebulous concept'.[62] Actually, most of the delegations arguing against the inclusion of this provision adopted a similar stance: they were not against the concept in itself, as most even deemed its translation into a legal one to be legitimate but rather they challenged its premature insertion into an immature branch of law. As William Schabas has pointed out:

> This was not really a rejection of [Lemkin's] thesis by which a group may be destroyed through attacks on its economy, its cultural bodies and its political institutions. Rather, it was simply a case of the world not being ready for such an innovative proposal in a binding treaty.[63]

The only precedent existing in relation to 'group culture' was the inter-war minority rights system, which, at the time of the negotiations, was openly recalled as a 'failure'.[64] Following the reshaping of Eastern and Central Europe post-First World

[60] Abtahi and Webb (n 39) preface, p. xxvii.

[61] Egypt, Ethiopia, Liberia, South Africa all became members between October and November 1945, cf. http://www.un.org/en/members/ last accessed 3 July 2016.

[62] Antonio Cassese, *International Criminal Law* (2nd edn., Oxford: Oxford University Press, 2008) p. 130.

[63] Schabas, 'Preface' in Lemkin, *Axis Rule in Occupied Europe* (n 3) p. xiii.

[64] Patrick Thornberry, *International Law and the Rights of Minorities* (Oxford: Clarendon Press; New York: Oxford University Press, 1991) pp. 48–9; Mark Mazower, 'The Strange Triumph of Human Rights, 1933–1950' (2004) 47 *The Historical Journal* 379, p. 379 (abstract). This minority rights system will be further analysed in the next section, in relation to the draft minority provision of the UDHR.

War, bilateral treaties had been concluded between those countries hosting new national minorities and their countries of origin, in order to ensure the protection of the rights of these minorities. The violation of German minorities' rights abroad, and therefore of the related minority treaties, had been used as a pretext by Nazi Germany to invade and annex or occupy the Central European territories where those minorities were living.

The prevailing argument was that 'there was a considerable difference between the so-called "physical" genocide (including biological genocide) and "cultural" genocide. Only physical genocide presented those exceptionally horrifying aspects which had revolted the conscience of humanity'.[65] As Venezuela pointed out, 'the general public would find it difficult to understand how, under the concept of genocide, massacres of human groups and denial of the right to teach a particular language in schools could be put on the same plane'.[66] Raphael Lemkin himself had publicly agreed to have cultural genocide addressed in another *corpus* of rules, drawing a distinction between 'physical and biological genocide', which affected the right to life, and cultural genocide, which concerned the 'right to development'.[67] Nevertheless, he would later write that '[c]ultural genocide [was] the most important part of the Convention'.[68]

Notwithstanding, beyond these convincing arguments, one cannot prevent oneself from questioning the underlying sincerity of other states' arguments. The main states opposing cultural genocide were the United States, Canada, and France,[69] all either being or having been involved in widespread campaigns of colonization to conquer territories already inhabited by other peoples. Some countries, such as Brazil and Egypt, 'expressed the fear that the concept of cultural genocide might hamper a reasonable policy of assimilation which no State aiming at national unity could be expected to renounce'.[70] This illustrative statement tends to confirm the idea that '[t]he wording of the (1948) Convention was shaped by the desire of its framers not to criminalize their own behaviour'.[71] The most powerful agreement was undoubtedly on the idea that cultural genocide was overall a minority rights issue to be included in the framework of the discussions related to the draft UDHR rather than in the

65 ECOSOC 'Ad Hoc Committee on Genocide, Commentary on Articles Adopted by the Committee' UN Doc. E/AC.25/W.1 (26 April 1948), in Abtahi and Webb (n 39) p. 982.

66 ECOSOC 'Two Hundred and Eighteenth Meeting: Draft Convention on the Crime of Genocide' E/SR.218 (26 August 1948), Canadian Delegate's Statement, in Abtahi and Webb (n 39) p. 1223.

67 Raphael Lemkin, 'Le Crime de Génocide' (Paris: La Documentation Française, Notes Documentaires et Etudes No 417, 1946) in Raphael Lemkin, *Qu'est-ce qu'un Génocide*, Préface de Panné J.-L. (Monaco: Editions du Rocher, 2008) p. 254 ('Mémorandum sur la Nécessité d'Inclure les Clauses Contre le Génocide dans les Traités de Paix').

68 Raphael Lemkin, 'Memorandum on the Genocide Convention', AHJS, P-154, Box 6, Folder 5, quoted in Moses 'Empire, Colony, Genocide' (n 19) pp. 12–13.

69 See e.g. ECOSOC 'Two Hundred and Eighteenth Meeting: Draft Convention on the Crime of Genocide' E/SR.218 (26 August 1948), Canadian Delegate's Statement, in Abtahi and Webb (n 39) p. 1224.

70 UN Doc. A/C.6/SR.63, General Assembly Sixth Committee, 63rd meeting, Thursday 30 September 1948, Egyptian Delegate's Statement, in Abtahi and Webb (n 39) p. 1293; Brazilian Delegate's Statement, p. 1292.

71 Christopher Powell, 'What Do Genocides Kill? A Relational Conception of Genocide' (2007) 9 *J.G.R.* 527, p. 532.

Genocide Convention.[72] The proceedings before the UNGA Third Committee, in charge of drafting the Universal Declaration, actually tend to confirm the doubts as to the sincerity of the delegations that opposed the cultural genocide draft provision in front of the Sixth Committee. Indeed, the same delegations—with the exception of Denmark—that had argued that the issue of cultural genocide would best be addressed by the UDHR, later reversed their position and voted against the inclusion of a draft provision on minority rights in this same Declaration.

2.2.2 The fate of the 'minority rights' provision in the draft Universal Declaration of Human Rights

> How (. . .) can we imagine an agreement of minds between men who are gathered together precisely in order to accomplish a common intellectual task, men who come from the four corners of the globe and who not only belong to different cultures and civilizations, but are of antagonistic spiritual associations and schools of thought. . .?[73]

This sentence introduced a report initiated by the UN Educational, Scientific, and Cultural Organisation (UNESCO), which aimed to gather the perspectives of worldwide experts on the content of a potential international bill of rights. One specific provision of the draft document became particularly illustrative of these cultural differences, the 'minority rights provision', which was drafted as follows:

> In States inhabited by a substantial number of persons of a race, language or religion other than those of the majority of the population, persons belonging to such ethnic, linguistic or religious minorities shall have the right, as far as compatible with public order and security to establish and maintain schools and cultural or religious institutions and to use their own language in the Press, in public assembly and before the courts and other authorities to the State.[74]

Although the principle underlying this provision had already been stated by the Permanent Court of International Justice (PCIJ),[75] it became quite controversial in the course of the negotiations. The emphasis fell on the protection of particular groups' religious and cultural institutions, their right to educate their children according to their own traditions and beliefs, and their right to use their own language in the public intercourse. These three specific features were also—and still are—contained in other provisions of the draft Universal Declaration,[76] though

[72] ECOSOC 'Two Hundred and Eighteenth Meeting: Draft Convention on the Crime of Genocide' E/SR.218 (26 August 1948), Venezuelan Delegate's Statement, in Abtahi and Webb (n 39) p. 1223.

[73] Jacques Maritain, 'Introduction' in Unesco, *Human Rights: Comments and Interpretations* (Paris: Unesco, 1948), UNESCO/PHS/3 (Rev) p. ii.

[74] UNCHR 'Report of the Drafting Committee to the Commission on Human Rights' E/CN.4/95 (21 May 1948) Draft art. 31.

[75] *Minority Schools in Albania* (Advisory Opinion) 6 April 1935, PCIJ Rep. Series AB No. 64, pp. 18–20.

[76] E/CN.4/95 (n 74) arts. 16, 21, 22, 26; Universal Declaration of Human Rights (adopted 10 December 1948) UNGA Res. 217 A(III) (UDHR) arts. 18, 26. The only mention of 'language' is to be found in art. 2 on non-discrimination.

formulated in individual rights whereas the minority provision had an explicit collective dimension, reflecting the 'cultural genocide' draft provision. According to Johannes Morsink, the added value would rest not on the nature of the rights protected as such but on the protection of 'ethnicity and language'.[77]

In contrast to the 'cultural genocide provision', the fate of the 'minority rights provision' of the draft International Bill of Rights—which would become the UDHR—was not foreseeable when the negotiations were initiated. As was the case for the negotiations of the draft Genocide Convention, the negotiations of the Universal Declaration were split into successive stages: the Secretariat's draft was first discussed and compiled by a drafting committee, which gathered for three sessions in Geneva; the outcome—the 'Geneva draft'—was subsequently discussed before the Third Committee prior to the final vote of the UNGA. The draft minority provision cited above was set out in Article 31 of the Geneva Draft and accompanied by a number of proposed alternative texts, the vast majority of which aimed at amending the Draft Committee's text and not at deleting it.[78] Only the delegation of the United States, led by Eleanor Roosevelt, clearly displayed its opposition to the draft provision; it proposed that the draft Article 31 should be substituted with a consolidation of two other draft provisions, so as to become: the right to 'rest and leisure, to participate in the custom and the cultural life of the community and of groups in the community, to enjoy the arts, and to share in the benefits that result from scientific discoveries'.[79]

The discussions within the Drafting Committee nevertheless evolved from one session to another. If a United States-sponsored amendment to delete the provision was first defeated, the draft provision was eventually rejected at the third session of the Drafting Committee.[80] According to Morsink, 'the negative mood (. . .) was caused by the worries that had been stirred up by [the] other discussions' on draft Article III of the Genocide Convention. The Cold War-tainted divide, which had already emerged in relation to the cultural genocide provision, arose again in relation to the minority rights provision.[81] Throughout the negotiations, the opposition to the draft provision increased, mainly advanced by representatives of the American continent. Latin American countries and the United States thus repeatedly argued, in the line of the arguments of Brazil and Egypt before the Sixth Committee, that a minority rights provision would impede the assimilationist policies, especially in relation to migrants, that were generally practised in those states. Emblematic of this position was Brazil's statement that:

> [i]f groups of foreigners living within a State remained too closely attached to the country of their origin, their assimilation into the country that had received them would be

[77] Johannes Morsink, *The Universal Declaration of Human Rights, Origins, Drafting and Intent* (Philadelphia: University of Pennsylvania Press, 2000) p. 269.

[78] E/CN.4/95 (n 74) pp. 13–14: alternative texts proposed by the Sub-Commission on the Prevention of Discrimination and the Protection of Minorities, France and the United Kingdom.

[79] Ibid. Alternative text proposed by the United States.

[80] ECOSOC 'Commission on Human Rights, Third Session, Summary Record of the Seventy-third meeting, Lake Success, New York, 15 June 1948' (24 June 1948) E/CN.4/SR.73.

[81] Morsink, *The Universal Declaration of Human Rights* (n 77) p. 274.

jeopardized. That country would be pursuing a policy of national suicide if it were to harbour groups of foreign agents who might prove to be extremely dangerous.[82]

This group of countries was joined in its opposition by Australia, for which 'the issue was one of assimilation and not of protection of minorities' and which stated that 'it desired the dispersal of groups rather than the formation of minorities'.[83] Several countries further stated that minority issues were not a universal problem but merely a European matter, with which they were not concerned.[84] Other delegations feared that a minority rights provision would harm the universal character of the Declaration.[85] Finally, a number of delegations expressed opposition or reluctance to revive the system of minority protection introduced by the League of Nations, the failure of which was deemed to be partly responsible for triggering the Second World War.[86] Some scholars therefore consider that the memory and the failure of the minority treaty system constituted the main reason for the rejection of the minority rights provision.[87]

By contrast, the USSR, Yugoslavia, and Denmark each submitted amendments in order to reintroduce the minority rights provision in front of the Third Committee.[88] The formulation of these submissions varied in their content. The Danish proposal focused only on minority rights related to education, while the two other amendments had a broader scope and also covered minority linguistic and cultural rights. Poland criticized the limited scope of the Danish proposal in a statement which illustrated the strong connection between the minority rights provision and the cultural genocide provision:

National culture, which was not mentioned in the Danish text, was the very expression of the life of the national community. In Poland, the first measures taken by the Nazis had been directed against education, and also against the expression of national cultural life.[89]

The Yugoslavian proposal focused largely on 'ethnical rights', as its representative argued that the minority rights provision should be nothing more than the

[82] UNGA Third Committee '161st Meeting, Draft International Declaration of Human Rights (E/800), Proposal concerning the Protection of Minorities' (27 November 1948) A/C.3/SR.161, p. 721. See also p. 722 (Chile).

[83] Ibid., pp. 725–6 (Australia).

[84] See e.g. A/C.3/SR.161 (n 82) p. 721 (Mexico), p. 725 (Australia), p. 726 (United States); UNGA Third Committee '162nd Meeting, Draft International Declaration of Human Rights (E/800)' Proposal concerning the Protection of Minorities (27 November 1948) A/C.3/SR.162, p. 729 (Canada).

[85] Johannes Morsink, 'Cultural Genocide, the Universal Declaration and Minority Rights' (1999) 21 *H.R.Q.* 1009, pp. 1057–8.

[86] See e.g. A/C.3/SR.161 (n 82) pp. 722–3 (France); A/C.3/SR.162 (n 84) p. 727 (Greece).

[87] Morsink, 'Cultural Genocide, The Universal Declaration and Minority Rights' (n 85) p. 1057.

[88] UNGA Third Committee 'Additional Articles Proposed for the Draft Declaration "Yugoslavia"' (6 November 1948) A/C.3/307/Rev.1/Add.1; UNGA Third Committee 'Denmark: addendum' (19 November 1948) A/C.3/307/Rev. 1/Add.2; UNGA Third Committee 'Additional Articles Proposed for the Draft Declaration, Corrigendum to Document E/800, Union of Soviet Socialist Republic' (27 November 1948) A/C.3/307/Rev.2/Corr.2.

[89] See e.g. A/C.3/SR.161 (n 82) p. 724.

recognition of the existence of minorities, coupled with the granting of individual rights to its members.[90] Eastern European countries strongly supported these amendments, along with a few other delegations such as Belgium and Denmark, but their efforts remained in vain. Some of them underlined the fundamental character of these rights. In an incisive statement, the Byelorussian delegate replied to those countries which argued that they were not concerned by the issue of minorities:

> It was impossible to ignore the fact that, at one time, Australia had carried out a policy of forceful elimination of its aboriginal group and that the North American Indian had almost ceased to exist in the United States. In colonial territories, there were no signs that indigenous culture was being developed and encouraged, and yet the representatives of metropolitan Powers made contant [sic.] references to the spread of civilization.[91]

The argument was also used by the USSR in an attempt 'to effect a division between the "Colonial Powers" and the Latin American countries'.[92] Poland described the provision as 'represent[ing] the positive aspect of the principle of non-discrimination'.[93] This same argument was finally used against the defenders of the provision, who argued that the minority rights provision was redundant in light of the non-discrimination provision already contained in the draft Declaration, the final and current version of which reads as follows:

> Everyone is entitled to all the rights and freedoms set forth in this Declaration, without distinction of any kind, such as race, colour, sex, language, religion, political or other opinion, national or social origin, property, birth or other status. Furthermore, no distinction shall be made on the basis of the political, jurisdictional or international status of the country or territory to which a person belongs, whether it be independent, trust, non-self-governing or under any other limitation of sovereignty.[94]

Considering that 'the protection of minorities would amount to an increase of discrimination',[95] Haiti proposed to settle the discussions by deferring the matter to the United Nations Sub-Commission on Prevention of Discrimination and Protection of Minorities.[96] Finally, the Chair decided to postpone the vote on these amendments after the discussion of the Haitian proposal, which was adopted by thirty-five votes, with five abstentions,[97] thus closing the discussions on the minority rights provision. An additional Yugoslavian amendment, related to national minorities and their development, was also discussed but similarly rejected.[98]

[90] Ibid., p. 720. [91] A/C.3/SR.162 (n 84) p. 728. [92] Thornberry (n 64) p. 136.
[93] A/C.3/SR.161 (n 82) p. 724. [94] UDHR (n 76) art. 2.
[95] See e.g. A/C.3/SR.161 (n 82) p. 724.
[96] UNGA Third Committee 'Haiti: Draft Resolution' (27 November 1948) A/C.3/373.
[97] A/C.3/SR.162 (n 84) p. 734.
[98] A/C.3/307/Rev.1/Add.1 (n 88) part B, discussed in UNGA Third Committee '163rd meeting, Draft International Declaration of Human Rights (E/800)' Proposal concerning the Protection of Minorities (29 November 1948) A/C.3/SR.163.

The rejection of the minority rights provision marks the anchoring of human rights in an individualist perspective. The final outcome of the UDHR was very much criticized, in particular for reflecting a Western ethno-centred view of human rights and therefore, of human beings. The American Anthropological Association (AAA) thus openly asked: 'How can the proposed Declaration be applicable to all human beings, and not be a statement of rights conceived only in terms of the values prevalent in the countries of Western Europe and America?'[99] The AAA statement would later come to reflect 'cultural relativism', the idea of which is very blatant in its following proposal:

> Standards and values are relative to the culture from which they derive so that any attempt to formulate postulates that grow out of the beliefs or moral codes of one culture must to that extent detract from the applicability of any Declaration of Human Rights to mankind as a whole.[100]

This statement itself was similarly criticized, but, as Sally Engle Merry notes, '[t]his was a reasonable worry in 1947, still a deeply colonial era, as it is today under the pressures of globalizing capitalism'.[101] As she illustrates, the AAA's criticism proved to be a well-founded one in light of the subsequent development of international law, which predominantly saw culture as an 'obstacle' to universalism.[102] Reading the negotiations of the UDHR may indeed remind of Hannah Arendt's ironic report on the nature of those international lawyers who drafted international human rights instruments: '[t]he groups they formed, the declarations they issued, showed an uncanny similarity in language and composition to that of societies for the prevention of cruelty to animals'.[103]

Half a decade later, the AAA attenuated its position in a 'Declaration on Anthropology and Human Rights', in which it undertook to define the basis for its involvement in human rights: 'People and groups have a generic right to realize their capacity for culture, and to produce, reproduce and change the conditions and forms of their physical, personal and social existence, *so long as such activities do not diminish the same capacities of others*'.[104] This Declaration thus reasserted the notion that the anthropological approach to human rights should be based on 'anthropological principles of respect for concrete human differences, both collective and individual, rather than on the abstract legal uniformity of Western tradition'. At the same time, it acknowledged the need to set limits to the unconditional tolerance of cultures that it had advocated in 1947, thus implicitly endorsing Article 30 UDHR, which provides that: 'Nothing in this Declaration may be interpreted as implying for any State,

99 AAA, the Executive Board, 'Statement on Human Rights', *American Anthropologist*, New Series, Vol. 49, No. 4, 1947, p. 539.

100 Ibid., p. 542.

101 Sally Engle Merry, 'Human Rights Law and the Demonization of Culture (and Anthropology along the Way)' (2003) 26 *A.A.A* 55, p. 67.

102 Ibid., p. 71.

103 Arendt, *Origins of Totalitarianism* (n 15) p. 371.

104 AAA, 'Declaration on Anthropology and Human Rights Committee', 1999, available at: http://www.aaanet.org/about/Policies/statements/Declaration-on-Anthropology-and-Human-Rights.cfm (last accessed 1 February 2015) (emphasis added).

group or person any right to engage in any activity or to perform any act aimed at the destruction of any of the rights and freedoms set forth herein.'[105]

2.3 From Cultural Genocide to Ethnocide

The legal vacuum surrounding the concept of cultural genocide constituted a fertile ground for those groups who would later argue in favour of having their experience of 'cultural destruction' recognized as genocide. As a result of the evolution of the concept outwith the legal sphere, 'cultural genocide' underwent further distortions, deriving either from its defenders or its opponents. The former multiplied the '-cide words' to qualify the specificity of some experience of victimhood, whereas the latter saw in 'cultural genocide' an argument to dismiss alleged claims of genocide.

2.3.1 The resurgence of ethnocide in the socio-anthropological sphere

The resurgence of 'ethnocide' first occurred in the anthropological literature of the 1960s and 1970s; it was engaged to describe the experiences of indigenous groups in Latin America, not their blatant extermination as such but rather the so-called 'vanishing' of indigenous groups in the Amazonian region, whose land had subsequently become that of extractive industries and others, thus destroying their traditional ways of life.[106] In a book entitled *La Paix Blanche ou Introduction à l'éthnocide*, Robert Jaulin reported on several years of anthropological observations in Colombia, during which time he witnessed the progressive assimilation of the Bari Indians within the dominant 'White population'. The purpose of the latter group—which was mainly composed of missionaries and industries—was to neutralize and control the Bari, and *a fortiori,* their lands and resources, with the support of the local authorities. Jaulin described this phenomenon as 'cultural criminality' and defined 'ethnocide' as 'a consequence of the extension of ourselves',[107] and thus, as a reflection of the tendency of the Western culture to envision itself as a superior civilization, in order to justify the eradication of other cultures.

[105] Ibid. In the Declaration, the AAA explicitly recognizes that its approach builds on international human rights treaties and customary law: 'the Universal Declaration of Human Rights (UDHR), the International Covenants on Civil and Political Rights, and on Social, Economic, and Cultural Rights, the Conventions on Torture, Genocide, and Elimination of All Forms of Discrimination Against Women, and Other Treaties which Bring Basic Human Rights within the Parameters of International Written and Customary Law and Practice'.

[106] Cuche (n 23) p. 64; Robert Jaulin, *La Paix Blanche. Introduction à l'Ethnocide* (Paris: Seuil, 1970); Pierre Clastres, 'Ethnocide' (1988) 28 *Art & Text* 51 (First published in 'De l'Ethnocide' (1974) 14 *L'Homme* 101; translated by Julian Pefanis and Bernadette Maher). For a criticism of the use of 'vanishing', see Elazar Barkan, 'Genocide of Indigenous Peoples' in Robert Gellately and Ben Kiernan (eds.), *The Specter of Genocide: Mass Murder in Historical Perspective* (Cambridge: Cambridge University Press, 2003) pp. 119–20.

[107] Robert Jaulin, *La Paix Blanche. Introduction à l'Ethnocide* (Paris: Seuil, 1970) p. 10.

A few years later, Pierre Clastres would advance a more systematic conceptualization of the concept of 'ethnocide'; Clastres characterized it as a 'new' word to describe either 'something new to be thought—or else something old, but as yet unthought'.[108] This was only partially true if one recalls Lemkin's use of the term 'ethnocide', which was therefore not a neologism. However, the anthropological concept was new to the extent that Lemkin's conceptualization of 'ethnocide' was synonymous with the generic concept of 'genocide',[109] as he considered the Latin roots of *ethnos* and *genos* to be interchangeable. In contrast with Lemkin's focus on the victim group, the anthropological conception tended to redefine the concept by understanding *ethnos* as the targeted feature of the group: its culture. Clastres rather defined 'ethnocide' as 'the systematic destruction of the modes of life and thought of people who are different from those who carry out this destructive enterprise. In short, genocide kills their bodies, while ethnocide kills their spirit'.[110] He opposed genocide and ethnocide as 'two perverse forms of pessimism and optimism';[111] the latter would not reach the stage of extermination but aim at the 'improvement' of the 'Other', while the former would rather imply some form of group destruction. Clastres thus ultimately defined ethnocide as 'forced assimilation'[112]; this understanding was especially reflected in his statement that: 'ethnocide is the dissolution of the many in the One'.[113]

This term has been engaged in one international instrument, the Declaration of San Jose of 11 December 1981, entitled 'UNESCO and the Struggle against Ethnocide', which declares 'that ethnocide, that is cultural genocide, is a violation of international law equivalent to genocide, which was condemned by the [1948 Genocide Convention]'.[114] This Declaration can be read in line with the 1971 Declaration of Barbados,[115] in which a pool of anthropologists had already demanded that Latin American States and religious institutions halt 'acts of aggression directed against aboriginal groups and culture' and 'both active interventions to "protect" Indian society as well as massacres and forced migrations from the homelands'. The Declaration further listed a set of measures to be adopted immediately, in which case they would 'be held responsible by default for crimes of ethnocide and connivance with genocide'.[116] In the Declaration of San Jose, 'ethnocide' is defined in the preamble:

[108] Pierre Clastres, 'Ethnocide' (1988) 28 *Art & Text* 51 (First published in 'De l'Ethnocide' (1974) 14 *L'Homme* 101; translated by Julian Pefanis and Bernadette Maher) p. 51.

[109] Lemkin, *Axis Rule in Occupied Europe* (n 3) p. 79, fn. 1.

[110] Clastres (n 108) p. 52.

[111] Ibid., p. 53.

[112] The idea of 'forced assimilation' will be studied in more depth in the next Section 2.3.2.1.

[113] Clastres (n 108) pp. 54–5.

[114] Declaration of San Jose, 'UNESCO and the Struggle against Ethnocide' (adopted 11 December 1981) preamble, para. 2. Robert Jaulin took part in its drafting.

[115] World Council of Churches and Programme to Combat Racism PCR 1/71 (E), 'Declaration of Barbados' available at: http://www.nativeweb.org/papers/statements/state/barbados1.php (last accessed 1 February 2015).

[116] The threat of being 'held responsible (. . .) for crimes of ethnocide' is mentioned in the set of measures intended to apply to religious missions but its formulation clearly indicates that states are the parties predominantly responsible for such crimes.

It means that an ethnic group is denied the right to develop and transmit its own culture and its own language, whether collectively or individually. This involves an extreme form of massive violation of human rights and, in particular, the right of ethnic groups to respect for their cultural identity.

The emphasis is again placed on the notions of 'development' and 'intergenerational transmission' of the group culture. Throughout the Declaration, ethnocide clearly appears as a concept tailored to indigenous peoples. It has operated to create and establish a border with the legal concept of genocide, which has increasingly become associated with physical-biological conceptions of group destruction.

Through these anthropological discussions of the concept, one can see that the core element of the debate remains the concept of group destruction, which lies at the heart of the definition of genocide and its *mens rea*. While anthropologists have framed their discussion outside the legal concept of genocide, to advocate instead for the recognition of a new international crime, other scholars, predominantly sociologists and philosophers, have focused their reflections on the legal definition of genocide itself and provided innovative interpretations of the notion of group destruction, mostly based on Lemkin's early conceptualization.

In this regard, the argument is that 'group destruction' should be understood in social terms, following Lemkin's powerful idea that genocide targets 'group foundations'.[117] For instance, in a speech as eloquent as it was controversial, Jean-Paul Sartre characterized the United States war in Vietnam as 'genocide', not from the perspective of the killings themselves but because 'the social structure [was] destroyed'.[118] This comes back to Lemkin's idea that physical and cultural destruction were two sides of the same coin. While Lemkin's thought has sometimes seemed to lack scientific support,[119] his intuition has not necessarily been contradicted by further research on the harm of group destruction, especially with the development of a sociological branch within the field of genocide studies. For instance, Christopher Powell implemented Norbert Elias's theory of groups as 'figurations' in relation to the *genos* of genocide, which he consequently defined as a 'network of practical social relations'. Genocide would thus be deemed to occur when the relational process is forcibly disrupted,[120] which seems more likely to take into account processes of ethnic cleansing or forced assimilation and of forced transfers of children.[121]

[117] Lemkin, *Axis Rule in Occupied Europe* (n 3) p. 79.

[118] Jean-Paul Sartre, Statement *'On Genocide'*, Second Session of the Bertrand Russell International War Crimes Tribunal on Vietnam, Denmark (November 1967): He saw in the United States position a 'blackmail' towards the Vietnamese peoples of both parts of the Seventeenth parallel, who were left with the choice of 'extermination (. . .) or capitulation', in other words, 'collective death or disintegration'.

[119] Damien Short, 'Cultural Genocide and Indigenous Peoples: A Sociological Approach' (2010) 14 *I.J.H.R.* 833, p. 841. The author refers to Moses 'Empire, Colony, Genocide' (n 19) p. 16.

[120] Christopher Powell, *Barbaric Civilization: A Critical Sociology of Genocide* (Montreal: McGill-Queen's University Press, 2011) p. 538.

[121] Damien Short, 'Australia: A Continuing Genocide?' (2010) 12 *J.G.R.* 45, p. 52.

In parallel, increasing emphasis has been placed on the harm caused to the 'social and cultural vitality' of the victim group.[122] On this basis, Claudia Card has theorized the ultimate harm of genocide under the concept of 'social death':

> Specific to genocide is the harm inflicted on its victims' social vitality. It is not just that one's group membership is the occasion for harms that are definable independently of one's identity as a member of the group. When a group with its own cultural identity is destroyed, its survivors lose their cultural heritage and may even lose their intergenerational connections.[123]

Focusing on the harm of genocide thus sheds new light on its cultural dimension, as illustrated by Mohammed Abed, who further advanced Card's theory and identified the necessary 'features that make a group susceptible to the harm of genocide', emphasizing among others its cultural 'comprehensiveness': 'a group must possess traditions, practices, and rituals that influence more than a single area or a few areas of the life of an individual'.[124]

From these socio-legal variations, it appears that the cultural dimension of the crime of genocide could possibly be re-introduced at the level of its *mens rea*, an argument that has been brought at several occasions into the legal sphere.

2.3.2 The persistence of the cultural genocide question in the legal sphere

The concept of cultural genocide has re-emerged in the legal sphere in two main contexts. The first is that of the forcible transfer of aboriginal and indigenous children in Australia and North America during the nineteenth and twentieth centuries. Although such acts seem *a priori* to fit within the definition of genocide, and in particular subparagraph II(e), states and tribunals have been quite reluctant to recognize such experiences of victimization as genocide, rather arguing that these were processes of 'forced assimilation'. The second case concerns the crimes of 'ethnic cleansing' that were perpetrated in the Former Yugoslavia in the 1990s and the way in which 'cultural genocide' has been used and analysed in the course of the related judicial process. In both contexts, the use of the 'cultural genocide' rhetoric has contributed to the dismissal of claims of genocide through the requalification of the facts under different labels, which are often considered as euphemisms of genocide.

2.3.2.1 Cultural genocide and forced assimilation

The thin line between ethnocide and forced assimilation, as conceptualized by Clastres, has also been used as an argument to dismiss the genocidal character of ethnocide. Jean-Michel Chaumont has thus argued for the clear distinction

[122] Short 'Cultural Genocide and Indigenous Peoples' (n 119) pp. 839–44.

[123] Claudia Card, 'Genocide and Social Death' in John K. Roth (ed.), *Genocide and Human Rights: A Philosophical Guide* (Houndmills, Basingstoke, Hampshire; New York: Palgrave Macmillan, 2005) p. 248. Claudia Card first coined the concept of 'social death' in 2003.

[124] Mohammed Abed, 'Clarifying the Concept of Genocide' (2006) 37 *Metaphilosophy* 308, pp. 314–15. The other features are the individual 'consent' to be member of the group and the 'arduous exit'.

between genocide and ethnocide, on the basis of the difference between the statuses of victims. To him, victims of ethnocide are considered as 'perfectible', while those of genocide are not. While Clastres had identified the same distinction, Chaumont made it essential.[125] This shift of perspective on the perpetrators' intent has been the predominant reason for the rejection of the legal qualification of acts of cultural genocide and processes of ethnocide as genocide.

'Forced assimilation' and 'cultural genocide' have been intertwined since Lemkin's conceptualization of genocide was advanced.[126] It is theoretically possible to construct a scale of gradation between these various concepts, and in particular between 'acculturation', 'assimilation', and 'ethnocide' or 'cultural genocide'. While the two former concepts can be regarded as 'inevitable process[es] of history',[127] 'more or less forced', the latter necessarily involves some coercive and intentional elements.[128] Yet, when assimilation is 'forced' and involves 'State policies and programs',[129] its differentiation from ethnocide becomes less obvious; that is, the process is opened up to various possible interpretations. Neither 'cultural genocide' nor 'forced assimilation' is defined in international law, which tends to strengthen the uncertainties as to their respective conceptual borders. It is generally assumed that 'forced assimilation' is prohibited through provisions related to the protection of culture,[130] including, in particular the negative obligations of states not to interfere in minority cultures.[131]

These inherent ambiguities have been displayed very clearly in cases of forcibly transferred children. A brief consideration of recent global history reveals that this practice is far from isolated. Throughout the nineteenth and twentieth centuries, 'settlers' colonial societies' organized the removal of indigenous children from their families, and their transfer either to settlers' families or residential schools, in order to 'de-Indianize' them. The underlying motto of such a campaign has been formulated in the United States as: 'Kill the Indian, save the man.'[132] Children

[125] Jean-Michel Chaumont, 'Génocide et Ethnocide' in Katia Boustany and Daniel Dormoy (eds.), *Génocide(s)* (Bruxelles: Bruylant; Editions de l'Université de Bruxelles, 1999) p. 254: 'le statut des victimes est complètement différent dans les deux crimes: pour l'ethnocidaire, les victimes sont perfectibles, elles sont susceptibles d'être "civilisées" et, à cette condition, intégrées dans la communauté dominante; pour le génocidaire, à l'inverse, les victimes sont irréductiblement ce qu'elles sont, et, à ce titre, incurables'.

[126] Lemkin, *Axis Rule in Occupied Europe* (n 3) p. 80.

[127] Thornberry (n 64) p. 141.

[128] Cuche (n 23) p. 64. Damien Short also puts the emphasis on coercion to argue that forced transfers of children, which have occurred in Australia, 'are producing something more than mere cultural change', in Short, 'Australia: A Continuing Genocide?' (n 121) p. 62.

[129] Rogers Brubaker, *Ethnicity without Groups* (Cambridge, Mass.: Harvard University Press, 2004) p. 119.

[130] Walter Kälin, 'Assimilation, Forced' in *Max Planck Encyclopedia of Public International Law* (Heidelberg and Oxford University Press, article last updated October 2010) paras. 8–11; Sub-Commission on Prevention of Discrimination and Protection of Minorities (53rd Session), 'Commentary to the Declaration on the Rights of Persons Belonging to National or Ethnic, Religious and Linguistic Minorities, by Asbjørn Eide,' (2 April 2001), E/CN.4/Sub.2/AC.5/2001/2 (Eide's commentary on the Minority Rights Declaration) para. 27.

[131] See e.g. UDHR (n 76) art. 27; International Covenant on Economic, Social and Cultural Rights (adopted 16 December 1966, entered into force 3 January 1976) 993 UNTS 3 (ICESCR) art. 15; International Covenant on Civil and Political Rights (adopted 16 December 1966, entered into force 23 March 1976) 999 UNTS 171 (ICCPR) art. 27. Detailed in Chapter 4.

[132] Statement made by Lieutenant Richard Henry Pratt, founder of the first residential school in Pennsylvania. See Patrick Wolfe, 'Settler Colonialism and the Elimination of the Native' (2006) 8 *J.G.R.* 387, p. 397; Vinodh Jaichand, 'Residential Schools' in Dinah L. Shelton (ed.), *Encyclopedia*

from nomadic societies in Iran and Syria,[133] as well as Roma children in several European countries also endured the same fate.[134] Examples of such schools can also be found in East Africa, 'generally patterned on colonial modes of education'[135] and in the Middle East, where they 'actually targeted the elites of indigenous communities'.[136] In the course of the Argentinean 'dirty war', led by the military Junta from 1976 to 1983, the dictatorship physically targeted political opponents while stealing their children to transfer them to families supporting the regime. All of these cases encompassed acts that are criminalized in the Genocide Convention, but nevertheless raised the question of whether they reached and satisfied the level of intent required. This section will focus on the cases of Australia and Canada, where commissions of inquiry have been established in order to promote truth and reconciliation and to redress the damage caused to these 'Stolen Generations'.

The Australian programme ran from 'the first days of the European occupation of Australia'[137] until the 1960s; the last school closed in 1988.[138] During the first stage, the programme focused on the so-called 'half-cast' children, before being generalized and administered in respect of all aboriginal children in 1940. The children were transferred either to boarding schools or to White Australian families in order to be acculturated and assimilated. This process was organized through federal and state laws, the coercive intensity of which varied across time and between states. One recurrent pattern was the placement of indigenous children under the 'guardianship' of a public 'Protector', who was invested with the discretion to remove them from their family in case of neglect. In practice, some authorities would systematically consider indigenous children to be neglected. No judicial authority was empowered to review the administrative decisions until 1972. In most cases, these transfers occurred without the consent of the parents; in some cases, their consent was required but authorities would not hesitate to pressure and threaten parents in case of their initial refusal.[139] Despite 'the apparent closeness of fit between the language contained in this provision and the many programs of mass child removal that have been carried out over the past two centuries',[140] Article II(e)

of Genocide and Crimes Against Humanity, vol. 2 (New York: Macmillan Reference USA; Thomson Gale, 2004) p. 900. Permanent Forum on Indigenous Issues, 'Indigenous Peoples and Boarding Schools: A Comparative Study (Prepared by Andrea Smith)' (26 January 2009) UN Doc. E/C.19/2009/CRP.1, p. 5; Tove Skutnabb-Kangas and Robert Dunbar, 'Indigenous Children's Education as Linguistic Genocide and a Crime Against Humanity? A Global View' (2010) 1 *Gáldu čála – Journal of Indigenous Peoples Rights*, p. 66.

133 Robert K. Hitchkock, 'Indigenous Populations, Genocide of' in Israel W. Charny (ed.), *Encyclopedia of Genocide*, vol. 1 (Toulouse; Santa Barbara: ABC-Clio, 1999) pp. 349–54.

134 Ian Hancock, 'Romanis' in Dinah L. Shelton (ed.), *Encyclopedia of Genocide and Crimes Against Humanity*, vol. 2 (New York: Macmillan Reference USA; Thomson Gale, 2004) p. 922.

135 United Nations Permanent Forum on Indigenous Issues (UNPFII), 'Indigenous Peoples and Boarding Schools' (n 132) p. 4.

136 Ibid.

137 Australian Human Rights Commission, *Bringing Them Home, Report of the National Inquiry into the Separation of Aboriginal and Torres Strait Islander Children from Their Families* (April 1997) p. 22.

138 Ibid., p. 30. 139 Ibid., pp. 5–9.

140 Kurt Mundorff, 'Other Peoples' Children: A Textual and Contextual Interpretation of the Genocide Convention, Article 2(e)' (2009) 50 *Harv.Int'l L.J.* 61, p. 63.

remained dormant until its revival in the mid-1990s in Australia, when that country's Human Rights and Equal Opportunity Commission was petitioned to conduct a 'national inquiry into the separation of Aboriginal and Torres Strait Islander Children from their families'.[141] In particular, the Commission was required by the Attorney General of Australia to trace back the history of the legal and political processes underlying this programme, and to consider adequate remedies. In April 1997, the Commission released a report entitled *Bringing Them Home*, which contains the testimonies of the victims of such removals as well as assorted evidence of the harm caused by those removals. The report triggered an important polemic within Australian society as it considered that the persistent and systematic policy of removals fell under the category of genocide.[142] Following the report, the Australian Prime Minister apologized in 2007 to the 'Stolen Generation' for 'the laws and policies of successive Parliaments and governments that have inflicted profound grief, suffering and loss' upon them.[143] A 'Sorry Day' was introduced to commemorate the 'Stolen Generation', the webpage of which qualifies the process as 'assimilation', without reference to the genocide label, despite the conclusions of the *Bringing Them Home* report.[144]

In Canada, the practice of removing native children from their families to send them to residential schools was also widespread from the 1870s until the 1970s, at which time these schools started to shut down.[145] The conditions inflicted on the children were very similar to those inflicted on Australian aboriginal children. In addition to the harm resulting from cultural, physical, and sexual violence, residential schools also sometimes involved other egregious aspects, including programmes of forced sterilizations of the children in the Provinces of Alberta and British Columbia,[146] and programmes of nutritional experimentation on malnourished children in the late 1940s.[147] During the 1980s and 1990s, 'Survivors' from the residential school system started to increasingly claim damages for the prejudice suffered, which pushed the Canadian government to conclude, in 2006, the *Indian Residential School Settlement Agreement* with both the communities affected by the Residential School System and the participation of the Churches involved in the system. Among others, the Agreement established a compensation scheme—which

141 Australian Human Rights Commission (n 137) p. 2 (terms of reference).

142 Ibid., p. 239.

143 Prime Minister Kevin Rudd, MP, Apology to Australia's Indigenous Peoples (13 February 2008), available at: http://australia.gov.au/about-australia/our-country/our-people/apology-to-australias-indigenous-peoples (last accessed 1 February 2015).

144 Australian government's webpage on 'Sorry Day and the Last Generation', available at: http://australia.gov.au/about-australia/australian-story/sorry-day-stolen-generations (last accessed 1 February 2015).

145 In Canada, the last school closed in 1996. See Truth and Reconciliation Commission of Canada (TRC), 'Canada, Aboriginal Peoples and Residential Schools: They Came for the Children' (2012) p. 20.

146 Zia Akhtar, 'Canadian Genocide and Official Responsibility' (2010) 10 *Int.C.L.R.* 111, pp. 116–17.

147 Ian Mosby, 'Administering Colonial Science: Nutrition Research and Human Biomedical Experimentation in Aboriginal Communities and Residential Schools, 1942–1952' (2013) 46 *Social History* 145, pp. 158–64.

will be discussed in Chapter 7—and created the Truth and Reconciliation Commission, mandated with the goals of reconstituting the history and legacy of the residential school system, promoting awareness and formulating recommendations to the Government of Canada.[148] The latter was constituted in 2009 and ended its activities in 2015 with the release of a 'final report'. Even though the legal qualification of the acts was not part of the Commission's mandate, the introduction of the report sets the tone by qualifying the residential school system as 'cultural genocide':

Physical genocide is the mass killing of the members of a targeted group, and *biological genocide* is the destruction of the group's reproductive capacity. *Cultural genocide* is the destruction of those structures and practices that allow the group to continue as a group. States that engage in cultural genocide set out to destroy the political and social institutions of the targeted group. Land is seized, and populations are forcibly transferred and their movement is restricted. Languages are banned. Spiritual leaders are persecuted, spiritual practices are forbidden, and objects of spiritual value are confiscated and destroyed. And most significantly to the issue at hand, families are disrupted to prevent the transmission of cultural values and identity from one generation to another.

In its dealing with Aboriginal people, Canada did all these things.[149]

The report provides an exhaustive analysis of the history and legacy of the residential school system, and includes a long list of recommendations, 'a call for action', in order to deal with the legacy of genocide and discrimination, and foster reconciliation between Aboriginal and non-Aboriginal Canadians. It remains to be seen whether and how the call for action will be followed-up, but the use of the term 'cultural genocide' itself seems to have been quite well accepted by Canadian society,[150] whose government had already formulated an official apology in 2008. Prime Minister Stephen Harper then recognized the extent of the harm caused by Canadian State laws and policies: 'This policy was wrong, caused great harm and has no place in our country'.[151]

Notwithstanding, the two Commissions' conclusions remain non-binding. In both cases, the governments and courts have so far refused to acknowledge the qualification of genocide. As Dirk Moses has noted, 'they cannot apologize for their own existence',[152] which is based on settler colonialism and the corollary 'logic of elimination' of aboriginal peoples that followed.[153] In Australia, the *Kruger* case

[148] Indian Residential Schools Settlement Agreement (8 May 2006) (IRS Canada) Schedule N, art. 1.

[149] Truth and Reconciliation Commission of Canada (TRC), *Honouring the Truth, Reconciling for the Future—Summary of the Final Report of the Truth and Reconciliation of Canada* (2015) p. 1.

[150] Laura Hensley, 'Residential School System Was "Cultural Genocide," Most Canadians Believe According to Poll', *National Post*, 9 July 2015, available at: http://news.nationalpost.com/news/canada/residential-school-system-was-cultural-genocide-most-canadians-believe-according-to-poll (last accessed 10 April 2016).

[151] Prime Minister Stephen Harper, 'Statement of Apology to Former Students of Indian Residential Schools' (8 June 2008).

[152] A. Dirk Moses, 'Genocide', 55 (2013) *Austl. Human. Rev.* 23, p. 39.

[153] Wolfe (n 132).

has been particularly emblematic of this trend; a complaint was filed both by individuals who had been forcibly removed from their families during their childhood and the parents of children who had met the same fate. They asked the Australian courts to declare unconstitutional the legal provisions of the so-called 'Aboriginal Ordinance', which made such removals possible. They especially based their claim on both the Australian Constitution, which, they alleged, granted them a 'constitutional right to freedom from and/or immunity from any law, purported law or executive act: (. . .) providing for or having a purpose, the effect or the likely effect of the destruction in whole or in part of a racial or ethnic group, or the language and culture of such a group',[154] and on the Genocide Convention. In respect of the latter, they relied particularly on paragraphs (b), (c), and (e) of the definition, as well as the prohibition of 'the free exercise of a religion contrary to section 116 of the Constitution'.[155] While recognizing the occurrence of some of the alleged acts—such as the forcible transfer of children or 'mental harm in at least some cases'[156]—and further, acknowledging the possibility that the Chief Protector's powers could have been misused,[157] the High Court judges did not find anything in the ordinance that 'would authorize the doing of acts "with intent to destroy, in whole or in part" the aboriginal race'.[158] Justice Dawson was more explicit in relation to 'cultural genocide'. Identifying a basis to reject the plaintiffs' request, he qualified the alleged acts as 'cultural genocide' whereas, '[t]he Genocide Convention is not concerned with cultural genocide, references to cultural genocide being expressly deleted from it in the course of its being drafted (. . .)'.[159] Yet, the plaintiffs had not explicitly formulated a claim of 'cultural genocide'. Their claim of cultural destruction was based on the Australian Constitution while their claim of genocide mainly involved acts criminalized in the Genocide Convention. Acts related to the prohibition of religion were the only ones to be grounded on the Genocide Convention while not being encompassed in Article II.

This tendency to use the cultural dimension of the Australian aboriginal experience to dismiss claims of genocide can also be found in the *Nyularimma* case,[160] in which the appellants aimed to strike out domestic provisions, the application of which resulted in the extinguishment of their Native land title, as well as the Australian governmental decision not to register native land on the World Heritage List. They notably argued that these legal acts amounted to genocide in the context of the historical injustice endured by their community. The three judges dismissed the appeal, predominantly on the basis that they did not have jurisdiction to review acts of genocide since the Genocide Convention had not yet been incorporated into Australian law. Nevertheless, they took care to provide their view on the relevance of the genocide term 'to describe the conduct of non-indigenes towards the indigenous population'.[161] As in the *Kruger* case, they concluded as to the inexistence of

[154] *Kruger v. Commonwealth* (1997) 190 CLR 1 (31 July 1997) High Court of Australia.
[155] Ibid., p. 12 (iv. C. vi). [156] Ibid., p. 13 (Brennan). [157] Ibid.
[158] Ibid., p. 93 (McHugh). [159] Ibid., p. 38 (Dawson).
[160] *Nulyarimma v. Thompson* (1999); *Buzzacott v. Hill* (1999), FCA 1192 (1 September 1999) Federal Court of Australia.
[161] Ibid., para. 5 (Wilcox).

an intent to destroy the group.[162] One judge, Justice Merkel J, emphasized in particular the fact that '[s]pecific international instruments have dealt with particular aspects of cultural protection'[163] as a basis to better dismiss the claim: 'Aboriginal people genuinely believe that they have been subjected to genocide'.[164]

The same trend has been observed in Canadian case law prior to the release of the Truth and Reconciliation Commission's final report, with the civil courts repeatedly dismissing claims of 'genocide' and 'cultural genocide'. In the *Raubach* and the *Indian Residential Schools* cases, the judges thus considered that they lacked 'the jurisdiction to award a declaratory order on the basis of a non-legal or political code of conduct', the judges' way to qualify the 1948 Genocide Convention.[165] In comparison with the Australian cases, the Canadian ones involved more straightforward claims of 'cultural genocide'. For instance, in the *Raubach* case, the plaintiffs sought reparation for the assaults they had endured at the residential schools, which they alleged had taken 'place in the context of a deliberate program to eradicate their culture. They sa[id], for example, that some of the assaults were designed to prevent them from speaking their language or following their customs. They describe this as a policy of cultural genocide'.[166] Beyond the formalist arguments which led to the rejection of the claims, the judge's rationale in the *Indian Residential Schools, Re* case is noteworthy, as he found that the provision of the domestic Criminal Code which referred to genocide, on the basis of which the claim was grounded, 'referred only to the physical destruction of peoples and not "cultural genocide" which appears to be the subject of the United Nations Convention'.[167] This statement, read in conjunction with the Canadian Truth and Reconciliation Commission's Conclusion, tends to illustrate the level of acceptance of the 'cultural genocide' rhetoric as a way to label the Canadian indigenous peoples' experience. Cultural genocide has thus been qualified as a 'moral descriptor anchored in a legal historical process and as such is a useful ground floor'.[168] References to the term can also be found in civil and criminal cases, involving aboriginal accused, who use the cultural genocide argument to contextualize their behaviours and establish mitigating circumstances.[169]

One should nevertheless be careful not to dismiss too rapidly the qualification of 'forced assimilation'. This section is dedicated to the use of 'cultural genocide' as a rhetorical tool, which might be engaged either to bring or dismiss claims at the legal level. The aim is not to adopt a definitive stance on those debates that enliven various societies around the world. Rather, it should be noted that there is

[162] Ibid., para. 12 (Wilcox): 'However, deplorable as our history is, in considering the appropriateness of the term "genocide", it is not possible too long to leave aside the matter of intent.'

[163] Ibid., para. 201 (Merkel J). [164] Ibid., para. 202 (Merkel J).

[165] *Indian Residential Schools, Re* [2000] A.J. No. 638 (Alta. Q.B.) (31 May 2000) Alberta Court of Queen's Bench, para. 73; *Raubach et al. v. The Attorney General of Canada et al.*, [2005] 1 WWR 334 (6 July 2004) Manitoba Court of Queen's Bench, para. 12.

[166] *Raubach et al.* (n 165) para. 10.

[167] See inter alia *Indian Residential Schools, Re* (n 165) para. 69.

[168] David B. MacDonald and Gordon Hudson, 'The Genocide Question and Indian Residential Schools in Canada' (2012) 45 *Can.J.Pol.Sc.* 427, p. 431.

[169] *R. v. B. (J.J.B.)* [2007] BCPC 426 (19 December 2007) British Columbia Provincial Court, para. 32; *R. v. Ladue* [2011] BCCA 101 (8 March 2011) British Columbia Court of Appeal, para. 6.

no reason to understand the use of one term or another as a zero-sum game. The recognition of genocide, as it was identified by the drafters of the *Bringing Them Home* report, does not prevent the process of forced transfer of children in Australia, as well as wider policies targeting the aboriginal population, from being labelled as 'forced assimilation'. Indeed, the term is actually used by Robert van Krieken, a scholar who has also advocated for the recognition of genocide in the Australian context.[170] However, other scholars have outlined the inadequacy of the term 'forced assimilation' to characterize the Australian and Canadian processes. MacDonald and Hudson thus argue that '[c]ultural genocide is more accurate than "forcible assimilation," because groups with clearly defined identities were targeted as groups, rather than as individuals'.[171] In light of the recognition of the living conditions endured by those children who were forcibly transferred, such as the above-mentioned acts of sexual assaults and instances of forced sterilizations in Canada, the qualification of 'forced assimilation' emerges as a euphemism. As Skutnabb-Kangas and Dunbar have noted, such a label raises the question of 'what exactly were/are Indigenous and Tribal children being assimilated into?'[172] Many studies have indeed pointed out that the aim of such policies was not to assimilate the children per se, that is to make them part of a homogenous group, but rather to serve the already-established dominant group, namely the wider Australian and Canadian societies, since the aboriginal children mainly received a low-level education, aimed at training them for unqualified positions.[173] The Canadian Truth and Reconciliation Commission's report on the legacy encapsulates the paradox well: 'Given all the damage caused by the residential schools—the physical and mental abuse, the loss of culture and language, the forced separation of families—it is a bitter irony that one of the schools' greatest failings was the very quality of the schooling they provided.'[174]

As problematic as it may be, the conceptual confusion between genocide, cultural genocide, and forced assimilation might nevertheless be understandable from the historical–legal point of view, especially if one remembers the debates that led to the inclusion of Article II(e) in the ultimate definition of genocide. In respect of the next case of 'ethnic cleansing', the use of cultural genocide emerges however as a rather artificial construction.

2.3.2.2 *Cultural genocide and ethnic cleansing*

The cultural genocide issue has found an interesting scope for renewal in front of the ICTY, in relation to the legal debate on the relationship between 'ethnic

[170] Robert van Krieken, 'Rethinking Cultural Genocide: Aboriginal Child Removal and Settler-Colonial State Formation' (2004) 75 *Oceania* 125, p. 127.

[171] MacDonald and Hudson (n 168) p. 431.

[172] Skutnabb-Kangas and Dunbar (n 132) p. 46.

[173] Jaichand (n 132) p. 900; Skutnabb-Kangas and Dunbar (n 132) p. 46.

[174] Truth and Reconciliation Commission (TRC) of Canada, 'Canada's Residential Schools: The Legacy', in *The Final Report of the Truth and Reconciliation Commission of Canada*, vol. 5 (2015) p. 6 ('The failure to educate').

cleansing' and genocide in the context of the regional armed conflict that followed the dissolution of Yugoslavia post-1991.[175] 'Ethnic cleansing', a journalistic expression derived from Serbian propaganda,[176] was soon incorporated into common political language. It is defined in *Encyclopaedia Britannica* as:

> the attempt to create ethnically homogeneous geographic areas through the deportation or forcible displacement of persons belonging to particular ethnic groups. Ethnic cleansing sometimes involves the removal of all physical vestiges of the targeted group through the destruction of monuments, cemeteries, and houses of worship.[177]

It should be emphasized that all of the parties to the conflict have in one way or another attempted to fulfil this general objective of 'ethnically purified territory' through the perpetration of some of the acts encompassed in the definition. The crimes have been particularly egregious on the territory of Bosnia and Herzegovina, especially within the self-proclaimed autonomous Bosnian Serb Republic, *Republika Srpska*, culminating, in July 1995, in the massacre of military-aged men of the enclave of Srebrenica.

The acts covered by the 'ethnic cleansing label' were thoroughly detailed in the final report of the Commission of Experts, which was established to investigate war crimes committed on the territory of the former Yugoslavia:

> mass murder, torture, rape and other forms of sexual assault; severe physical injury to civilians; mistreatment of civilian prisoners and prisoners of war; use of civilians as human shields; destruction of personal, public and cultural property; looting, theft and robbery of personal property; forced expropriation of real property; forceful displacement of civilian population; and attacks on hospitals, medical personnel and locations marked with the Red Cross/Red Crescent emblem.[178]

Most of these acts could *prima facie* constitute the *actus reus* of both crimes against humanity and of genocide. Some other acts were deliberately rejected during the negotiations of the 1948 Convention; the 'forceful displacement of civilian population' and the 'destruction of (. . .) cultural property' are examples of such excluded acts. However, these were also particularly prominent features of the campaign of ethnic cleansing in the Former Yugoslavia. This contrast gave rise to two antagonist movements within the legal scholarship, especially in relation to whether these crimes fulfilled the legal requirement of an intent to destroy the group.[179] On the one hand, ethnic cleansing was considered to be a crime distinct from that of genocide as the underlying intent was not to destroy the

[175] William A. Schabas, *Genocide in International Law: The Crime of Crimes* (2nd edn., Cambridge: Cambridge University Press, 2009) p. 221.

[176] George J. Andreopoulos, 'Ethnic Cleansing' in *Encyclopædia Britannica Online Academic Edition*. Encyclopædia Britannica Inc., 2013, available at http://www.britannica.com/EBchecked/topic/194242/ethnic-cleansing (last accessed 1 February 2015).

[177] Ibid. See also Eric Markusen, 'Ethnic Cleansing and Genocide' in Charny (n 133) p. 215.

[178] UNSC 'Final Report of the Commission of Experts Established Pursuant to Security Council Resolution 780 (1992)' (27 May 1994) UN Doc. S/1994/674, para. 134.

[179] Cécile Tournaye, 'Genocidal Intent before the ICTY' (2003) 52 *Int'l & Comp.L.Q.* 447, p. 447.

group as such but rather to displace a group for the purposes of making a territory homogenous.[180] Others considered ethnic cleansing to be a 'euphemism' for genocide, the explanation for this underlying rhetoric being of a political rather than legal nature.[181] In the 1992 UNGA Resolution 47/121, the UN Member States expressed their grave concern in relation to the pursuit of 'the abhorrent policy of "ethnic cleansing," which is a form of genocide' in the Republic of Bosnia and Herzegovina.[182] Eventually, only the crimes perpetrated in Srebrenica have been legally recognized as acts of 'genocide' in Bosnia and Herzegovina. In other municipalities, the ICTY did not follow the Commission of Experts and rather considered that the intent was not to destroy the group as such but rather to remove the group permanently, so as to fall instead within the category of crimes against humanity.[183]

In respect of the overall context of ethnic cleansing, cultural genocide has firstly been used in its narrow sense to describe one specific feature of this campaign, namely the widespread destruction of cultural and religious heritage.[184] These destructions targeted sites registered on the UNESCO World Heritage List, such as the old city of Dubrovnik in Croatia and the Mostar Bridge in Bosnia and Herzegovina, and included the systematic destruction of religious buildings. The Commission highlighted in particular that '[t]he purpose of this destruction is to eradicate cultural, social and religious traces that identify the ethnic and religious groups',[185] a statement which recalls a crime once formulated as 'cultural genocide'. Yet, whether 'cultural genocide' or not, cultural destruction was one part of the whole process, as a result of which the Commission considered that those involved in this campaign of ethnic cleansing '[were] also susceptible to charges of genocide and crimes against humanity, in addition to grave breaches of the Geneva Conventions and other violations of international humanitarian law'.[186] It should be noted that the Commission did not qualify any acts as genocidal but merely reviewed the different crimes committed during the conflict as well as the potentially applicable law. The question was nevertheless settled in a different way by the ICTY in the *Krstić*

[180] See e.g. Schabas, *Genocide in International Law* (n 175) p. 234.

[181] See e.g. John B. Quigley, *The Genocide Convention: An International Law Analysis* (Aldershot, England; Burlington, VT: Ashgate Pub., 2006) p. 193; Martin Shaw, *What Is Genocide?* (Cambridge: Polity Press, 2007) pp. 49–54.

[182] UNGA Res. 47/121 (18 December 1992) 'The situation in Bosnia and Herzegovina', Preambular para. 9.

[183] The latest confirmation of this can be found in: *Karadžić Case* (Trial Judgment) IT-95-5/18-I (24 March 2016).

[184] Lorie Fisler Damrosch, 'Genocide and Ethnic Conflict' in David Wippman (ed.), *International Law and Ethnic Conflict* (Ithaca; London: Cornell University Press, 1998) p. 266; András J. Riedlmayer, 'Destruction of Cultural Heritage in Bosnia-Herzegovina, 1992–1996: A Post-War Survey of Selected Municipalities' (International Criminal Tribunal for the Former Yugoslavia, Exhibit Number P486, 2002); Bevan (n 16); András J. Riedlmayer, 'Crimes of War, Crimes of Peace: Destruction of Libraries during and after the Balkan Wars of the 1990s' (2007) 56 *Library Trends* 107, pp. 127–8; Donna-Lee Frieze, The Destruction of Sarajevo's *Vijecnica*: A Case of Genocidal Destruction? in Adam Jones (ed.), *New Directions in Genocide Research* (London; New York: Routledge, 2009) pp. 57–74.

[185] 'Final Report of the Commission of Experts' (n 178) para. 136.

[186] Ibid., para. 150.

case, the first case in which the ICTY convicted an accused for 'aiding and abetting' genocide in Srebrenica.[187]

In the *Krstić* case, the judges addressed the issue of 'ethnic cleansing' in the context of the debate on 'cultural genocide', which they defined as ' "cultural" destruction of the group':[188]

> The Trial Chamber is aware that it must interpret the Convention with due regard for the principle of *nullum crimen sine lege*. It therefore recognises that, *despite recent developments, customary international law limits the definition of genocide to those acts seeking the physical or biological destruction of all or part of the group*. Hence, an enterprise attacking only the cultural or sociological characteristics of a human group in order to annihilate these elements which give to that group its own identity distinct from the rest of the community would not fall under the definition of genocide. The Trial Chamber however points out that *where there is physical or biological destruction there are often simultaneous attacks on the cultural and religious property and symbols of the targeted group as well, attacks which may legitimately be considered as evidence of an intent to physically destroy the group*. In this case, the Trial Chamber will thus take into account as evidence of intent to destroy the group the deliberate destruction of mosques and houses belonging to members of the group.[189]

According to this paragraph, cultural genocide as a process of its own cannot amount to genocide while cultural genocide as a technique may serve as evidence of its perpetrator's *mens rea*. It is noteworthy that the definition of cultural genocide offered in this paragraph, 'an enterprise attacking only the cultural or sociological characteristics of a human group', reflects the evolved and broadened understanding of the concept as a form of genocide, that is, beyond a technique.[190] Yet in this judgment, the concept has been broadened even more, so as to encompass the whole non-physical-biological dimension of genocide. The blurring of the concept of cultural genocide thus tends to make its identification, as an object of inquiry, an arduous task in relation to the determination of the applicable norms of international law.

2.4 Concluding Remarks

This study of the legal history of the concept of cultural genocide has allowed for some conceptual tensions and legal challenges to be underlined, including: the gradual stretching of the concept of cultural genocide, the tendency to oppose cultural genocide to physical and biological genocide, and its positioning in law at the crossroads of international human rights law and international criminal law. The roots for the conceptual stretching can be traced back to Lemkin's writings, as well as to the draft Genocide Convention itself and its related negotiations. The second

[187] *Krstić Case* (Appeals) IT-98-33 (19 April 2004) para. 144.
[188] *Krstić Case* (Trial) ICTY-98-33 (2 August 2001) para. 576.
[189] Ibid., para. 580 (emphases added).
[190] Ibid. The finding is discussed at length in Chapter 3.

draft provision on cultural genocide, which was ultimately rejected, was already isolated from the physical-biological definition of genocide. Even though this was mainly due to formalities, namely, to leave scope for states to make reservations on this specific dimension of genocide, this nevertheless rendered 'cultural genocide' an autonomous form of genocide. Thus, if the outcome of the negotiations had been different and the draft provision on cultural genocide had been adopted, 'cultural genocide' would have been a crime of its own, unless subsequently reintroduced in the core of the definition of genocide.

Not only has the early treatment of the concept of cultural genocide illustrated the tension between cultural genocide as a technique and cultural genocide as a process but it has also operated to anchor the very concept of genocide within closed categories: cultural, physical, and biological, so as to overlook Lemkin's conceptualization of genocide as a '*coordinated* plan'.

The blurring of the conceptual borders has also made the legal issue more acute, in terms of the determination of the branch of international law that should address the concept. This question was formulated in the 1940s as either genocide or human rights, but no answer was then identified. The evolution of the concept renders the dichotomy less and less convincing since the answer in law might depend on whether we talk of 'the events, the intentions, or the consequences'.[191] The question is actually relevant to the overall concept of cultural genocide, which focuses considerably on the intergenerational dimension of the harm and hence the 'consequences'. There is a foreseeable distinction to be drawn between cultural destruction understood as a result and the intent to culturally destroy a group. Only in the latter case can the question of the legal qualification be raised as genocide.

[191] Elazar Barkan, 'Genocide of Indigenous Peoples' in Robert Gellately and Ben Kiernan (eds.), *The Specter of Genocide: Mass Murder in Historical Perspective* (Cambridge: Cambridge University Press, 2003) p. 135. The author has formulated the dilemma in relation to processes of forcible transfers of children.

3

The Cultural Dimension of the Crime of Genocide

In spite of repeated calls to extend it, the law of genocide has literally been kept intact.[1] In its Draft Code of Crimes against the Peace and Security of Mankind, the International Law Commission (ILC) reproduced Article II of the Genocide Convention, considering that the provision 'is widely accepted and generally recognized as the authoritative definition of this crime'.[2] The definition was not subject to intense debates during the elaboration of the Statute of the International Criminal Court (ICC).[3] Still, the terms of the debate have evolved considerably since 1948. On the one hand, the meaning of cultural genocide has shifted from a mere technique of genocide towards the cultural destruction of certain groups. On the other hand, the rise of 'ethnic conflicts' during the 1990s has called for the implementation of this definition, and *a fortiori,* its interpretation, in contexts that would differ sharply from the post-Holocaust context of its initial formulation.

Considering these two evolutions, the question of the reintroduction of cultural genocide into the ambit of the legal definition of genocide brings the focus to the interpretation of its *mens rea*, that is 'the intent to destroy, in whole or in part, a national, ethnic, racial or religious group, as such', so as to determine whether it may encompass the notion of group cultural destruction. Genocide is often described as a 'crime of *mens rea*',[4] which attributes enormous weight to the

[1] See e.g. Sub-Commission on Prevention of Discrimination and Protection of Minorities (38th Session), 'Revised and Updated Report on the Question of the Prevention and Punishment of the Crime of Genocide Prepared by Mr. Benjamin Whitaker' (2 July 1985), UN Doc. E/CN.4/Sub.2/1985/6 (Whitaker Report) para. 33.

[2] ILC (48th Session), 'Draft Code of Crimes against the Peace and Security of Mankind with Commentaries', *Yearbook of the International Law Commission,* 1996, vol. II, Part Two (ILC 1996 Draft Code of Crimes) Commentary on art. 17, para. 3. This statement sits in full contradiction to Claudia Card's definition of genocide as 'social death', in Claudia Card, 'Genocide and Social Death' in John K. Roth (ed.), *Genocide and Human Rights: A Philosophical Guide* (Houndmills, Basingstoke, Hampshire; New York: Palgrave Macmillan, 2005) pp. 238–54, discussed in Section 2.3.1.

[3] Herman von Hebel, Darryl Robinson, 'Crimes within the Jurisdiction of the Court' in Roy S. Lee, *The International Criminal Court: The Making of the Rome Statute* (The Hague; London; Boston: Kluwer Law International), p. 89: A few proposals to expand the definition were made during the 1996 sessions of the Preparatory committee. (…) At the Rome Conference, the definition of the crime of genocide was not discussed in substance, but was referred directly to the Drafting Committee'.

[4] *Prosecutor v. Omar Hassan Ahmad Al Bashir* (Decision on the Prosecution's Application for a Warrant of Arrest against Omar Hassan Ahmad Al Bashir) ICC-02/05-01/09 (4 March 2009) Pre-Trial Chamber I, fn. 140.

individual perpetrator's intent. The international legal definition of genocide is now firmly anchored in a criminal law perspective with emphasis placed on the perpetrators' *intent* to destroy one of the four groups as such, to the detriment of the early affirmation of group protection.[5] This *dolus specialis* or special intent, as international courts have labelled it,[6] is what distinguishes genocide from other war crimes or crimes against humanity. Looking more closely, these few words give rise to a wide range of questions, such as what is a group, how is it defined, how is it identified, how is it to be destroyed, what is the rationale for criminalizing this crime for 'only' four types of groups and what do the words 'as such' mean? When the time came to reply to these questions through judicial interpretation, not a single answer was offered. Diverging interpretations of the *mens rea* of genocide have thus been rendered, especially in respect of whether the notion of group destruction should be understood in merely physical and biological terms or in its broader socio-cultural terms.

Against this backdrop, this chapter thus aims to cut through these conflicting interpretations and reconstruct the meaning of the *mens rea* according to the various principles of both international criminal law and general international law applicable to the interpretation of the definition of genocide.

3.1 The Interpretive Dilemma of 'Group Destruction'

The unique and universal definition of genocide has given rise to two conflicting interpretations of the notion of 'group destruction'. The following study will focus on the socio-legal and methodological underpinnings of these conflicting interpretations.

3.1.1 One law, two interpretations

The rejection of the draft provision on cultural genocide during the negotiations of the Genocide Convention led the ILC to consider, in its work on the codification of crimes against peace and security of mankind, that '[t]he definition of the word "destruction" (. . .) must be taken only in its material sense, its physical or biological sense'.[7] While this interpretation seemed obvious to the experts of the ILC—at a time when almost no tribunal in the world had had the occasion to review alleged acts of genocide—it was actually the object of further discussion when the time

[5] UNGA Res. 96(1) (11 December 1948) 'The Crime of Genocide'; *Reservations to the Convention on the Prevention and Punishment of the Crime of Genocide*, (Advisory Opinion) [1951] ICJ Rep. 15 (*Reservations to the Genocide Convention*) p. 12.

[6] *Akayesu Case* (Trial) ICTR-96-4-I (2 September 1998) para. 122.

[7] ILC (43rd Session), 'Draft Code of Crimes against the Peace and Security of Mankind with Commentaries', *Yearbook of the International Law Commission*, 1991, vol. II (ILC 1991 Draft Code of Crimes) Commentary on art. 19, para. 4; ILC 1996 Draft Code of Crimes (n 2) Commentary on art. 17, para.12.

came for the concrete implementation of the long-dormant provision. This was especially true in the International Criminal Tribunal for the Former Yugoslavia (ICTY) within which a clear trend towards a physical understanding of genocide emerged, albeit with many dissents.

Beginning in the 1990s, the judicial processes related to the punishment of the crimes perpetrated in the Former Yugoslavia gave rise to an important judicial dialogue in respect of what genocide means. Five different levels of courts received a mandate to review the crimes, including alleged acts of genocide, perpetrated in Bosnia and Herzegovina. Within the *ad hoc* tribunal of the ICTY, prosecutors soon focused on 'the most responsible'[8] while the other perpetrators were deferred to a hybrid tribunal in Bosnia, the Bosnian War Crimes Chamber.[9] In the meantime, some national tribunals, based in non-territorial states, were entitled to exercise universal jurisdiction, triggering the jurisdiction of the European Court of Human Rights (ECtHR) in one case.[10] Finally, the International Court of Justice (ICJ) reviewed potential state responsibility.[11] The interpretive process focused on the intent to destroy the group.

At the early stages of the functioning of the ICTY the Trial Chamber requested that the Prosecutor 'consider broadening the scope of the characterisation of genocide' in the 'review of the indictments pursuant to rule 61' in the *Mladić and Karadžić* case.[12] The Prosecutor had only included the acts of 'interment of civilians in detention facilities and inhumane treatment therein' under the genocide count, while the other acts were dealt with under the offence of persecution, a crime against humanity. Reviewing those alleged acts of crimes against humanity, the Chamber examined 'whether the pattern of conduct of (. . .) "ethnic cleansing", taken in its totality, reveals such a genocidal intent'.[13] The 'taken in its totality' part is noteworthy since the subsequent developments of the review dedicated particular attention to the acts targeting 'the very *foundation of the group*—acts which are not in themselves covered by the list in Article 4(2) but which are committed as part of the same pattern of conduct':[14]

[8] This selectivity first originated from a prosecutorial strategy and was later enshrined in the ICTY Completion Strategy. See Website of the ICTY, 'About the ICTY': http://www.icty.org/sid/3 (last accessed 1 February 2015).

[9] See Law on the Transfer of Cases from the ICTY to the Prosecutor's Office of BIH and the Use of Evidence Collected by ICTY in Proceedings Before the Courts in Bosnia and Herzegovina (BiH), "Official Gazette" of Bosnia and Herzegovina, No. 61/04. A 'programme of international judges' has also been established in Kosovo, http://www.trial-ch.org/en/resources/tribunals/hybrid-tribunals/programme-of-international-judges-in-kosovo.html (last accessed 1 February 2015).

[10] *Jorgić v. Germany*, App. No. 74613/01 (ECtHR) 12 July 2007.

[11] See Convention on the Prevention and Punishment of the Crime of Genocide (adopted 9 December 1948, entered into force 12 January 1951) 78 UNTS 277 (Genocide Convention) art. IX; *Application of the Convention on the Prevention and Punishment of the Crime of Genocide (Bosnia and Herzegovina v. Serbia and Montenegro)* (Judgment) [2007] ICJ Rep. 43.

[12] *Karadžić & Mladić Case* (Review of the Indictments Pursuant to Rule 61 of the Rules of Procedure and Evidence) IT-95-5-R61; IT-95-18-R6I (11 July 1996) para. 95.

[13] Ibid., para. 94. [14] Ibid., (emphasis added).

The systematic rape of women, to which material submitted to the Trial Chamber attests, is in some cases intended *to transmit a new* ethnic *identity to the child.* In other cases, humiliation and terror serve to dismember the group. *The destruction of mosques or Catholic Churches is designed to annihilate the centuries long presence of the group or groups; the destruction of the libraries is intended to annihilate a culture which was enriched through the participation of the various national components of the population.*[15]

It is on these bases that the court requested the Prosecutor to envisage the genocide count for ethnic cleansing, an approach that he actually adopted.[16] There was therefore a clear trend towards broadly labelling the crimes perpetrated in the Former Yugoslavia as genocide.

The step was actually taken in the *Jorgić* case, which was decided by German courts through their exercise of universal jurisdiction.[17] This case involved a Bosnian-Serb living in Germany who had been the leader of a paramilitary group during the Yugoslavian conflict. He was accused of a series of crimes committed in his homeland, the region of Doboj, against the local Bosnian-Muslim population. The Higher State Court of Düsseldorf rendered the first judgment in 1997, which was successively appealed before the Federal Supreme Court of Germany in 1999 and the German Federal Constitutional Court in 2000. The German courts, which were among the first courts to rule on the crimes committed during the conflict in the Former Yugoslavia, concluded that the intent to destroy the group could be conceived as an intent to destroy it as a 'social unit' and therefore convicted Jorgić for his participation in 'genocide'.

The case was subsequently heard before the ECtHR, which rendered its judgment in 2007,[18] an original situation since the Strasbourg judges are rarely confronted with alleged acts of genocide. They were not asked to qualify the acts in legal terms—in other words, to give an interpretation of the genocide definition with regard to facts—but rather to evaluate the accuracy and foreseeability of the interpretation given by the national courts. The defendant challenged his conviction on the basis of Articles 6—right to a fair trial—and 7(1) of the European Convention on Human Rights (ECHR), which is a materialization of the *nullum crimen sine lege* principle.[19] On this latter ground, Jorgić contested the 'broad' interpretation

[15] Ibid., (emphasis added).

[16] *Karadžić Case* (Third Amended Indictment) IT-95-5/18-I (27 February 2009). Yet, it was finally decided that the count related to genocide would only concern the crimes perpetrated in Srebrenica in *Karadžić Case* (Transcript; 98*bis* Ruling) IT-95-5/18-I (28 June 2012) pp. 28763–74. This 98*bis* ruling was ultimately overturned in *Karadžić Case* (Appeals Rule 98*bis*) IT-95-5/18-I (11 July 2013) para. 51.

[17] *Jorgić* (Trial) IV-26/96; 2StE 8/96 (26 September 1997) Higher State Court of Düsseldorf; English version available at: http://www.legal-tools.org/doc/bd3e74/ (last 3 July 2016); *Nikola Jorgić* (Appeals) 3 StR 215/98 (30 April 1999) Federal Supreme Court of Germany; English version available at: http://www.legal-tools.org/doc/85b784/ (last accessed 3 July 2016); *Nikola Jorgić* (Constitutional Appeals) 2 BvR 2190/99 (12 December 2000) German Federal Constitutional Court; English version in *International Law Report*, Vol. 135, pp. 152–67.

[18] *Jorgić v. Germany* (n 10).

[19] Convention for the Protection of Human Rights and Fundamental Freedoms (European Convention on Human Rights, as amended) (adopted 4 November 1950, entered into force 3 September 1953) CETS No.: 005 (ECHR), art. 7 para. 1: *No one shall be held guilty of any criminal offence on account of any act or omission which did not constitute a criminal offence under national or*

made by the German courts of the *mens rea* of genocide. Jorgić argued that the ethnic cleansing in which he took part 'had been aimed only at driving all Muslims away from that region by force, that is, at expelling that group, not destroying its very existence'. It therefore could not be considered as genocide within the meaning of Article 220a of the Criminal Code'.[20] This German provision criminalizes 'genocide' in the exact same terms as Article II of the Genocide Convention. The ECtHR upheld the interpretation rendered by the German government and courts, which had proceeded to a 'systematic interpretation'[21] of the definition of genocide. In particular, they relied on the last two paragraphs of the definition of genocide (imposition of measures to prevent births, forcible transfer of children) to demonstrate that genocide 'did not necessitate a physical destruction of living members of the group in question', which, according to the European court, 'does not appear unreasonable'.[22] The applicant further emphasized the conflict of interpretation existing between the German courts and the international jurisdictions,[23] since in the meantime, the ICTY had settled the issue in the opposite way in the *Krstić* case.

Indeed, the position of the German courts had quickly been relegated to the status of a minority view. Soon after the German Federal Constitutional Court's judgment, the ICTY Trial Chamber ruled in 2001 that the group destruction should be understood in physical or biological terms only,[24] therefore emphasizing the harm caused to the individual group members. The Appeals Chamber affirmed the *Krstić* trial judgment in 2004.[25] The trend towards broadly labelling the crimes perpetrated in the Former Yugoslavia as genocide did not evaporate immediately after the *Krstić* trial and the appeals judgments. Rather, subsequent case law within the ICTY shows the discomfort that some judges felt when trying to take a position on this issue. Even in the *Krstić* case, the Appeals Chamber recalled that '[t]hose who devise and implement genocide seek to deprive humanity of the manifold richness its nationalities, races, ethnicities and religions provide'.[26] It also justified the Trial Chamber's conclusion that genocide had occurred by underlying the 'potential extinction' of the patriarchal based-community of Srebrenica.[27] As noted by Zahar, '[t]he Appeals Chamber here pretends to be talking about biological destruction but keeps sliding back into the area of cultural destruction'.[28] The final decision of the Appeals Chamber also gave rise to a strong dissenting opinion specifically on this subject-matter from Judge Shahabuddeen, in which he concluded that 'the intent to destroy the group as a group is capable of being proved by evidence of an

international law at the time when it was committed. Nor shall a heavier penalty be imposed than the one that was applicable at the time the criminal offence was committed.

[20] *Jorgić v. Germany* (n 10) para. 92. [21] Ibid., para. 105. [22] Ibid.
[23] Ibid., para. 93. [24] *Krstić Case* (Trial) ICTY-98-33 (2 August 2001) para. 580.
[25] *Krstić Case* (Appeals) ICTY-98-33 (19 April 2004), para. 25. [26] Ibid., para. 36.
[27] Ibid., para. 28.
[28] Alexander Zahar, 'Commentary on the Judgment of the ICTY Appeals Chamber in the Case of Prosecutor v. Radislav Krstić' (2004) 19 *Annotated Leading Cases of International Criminal Tribunals* 629, p. 636.

intent to cause the non-physical destruction of the group in whole or in part, except in particular cases in which physical destruction is required by the Statute'.[29]

A year after the appeals judgment in the *Krstić* case, the ICTY again reviewed crimes perpetrated in the enclave of Srebrenica in the *Blagojević* case. This case was distinguishable from the first one since Blagojević's responsibility for genocide was mainly sought in respect of his participation in acts of population transfers and corollary 'opportunistic killings' rather than the mass killings of the military-aged men. The former crimes were addressed as both 'acts of inflicting serious mental harm' and at the level of the *mens rea*, under the term 'destroy'.[30] The Trial Chamber pointed out the confused analogy made in the *Krstić* case between forms of genocidal destruction other than physical, on the one hand, and cultural genocide, on the other hand.[31] The Trial Chamber decided to rely on Judge Shahabuddeen's dissenting opinion and the German *Jorgić* case to challenge the *Krstić* Trial and Appeals Chambers' holdings, by stating that:

A group is comprised of its individuals, but also of its history, traditions, the relationship between its members, the relationship with other groups, the relationship with the land. The Trial Chamber finds that the physical or biological destruction of the group is the likely outcome of a forcible transfer of the population when this transfer is conducted in such a way that the group can no longer reconstitute itself.[32]

The Trial Chamber's claim to follow Shahabuddeen finally resulted in an understanding of genocidal intent that mirrors the definition established in *Krstić* as it found an intent to physically destroy the group through acts intended to harm its socio-cultural structure. The Appeals Chamber dismissed the conviction for genocide and held that the acts attributed to Blagojević did not demonstrate sufficient intent to destroy the group, since his knowledge of the mass killings could not be proven. In contrast, such knowledge had been 'key to the finding that genocide had been committed' in the *Krstić* case.[33] The Appeals Chamber did not enter into much detail on the meaning of group destruction. It simply noted that it was 'not convinced by the Trial Chamber's reasoning that the forcible transfer operation alone or coupled with the murders and mistreatment in Bratunac town would suffice to demonstrate the principal perpetrators' intent to "destroy" the protected group'.[34] It would undoubtedly have reached the same conclusion had the Trial Chamber explicitly understood the intent in non-physical or biological terms.

Another illustration of this putative uneasiness created by the *Krstić* interpretation can be found in the *Krajišnik* case, more specifically in a footnote of the trial judgment:

It is not accurate to speak of 'the group' as being amenable to physical or biological destruction. Its members are, of course, physical or biological beings, but the bonds among its members, as well as such aspects of the group as its members' culture and beliefs, are neither

[29] *Krstić Case* (Appeals) (n 25) Judge Shahbuddeen's dissenting opinion, para. 54.
[30] *Blagojević & Jokić Case* (Trial) IT-02-60 (17 January 2005) para. 665.
[31] Ibid., para. 658. [32] Ibid., para. 666.
[33] *Blagojević & Jokić* (Appeals) IT-02-60 (9 May 2007) para.122. [34] Ibid., para.123.

physical nor biological. Hence the Genocide Convention's 'intent to destroy' the group cannot sensibly be regarded as reducible to an intent to destroy the group physically or biologically, as has occasionally been said.[35]

This footnote referred to a statement made in the body of the decision, in which the Court considered that a group might be destroyed in ways other than those that are physical or biological, such as 'by severing the bonds among its members'.[36] This rather innovative statement was made just between the two *Blagojević* judgments. The case differed since the Chamber was reviewing the genocidal intent underlying the killings of the leading members of the Bosnian Muslim and Bosnian Croat communities. The physical *actus reus* was established but the court did not find enough evidence of the related intent.[37] Since the charge of genocide was dismissed, the Appeals Chamber did not have the opportunity to comment on the Trial Chamber's finding and this part of the judgment escaped the fate of the *Blagojević* judgment.

Other tribunals have also addressed the issue. In its two judgments on the *Application of the Convention on the Prevention and Punishment of the Crime of Genocide*, the ICJ adopted the 'physical destruction' understanding of the group on the basis of the ILC and ICTY's findings, without any preliminary critical assessment.[38]

The International Criminal Tribunal for Rwanda (ICTR) also predominantly adopted the ILC's interpretation of a 'material' destruction.[39] Unlike the Bosnian case, the nature of the *mens rea* did not have practical implication, as the destruction of the Tutsi group was indeed primarily physical.[40] Yet, the reasoning was less straightforward in the *Akayesu* case, which was the first to assess charges of genocide and in which an issue of criminal qualification therefore arose. The Tribunal stated, using a language that reminds one of Lemkin's, that:

[t]he intent may also be inferred from the perpetration of acts which violate, or which the perpetrators themselves consider to violate the *very foundation of the group*—acts which are not in themselves covered by the list in Article 4(2) but which are committed as part of the same pattern of conduct'.[41]

[35] *Krajišnik Case* (Trial) IT-00-39 (27 September 2006) fn. 1701.

[36] Ibid., para. 854.

[37] Ibid., para. 1092.

[38] *Application of the Genocide Convention (Bosnia and Herzegovina v. Serbia and Montenegro)* (Judgment) (n 11) paras. 90, 344; *Application of the Convention on the Prevention and Punishment of the Crime of Genocide (Croatia v. Serbia)* (Judgment) [2015] ICJ Rep. 24, para. 136. This conception has been heavily criticized by Judge Cançado Trindade in his dissenting opinion to the *Croatia v. Serbia* Judgment, para. 422: 'To attempt to dissociate physical/biological destruction from the cultural one, for the purpose of the determination of genocide, appears to me an artificiality.'

[39] See e.g. *Semanza Case* (Trial) ICTR-97-20 (15 May 2003) para. 315; *Kajelijeli Case* (Trial) ICTR-98-44A (1 December 2003) para. 808.

[40] Larissa van den Herik, 'The Schism between the Legal and the Social Concept of Genocide in Light of the Responsibility to Protect', available at: http://ssrn.com/abstract=1989847 (last accessed 1 February 2015) p. 2.

[41] *Akayesu Case* (Trial) (n 6) para. 523 (emphasis added): the question was whether certain acts—namely, rape and sexual violence—could be treated as acts of genocide, despite not being enumerated in the list in the Convention; see also *Kayishema et al. Case* (Trial) ICTR-95-1 (21 May 1999) para. 95.

This finding was actually reiterated in the *Krstić* trial judgment six years later, with the difference that in the latter judgment, the judges felt the need to qualify the nature of the intent to destroy the group as physical and biological.

We have therefore reached a somewhat puzzling situation where, depending on the court, one might or might not be convicted of genocide, notwithstanding that the same law and principles apply. These various judicial statements reflect strong socio-legal divergences on the meaning of 'destruction' in relation to 'group'. Hence, the definition of the latter will necessarily have an impact on the understanding of the former. That is to say, in order to reach a conclusion that the destruction can be understood in socio-cultural terms, judges will rather emphasize the existence of intra-group bonds, as in the *Blagojević* and *Krajišnik* trial judgments. Those who instead reach the opposite conclusion, of a physical-biological understanding destruction of the group, do not necessarily deny the existence of such bonds within a group. However, they consider genocide as a legal fiction, which, once again, is not necessarily aimed at reflecting the 'reality' of group destruction. Nevertheless, their conclusion implies that the group is understood as an aggregate of individual members, which contrasts with most of the academic literature on the topic.

3.1.2 The socio-legal foundations of conflicting interpretations

The account of the interpretive dilemma in the Bosnian and Herzegovinian-related case law raises a number of questions, which come back to the socio-anthropological debates identified in Chapter 2: how to define 'groups' in the definition of genocide and how to understand their destruction. In this regard, one should keep in mind the concept of 'legal fiction', already mentioned in the introduction, which implies that legal concepts may not necessarily follow the concepts as developed by other disciplines. According to the definition of the *Dictionary of Sociology*, a '(social) group' can be understood as a '[a] number of individuals, defined by formal or informal criteria of membership, who share a feeling of unity or are bound together in relatively stable patterns of interaction'.[42] This definition articulates various theories of the social group: a mere aggregate of individuals, a collective entity that subsumes its individual members, or a network of interaction between individuals.

Cutting through most contemporaneous theories of the social group, the ILC considers that only membership is relevant to define genocide, not individual identity.[43] The ILC thus facilitates a disconnection between the definition of the group, on the one hand, and its destruction, on the other, which enables it to conclude that: 'The national or religious element and the racial or ethnic element are not taken into consideration in the definition of the word "destruction", which must be taken only in its material sense, its physical or biological sense'.[44] Consequently,

[42] Gordon Marshall and John Scott (eds.), 'Group (social group)' in *A Dictionary of Sociology* (3rd rev. ed. Oxford: Oxford University Press, 2009), available at: http://www.oxfordreference.com.ezproxy.eui.eu/views/ENTRY.html?subview=Main&entry=t88.e958 (last accessed 1 February 2015).

[43] ILC 1996 Draft Code of Crimes (n 2) Commentary on art. 17, para. 6.

[44] Ibid. Commentary on art. 17, para. 12.

the four epithets of 'national, ethnic, racial and religious' only serve the purpose of identifying potential victims of genocide, not the harm of genocide. From the ILC's perspective, the group thus has a mere functional dimension, that of distinguishing the crime of genocide from other crimes against humanity, which primarily target individuals. By contrast, in a 1960 report on China's policy in Tibet, the International Commission of Jurists (ICJ) found that Tibetans were victims of genocide as a religious group on the basis of the ultimate target: the group's 'faith and belief'[45] and not the individual members themselves.

The ILC's position therefore seems paradoxical since, on the one hand, the Commission firmly anchors the crime of genocide within the social conception of the group when it states that 'the intention must be to destroy a group and not merely one or more individuals who are coincidentally members of a particular group' and, on the other hand, it ultimately defines the crime as merely targeting one or more individual members of the group. William Schabas also tends to fit into this line of thought, when he suggests that on the basis of Article 30 UDHR 'the ordinary meaning of "group"' should be read as 'an entity composed of more than one individual'.[46] It seems difficult to read such an 'ordinary' meaning from Article 30, which prevents any group from 'destroying' the rights and freedoms set out in the UDHR. The inclusion of the word 'group' in this provision was originally intended to cover criminal organizations such as the Nazis or the Ku Klux Klan,[47] which were indeed 'entit[ies] composed of more than one individual' but not the kind of 'group' mentioned in the Genocide Convention. Furthermore, Article 30 is often invoked in order to warn against the possibility of human groups, such as ethnic groups, restraining their individual members' rights and freedoms, which again tends to confirm the social understanding of the notion of group.

In brief, a sociological approach to the notion of group destruction inherently questions the ILC position, since, as Larry May states, '[c]onceptually, destroying a group must be different from merely killing the group's members'.[48] This concern also emerges from the various statements made by either the German judges or some ICTY judges, when they refer to the 'group foundations' or the idea of 'social unit'. The question that remains, therefore, is how to cut through these various interpretations from a legal perspective. In order to do so, the range of methodological tools of interpretation that international law offers needs to be mobilized before a final answer can ever be provided.

[45] International Commission of Jurists, 'Tibet and the Chinese People's Republic' (Geneva: ICJ, 1960) p. 12. The ICJ considered that the Tibetans could not be concluded as a national group on the basis of the Genocide Convention based on the following argument: 'Violation of their right to exist as a religious group was proven; violation of their right to exist as a national, ethnical or racial group was not. The dividing line is that a Tibetan who would not give up his religion was killed or ran the risk of being killed; he could never give up being a Tibetan.'

[46] William A. Schabas, *Genocide in International Law: The Crime of Crimes* (2nd edn., Cambridge: Cambridge University Press, 2009) p. 122.

[47] Johannes Morsink, *The Universal Declaration of Human Rights, Origins, Drafting and Intent* (Philadelphia: University of Pennsylvania Press, 2000) pp. 87–8.

[48] Larry May, *Genocide: A Normative Account* (Cambridge; New York: Cambridge University Press, 2010) p. 7.

3.2 'Group Destruction' in Light of Methods and Principles of Interpretation in International Law

The legal methods of interpretation may emerge as useful tools to get out of the interpretive dilemma and overcome the sociological and philosophical deadlock that seems to taint the question of group destruction. Still, the various socio-legal rationales are important to keep in mind during this exercise, as legal interpretation is not an autopoietic exercise. The definition of genocide is predominantly enshrined in treaty law, starting with the Genocide Convention, and further in the statutes of international criminal tribunals. As such, one should first refer to the rules of treaty interpretation, as set out in the Vienna Convention on the Law of Treaties (VCLT).[49]

The VCLT involves an interpretative process encompassing two main steps. First, according to the general rule of interpretation set out in Article 31(1) VCLT, '[a] treaty shall be interpreted in good faith in accordance with the ordinary meaning to be given to the terms of the treaty in their context and in the light of its object and purpose'. Thereafter, and only if the meaning of the provision or of one specific term remains 'ambiguous' or 'manifestly absurd or unreasonable' does Article 32 VCLT authorize recourse to the intent of the authors as supplementary means of interpretation, that is the 'preparatory works of the treaty and the circumstances of its conclusion'. These two articles reflect a pragmatic compromise between privileging the text of the treaty on its face, its purpose, and the intent of the authors, which 'emphasises the primacy of the basis for the interpretation of a treaty, while at the same time giving a certain place to extrinsic evidence of the intentions of the parties and to the objects and purposes of the treaty as means of interpretation'.[50] Articles 31 and 32 of the VCLT provide courts with a wide range of interpretative tools, which may potentially conflict with one another. As the ILC suggests in its commentary on the VCLT, 'recourse to many of these principles is discretionary rather than obligatory and the interpretation of documents is to some extent an art, not an exact science'.[51] The interpreter's reasoning will nevertheless necessarily evolve within some well-defined boundaries, and in particular the hierarchy established between the two articles.

These rules are considered as constituting a codification of already-existing principles of customary international law,[52] which means that they also apply to treaties that entered into force before the VCLT itself, such as the 1948 Genocide

[49] Vienna Convention on the Law of Treaties (adopted 23 May 1969, entered into force 27 January 1980) 1155 UNTS 331 (VCLT).

[50] ILC (18th Session), 'Draft Articles on the Law of Treaties with Commentaries', *Yearbook of the International Law Commission*, 1966, vol. II (ILC Draft Articles on the Law of Treaties), Commentary to Article 27 [later Article 31], para. 2.

[51] Ibid., para. 4.

[52] *Oil Platforms (Islamic Republic of Iran v. United States of America)* (Judgment) [1996] ICJ Rep. 803, para. 23.

Convention.[53] Any attempt to interpret the terms of the definition of genocide should therefore respect, as a matter of principle, these two steps. This is true with regard to the interpretation of Article II of the Genocide Convention.

The question remains open as to the interpretation of the definitions contained in the statutes of international criminal tribunals and national criminal codes, which reproduce the words of Article II. Hence, when it comes to the implementation of these domestic provisions, the judicial actor necessarily interprets the international provision[54] whereas he or she is acting in a different institutional and statutory context than the one set out in the Genocide Convention. Both the ICTY Trial Chamber[55] and the German courts[56] thus affirmed the applicability of the interpretive principles of the VCLT, though without providing equal weight to the available principles. While the German courts clearly anchored their interpretation in the general rule of interpretation established in Article 31 VCLT, the ICTY gave more weight to the *travaux préparatoires*. These principles should in turn be articulated and sometimes balanced with other principles that transcend the legal discipline in which they are implemented (for example, principles of criminal law). When it comes to the implementation of the definition of genocide, this may occur in two different settings: either in international criminal law or the law of state responsibility. A further question arises as to the possibility of reaching different outcomes in each of these settings.

This section will thus reconstruct the interpretive process of the concept of 'group destruction' in light of the general rule of interpretation, as set out in Article 31 VCLT. The question as to the importance that should be attributed to the *travaux préparatoires* will then be discussed, and the consequences that should be attached to the principles of either international criminal law or state responsibility subsequently assessed.

3.2.1 The meaning of 'group destruction' in light of its context, object, and purpose

Article 31 VCLT firstly requires that we look for the 'ordinary' meaning of the terms. Some authors thus consider that '[t]his follows from the simple grammatical observation that it is not accurate to speak of 'the group' as being amenable to physical or biological destruction'.[57] However, an endeavour of the ordinary meaning ultimately reflects the sociological and philosophical divergence on the issue, of particular relevance in a multilingual context. This can be illustrated with reference to the term 'destroy'; in *The New Oxford Dictionary of English*, spiritual destruction—to 'ruin emotionally or spiritually'—is listed first, before reference is made to material destruction,[58] while *Le Nouveau Petit Robert* clearly gives priority

[53] *Jelisić Case* (Trial Judgment) IT-95-10 (14 December 1999) para. 61.

[54] See e.g. *Jorgić v. Germany* (n 10) para.106.

[55] *Krstić Case* (Trial) (n 24) para. 544.

[56] *Nikola Jorgić* (Constitutional Appeals) (n 17) p. 162.

[57] Alexander Zahar and Goran Sluiter, 'Genocide Law: An Education in Sentimentalism' in A. Dirk Moses (ed.), *Genocide* (Abingdon; New York, NY: Routledge, 2010, Vol. 6) p. 138.

[58] Judy Pearsall and Patrick Hanks (eds.), *The New Oxford Dictionary of English* (Oxford: Clarendon Press, 1998): 'ruin (someone) emotionally or spiritually, defeat (someone utterly)'.

to the material destruction by equating 'destroy' with 'kill' and 'exterminate' before envisaging it to be the disintegration of some organized structure.[59] The other steps established in Article 31 VCLT must therefore be implemented; this requires that we look at the context of the words to be interpreted—'systemic interpretation'—and the overall purpose and object of the Treaty, known as 'teleological interpretation'.[60]

3.2.1.1 *The legal context of 'group destruction'*

Article 31(2) requires that the context of the provision be taken into account through 'the text, including its preamble and annexes'. This consideration of context thus involves broadening the focus, from the terms themselves, to the provision in which it is contained, the rest of the treaty, as well as other relevant rules of international law. The initial exercise consists of looking at the entirety of Article II. As a first step, the original twofold structure of the provision should be recognized: a crime is necessarily composed of criminal acts, associated with an intent to perpetrate the act. While this conception is present from subparagraphs (a) to (e) of the definition of genocide, the first paragraph of the definition adds an element to the common definition of a crime. The *mens rea* of genocide, as examined in this chapter, is more than the simple intent to perpetrate the five criminalized acts; it is the intent to destroy a group as such. The qualification of this *mens rea* as '*dolus specialis*' tends to cover a double meaning. On the one hand, it describes the additional *mens rea*. On the other, it describes the degree of criminal intent required for the crime, which is considered to be more than the mere knowledge that the criminal acts may lead to the destruction of the group; rather, the perpetrator needs to endorse this intent.[61] Only the first dimension of the *dolus specialis* is relevant for the present study. International tribunals have consistently stated that the evidence of the *mens rea* might be found in the perpetration of acts other than those mentioned in the definition of genocide,[62] as illustrated by the *Krstić* finding in relation to the use of acts of cultural genocide as evidence of the genocidal intent. As the international criminal tribunals have interpreted it, the special *mens rea* in genocide allows for

[59] Paul Robert, Josette Rey-Debove, and Alain Rey (eds.), *Le Nouveau Petit Robert: Dictionnaire Alphabétique et Analogique de la Langue Française* (Paris: Dictionnaires Le Robert, 2000) p. 705: 'Détruire'.

[60] Mark E Villiger, *Commentary on the 1969 Vienna Convention on the Law of Treaties* (Leiden, Boston: Martinus Nijhoff Publishers, 2009) p. 421.

[61] *Akayesu Case* (Trial) (n 6) para. 498. Some authors rather argue for a lesser degree of intent to be recognized, at least for low-level perpetrators, cf. Kai Ambos, 'What Does 'Intent to Destroy' in Genocide Mean?' (2009) 91 *International Review of the Red Cross* 833, pp. 845–50; Katherine Goldsmith, 'The Issue of Intent in the Genocide Convention and its Effect on the Prevention and Punishment of the Crime of Genocide: Toward a Knowledge-Based Approach' (2010) 5 *G.S.P.* 238, pp. 238–57.

[62] This was repeatedly asserted in the international criminal case law and academic scholarship. See e.g. *Akayesu Case* (Trial) (n 6) para. 523; *Application of the Genocide Convention (Bosnia and Herzegovina v. Serbia and Montenegro)* (Judgment) (n 11) para. 197; *Application of the Genocide Convention (Croatia v. Serbia)* (Judgment) (n 38) paras. 382, 390; Otto Triffterer, 'Genocide: Its Particular Intent to Destroy in Whole or in Part the Group as Such' (2001) 14 *L.J.I.L.* 399, pp. 399–408.

the reintroduction of a wide-range of acts that are not directly encompassed in the *actus reus* of genocide. The question therefore arises as to whether the *mens rea* of genocide should reflect its *actus reus* or could be understood in broader terms. In other words, should the perpetrator seek to achieve the physical and/or biological annihilation of the group as such or would an intent to eliminate the group, as a social entity, be 'enough' to constitute the *mens rea* of genocide?

Returning to the ILC statement on the 'physical-biological understanding' of the word destruction,[63] therein it seems to assume that the material and mental elements of genocide should conflate. However, the structure of the definition of genocide can be interpreted in a different way. At first glance, it seems that the *mens rea* concerns 'groups as such'—whether the 'as such' relates to the national, ethnic, racial, or religious identity of the group or the overall entity—while the *actus reus* targets individual members. Therefore, even though the group is harmed through the harm to its individual members, it might also be expected that additional acts will be perpetrated against its own characteristics. There is thus no structural reason to consider that if the *actus reus* only includes acts of physical and biological destruction, the *mens rea* should necessarily be understood as meaning the physical and biological destruction of the group. In his dissenting opinion to the *Krstić* Appeals judgment, Judge Shahabuddeen advanced strong arguments in this regard, especially when he stated that '[f]rom their nature, the listed (or initial) acts must indeed take a physical or biological form, but the accompanying intent, by those acts, to destroy the group in whole or in part need not always lead to a destruction of the same character'.[64]

Depending on the reading that one will make about the five acts, one will either consider that genocide is only about physical and biological destruction of the group, or that it actually goes beyond such a narrow understanding. Partisans of the physical-biological interpretation will read the whole definition of genocide as the ILC does: 'Subparagraphs (a) to (c) of the article list acts of "physical genocide", while subparagraphs (d) and (e) list acts of "biological genocide" '.[65] Defenders of a more socio-cultural position, such as the German courts,[66] will place emphasis on the 'mental harm' of subparagraph (b) and the cultural origins of subparagraph (e). Some will go as far as to challenge the respective physical and biological dimensions of subparagraphs (c) and (d).[67] Another way of proceeding is to reason *a contrario*,

[63] ILC 1996 Draft Code of Crimes (n 2) Commentary on art. 17, para. 12.

[64] *Krstić Case* (Appeals) (n 25) Judge Shahabuddeen's dissenting opinion, para. 48.

[65] ILC 1996 Draft Code of Crimes (n 2) Commentary on art. 17, para. 12.

[66] *Nikola Jorgić* (Appeals) (n 17) p. 26; *Nikola Jorgić* (Constitutional Appeals) (n 17) p. 160; Confirmed by *Jorgić v. Germany* (n 10) para. 96.

[67] Patrick Wolfe, 'Settler Colonialism and the Elimination of the Native' (2006) 8 *J.G.R.* p. 401; the author argues that subparagraph (d) could be interpreted as encompassing acts other than 'biological means', such as a gender-based separation of group members. See also *Tolimir*, IT-05-88/2-T, 'Trial Judgment' (12 December 2012), para. 768: the ICTY reviewed and ultimately rejected a similar argument made by the Prosecutor, who emphasized 'the fact that as a consequence of the choice of many of the women who were transferred not to remarry because of "the lack of military-aged men, the loss of a husband's pension upon remarriage, the social stigma of remarriage and feelings of guilt" the birth rate in the community may have decreased.' Zdravko Tolimir was eventually convicted for genocide and conspiracy to commit genocide in Srebrenica.

as did Judge Shahabuddeen when he noted that only subparagraphs (c) and (d) contained a specification of the nature of the intent required in relation to the respective acts of physical and biological destruction: '*[a] contrario*, it would seem that, in other cases, the Statute itself does not require an intent to cause physical or biological destruction of the group in whole or in part'.[68] Since they catalyse much of the debate related to the reintroduction of cultural genocide, whether as a technique or a process, subparagraphs (b), (c), and (e) will be analysed in more detail below.

Subparagraph (b) 'mental suffering'

The inclusion of subparagraph (b) in the final definition of genocide is a result of China's efforts to have the experience of its people during the Second World War recognized, and in particular the consequences of the spreading of opium by Japanese troops, which would render Chinese addicted to this drug and consequently make them lose their capacities of judgment and resistance.[69] By the same token, 'mental harm' could be used to qualify acts of cultural genocide, on the basis of the harm that such acts engender. This could apply to the harm endured by the group members following the destruction of cultural heritage, or the consequences resulting from forced transfers of children, such as alcoholism or violent behaviours observable at the adult age.[70]

'Mental harm' lacks a well-anchored definition in international law. For instance, the ICC Elements of Crimes note, in a footnote to the elements of Article 6(b), that '[t]his conduct may include, but is not necessarily restricted to, acts of torture, rape, sexual violence or inhuman or degrading treatment'.[71] Beyond genocide, 'mental harm' is a characteristic feature of the international legal framework on the prohibition of torture, which defines torture as 'any act by which severe pain or suffering, whether physical or mental, is intentionally inflicted on a person (. . .)'.[72] Shue and Luban define mental pain and suffering as:

> the kind of pain or suffering we describe using psychological terms like *anxiety*, *terror*, *humiliation*, *despondency*, *brokenheartedness*, *grief*, and so on. (. . .). What makes them mental is that the terms name emotional states; what makes them pain and suffering is that they feel bad, and what makes them severe is how bad they feel.[73]

68 *Krstić Case* (Appeals) (n 25) Judge Shahabuddeen's dissenting opinion, para. 48.

69 ECOSOC 'Ad Hoc Committee on Genocide: Summary Record of the Fifth Meeting' E/AC.25/SR.5 (16 April 1948), in Hirad Abtahi and Philippa Webb, *The Genocide Convention—The Travaux Préparatoires*, 2 vols. (Leiden; Boston: Martinus Nijhoff Publishers, 2008) p. 731.

70 Australian Human Rights Commission, *Bringing Them Home, Report of the National Inquiry into the Separation of Aboriginal and Torres Strait Islander Children from Their Families* (April 1997) pp. 481–2. See also Tove Skutnabb-Kangas and Robert Dunbar, 'Indigenous Children's Education as Linguistic Genocide and a Crime Against Humanity? A Global View' (2010) 1 *Gáldu Čála: Journal of Indigenous Peoples Rights*, p. 84; David B. MacDonald and Gordon Hudson, 'The Genocide Question and Indian Residential Schools in Canada' (2012) 45 *Can.J.Pol.Sc.* 427, p. 440.

71 ICC Elements of Crimes, ICC-ASP/1/3(part II-B) (adopted and entered into force 9 September 2002) art. 6(b) para. 1, fn. 3.

72 Convention against Torture and Other Cruel, Inhuman or Degrading Treatment or Punishment (adopted 10 December 1984, entered into force 26 June 1987) 1465 UNTS 85, art. 1(1).

73 David Luban and Henry Shue, 'Mental Torture: A Critique of Erasures in U.S. Law' (2012) 100 *Geo. L.J.*, 823, p. 830 (emphasis added).

Amongst the numerous examples of mental pain and suffering, 'desecration' is often invoked as the 'forcing victims to witness or engage in the violation of religious practices (irreverence, blasphemy, profanity, defilement, sacrilege, incest, Satanism)'.[74] Even the United States, which has a particularly restricted understanding of the notion of torture, recognizes 'acts intended to denigrate the religion, religious practices, or religious objects of the individual' as acts of torture.[75] Yet, while the terms are the same, international criminal law precludes the interpretation of a criminal provision by analogy,[76] which means that developments occurring in the legal framework against torture cannot be transposed as such in the context of international criminal law, unless such findings could actually be considered to reflect the adequate, if not ordinary, meaning of the criminal provision at stake.

Subparagraph (b) has actually received extensive interpretation so as to allow for the inclusions of a wide-range of acts not anticipated by the drafters of the Convention, as a result of the finding that 'causing serious bodily or mental harm does not necessarily mean that the harm is permanent and irremediable'.[77] The most emblematic inclusion may be that of rape, which has increasingly been used as a tool of group destruction, especially during the Rwandese genocide. Notwithstanding, these acts would not naturally fall within any of the *actus reus* listed in the definition of genocide. In the *Akayesu* judgment, the ICTR Trial Chamber concluded that such acts would fall within subparagraph (b) of the definition of genocide, related to 'serious bodily and mental harm'. The Chamber justified its reasoning with explicit reference to the Tutsi identity of the victims,[78] as well as the specific harm that these rapes caused:

> These rapes resulted in physical and psychological destruction of Tutsi women, their families and their communities. Sexual violence was an integral part of the process of destruction, specifically targeting Tutsi women and specifically contributing to their destruction and to the destruction of the Tutsi group as a whole.[79]

The emphasis on the expanded victimhood which extends from rape, which also impacts on 'families and communities', implicitly refers to the cultural context of the victims. It explains why, in the Rwandese context, rapes are understood as more than individual acts of sexual violence, and become actual acts of genocide. As Kurt Mundorff has noted, such a 'case law destabilizes the ILC's distinction between physio-biological and cultural genocide'.[80]

Furthermore, on the basis of the Eichmann judgment, the ICTR has also included persecutory acts in the scope of subparagraph (b), when perpetrated with the intent to destroy a group.[81] The notion of persecution will be further developed

[74] Almerindo E. Ojeda, 'What is Psychological Torture?' in Almerindo E. Ojeda (ed.), *The Trauma of Psychological Torture* (Westport, Conn.; Praeger, 2008) p. 3.

[75] Exec. Order No. 13,440, 3 C.F.R. 229 (2007) quoted by Luban and Shue (n 73) fn. 103.

[76] Rome Statute of the International Criminal Court (adopted 17 July 1998, entered into force 1 July 2002) 2187 UNTS 3 (ICC Rome Statute) art. 22(2).

[77] *Akayesu Case* (Trial) (n 6) para. 502. [78] Ibid., para. 732. [79] Ibid., para. 731.

[80] Kurt Mundorff, 'Other Peoples' Children: A Textual and Contextual Interpretation of the Genocide Convention, Article 2(e)' (2009) 50 *Harv.Int'l L.J.* 61, p. 113.

[81] *Akayesu Case* (Trial) (n 6) paras. 503–4.

in Chapter 5. At this stage, it is worth noting that this finding is interesting since this crime against humanity, which is defined as 'serious violations of fundamental rights',[82] was also used by the ICTY to criminalize the destruction of religious cultural heritage in Bosnia. Yet the ICTY has been very cautious not to open to too great an extent the interpretation, by adding that: '[a] distinction must thus be drawn between serious mental harm and emotional or psychological damage or attacks on the dignity of the human person not causing lasting impairment'.[83] It further stated that:

> serious harm need not cause permanent and irremediable harm, but it must involve harm that goes beyond temporary unhappiness, embarrassment or humiliation. It must be harm that results in a grave and long-term disadvantage to a person's ability to lead a normal and constructive life. In subscribing to the above case-law, the Chamber holds that inhuman treatment, torture, rape, sexual abuse and deportation are among the acts which may cause serious bodily or mental injury.[84]

This list of examples seems to exclude *prima facie* acts of cultural genocide, which thus far, have not been argued before the ICTY on the basis of Article II(b). However, the recent evolution of the ICTY's case law in relation to acts of forcible transfer of population is noteworthy in this regard. In the *Blagojević & Jokić* case, the Appeals Chamber had refused to consider them as *actus reus,* and only acknowledged them at the level of the *mens rea*, to support the evidence of the genocidal intent associated with the perpetration of mass killings,[85] therefore anchoring the forced transfers in a biological-physical understanding of the group. In the *Karadžić* case, the Trial Chamber formally included such acts within the scope of subparagraph (b), highlighting 'the atmosphere of panic in Potocari'.[86] It especially found 'that the mental harm caused to the women, children, and some elderly men as a result of the killing of the men and boys and the *forcible removal of the remainder of Bosnian Muslims* had long-lasting effects on the respective abilities of the surviving women, children, and some elderly men to live normal and constructive lives'.[87] Still, the recognition of acts of 'forcible removal' is narrowly intertwined with the killings of the Bosnian Muslim males of Srebrenica.

Furthermore, we find examples of the domestic implementation of this provision that include acts of cultural destruction. For example, in Guatemala, the Commission of Historical Clarification (CEH) found that the Mayan population had been victim of genocide in the early 1980s, notably in respect of acts criminalized under Article II(b) of the Genocide Convention, within which it considered 'the occupation or destruction of Mayan sacred places'.[88] As for the special intent to perpetrate genocide by inflicting 'serious physical or mental harm' on the

[82] ICC Rome Statute (n 76) art. 7(2)(g). [83] *Krstić Case* (Trial) (n 24) para. 510.
[84] Ibid., para. 513. [85] *Blagojević & Jokić Case* (Appeals) (n 33) para. 123.
[86] *Karadžić Case* (Trial Judgment) IT-95-5/18-I (24 March 2016) para. 5662.
[87] Ibid., para. 5664.
[88] Comisión para el Esclaracimiento Histórico (CEH), *Guatemala: Memoria del Silencio*, 1999, available at: http://www.centrodememoriahistorica.gov.co/descargas/guatemala-memoria-silencio/guatemala-memoria-del-silencio.pdf (last accessed February 2015) para. 1012.

group members, the Commission underlined that it could be identified through the actual 'effect of destroying the social cohesion of the group, which characterized such acts', emphasizing that such effect 'correspond[ed] to the intention of both physically and *spiritually* destroying the group'.[89]

Subparagraph (c) 'Conditions of life calculated to bring about its physical destruction'

The engagement of this subparagraph in order to support claims of non-physical or biological group destruction may seem contradictory, as this is the only genocidal act in respect of which the intent to physically destroy the group is explicit. Notwithstanding, this provision may be used in two ways for the purpose of reinterpreting the *mens rea* of genocide.

Firstly, it is possible to argue that if the drafters took care to underline the notion of 'physical destruction', *a contrario*, it means that the other acts criminalized by the definition of genocide do not necessarily entail its physical destruction.[90] Still, it remains to be seen whether such other acts would not only go beyond physical destruction but also beyond biological destruction, which is the second possible means of destruction recognized by the ILC, the ICTY, and the ICJ. In this regard, it is possible to identify some bias in the approach adopted by the German courts, as they only opposed the physical *versus* social understanding while the broader debate deals with the distinction between the physical-biological understanding, on the one hand, and the more socio-cultural conception, on the other.[91]

Furthermore, this provision can also be used to advance the inclusion of a more socio-cultural understanding of the crime of genocide, by interpreting broadly the notion of 'group conditions of life' and trying to relate it to the physical group destruction. Federico Lenzerini accordingly argues that:

> on account of the special spiritual link that members of indigenous communities have with their own ancestral lands, lifestyle, traditions and cultural roots, their forcible removal from their lands and the consequent sudden impact with the Western society could be considered as a treatment entailing both 'serious . . . mental harm' to the prejudice of such people and infliction 'on the group [of] conditions of life calculated to bring about its physical destruction in whole or in part'. These acts (. . .) may in fact lead many indigenous persons to a physical and psychological decline that may eventually bring them to death.[92]

[89] Ibid., para. 1243: 'La CEH concluye que, entre los actos perpetrados con la intención de destruir total o parcialmente a numerosos grupos mayas, también se cometieron múltiples acciones que constituyeron "lesiones graves a la integridad física o mental de los miembros de los grupos" mayas afectados (artículo II, letra "b" de la Convención). El efecto de destruir la cohesión social del grupo, característico de estos actos, se corresponde con la intención de aniquilar física y *espiritualmente* al grupo.' (emphasis added).

[90] See *Krstić Case* (Appeals) (n 25) Judge Shahabuddeen's dissenting opinion, paras. 48–9; Skutnabb-Kangas and Dunbar (n 70) p. 85.

[91] *Nikola Jorgić* (Constitutional Appeals) (n 17) p. 160.

[92] Federico Lenzerini, 'The Trail of Broken Dreams: The Status of Indigenous Peoples in International Law' in Federico Lenzerini (ed.), *Reparations for Indigenous Peoples: International and Comparative Perspectives* (Oxford: Oxford University Press, 2008) p. 103.

Other scholars have formulated similar arguments in relation to the forced transfers of aboriginal children, and that 'the social, economic and cultural conditions which states impose[d] upon indigenous peoples [were] calculated to bring about the physical destruction of indigenous groups, and they cite as evidence levels of alcoholism, infant mortality, suicide and disease'.[93] The extent to which these consequences were 'calculated'—that is intended—with a view to destroying the group, and not simply the result of negligent and possibly criminal policies, remains to be proven.

International courts were led to review arguments of acts of non-physical or biological group destruction based on Article II(c). For instance, Bosnia claimed before the ICJ 'that throughout the conflict in Bosnia and Herzegovina, Serb forces engaged in the deliberate destruction of historical, religious and cultural property of the protected group in "an attempt to wipe out the traces of their very existence" '.[94] The argument was rejected by the Court, which considered that these acts could not fall within the meaning of Article II(c).[95] A few years later in its *Popović* judgment, a Trial Chamber dismissed a charge of genocide based on subparagraph (c) of its definition, on the basis that it was not satisfied that 'the destruction of the social structure of the community and the inability of those who were forcibly transferred to reconstruct their lives (. . .) [were] the kinds of conditions intended to be prohibited by Article 4(2)(c) of the Statute'.[96] Although this judgment is clearly inscribed in the *Krstić* line, it can also be read as confirming the *a contrario* analysis of Judge Shahabuddeen—who indeed noted the explicit reference to 'physical destruction' under subparagraph (c)[97]—rather than the absolute biological-physical conception of the *Krstić* Trial and Appeals Chambers.

Finally, this subparagraph has received extensive interpretation so as to include forced evictions of populations from their homes. The *Akayesu* trial judgment was the first decision to mention it.[98] This act was soon after integrated as an Element of Crime of subparagraph (c) of the ICC definition of genocide in the following words: 'forced transfers of population, when committed with the intent to destroy the group'.[99] The concrete implementation of these types of acts as genocidal could occur in the *Al Bashir* case, the indictment of which for genocide encompasses such a crime under subparagraph (c),[100] in contrast to the strategy of indictments within the

[93] Skutnabb-Kangas and Dunbar (n 70) p. 82 (quoting Chris C. Tenant and Mary Ellen Turpel, 'A Case Study of Indigenous Peoples: Genocide, Ethnocide and Self-Determination', *Nordic Journal of International Law*, Vol. 59, No. 3, 1990, p. 296); MacDonald and Hudson (n 70) p. 440.

[94] *Application of the Genocide Convention (Bosnia and Herzegovina v. Serbia and Montenegro)* (Judgment) (n 11) para. 335. The same argument was formulated by Croatia in *Application of the Genocide Convention (Croatia v. Serbia)* (Judgment) (n 38) paras. 386–90.

[95] *Application of the Genocide Convention (Bosnia and Herzegovina v. Serbia and Montenegro)* (Judgment) (n 11) para. 344.

[96] *Popović et al. Case* (Trial) IT-05-88 (10 June 2010) para. 854.

[97] *Krstić Case* (Appeals) (n 25) Judge Shahabuddeen's dissenting opinion, para. 48.

[98] *Akayesu Case* (Trial) (n 6) para. 506.

[99] ICC Elements of Crimes (n 71) art. 6(c) para. 4, fn. 4.

[100] *Prosecutor v. Omar Hassan Ahmad Al Bashir* (Second Arrest Warrant) ICC-02/05-01/09 (12 July 2010) Pre-Trial Chamber I, pp. 7–8. The status of this case is uncertain at the time of writing, since the ICC Prosecutor has announced in her December 2014 report to the Security Council her intent to

ICTY, where acts of forced transfers of population have rather been reviewed under subparagraph (b) of the definition of genocide, as serious mental harm imposed on members of the group.[101] It is noteworthy that the ICC Elements of Crimes illustrate the term 'conditions of life' with the 'deliberate deprivation of resources indispensable for survival, such as (. . .) systematic expulsion from homes'.[102] This was exactly what was at stake in the cases adjudicated by the ICTY and it will certainly be interesting to follow the way in which the ICC will apply this specific provision and the basis on which it will connect such acts with an intent to physically destroy the group, which is still required by Article 6(c) of the Rome Statute.

Subparagraph (e) 'Forcibly transferring children from one group to another'

The history of subparagraph (e) and its late reintegration into the provision on genocide has led William Schabas to qualify it as 'enigmatic',[103] even as an 'anomaly'.[104] Mundorff speaks of its 'dormant and anachronistic status'.[105] Indeed, those who defend a physical-biological interpretation of the crime of genocide might feel somewhat puzzled when confronted with this provision, the physical-biological dimension of which is not particularly self-evident.[106] Each of the antagonistic positions adopted will therefore tend to rely on the history of this provision: the Greek emphasis on its biological dimension at the moment of its reintroduction in the definitive definition of genocide;[107] a crime of cultural genocide in the first draft of the Genocide Convention.[108] Furthermore, 'biological genocide' was initially conceived as a set of measures aimed at preventing the group from biologically reproducing itself,[109] which is not necessarily the consequence of the forced transfer of children. Consequently, there are very few legal cases, and even fewer criminal cases, in which the issue has been addressed. There is one example, the occurrence of which preceded the negotiations and adoption of the Genocide Convention: namely, the *RuSHA* case, tried by the United States International Military Tribunal of Nuremberg, which dealt mainly with forced transfers of 'racially

slow down investigations in the Al-Bashir case, as a measure of protection against the Security Council's passive approach to having its resolutions enforced by UN Member States.

[101] *Blagojević & Jokić Case* (Trial) (n 30) para. 650; *Karadžić Case* (Trial) (n 86) paras. 5662–65.

[102] ICC Elements of Crimes (n 71) art. 6(c), para. 4, fn. 4.

[103] Schabas, *Genocide in International Law* (n 46) p. 201.

[104] William A. Schabas, 'Judicial Activism and the Crime of Genocide' in Shane Darcy and Joseph Powderly (eds.), *Judicial Creativity at the International Criminal Tribunals* (Oxford: Oxford University Press, 2010) p. 75.

[105] Mundorff (n 80) p. 63.

[106] Micol Sirkin, 'Expanding the Crime of Genocide to Include Ethnic Cleansing: A Return to Established Principles in Light of Contemporary Interpretations' (2010) 33 *Seattle U.L. Rev.* 489, p. 514.

[107] UNGA Sixth Committee (3rd Session) 'Eighty-Second Meeting' (23 October 1948) UN Doc. A/C.6/SR.82, in Abtahi and Webb (n 69) p. 1492.

[108] ECOSOC 'Draft Convention on the Crime of Genocide' E/447 (26 June 1947), in Abtahi and Webb (n 69) p. 215, art. I(II)(3)(a).

[109] Raphael Lemkin, *Axis Rule in Occupied Europe: Laws of Occupation—Analysis of Government—Proposals for Redress* (2nd edn., first published 1944, Clark, N.J.: Lawbook Exchange, Ltd., 2008) pp. 86–7; ECOSOC 'Draft Convention on the Crime of Genocide' E/447 (n 108) p. 234.

valuable Polish children' to Nazi Germany to be educated in the Nazi ideology, for which the accused were convicted of war crimes and crimes against humanity.[110] While the tribunal did not have the jurisdiction to qualify such acts as genocide, the Prosecutor did not hesitate to use the neologism to describe this particular set of acts.[111] It should be pointed out that under the Third Reich, the transfers of children were accompanied by a wide-range of other acts targeting the biological and physical features of the group, such as forced sterilizations and the extermination of children. As such, the *RuSHA* case can only have limited precedence in the context of the processes that targeted indigenous children in Western democracies.

In its Draft Code of Crimes against the Peace and Security of Mankind, the ILC remained quite neutral in its appreciation of the provision, noting that '[t]he forcible transfer of children would have particularly serious consequences for the future viability of a group as such'.[112] This should nonetheless be read in light of its former statement on the mere biological and physical nature of the crime of genocide and its rejection of the concept of cultural genocide.[113] A few criminal courts have had the occasion to deliver statements on Article II(e). In the *Akayesu* case, the ICTR considered that:

> With respect to forcibly transferring children of the group to another group, the Chamber is of the opinion that, as in the case of measures intended to prevent births, the objective is not only to sanction a direct act of forcible physical transfer, but also to sanction acts of threats or trauma which would lead to the forcible transfer of children from one group to another.[114]

In the *Jorgić* case, the German courts grounded their *ratio* on the nature of crime of 'forcibly transferring children', which does not call on any biological understanding per se,[115] but did not review acts of the forcible transfer of children as such. Judge Shahabuddeen further noted that:

> It is not apparent why an intent to destroy a group in a non-physical or non-biological way should be outside the ordinary reach of the Convention on which the Statute is based, provided that that intent attached to a listed act, this being of a physical or biological nature.[116]

The ICJ also had to look at this provision in its 2007 judgment, in the *Bosnia v. Serbia* case, in which Bosnia claimed:

> that rape was used as a 'way of affecting the demographic balance by impregnating Muslim women with the sperm of Serb males' or, in other words, as 'procreative rape'. The applicant argues that children born as a result of these 'forced pregnancies' would not be considered to be part of the protected group and considers that the intent of the perpetrators was to transfer the unborn children to the group of Bosnian Serbs.[117]

[110] *Ulrich Greifelt et al. (RuSHA case)* Judgment (1949) United Nations War Crimes Commission, XIII Law Reports of Trials of War Criminals 1, United States Military Tribunal, Nuremberg.
[111] Ibid., para. 2.
[112] ILC 1996 Draft Code of Crimes (n 2) Commentary on art. 17, para. 17.
[113] Ibid. Commentary on art. 17, para. 16.
[114] *Akayesu Case* (Trial) (n 6) para. 509.
[115] *Nikola Jorgić* (Appeals) (n 17) p. 26.
[116] *Krstić Case* (Appeals) (n 25) Judge Shahabuddeen's dissenting opinion, para. 49.
[117] *Application of the Genocide Convention (Bosnia and Herzegovina v. Serbia and Montenegro)* (Judgment) (n 11) para. 362.

The Court rejected the argument for lack of evidence, without commenting on its legal accuracy, even though it outlined the apparent absence of 'any aim to transfer children of the protected group to another group *within the meaning* of Article II(e) of the Convention'.[118] In a separate opinion, Judge Kreca, the *ad hoc* judge appointed by Serbia-Montenegro, interpreted the provision as involving physical-biological destruction: '[e]ven if it is accepted that the act covered by subparagraph (e) constitutes "cultural" or "sociological" genocide, its meaning is *in concreto* of limited importance'.[119] As an exception to the 'principle of material genocide', he considered that it 'would be subject to restrictive interpretation'.[120] The rationale is quite hard to follow since no argument exists to address any kind of hierarchy between the acts listed in Article II. Such a statement nevertheless reveals the lesser consideration that some lawyers might dedicate to this *sui generis* provision. In its 2015 judgment, the ICJ touched again upon the issue, even though Croatia had not even raised the issue in its application, in order to emphasize the potential 'physical' destruction entailed by forcible transfers of children from one group to another, 'since it can have consequences for the group's capacity to renew itself, and hence to ensure its long-term survival'.[121] This assertion, which would rather correspond to the definition of 'biological destruction', does not seem to be supported by any reliable source so that it can be concluded that the ICJ case law is not particularly convincing when it comes to interpreting Article II(e).

More recently, a scholar, Sonja Grover, has advocated for the ICC to address the enrolment and use of child soldiers in the various situations under its review as the 'forcible transfer of children from one group to another'. The argument is interesting as it relies almost exclusively on social and cultural concerns:

> the intent of these armed groups or forces is to appropriate the children indefinitely and not just for the duration of the armed conflict, to permanently alienate the children from their families and home communities, and to obliterate the personal and cultural identity of the children and substitute the perpetrator identity and credo.[122]

Yet one major obstacle arises in respect of the definition of the victim group, since the notion of 'national, ethnic, racial or religious (victim) group' has so far been interpreted as different from the perpetrator group.[123] It is therefore difficult to envision the recognition of genocide against a group of children, or more broadly of families, who would share the same national, ethnic, and/or religious identities as the perpetrators. This issue has been especially acute in the context of the legal qualification of the Argentinean 'dirty war'. Amongst the numerous crimes perpetrated by the military junta, 500 children have been reported 'stolen' and illegally

[118] Ibid., para. 364 (emphasis added).
[119] Ibid. Dissenting Opinion of Judge *ad hoc* Kreca, para. 85. [120] Ibid.
[121] *Application of the Genocide Convention (Croatia v. Serbia)* (Judgment) (n 38) para. 136.
[122] Sonja Grover, 'Child Soldiers as Victims of "Genocidal Forcible Transfer": Darfur and Syria as Case Examples' (2013) 17 *I.J.H.R.* 411, pp. 411–12. The author also focuses on the concept of 'social death'.
[123] Ibid., pp. 414–15.

adopted by military families.[124] Most Argentinean national courts have rejected the qualification as genocide, based on the political dimension of the group.[125] A few others have, however, recognized the genocidal dimension of the repression, as evidenced by the forcible transfer of children.[126] Amongst the latter, one of the most influencing developments actually occurred in Spain, where Judge Garzón indicted ninety-eight Argentinean military members for crimes against humanity, crimes of torture, and genocide. Most of his decision relates to the nature of the victim group, which he qualified subjectively—that is according to the perpetrators' perception—as being, amongst others, national and religious. The fate of those 500 children was engaged as determinative evidence of the qualification of genocide. According to him, the fact that there are 'children, who disappeared and were separated from their families in order to be raised in accordance with the Christian ideology (...) is an essential element for the consolidation and qualification of the conduct as genocide of a cohesive group, according to the perpetrators, for its discrepancy with the Christian religious ideology (...)'.[127] This interpretation remains highly controversial.[128] Furthermore, when reviewed individually, acts of forcibly transferring children have rather been considered to fall within the 'crimes against humanity' category by the Argentinean courts.[129]

In Australia and Canada, the Truth and Reconciliation Commissions did not discuss in depth the nature of the *mens rea* and how it should be interpreted. The Australian Human Rights Commission did not enter into the biological *versus* cultural controversy, but rather assumed the cultural dimension of the process of forced transfers of children in Australia.[130] Its conclusions were based on the cultural multilevel harm caused by the practice: '[f]or Indigenous children their 'families' were constituted by their entire community. (...). Children removed from their families were also removed from their communities'.[131] Relying on the victims'

[124] Daniel Feierstein, 'National Security Doctrine in Latin America, The Genocide Question' in Donald Bloxham and A. Dirk Moses (eds.), *The Oxford Handbook of Genocide Studies* (Oxford: Oxford University Press, 2010) p. 46.

[125] *Riveros, Santiago O. y otros* (Decision on Sentence) 08/2009 (12 August 2009) Tribunal Oral en lo Criminal Federal No.1 de San Martín.

[126] *Etchecolatz, Miguel O.* (Judgment) 2251/06 (19 September 2006) Tribunal Oral Criminal Federal La Plata n. 1; *Von Wernich, Christian F.* (Judgment) 2506/07 (1 November 2007) Tribunal Oral Criminal Federal La Plata n. 1, para. 3.

[127] *Auto de Procesamiento a 98 Militares Argentinos* (Judgment) 19/97-L (2 November 1999) Audiencia Nacional Madrid, p. 154: '*El hecho de que existan niños desaparecidos que en Argentina fueron segregados de sus familias para que se desarrollaran en la ideología cristiana, en vez de en la atea o no cristiana de sus familias—según los genocidas—es un elemento esencial para la consolidación de la calificación de la conducta como genocidio de un grupo cohesionado, según los ejecutores de los delitos, por su discrepancia con la ideología religiosa cristiana*' [author's translation].

[128] Armando Kletnicki, 'Disappeared Children in Argentina: Genocidal Logic and Illegal Appropriation' (2006) 8 *J.G.R.*, 2006 181.

[129] See e.g. Lisa Avery, 'A Return to Life: The Right to Identity and the Right to Identify Argentina's "Living Disappeared"' (2004) 27 *Harv. W.L.J.* 235, p. 258.

[130] Australian Human Rights Commission (n 70) p. 237.

[131] Ibid., p. 10.

testimonies,[132] the report underlined the 'totality of separation',[133] as the children were prohibited to speak their own language and communicate with their family. We note here that the Commission could have made a greater case for the biological destruction of the group, which would have been more acceptable for those who are reluctant to attribute to such acts the genocide label. This biological dimension still transpires from parts of the report but always in conjunction with cultural considerations, as is clear from the following statement: '[a]boriginal children were not removed because their 'white blood' made them 'white children' and part of the 'white community'. . . They were removed because, if they stayed with 'their group', they would acquire their 'habits', their culture and traditions'.[134] Public speeches and acts clearly showed that the aim was to eliminate the indigenous groups 'as such', by means of cutting the intergenerational transmission of culture, preventing children from practising it as well as, in a longer-term perspective, promoting the genetic modification of the indigenous community by endeavouring to whiten it.[135] Mundorff goes even further and argues that the transfer 'was a physical act intended to destroy the group as a physical-biological entity. Therefore, this practice amounts to genocide, even though the means of destruction were often culturally mediated'.[136] This seems to constitute a broader understanding of the term 'physical', usually used to designate murderous genocidal processes.

The Canadian Truth and Reconciliation Commission also briefly touched upon the issue, for the purpose of emphasizing its call for justice for the victims rather than for the mere sake of using the 'genocide' label. As mentioned in Chapter 2, the Commissioners qualified the process of forced removal of Aboriginal children as 'cultural genocide' from the very first page of their report. Nevertheless, in the volume dedicated to the 'legacy' of the residential school system, they discussed the nature of group destruction in the definition of genocide. While acknowledging that 'cultural genocide' was deliberately rejected from the scope of the Genocide Convention, they considered that the wording of subparagraph (d) and (e) did not support the interpretation of 'group destruction' as being physical only:

> The forcible sterilization of women and girls for the purpose of preventing their group from repopulating itself would be an act of genocide, even though the individual female victim would be allowed to live. The forcible removal of children from their racial community in order to be indoctrinated into another racial community and thereby destroy their original group would likewise be an act of genocide, even though the children themselves continued to live as members of the new group.[137]

[132] Ibid., p. 112: 'I realised later how much I'd missed of my culture and how much I'd been devastated. Up until this point of time I can't communicate with my family, can't hold a conversation (. . .).'

[133] Ibid., p. 133.

[134] Ibid., p. 236. Reference omitted.

[135] Ibid., p. 24: Government officials theorized that by forcibly removing indigenous children from their families and sending them away from their communities to work for non-indigenous people, this mixed descent population would, over time, 'merge' with the non-indigenous population.

[136] Mundorff (n 80) pp. 111–12.

[137] Truth and Reconciliation Commission (TRC) of Canada, 'Canada's Residential Schools: The Legacy', in *The Final Report of the Truth and Reconciliation Commission of Canada*, vol. 5 (2015) pp. 125–6.

It should be noted that the Canadian Truth and Reconciliation Commission did not further consider the 'cultural' *versus* 'biological' debate in relation to Article II(e). In any event, the Commission took care to note that qualifying the acts as genocide would go outside the scope of its mandate. Its reflections on the topic would even tend towards the non-applicability of the Genocide Convention to these acts, at least when it came to those perpetrated in the nineteenth century.[138] Its reasoning on the nature of the *mens rea* is only aimed at advocating the recognition of these acts as a *legal wrong*, through pointing at the following paradox: while the acts *could* be deemed to fall under the Genocide Convention, Canada and its justice system do not even recognize them as constituting a legal wrong, in the civil law sense.

Both the Australian and Canadian reports have tended to overlook the interpretive debate around the nature of the intent that is inferred by Article II(e), which may indicate the practical irrelevance of the debate. If one really wanted to settle the issue, one could actually argue that the intent was dual. Firstly, the policies aimed at culturally destroying the group through the prevention of intergenerational transmission of its culture contributed to the creation of impermeable barriers between generations. Secondly, at least in the Australian case, the authorities also sought the group's biological destruction, as reflected in their openly expressed intention to genetically whiten the group.[139]

Still, the emphasis on the cultural dimension probably reflects better the facts since the authors of these transfers were animated by a clear intention to 'save' those children from a sub-culture.[140] These arguably 'good motives' may give rise to some confusion in relation to their distinction from the 'intent to destroy a group' that is required by the definition of genocide. In the Australian *Kruger* case, the judges thus used this argument to dismiss the claim that such an intent was pursued by the Aboriginals Ordinance, with one of them stating that: 'it is to my mind not possible to conceive of any acceptable definition of genocide which would embrace the actions authorized by the 1918 Ordinance, given that they were required to be performed in the best interests of the Aboriginals concerned or of the Aboriginal population'.[141] However, 'good motives' may not preclude an intent to destroy the group. As Damien Short has noted, '[a]lthough the resulting physical, cultural and mental harm may be the opposite of the alleged motivation and hence not prima facie intentional as such, in traditional British legal parlance "foresight and recklessness" as to the consequences of action are "evidence from which intent may be inferred." '[142]

The discussion of the biological and cultural dimension of group destruction by virtue of the forcible transfer of children from one group to another tends to

[138] Ibid., p.126. [139] Australian Human Rights Commission (n 70) p. 94.

[140] Sonja Starr and Lea Brilmayer, 'Family Separation as a Violation of International Law' (2003) 21 *Berkeley J. Int'l L.* 213, p. 237; Robert van Krieken, 'Rethinking Cultural Genocide: Aboriginal Child Removal and Settler-Colonial State Formation' (2004) 75 *Oceania* 125, p. 129.

[141] *Kruger v. Commonwealth* (1997) 190 CLR 1 (31 July 1997) High Court of Australia, p. 37 (Dawson).

[142] Damien Short, 'Australia: A Continuing Genocide?' (2010) 12 *J.G.R.* 45, p. 62 (footnotes omitted).

reflect a contrast between the victims' perceptions of their harm, which are mainly cultural, on the one hand, and the perpetrators' racist intent, grounded on biological considerations, on the other. It is paradoxical to consider that in order to fit within the current definition of genocide, the victims' perceptions of cultural destruction need to be discarded in favour of the perpetrators' racist motives of biological destruction. Outside of the criminal legal framework, it means that the claim should be distorted so as to fit the legal understanding of genocide. Besides, the issue of the intent is twofold in the case of forcibly transferred children: not only is the physical-biological dimension of the intended destruction to be proven but so also must the *dolus specialis* of the perpetrators, the policy-makers in this case. Both of these criteria have constituted insurmountable obstacles for aboriginal people in their endeavours to have their experience recognized as genocide before the domestic courts.[143] From a criminal perspective, this process is a difficult one to qualify since a substantial part of the facts happened not only before the conclusion of the Genocide Convention, but also before its ratification and implementation by Australia.[144] Moreover, criminal law, whether international or national, calls for the individualization of responsibilities and the identification of individual intents to perpetrate genocide. This would imply the identification of individual perpetrators, most of whom have died a long time ago. Attempts were made to challenge the legality of the Aboriginal Ordinance, which authorized such a forced transfer.

The Australian and Canadian cases underline well two intertwined issues: firstly, the difficulty in differentiating the *actus reus* and the *mens rea* in terms of 'nature' and secondly, the difficulty in labelling the 'forcible transfer of children' in biological or cultural terms. The arguments in favour of one interpretation or the other ultimately lose some of their persuasive power since they tend to reflect strategies more than efforts to accurately describe the process.

The context of Article II therefore illustrates that both positions can be supported by different interpretations of the *actus reus*, although its context more naturally tends towards interpreting the meaning of 'destroy' in socio-cultural terms. As for the more general context, beyond Article II, the preamble of the Genocide Convention also refers to the UNGA Resolution 96(1), the precursor of the Genocide Convention. As mentioned above, the preamble of this resolution both underscored the physical dimension of genocide, by drawing an ambiguous analogy with homicide,[145] and the socio-cultural understanding of the group destruction by underlying the 'great losses to humanity in the form of cultural and other contributions represented by these human groups'.[146]

[143] See e.g. *Indian Residential Schools, Re* [2000] A.J. No. 638 (Alta. Q.B.) (31 May 2000) Alberta Court of Queen's Bench; *Raubach et al. v. The Attorney General of Canada et al.*, [2005] 1 WWR 334 (6 July 2004) Manitoba Court of Queen's Bench before the Canadian courts, the judgments of which did not enter into the intent versus motives debate.

[144] *Kruger* (n 141).

[145] On the ambiguity of the analogy, see Martin Shaw, *What Is Genocide?* (Cambridge: Polity Press, 2007) p. 106.

[146] UNGA Res. 96(1) (n 5).

3.2.1.2 *The objects and purposes of the Genocide Convention*

The object and purpose of the Convention have been clearly identified by the ICJ in its 1951 advisory opinion on *Reservations to the Convention on the Prevention and Punishment of the Crime of Genocide*:

> The Convention was manifestly adopted for a purely humanitarian and civilizing purpose. It is indeed difficult to imagine a convention that might have this dual character to a greater degree, since its object on the one hand is to safeguard the very existence of certain human groups and on the other to confirm and endorse the most elementary principles of morality.[147]

Here, the key phrase is clearly 'to safeguard the very existence of certain human groups'. The ICJ made this statement predominantly on the basis of the UNGA Resolution 96(1).[148] The inclusion of 'very', to modify 'existence' would thus tend to imply a broad understanding of what it means for a group to exist.

This idea is illustrated by the German approach in the *Jorgić* case. In the first trial, in front of the Higher State Court of Düsseldorf, the social emphasis on the group destruction had been acknowledged, without any discussion on the potential debate that could arise from this assertion.[149] In the next two instances, the Federal Supreme Court and Federal Constitutional Court both developed the rationale by emphasizing the protected legal interest, that is that of the victim groups. The Constitutional Court thus stated that:

> the crime of genocide protects a legal interest that lies beyond the individual, namely the social existence of a group, finds it basis in the wording of the provision which requires that the intent to destroy be directed against the 'group as such'. The intent to destroy required by §220a of the German Criminal Code, *considering the natural meaning of the words*, has a broader meaning than physical-biological annihilation.[150]

Here, the German court implicitly implemented the VCLT, using, as a point of departure for its analysis, the ordinary meaning of the terms read in light of the object of the Genocide Convention.[151] This approach corresponds to some efforts to disentangle genocide from its international criminal law category and thus to shift the analysis from the sole focus on the perpetrators. Accordingly, it tries to reintegrate the victims, the group, into the framework.[152]

This argument can nonetheless be considered as biased itself, since it relies on only one object of the Genocide Convention, namely, the safeguarding of the very existence of human groups. Other objects and purposes can be identified: 'to confirm and endorse the most elementary principles of morality' in the ICJ words and punishment and prevention in the words of Article I of the Genocide Convention.

[147] *Reservations to the Genocide Convention* (n 5) p. 12 (emphasis added).
[148] Ibid.
[149] *Jorgić* (Trial) (n 17).
[150] *Nikola Jorgić* (Constitutional Appeals) (n 17) pp. 159–60 (emphasis added).
[151] The VCLT is explicitly mentioned in another part of the decision, about the subsequent practice: *Nikola Jorgić* (Constitutional Appeals) (n 17) p. 162.
[152] Goldsmith (n 61) p. 248.

These ideas are not easy to reconcile. The preventive dimension of the Genocide Convention would certainly help to reorientate the understanding of the crime towards a more socio-cultural understanding, so as to underline the process of genocide and its cultural dimension, as acts of cultural destruction may happen at rather early stages. From this perspective, physical destruction results from a process of escalation, involving a wide range of other steps.[153] Genocide being a complex and multifaceted process, it will often involve other acts that de facto play a role in the process of genocide and cannot as such be ignored by law.[154]

At the level of international criminal law, the notion of physical destruction bears the problem of the need to distinguish the crime of genocide from other crimes against humanity, especially the crime of extermination. Crimes against humanity are characterized by the existence of a widespread or systematic attack against a civilian population; genocide, by contrast, requires the intent to destroy the group as such, but not necessarily evidence of a widespread or systematic attack to do so.[155] Here, again, a purely 'physical' definition of genocide is problematic. By virtue of this definition, genocide is only recognized when acts of physical destruction are perpetrated, which generally involves the targeting of a 'substantial part of the group'.[156] From this perspective, the crime of genocide increasingly incorporates the 'widespread and systematic' element that is inherent to crimes against humanity while attenuating the group dimension, which is nevertheless pivotal to its conceptualization. As Cécile Tournaye notes, a broader interpretation of the *mens rea* would 'permit the distinction of genocide from the crime of extermination, which would be concerned with a massive physical destruction, the purpose of which is not necessarily the destruction of a human group, as such'. The focus would then shift to the group as such, and the fact that the acts target primarily the group, through but beyond its individual members.[157] This would also be reflected in the structure of Article II, where the intent concerns the group through acts perpetrated against its individual members.

However, such a teleological interpretation may turn out to be problematic in an international criminal law framework since the purpose of international criminal tribunals is mainly to punish perpetrators for international crimes, not directly

[153] Nazila Ghanea, 'Repressing Minorities and Getting Away With It: A Consideration of Economic, Social and Cultural Rights' in Nazila Ghanea and Alexandra Xanthaki (eds.), *Minorities, People and Self-Determination: Essays in Honour of Patrick Thornberry* (Leiden; Boston: Martinus Nijhoff Publishers, 2005) p. 199.

[154] Triffterer (n 62) p. 401.

[155] Although the ICC Elements of Crimes have added an element to each subparagraph of the definition of genocide, which tends to converge with the 'systematic' requirement of crimes against humanity: 'The conduct took place in the context of a manifest pattern of similar conduct directed against that group or was conduct that could itself effect such destruction.' See e.g. ICC Elements of Crimes (n 71) art. 6(a) para. 4.

[156] ILC 1996 Draft Code of Crimes (n 2) art. 17, para. 8; *Jelisić Case* (Trial) (n 53) para. 82; *Application of the Genocide Convention (Bosnia and Herzegovina v. Serbia and Montenegro)* (Judgment) (n 11) para. 198; on the different meanings of 'in part', see Schabas, *Genocide in International Law* (n 46) pp. 277–86.

[157] Cécile Tournaye, 'Genocidal Intent before the ICTY' (2003) 52 *Int'l & Comp. L.Q.* 447, pp. 456–7.

to protect their victims or 'safeguard the very existence of human groups'. The teleological method thus bears the risk of contravening the *nullum crimen sine lege* principle.[158] Accordingly, 'punishment' of individual perpetrators remains a crucial object of the framework established by the Genocide Convention, and certainly the most developed one. Notwithstanding, the interpretation of the word 'destroy' according to the methodology set out in the VCLT does not stand in favour of a physical-biological understanding of the special intent required by the definition of genocide. In the absence of any explicit reference to the nature of the destruction implied by genocide, a contextual reading of the definition of genocide clearly tends towards a broader understanding of this term, which only then reflects the added-value of criminalizing acts perpetrated against a 'group as such' in contrast to the crime against humanity of extermination, for instance.[159] Indeed, in respect of the sources quoted by the Trial Chamber in the *Krstić* judgment in the reaching of its conclusion, all of them tended towards such a conception, from Lemkin[160] to the UNGA Resolution 47/121, which labelled ethnic cleansing in the Former Yugoslavia as genocide[161] and the *Jorgić* case,[162] through the *RuSHA* case, tried by the US Military Tribunal in Nuremberg.[163] Only one source quoted tipped the scale in favour of a more restrictive understanding of the *mens rea*, the *travaux préparatoires* of the Genocide Convention.

3.2.2 The meaning of 'group destruction' in light of the drafters' intent

In the *Krstić* trial judgment, the reference to the *travaux préparatoires* of the Genocide Convention was made as follows:

> Although the Convention does not specifically speak to the point, the preparatory work points out that the 'cultural' destruction of a group was expressly rejected after having been seriously contemplated. The notion of cultural genocide was considered too vague and too removed from the physical or biological destruction that motivated the Convention.[164]

This simply constituted a reassertion of the ILC's opinion on the matter, reflected in its commentary on the 1996 Draft Code. The Chamber used this reasoning, and weighed all existing sources,[165] to reach the conclusion that 'despite recent

[158] Dov Jacobs, 'Positivism and International Criminal Law: The Principle of Legality as a Rule of Conflict of Theories' in Jean d'Aspremont and Jörg Kammerhofer (eds.), *International Legal Positivism in a Post-Modern World* (Cambridge: Cambridge University Press, 2014) p. 468.

[159] Tournaye (n 157) p. 456.

[160] *Krstić Case* (Trial) (n 24) para. 575.

[161] Ibid., para. 578, reference to UNGA Res. 47/121 (18 December 1992) 'The Situation in Bosnia and Herzegovina'.

[162] Ibid., para. 579, reference to *Nikola Jorgić* (Constitutional Appeals) (n 17).

[163] Ibid., para. 575; reference to *Ulrich Greifelt et al.* (n 110): the Prosecutor's indictment mentioned 'a systematic program of genocide, aimed at the destruction of foreign nations and ethnic groups, in part by murderous extermination, and in part by elimination and suppression of national characteristics'.

[164] *Krstić Case* (Trial) (n 24) para. 576 (footnotes omitted).

[165] Ibid., paras. 571–9. The Trial Chamber referred to, amongst others: UNGA Res. 96(1) (n 5); ECOSOC 'Draft Convention on the Crime of Genocide' E/447 (n 108); UNGA Res. 47/121 (n 161); ILC 1996 Draft Code of Crimes (n 2); *Nikola Jorgić* (Constitutional Appeals) (n 17) pp.152–67.

developments, customary international law limits the definition of genocide to those acts seeking the physical or biological destruction of all or part of the group'.[166] In spite of its earlier statement that it would interpret the definition of genocide according to the VCLT rules,[167] the Trial Chamber started by quoting the *travaux préparatoires* of the Convention,[168] without any preliminary attempt to interpret the words themselves. While it could be deduced that the Chamber implicitly acknowledged the ambiguity of the word 'destroy', thus justifying the recourse to the *travaux préparatoires*, the weight granted to these documents raises a number of questions, in relation to both the reference to the draft provision on cultural genocide and the content of the discussions in relation to the meaning of the word 'destroy'.

First and foremost, the alignment of the issue of the nature of group destruction with the discussions related to the concept of 'cultural genocide' is questionable. Indeed, cultural genocide was discussed at the level of the *actus reus*, whereas in *Krstić*, the legal issue concerned the meaning of the *mens rea*, in order to determine the legal significance of the forcible transfer of the population of Srebrenica, which was carried out in conjunction with the murder of military-aged men. If one looks back to the facts of the case, it is only the destruction of the main mosque of Srebrenica that could be labelled 'cultural genocide' from the perspective of the draft Genocide Convention. Nowhere in the indictment can any mention of destruction of cultural heritage or attack on the language of the group be found, in contrast to the content of the draft provision on 'cultural genocide'.[169] The issue arose on several occasions during the hearings. At the early stage of the trial, films and photos describing Srebrenica were screened. By virtue of these documents, it was possible to identify the various stages of the destruction of the main Mosque of Srebrenica, from the dynamiting of its dome and minaret[170] to its complete destruction and transformation into a parking lot,[171] with the erection of an Orthodox Church in the background.[172] As the investigation team leader at the ICTY testified, apart from knowing that at the time of the massacre, there were people in Srebrenica, '[f]or the rest, in fact, the only elements we have are the destructions of the mosques'.[173] Two witnesses were also interrogated in order to determine individual responsibilities for the destruction of the mosques but they were unable to answer.[174] In the framework of the Prosecution's closing statement, Mark Harmon, from the Office of the Prosecutor (OTP), invited the court to consider:

166 *Krstić Case* (Trial) (n 24) para. 580.
167 Ibid., para. 541.
168 Ibid., para. 571.
169 ECOSOC 'Draft Convention on the Crime of Genocide' E/447 (n 108); ECOSOC 'Ad Hoc Committee on Genocide: Summary Record of the Fourteenth Meeting' UN Doc. E/AC.25/SR.14 (27 April 1948), in Abtahi and Webb (n 69) p. 892.
170 *Krstić Case* (Transcript) ICTY-98-33 (13 March 2000) p. 521, at. 18–19, p. 542 at 1–5.
171 Ibid., at 6–7, p. 543, at 5–9.
172 Ibid., p. 542, at 8–22.
173 Ibid., pp. 544–5, at 12–13.
174 See *Krstić Case* (Transcript) ICTY-98-33 (22 May 2000), Testimony of Mr. Erdemovic, p. 3173, at 24–5, p. 3174, at 1–2; *Krstić Case* (Transcript) ICTY-98-33 (24 November 2000), Testimony Witness DE, p. 7740, at 7–25.

even though the genocide convention does not prohibit cultural genocide, (. . .) what happened to the religious monuments in the Srebrenica enclave after the capture by General Krstić's soldiers. All of the mosques within the town of Srebrenica were dynamited; the main mosque in Srebrenica was completely destroyed and it's now a parking lot.[175]

During the discussion, Judge Rodrigues explicitly asked Harmon to provide clarification on what exactly he meant by bringing cultural destruction within the interpretation of genocide. In his answer, the latter reiterated his previous statement:

The genocide convention doesn't recognise cultural destruction as being genocide, the cultural monuments and the like being genocide. My submission to Your Honours was not that the destruction of the mosques equalled *[sic.]* genocide, but that it is a factor in the matrix of all the other factors that you could consider when assessing whether or not there was genocidal intent. We know that immediately on the heels of the deportations and immediately during or after the mass executions, the traces of the Muslim community were being erased. So that is my only submission on that point.[176]

These were the only few mentions of mosques during the two years of the trial of Krstić and they were never used for the purpose of orientating the judges towards the recognition of cultural genocide. Consequently, in its judgment, the Trial Chamber made scarce use of the destruction of the Srebrenica Mosque to demonstrate Krstić's intent to destroy the Bosnian Muslim group of Srebrenica.[177]

The weight given to the *travaux préparatoires* and the 1940s debate on cultural genocide is therefore surprising because it does not cover much of the acts that the Tribunal was reviewing. In this regard, it would have perhaps been more relevant to refer to the debate on the Syrian amendment to include in the list of genocidal acts the act of 'imposing measures intended to oblige members of a group to abandon their homes in order to escape the threat of subsequent ill-treatment',[178] a reference which the ICJ subsequently made.[179] While the latter simply noted the rejection of the amendment, it is worth noting that the discussions on the Syrian proposal were again inspired by individual self-interests, such as the concern for the Western States not to self-incriminate, as they were in the meantime proceeding with the evacuation of the German population out of the Eastern European territories in particularly ruthless conditions.[180] There therefore arises an issue of qualification of the facts themselves, especially when analysed in relation to the legal issues addressed during the negotiations of the Genocide Convention. This was implicitly noted by the Trial Chamber which, in its concluding paragraph, took care to extend its reasoning to the 'cultural and *sociological* characteristics of a human group'.[181]

[175] *Krstić Case* (Transcript) ICTY-98-33 (27 June 2001) p. 9994, at 9–14.

[176] Ibid., p. 10028, at 23; p. 10029, at 1–6.

[177] *Krstić Case* (Trial) (n 24) para. 595.

[178] UNGA Sixth Committee (3rd Session) 'Eighty-First Meeting' (22 October 1948) UN Doc. A/C.6/SR.81, in Abtahi and Webb (n 69) p. 1479.

[179] *Application of the Genocide Convention (Bosnia and Herzegovina v. Serbia and Montenegro)* (Judgment) (n 11) para. 190.

[180] Daniele Conversi, 'Cultural Homogenization, Ethnic Cleansing and Genocide' in Robert A. Denemark (ed.), *The International Studies Encyclopedia*, vol. 1 (Oxford; Boston, MA: Wiley-Blackwell/ISA, 2010) p. 728.

[181] *Krstić Case* (Trial) (n 24) para. 580 (emphasis added).

Thus, it is possible to conclude that the Tribunal crafted and deployed an incorrect analogy regarding the meaning of the rejection of the cultural genocide provision. In the same way as there was no factual reason for the ICTY to adopt such a perspective, there is no reason to see in the *Jorgić* finding, a 'reintroduction of cultural genocide through the frontdoor'.[182] Neither the German courts, nor the ECtHR actually qualified the acts as 'cultural genocide'. Judge Shahabuddeen also explicitly took distance from such a concept, adding that 'the foregoing is not an argument for the recognition of cultural genocide. It is established that the mere destruction of the culture of a group is not genocide: none of the methods listed in Article 4(2) of the Statute need be employed'.[183]

Though the analogy might turn out to be useful, there would nevertheless continue to be some limits to the actual use of the 1940s discussions on 'cultural genocide'. It remains to be seen whether the *travaux préparatoires* of the Genocide Convention would allow for the confirmation of any of the two potential meanings of the intent to destroy the group. As a matter of principle '[n]ot only should the *travaux* be used judiciously, their significance should not be distorted'.[184] On both issues, it is very doubtful that the *travaux préparatoires* of the Genocide Convention correctly accomplishes these goals in the precise case of the *mens rea* of genocide. Firstly, as it has been illustrated in Chapter 1, the rejection of 'cultural genocide' has been grounded on a number of arguments, some of which were particularly questionable, such as the idea that it would 'hamper a reasonable policy of assimilation'.[185] This tends to strengthen the political dimension of the *travaux préparatoires* and the need to take adequate distance when referring to them. It is noteworthy that the ICJ has already considered the possibility of taking distance from the *travaux préparatoires* in respect of conventions adopted a substantial number of years in the past, considering that it 'must take into consideration the changes which have occurred in the supervening half-century, and its interpretation cannot remain unaffected by the subsequent development of law'.[186] Such a statement confirms the idea that international treaties and conventions can and should, if necessary, receive an evolutionary interpretation.[187] Moreover, Pierre-Marie Dupuy argues that the ambiguity of international instruments is often due to confused negotiations, which renders very unlikely the clarification of the notion by virtue of reference to the *travaux préparatoires*.[188]

[182] Antonio Cassese et al. (eds.), *International Criminal Law: Cases and Commentary* (Oxford: Oxford University Press, 2011) p. 228.

[183] *Krstić Case* (Appeals) (n 25) Judge Shahabuddeen's dissenting opinion, para. 53.

[184] Schabas, 'Judicial Activism and the Crime of Genocide' (n 104) p. 79.

[185] Egyptian Delegate's Statement in UN Doc. A/C.6/SR.63, General Assembly Sixth Committee, 63rd Meeting, Thursday 30 September 1948, in Abtahi and Webb (n 69) p. 1293.

[186] *Legal Consequences for States of the Continued Presence of South Africa in Namibia (South West Africa) notwithstanding Security Council Resolution 276 (1970)* (Advisory Opinion) [1971] ICJ Rep. 16, para. 53.

[187] Georg Nolte, *Introductory Report for the Study Group on Treaties over Time: Jurisprudence of the International Court of Justice and Arbitral Tribunals of Ad Hoc Jurisdiction Relating to Subsequent Agreements and Subsequent Practice*, 2010, reproduced in Georg Nolte (ed.), *Treaties and Subsequent Practice* (Oxford: Oxford University Press, 2013) pp. 169–209.

[188] Pierre-Marie Dupuy and Yann Kerbrat, *Droit International Public* (11ème ed., Paris: Dalloz, 2012) p. 361, para. 315.

Nevertheless, the historical value of these works is undeniable and the interpretation rendered might benefit, to the extent that it can be determined, for instance, the interests that were at stake at the time of the negotiation or why one particular wording has been retained instead of another. Yet, with regard to the issue of the nature of the *mens rea* of genocide, Dupuy's statement above is verified; the reader of the preparatory works will be disappointed to see that this issue was never discussed. Schabas notes that '[w]hile these questions were not specifically debated during the drafting of Article II, the *spirit* of the discussions resists extending the concept of destruction beyond physical and biological acts'.[189] However, the relevant rule of interpretation on this subject matter, Article 32 VCLT, does not refer to the 'spirit of the discussion' but to the content of the discussion. In the same way as it was questionable to analogize the issue of the *mens rea* with the debate on 'cultural genocide', it was also questionable to simply assume that the drafters' intention was to connect the nature of the *mens rea* to that of the *actus reus*. During the negotiations of the Genocide Convention, the crime was actually discussed as a whole, from a rather macro-perspective, without concretely addressing its twofold structure. At no stage was the meaning of the term 'destroy' discussed in-depth. Only France expressed its concern about the ambiguity as it considered that it would introduce a confusion between the 'final result and the means employed to obtain the result', that is between the *actus reus* and *mens rea* of genocide. It was concerned that 'destruction' in French was not the criminal act but the means to achieve it.[190] These doubts were not followed by any debate, nor were they reiterated at a further stage during the negotiations.

The rejection of Draft Article III on 'cultural genocide' undoubtedly contributed to shape the final definition of genocide. To some extent, Article II might therefore be considered as reflecting a physical conception of genocide. The first draft of the Convention itself contemplated that 'acts of violence by individuals of communities not aimed at the destruction of a group of human beings' were 'outside the notion of genocide so long as the intention physically to destroy a group of human beings is absent'.[191] Despite its repeated use, the term 'physical destruction' was not deployed with a consistent meaning. For some delegations, it implied equating genocide with 'extermination', not necessarily because it was deemed to be its 'proper' meaning,[192] but rather for the purpose of gathering a consensus.[193] For other delegations, 'physical destruction' was defined more holistically, to include

[189] Schabas, *Genocide in International Law* (n 46) p. 271.

[190] ECOSOC 'Ad Hoc Committee on Genocide: Summary Record of the Eleventh Meeting' UN Doc. E/AC.25/SR.11 (16 April 1948), in Abtahi and Webb (n 69) pp. 850, 852 (French Delegate's Statement).

[191] ECOSOC 'Draft Convention on the Crime of Genocide' E/447 (n 108) p. 232.

[192] Mainly France and the U.S. advocated for a strict physical understanding, equating to genocide. Cf. French Delegate's Statement in 'Summary Record of the Tenth Meeting' UN Doc. E/AC.25/SR.11 (16 April 1948), in Abtahi and Webb (n 69) p. 843.

[193] See e.g. UNGA Sixth Committee (3rd Session) 'Seventy-First Meeting' A/C.6/SR.71 (11 October 1948), in Abtahi and Webb (n 69) p. 1365 (Statement of the Dominican Delegate).

the 'destruction of the characteristics of the group', alongside the widely accepted 'extermination of its members'.[194]

Consequently, if the final definition is deemed to be of any use here, it is in its conclusion that genocide goes beyond 'extermination'. Instead of basing any legal reasoning on the latent confusion between the *mens rea* and the *actus reus* of genocide, which underpinned the 1940s negotiations, this confusion should rather be understood and engaged as a reason to moderate the inspiration one derives from the *travaux préparatoires.* Coming back to the language of the VCLT principles of interpretation, it can be concluded that the *travaux préparatoires* neither 'confirm' the physical-biological understanding of the *mens rea,* nor its 'socio-cultural' interpretation. Their usefulness is therefore doubtful in respect of the nature of the *mens rea.*[195]

3.2.3 The meaning of 'group destruction' in light of the context of interpretation

The *nullum crimen sine lege* principle implies opting for a restrictive interpretation that would benefit the accused, a principle that can itself be interpreted more or less restrictively. If its implementation gives rise to no doubt in the context of criminal trials, the opening of the genocide legal framework to state responsibility raises the question of the relevance of the transposition of the restrictive interpretation of the *mens rea* of genocide, which has been derived in a criminal context, to the context of state responsibility.

3.2.3.1 The restrictive interpretation induced by the nullum crimen sine lege *principle*

The *nullum crimen sine lege* principle is grounded in international human rights instruments, as it aims at protecting the rights of the accused. The International Covenant on Civil and Political Rights (ICCPR) defines the principle as follows: 'criminal legislation must abide by the principle of specificity, whereby rules criminalizing human conduct must be as specific and clear as possible, so as to guide the behaviour of citizens'.[196] This principle is part of the wider principle of legality, which is critical to criminal law and implies a restrictive interpretation of the criminal provision whenever it is not sufficiently defined in specific terms; indeed, this can be said to be the case with regard to the international legal definition of genocide, and especially the meaning of 'intent to destroy a group as such'.

194 UNGA Sixth Committee (3rd Session) 'Sixty-Sixth Meeting' UN Doc. A/C.6/SR.66 (4 October 1948), in Abtahi and Webb (n 69) p. 1325 (Statement of the Lebanese Delegate).

195 Skutnabb-Kangas and Dunbar (n 70) p. 84.

196 International Covenant on Civil and Political Rights (adopted 16 December 1966, entered into force 23 March 1976) 999 UNTS 171 (ICCPR) art. 15(1); Cassese, *International Criminal Law* (n 182) p. 32.

Before addressing the *nullum crimen sine lege* obstacle to the broad interpretation, it is worth discussing one argument which is often advanced to reject such a possible interpretation: namely, the risk of unduly extending the scope of the crime of genocide, which, because it is the most serious crime, the 'crime of crimes', should necessarily be interpreted restrictively.[197] This idea does not rely on any clear principle of international law. As with any crime, genocide needs to be interpreted restrictively and as with any international crime, the threshold of evidence is set high so that its recognition is indeed limited to serious cases. As stated by the ICTY Appeals chamber in the *Krstić* case: '[w]here these requirements are satisfied, however, the law must not shy away from referring to the crime committed by its proper name'.[198] The 'crime of crimes' rhetoric is mainly grounded on the specific *mens rea* of the crime of genocide, which distinguishes genocide from crimes against humanity.[199] However, if the debate is refocused on the group destruction, the selective dimension of the list of groups in the definition of genocide, which excludes political and social groups, attenuates the very idea of crime of crimes. As Payam Akhavan advances in relation to the distinction between the genocidal act of murder and the crime against humanity of persecution, '[i]t is unclear why mass murder against such groups "as such" is lesser in gravity than similar acts against members of "national, ethnic, racial, or religious" groups'.[200]

In the 'Report of the International Commission of Inquiry on Darfur to the United Nations Secretary-General', in which it defended the idea that all international crimes are equally serious, it was provided that:

> It is indisputable that genocide bears a special stigma, for it is aimed at the *physical obliteration* of human groups. However, one should not be blind to the fact that some categories of crimes against humanity may be similarly heinous and carry a similarly grave stigma (. . .).[201]

Thus, it is on the actual elements of genocide that reflection is necessary rather than on its abstract and absolute seriousness.

The VCLT and its principles have been drafted for inter-state relationship and are part of general international law. In contrast, the principles implied by the punishment purpose of the genocide legal framework are part of international criminal

[197] Schabas, *Genocide in International Law* (n 46) pp. 269–70; Laurence Burgorgue-Larsen, 'Le Génocide Oublié du Timor Oriental' in Katia Boustany and Daniel Dormoy (eds.), *Génocide(s)* (Bruxelles: Bruylant; Editions de l'Université de Bruxelles, 1999) p. 247: according to Burgorgue-Larsen, '*Appliquer la notion de génocide à chaque fois "que l'on veut dénoncer une pratique susceptible de porter atteinte à l'intégrité d'un groupe", entrainerait automatiquement un* mésusage *du concept, qui participerait activement à son* inflation, *et partant à sa* banalisation'.

[198] *Krstić Case* (Appeals) (n 25) para. 37.

[199] Goldsmith (n 61) p. 250; Richard May and Marieke Wierda, 'Is There a Hierarchy of Crimes in International Law?' in Lal Chand Vohrar *et al.* (eds.), *Man's Inhumanity to Man—Essays in International Law in Honour of Antonio Cassese* (The Hague; London; New York: Kluwer Law International, 2003) p. 514; Schabas, *Genocide in International Law* (n 46) p. 653.

[200] Payam Akhavan, *Reducing Genocide to Law: Definition, Meaning, and the Ultimate Crime* (Cambridge; New York: Cambridge University Press, 2012) p. 85.

[201] International Commission of Inquiry on Darfur, 'Report of the International Commission of Inquiry on Darfur to the United Nations Secretary-General, Pursuant to Security Council Resolution 1564 of 18 September 2004' (25 January 2005) para. 506 (emphasis added).

law, a specific branch of international law. Following the *lex specialis derogat generali* principle, principles of international criminal law are supposed to prevail over the VCLT principles in case of conflict. The question is therefore the following: can a broad interpretation of a criminal provision—which has been made possible by the careful implementation of some principles of customary international law—be neutralized by principles of international criminal law on the basis that it would entail the creation of a new element of the crime of genocide?

The ICTY replied affirmatively to this question, by virtue of reformulating the *mens rea* in 'cultural genocide' terms, considering that it should 'interpret the Convention with due regard to [the *nullum crimen sine lege*] principle'.[202] In the *Jorgić* case, the ECtHR found that the systematic interpretation undertaken by the German courts[203] was 'not (. . .) unreasonable'.[204]

To provide an updated answer to the above question, three evolutions should be taken into consideration: firstly, the subsequent ECtHR case law on the matter, secondly, the authority of the *Krstić* interpretation and thirdly, the changes brought about by the ICC Rome Statute. As for the former issue, three more recent cases illustrate well the implementation of such principle for the purpose of the present study, as they both involved international crimes, as in the *Jorgić* case. The first case, *Kononov v. Latvia*, concerned the conviction of a Russian national and former Red Partisan, for alleged war crimes, committed in 1944. The third section of the ECtHR considered that the Latvian conviction constituted a breach of Article 7(1) ECHR, mainly on the basis that the victims were combatants so that the offence of war crime was not constituted on the basis of customary international law, as applicable at the time of the events.[205] The Grand Chamber took a reverse approach, emphasizing the 'foreseeability' of the conviction, even in 1944.[206] In the *Korbely v. Hungary* case, the applicant was convicted by Hungarian courts for crimes against humanity, on the basis of common Article 3 of the 1949 Geneva Conventions, in relation to his participation in the 1956 repression of the popular upheaval during which he allegedly killed an opponent of the regime. For the purpose of determining whether the conviction for crimes against humanity was legal according to Article 7(1) ECHR, the ECtHR therefore reviewed the qualification of the alleged facts. It especially found that the context of crimes against humanity, that is a widespread and systematic attack, was not particularly obvious in the present case[207] and that the victim was not covered by the protected status of non-combatant according to common Article 3 of the Geneva Conventions,[208] so that the conviction for this specific international crime could not be considered as 'foreseeable' and therefore constituted a breach of Article 7(1).[209]

202 *Krstić Case* (Trial) (n 24) para. 580.

203 *Jorgić v. Germany* (n 10) paras. 92–105.

204 Ibid., para. 105.

205 *Kononov v. Latvia*, App. No. 36376/04 (ECtHR) 24 July 2008, paras. 131–7, 146.

206 *Kononov v. Latvia*, App. No. 36376/04 (ECtHR, Grand Chamber) 17 May 2010, paras. 234–44.

207 *Korbely v. Hungary*, App. No. 9174/02 (ECtHR, Grand Chamber) 19 September 2008, paras. 83–5.

208 Ibid., paras. 89–93.

209 Ibid., para. 95.

The third and most recent case, the *Vasiliauskas v. Lithuania* case, is particularly relevant as it also dealt with a conviction for the crime of genocide, based on a domestic implementation and interpretation of the international definition of genocide.[210] The case was brought in front of the ECtHR in 2009 and was settled by the Grand Chamber in 2015. The applicant had been convicted of genocide by Lithuanian domestic courts in 2004 and 2005 for his participation in the killing of two Lithuanian partisans in 1953. At the time, Lithuania was controlled by the USSR, which would violently repress any forms of resistance to its authority. After the collapse of the USSR, Lithuania ratified the Genocide Convention and enacted in 1992 the *Law on Responsibility for Genocide of Inhabitants of Lithuania*, the provisions of which were not covered by the principle of non-retroactivity. In 1999, the definition of genocide was codified in Article 99 of the Criminal Code and the list of victim groups was further expanded so as to include social and political groups. It was on the basis of this provision that Mr. Vasiliauskas was convicted of genocide, the Lithuanian courts considering that the two partisans were 'part of' the target group, the inhabitants of Lithuania, as members of a political group. Unlike the *Jorgić* case, the *Vasiliauskas* case did not relate to interpreting the meaning of 'group destruction' but rather of the words 'in part', thus touching upon the question of whether they should be interpreted in quantitative (substantial number of victims) or qualitative (the targeting of particularly prominent members, such as religious and political leaders, which may in turn threaten the group's survival) terms.[211] In front of the ECtHR, Mr. Vasiliauskas argued that his conviction violated Article 7(1) ECHR since the legal basis, the Lithuanian penal code, reflected a broader interpretation than the definition of genocide as prevailing at the time of the facts, which therefore resulted in a breach of the principle of non-retroactivity. In turn, the Lithuanian government argued that the characterization of 'political groups' here overlapped with the contours of the national group, which was ultimately targeted for destruction through the elimination of its political fringe.[212]

The Court found that in no way could customary international law be deemed to have criminalized genocide against 'political groups' in 1953.[213] Although it concurred with the Lithuanian argument that the 'resistance against the Soviet occupation was to be regarded as self-defence of the State of Lithuania',[214] it also found that in 1953, a 'qualitative interpretation' of the words 'in part' could not be foreseen, 'even with the assistance of a lawyer'. In spite of subsequent case law within various courts, especially the ICTY and the ICJ, the partial destruction of the national group should be interpreted as requiring a condition of 'substantiality', that is a quantitative threshold. In this regard, the ECtHR grounded its reasoning

[210] *Vasiliauskas v. Lithuania*, App. No. 35343/05 (ECtHR, Grand Chamber) 20 October 2015.

[211] This refers to the question of whether the words 'in part' should be interpreted in quantitative (substantial number of victims) or qualitative (the targeting of particularly prominent members, such as religious and political leaders, which may in turn threaten the group's survival). The ICTY case law does not cut through the two interpretations. See e.g. *Jelisić Case* (Trial) (n 53) paras. 80–2, *Krstić Case* (Trial) (n 24) para. 580.

[212] Ibid., paras. 139, 142, 148. [213] Ibid., paras. 175–8. [214] Ibid., para. 180.

in Article 31(1) VCLT and emphasized that since the meaning of the words 'in part' was ambiguous, the Lithuanian courts' characterization of the partisans as a 'national group' corresponded to an interpretation 'by analogy' and was again not foreseeable.[215] This final conclusion was the object of several dissenting opinions, in which a number of European judges considered that a qualitative interpretation of the words 'in part' could have reasonably been foreseen in 1953, especially if one takes into account the context of the crimes, that is 'the Soviet authorities' operations to eradicate the Lithuanian partisans as a significant part of the nation in 1944–53 *with the intent of destroying the fabric of the nation of Lithuania*'.[216] The judges thus referred to the *Jorgić* judgment to 'confirm the principle (. . .) that an interpretation of the scope of the offence which is consistent with the essence of that offence "must, as a rule, be considered as foreseeable" '.[217]

These European cases illustrate the difficult task of assessing an interpretation without interfering in the assessment of the facts themselves. Even though the *Vasiliauskas* case embraces a much more cautious approach to potentially broad interpretations of the definition of genocide, it could still be read as confirming the seriousness of the ECtHR test of foreseeability.[218] As such, it would still be possible to question the interpretative outcome of the *Krstić* judgment and the weight it gave to the *nullum crime sine lege* principle, while the ECtHR considered that the same interpretation would pass its test.

However, it is unclear whether the *Jorgić* interpretation would still be possible almost a decade later, in light of both the ECtHR's own case law related to the interpretation of international crimes and the authority since then acquired by the *Krstić* interpretation. In the *Jorgić* case, the ECtHR's own reasoning seemed to be mainly inspired by chronological concerns. The German courts' interpretation of the definition of genocide occurred before the ICTY and the ICJ were able to give their own interpretation. As a result, if we look strictly at the question that was submitted to the ECtHR, the applicant, Jorgić, could not have expected to be judged according to the narrower interpretation, as the latter was not yet prevailing. It should nevertheless be noted that the physical-biological understanding of group destruction had already been stated on two occasions by the ICL, in its 1991 and 1996 Draft Codes of Crimes against the Peace and Security of Mankind;[219] these Draft Codes, however, do not have any particular interpretive authority. Nevertheless, one cannot deny that the interpretation developed in *Krstić*, which is itself based on the

[215] Ibid., para. 183.

[216] Ibid. Joint dissenting opinion of Judges Villiger, Power-Forde, Pinto De Albuquerque and Kūris, paras. 26, 36 (emphasis added).

[217] Ibid. Joint dissenting opinion, para. 30.

[218] See also: *C.R. v. The United Kingdom*, App. No. 20190/92 (ECtHR) 22 November 1995, para. 34; *S.W. v. The United Kingdom*, App. No. 20166/92 (ECtHR) 22 November 1995, para. 36; ECHR *K.-H.W. v. Germany*, App. No. 37201/97 (ECtHR) 22 March 2001, para. 85; see also Mohammed Shahabuddeen, 'Does the Principle of Legality Stand in the Way of Progressive Development of Law?' (2004) 2 *J.I.C.J.* 1007.

[219] ILC 1991 Draft Code of Crimes (n 7) Commentary on art. 19, para. 4; ILC 1996 Draft Code of Crimes (n 2) Commentary on art. 17, para. 12

ILC's commentary on its 1996 Draft Code of Crimes against the Peace and Security of Mankind,[220] was constantly reaffirmed by the ICTY Appeals Chamber[221] and later endorsed by the ICJ in its 2007 judgment on the *Application of the Genocide Convention* case.[222] It has now been attributed considerable weight in international law and recognized as customary international law despite its flaws.[223] As Schabas has noted, even Judge Shahabuddeen has implicitly concurred with the *Krstić* interpretation, as he did not dissent in the *Blagojević* appeals judgment.[224] In particular, the ICTY Appeals Chamber overturned the conviction for genocide of the accused, which the Trial Chamber had grounded on an interpretation explicitly borrowed from Judge Shahabuddeen's dissenting opinion in the *Krstić* case.[225] As such, it may be considered as constituting 'subsequent practice' in the sense of Article 31(3)(b) VCLT, which shall be taken into account when interpreting the relevant piece of law.

Furthermore, Larissa van den Herik pointed out that the German rationale 'may well have been inspired by the lack of jurisdiction over crimes against humanity. (. . .) The implementation of the ICC Statute in the jurisdictions of state parties has undercut this development to some extent'.[226] Unlike the statutes of other international criminal tribunals, the ICC Rome Statute has introduced provisions on both the applicable law and methodologies of interpretation for the Court. Article 21, on the 'applicable law', introduces a hierarchy between the sources, which the Permanent Court 'shall' or 'might' apply. Within the first category of mandatory sources, a further hierarchy is introduced between: i) the ICC primary sources (Statute, Elements of Crimes, and Rules of Procedure and Evidence); ii) relevant international treaties and principles; iii) general principles of law based on a comparative assessment of domestic legal systems.[227] Article 22 codified the *nullum crimen sine lege* principle in a strict manner,[228] considering in particular that '[i]n case of ambiguity, the definition shall be interpreted in favour of the person being investigated, prosecuted or convicted'.[229]

The ICC has provided its own understanding of these two provisions in the *Katanga* judgment pursuant to Article 74 of the Statute. When it comes to the methods of interpretation, it considered that applicable law set out at Article 21 of

[220] ILC 1996 Draft Code of Crimes (n 2) Commentary on art. 17, para. 12.

[221] *Blagojević & Jokić Case* (Appeals) (n 33) para. 123; *Popović et al. Case* (Trial) (n 96) para. 854.

[222] *Application of the Genocide Convention (Bosnia and Herzegovina v. Serbia and Montenegro)* (Judgment) (n 11) para. 344.

[223] *Krstić Case* (Trial) (n 24) para. 580; *Krstić Case* (Appeals) (n 25) para. 25; William A. Schabas, *The International Criminal Court: A Commentary on the Rome Statute* (Oxford; New York: Oxford University Press, 2010) p. 410.

[224] Schabas, 'Judicial Activism and the Crime of Genocide' (n 104) p. 77; see *Blagojević & Jokić Case* (Appeals) (n 33) para. 123.

[225] *Blagojević & Jokić Case* (Trial) (n 30) para. 666.

[226] Larissa van den Herik, 'The Meaning of the Word "Destroy" and its Implications for the Wider Understanding of the Concept of Genocide' in Harmen G. van der Wilt (ed.), *The Genocide Convention: The Legacy of 60 Years* (Leiden; Boston: Martinus Nijhoff Publishers, 2012) pp. 57–8.

[227] ICC Rome Statute (n 76) art. 21(1).

[228] Cassese, *International Criminal Law* (n 182) p. 40.

[229] ICC Rome Statute (n 76) art. 22(2).

the Rome Statute should be interpreted according to Articles 31 and 32 VCLT,[230] which should prevail over precedents from other international criminal tribunals.[231] It further emphasized the importance of the principle of effectiveness of a provision: 'Thus, in interpreting a provision of the founding texts, the bench must dismiss any solution that could result in the violation or nullity of any of its other provisions.'[232] If this so far goes in the direction of the argument previously constructed in this chapter, the Chamber's interpretation of Article 22 left little hope for a socio-cultural understanding of the *mens rea* of genocide. It emphasized in particular the 'principle of strict construction' according to which '[t]he Chamber therefore cannot adopt a method of interpretation that might broaden the definition of the crimes'. Here, it is noteworthy that the German courts themselves qualified their interpretation as broader than a physical understanding of the *mens rea*.[233] This would already undermine the possibility of an evolutionary interpretation had the ICC itself not qualified the teleological interpretation as 'antiethical to the principle of legality, and more specifically, to the rule of strict construction and the principle of *in dubio pro reo*'.[234] Interestingly, this very interpretation is based on the general rule of interpretation, since the ICC based its reasoning on the object and purpose of the Rome Statute, which is 'to put an end to impunity for the perpetrators of the most serious crimes within the jurisdiction of the Court'. As such, this methodology primarily concerns the ICC, although it can also be read as guidelines that other criminal jurisdictions may use when interpreting their own domestic criminal provisions, while exercising the principle of complementarity.

3.2.3.2 The relevance of a restrictive interpretation in the context of state responsibility for genocide

The ICJ's stance *vis-à-vis* the nature of the obligations established in the Genocide Convention has clearly shifted throughout its case law. While the 1951 Advisory opinion and the 1996 judgment related to the preliminary objections in the *Application of the Genocide Convention* case and seemed to reflect a human rights approach to the Convention, the 2007 judgment has rather taken a criminal turn. In its 1996 decision regarding the preliminary objections raised by Yugoslavia, the Court took care to clearly distinguish the underlying principles of state responsibility from those of criminal responsibility. Firstly, it prepared the ground for the 2007 finding that the provisions of the Genocide Convention, especially Articles IX and IV did not exclude state responsibility.[235] Second, when addressing Yugoslavia's preliminary objection on the jurisdiction *ratione temporis* of the Court, it rejected the potential application of the principle of non-retroactivity

[230] *Prosecutor v. Germain Katanga* (Judgment Pursuant to Article 74 of the Statute) ICC-01/04-01/07 (7 March 2014) Trial Chamber II, paras. 43–5.

[231] Ibid., para. 47.

[232] Ibid., para. 46.

[233] *Nikola Jorgić* (Appeals) (n 17) pp. 159–60.

[234] *P. v. Katanga* (n 230) paras. 52, 54.

[235] *Application of the Convention on the Prevention and Punishment of the Crime of Genocide (Bosnia and Herzegovina v. Yugoslavia)* (Preliminary Objections) [1996] ICJ Rep. 595, para. 32.

to inter-State disputes. Yugoslavia argued that the Court could only exercise its jurisdiction in relation to the events perpetrated after the two Parties had accessed the Genocide Convention—that is for Bosnia, either on 6 March 1992, the day of its independence or on 29 December 1992, the date of its Notice of Succession;[236] on 27 April 1992 for Yugoslavia[237]—on the model of criminal law. The ICJ replied the following:

In this regard, the Court will confine itself to the observation that the Genocide Convention - and in particular Article IX - does not contain any clause the object or effect of which is to limit in such manner the scope of its jurisdiction *ratione temporis,* and nor did the Parties themselves make any reservation to that end, either to the Convention or on the occasion of the signature of the Dayton-Paris Agreement. The Court thus finds that it has jurisdiction in this case to give effect to the Genocide Convention with regard to the relevant facts which have occurred since the beginning of the conflict which took place in Bosnia and Herzegovina. This finding is, moreover, in accordance with the object and purpose of the Convention as defined by the Court in 1951 and referred to above (see paragraph 31). As a result, the Court considers that it must reject Yugoslavia's sixth and seventh preliminary objections.[238]

The reference to the VCLT unambiguously anchored state responsibility on principles of general international law and several parts of the judgment may be interpreted as reflecting a human rights approach to the Genocide Convention. Thus, while it is not limited to this discipline, the reliance on the 'object and purpose' has become a distinctive feature of the interpretation of international human rights instruments.[239] This idea is strengthened by the reference to the 1951 Advisory opinion, which identified one of the objects of the Genocide Convention as the 'safeguard[ing] the very existence of certain human groups'.[240] Throughout the 1996 judgment, the ICJ repeatedly used the object and purpose of the Genocide Convention to provide a progressive interpretation of some of its provisions. For instance, it rejected Yugoslavia's argument that the dispute was not international according to the Genocide Convention, especially its Article IV, on the basis that the Genocide Convention created *erga omnes* obligations, thus rendering irrelevant territorial restrictions to the scope of the Genocide Convention.[241] It also interpreted broadly the possibility for states to become parties to this Convention, in spite of procedural flaws in the accession to this instrument, underlining the 'legal nature of the Genocide Convention', under which 'the contracting States do not have any interests of their own; they merely have, one and all, a common interest, namely, the accomplishment of those high purposes which are the *raison d'être* of the convention'.[242]

236 Ibid., para. 23. 237 Ibid., para. 17. 238 Ibid., para. 34.

239 Cf. *Tyrer v. the United Kingdom*, App. No. 5856/72 (ECtHR) 25 April 1978, para. 31; *The Right to Information on Consular Assistance in the Framework of the Guarantees of Due Process of Law*, Advisory Opinion, Inter-American Court of Human Rights, Series OC-16/99 (1 October 1999) para. 114.

240 *Reservations to the Genocide Convention* (n 5) p. 12.

241 *Application of the Genocide Convention (Bosnia and Herzegovina v. Serbia and Montenegro)* (Preliminary Objections) (n 235) para. 31.

242 *Reservations to the Genocide Convention* (n 5) p. 23; *Application of the Genocide Convention (Bosnia and Herzegovina v. Serbia and Montenegro)* (Preliminary Objections) (n 235) para. 22.

This potential for a broad and evolutionary interpretation of the terms of the Convention was not completely ignored in the 2007 judgment; this is clear from the outset with the very recognition of the principle of state responsibility, which was not self-evident in the Convention. However, unlike its previous statement on the principle of non-retroactivity, the Court made great use of standards of international criminal law.[243] Certainly, the ICJ was operating in a different and rather original context, since it was requested to address facts that had already been reviewed—and were being reviewed—at length by the ICTY. As of 2007, only one case had resulted in a conviction for genocide, the *Krstić* case, in relation to the crimes perpetrated in Srebrenica.

The ICJ thus faced two options: either to stick to the ICTY's qualification of the facts, held in the specific context of individual criminal responsibility, or to review the facts according to its own principles of interpretation, with the possibility of reaching diverging conclusions. Two paragraphs show that the first option was indeed favoured: the ICJ's use of the application of the *in dubbio pro reo* principle to a state and the review of Serbia's *dolus specialis*. While it had set its standard of evidence as 'fully conclusive',[244] the ICJ ultimately considered that 'it is not established *beyond any doubt* in the argument between the Parties whether the authorities of the FRY supplied — and continued to supply — the VRS leaders'.[245] As for the 'intent to destroy the group', the ICJ had already considered it to be a crucial element of the definition of genocide in its advisory opinion on the *Legality of the Nuclear Weapons*, while not having taken a stance on the implementation of such a criterion in a context of state responsibility.[246] In 2007, it required that:

> The *dolus specialis*, the specific intent to destroy the group in whole or in part, has to be convincingly shown by reference to particular circumstances, unless a *general plan* to that end can be convincingly demonstrated to exist; and for a *pattern of conduct to be accepted as evidence of its existence*, it would have to be such that it could only point to the existence of such intent.[247]

This gives rise to a very crucial question about the criminal elements on which state responsibility for genocide should be based. Although the ICJ correctly

[243] Antonio Cassese, 'On the Use of Criminal Law Notions in Determining State Responsibility for Genocide' (2007) 5 *J.I.C.J.* 875, pp. 879–81; Paola Gaeta, 'On What Conditions Can a State be Held Responsible for Genocide?' (2007) 18 *E.J.I.L.* 631, pp. 644–6; Anja Seibert-Fohr, 'State Responsibility for Genocide under the Genocide Convention' in Paola Gaeta (ed.), *The UN Genocide Convention: A Commentary*, (Oxford: Oxford University Press, 2009) p. 355.

[244] *Application of the Genocide Convention (Bosnia and Herzegovina v. Serbia and Montenegro)* (Judgment) (n 11) para. 209.

[245] Ibid., para. 422. The contrast is underlined in Seibert-Fohr (n 243) pp. 360–1; Theodor Meron, 'Human Rights Law Marches into Next Territory: The Enforcement of International Human Rights in International Criminal Tribunals (Marek Nowicki Memorial Lecture)' in Theodor Meron, *The Making of International Criminal Justice: The View from the Bench: Selected Speeches* (Oxford: Oxford University Press, 2011) p. 233.

[246] *Legality of the Threat or Use of Nuclear Weapons* (Advisory Opinion) [1996] ICJ Rep. 226, para. 26.

[247] *Application of the Genocide Convention (Bosnia and Herzegovina v. Serbia and Montenegro)* (Judgment) (n 11) para. 373 (emphasis added).

rejected the concept of 'State criminal responsibility', it could not fully escape the very nature of genocide: a crime, with a specific intent. Any crime would require the establishment of the *actus reus* and the review of the alleged perpetrator's intent in perpetrating the criminal act. By contrast, state responsibility requires the existence of a breach of international law attributable to a state.[248] Then, the question arises as to where the *dolus specialis*, a concept of criminal law which 'is part of the primary norm', fits in the perspective of state responsibility?[249] Unlike the usual regime of state responsibility, the objective existence of a breach of international law is hardly possible to establish since it inherently depends on individual intents. As Theodor Meron noted: 'Notably, knowledge of *mens rea* (...) is not an issue that the ICJ is often called upon to adjudicate. Intent is not normally a matter of relevance for treaty interpretations.'[250] Indeed, the ICJ eluded the issue and limited itself, for each of the alleged acts, to review the relevant ICTY's case law. The ICJ systematically concluded that they did not reveal any intent to destroy the group, except in the case of Srebrenica. For instance, when reviewing instances of killings, it indicated that it 'ha[d] carefully examined the criminal proceedings of the ICTY and the findings of its Chambers, cited above, and observed that none of those convicted were found to have acted with specific intent (*dolus specialis*)'.[251] This is a very surprising line of reasoning, since it implies that only a few perpetrators can be deemed responsible for the perpetration of the criminal acts, namely, those who were indicted in front of the ICTY. In this regard, Anja Seibert-Forh's analysis of the ICJ's methodology indicates well the flaws: the ICJ 'accumulated the jurisprudence of the ICTY to a macro-perspective in order to determine whether genocide had been committed'.[252]

The question remains as to the right approach to the *dolus specialis*, an explicit and pivotal element of genocide, in the context of state responsibility. Considering that the implications of the specific intent are twofold, materialized both in substantive and psychological elements, it is less certain that the psychological dimension is necessary in the context of state responsibility, while the substantive element remains part of the international wrongful act. Of course, state responsibility is a legal fiction and thus ultimately depends on individuals but there is no reason why a psychological element should be added in the context of state responsibility for

[248] ILC (53rd Session), 'Draft Articles on Responsibility of States for Internationally Wrongful Acts, with Commentaries', *Yearbook of the International Law Commission,* 2001, vol. II, Part Two (ILC 2001 Draft Articles on State Responsibility) art. 2.

[249] Seibert-Fohr (n 243) p. 367. See also Andrea Bianchi, 'State Responsibility and Criminal Liability of Individuals' in Antonio Cassese (ed.), *The Oxford Companion to International Criminal Justice* (Oxford: Oxford University Press, 2009) p. 18.

[250] Theodor Meron, 'The ICJ's Opinion in Bosnia and Herzegovina v Serbia and Montenegro' in Meron (n 245) p. 232.

[251] *Application of the Genocide Convention (Bosnia and Herzegovina v. Serbia and Montenegro)* (Judgment) (n 11) para. 277. Reiterated for the review of acts under art. II(b), para. 319, for art. II(c), para. 354.

[252] Seibert-Fohr (n 243) p. 359. The same opinion is shared by Douglas Singleterry, '"Ethnic Cleansing" and Genocidal Intent: A Failure of Judicial Interpretation?' (2010) 5 *GSP* 39, p. 58: 'The Court appears to treat these as separate, isolated episodes rather than as systemic patterns of abuse.'

genocide, which should rather follow the prescriptions of the 2001 ILC Articles on State Responsibility: The establishment of an international wrongful act and its attribution to a state. Schabas also argues against the need for establishing the state specific intent to perpetrate genocide:

> Instead of a mechanistic and unsatisfying attempt to impose concepts that belong to individual liability on the behavior of a State, it would be better to take the State policy as the starting point and attempt to relate this to individual guilt. Following this approach, the first issue to be resolved in a determination as to whether genocide is being committed is whether there exists a State policy. If the answer is affirmative, then the inquiry shifts to the individual, with the central question being not the individual's intent, but rather the individual's knowledge of the policy.[253]

However, Schabas's proposal ultimately comes back to the creation of an additional element to prove genocide, namely the existence of a state policy. This element can be found in the report of the Darfur commission[254] while the ICJ has considered that this requirement was not essential.[255] The 2007 findings were reiterated in the ICJ 2015 judgment in the *Croatia v. Serbia* case,[256] in spite of Croatia's request that the Court lower its threshold of evidence of the intent to perpetrate genocide in relation to state responsibility.[257] As it could be foreseen in light of the absence of genocide conviction in front of the ICTY in cases involving crimes perpetrated on the Croatian territory, the ICJ did not recognize that Serbia had perpetrated genocide in Croatia.

The issue of determining the intent to destroy the group in a context of state responsibility thus remains a sensitive and unsettled one in customary international law, as it challenges the principle underlying the regime of state responsibility in international law as 'objective in scope'.[258] The 2007 and 2015 ICJ judgments show how much the legal framework of genocide has been anchored into international criminal law. Accordingly the context of the interpretation of the definition of genocide only has a limited impact on the methodologies involved. Firstly, international criminal courts, as well as national German courts, have themselves anchored their interpretation in the methodology provided by the VCLT. Secondly, the ICJ has constrained itself with considerations of international criminal law when reviewing state responsibility for genocide. Although the possibility that other investigative and judicial bodies may adopt different methodological approaches is

[253] William A. Schabas, 'State Policy as an Element of International Crimes' (2008) 98 *J.Crim.L. & Criminology* 953, p. 971.

[254] Darfur Report (n 201) para. 642.

[255] The ICJ analysed whether such a state policy to perpetrate genocide existed in Bosnia and Herzegovina but only as a potential element of evidence, not as a requirement in itself. Cf. *Application of the Genocide Convention (Bosnia and Herzegovina v. Serbia and Montenegro)* (Judgment) (n 11) para. 190.

[256] *Application of the Genocide Convention (Croatia v. Serbia)* (Judgment) (n 38) para. 148.

[257] 'Croatia asks ICJ to lower standards for proving genocide', *dalje.com* (20 March 2014) available at: http://dalje.com/en-croatia/croatia-asks-icj-to-lower-standards-for-proving-genocide/503379 (last accessed 1 February 2015).

[258] Bianchi (n 249) p. 18.

not excluded,[259] the current state of the international law of genocide so far remains deeply anchored in criminal rhetoric and principles.

3.3 Concluding Remarks

There seems to be an inherent difficulty for the law of genocide to adequately address the idea of a 'single multidimensional process'.[260] Not only is this due to the definition itself and its restrictive list of genocidal acts, but it is also a result of its criminal nature, which limits the ability of the framework to reach states, notwithstanding that they are the main subjects of international law and, as such, certain essential actors of genocidal processes. Furthermore, the structure of international criminal law induces a compartmentalization of the process into a variety of perpetrators and sub-crimes, according to a dubious classification in physical, biological, and cultural terms. Hence, while most of the possible interpretative methods[261] implied by the VCLT tend towards a non-physical understanding of the *mens rea* of genocide, the physical-biological interpretation is becoming less and less challengeable from an international criminal legal perspective.

A 'broader' understanding of the *mens rea* would not absolve the legal definition of genocide from all its ambiguities, but it would certainly bring it some coherence, if only to clarify the status of subparagraph (e).[262] This is perhaps the most powerful argument towards a broad understanding, one which integrates another principle of interpretation that has not been explicitly enshrined in the VCLT into the loop of the interpretation: the principle of *effet utile*, or '*ut res magis valeat quam pereat*',[263] according to which any text or norm 'should be interpreted in such a way that a reason and a meaning can be attributed to every word. No word or provision may be disregarded or treated as superfluous, unless this is absolutely necessary to give effect to the terms read as a whole'.[264] This idea is somewhat intent-based as it is assumed that the authors of a Convention have intended to give such a meaning to a term so that the provision might receive implementation.[265] This principle has been used several times by the ICTY.[266] In the context of the *mens rea* of genocide, the principle of *effet utile* becomes helpful for the purposes of determining the right interpretation by outlining the one which engenders the most coherence, at the level of both the crime of genocide itself and the broader field of international criminal law.

[259] Cf. Darfur Report (n 201) p. 4; when addressing whether genocide occurred, the Commission looked at whether a genocidal policy had been pursued and implemented in Darfur.

[260] Christopher Powell, 'What Do Genocides Kill? A Relational Conception of Genocide' (2007) 9 *J.G.R.* 527, p. 534.

[261] Villiger (n 60) pp. 421–2.

[262] Starr and Brilmayer (n 140) p. 240.

[263] 'That the thing may rather have effect than be destroyed.'

[264] UNSC 'Final Report of the Commission of Experts Established Pursuant to Security Council Resolution 780 (1992)' (27 May 1994) UN Doc. S/1994/674, para. 90.

[265] Jean Salmon (ed.), *Dictionnaire du Droit International Public* (Bruxelles: Bruylant, 2001) p. 416.

[266] See e.g. *Tadić Case* (Appeals) IT-94-1 (15 July 1999) para. 284.

Furthermore, as noted by Schabas, such a broad interpretation would also satisfy grounds for implementation in cases of the 'destruction of aboriginal communities by a combination of violence, eradication of economic life and incitement to assimilation',[267] a paraphrase for the contemporary indigenous understanding of cultural genocide, or 'ethnocide'. This would allow for the rationalization of the discourse which, according to Bartolomé Clavero, unduly opposes ethnocide to genocide: '[e]thnocide as a category does not provide a basis for the international judicial defence of indigenous peoples. In international law, genocide, which does have that potential, has a meaning under the Convention which is far broader than physical destruction and which is lost with the new concept of ethnocide'.[268] However, as articulated by Judge Shahabuddeen in his dissenting opinion, the consequences of the ICTY case law should not be over-estimated, since even in the case of an alternative interpretation of the *mens rea*, the issue of 'cultural genocide' would still be confronted with the mainly biological and physical nature of the *actus reus*.

When it comes to proper acts of cultural genocide, considered as a technique of genocide, the current *Krstić* interpretation, although being progressive, does not completely solve the issue since these acts are now acknowledged as being part of the process of genocide, while their genocidal character is rejected for historical reasons. Ana Vrdoljak aptly describes this 'inconsistency' in the definition of genocide:

> That is, a group must have a distinct identity to attract the protection afforded by the Convention but acts which target their cultural heritage (and which render the group distinctive) are not prohibited per se. Confining such acts to establishing the *mens rea* of genocide alone, serves only to highlight this inconsistency rather than remedy it.[269]

The question is therefore one of remedying this inconsistency. In the current state of the interpretation of the 'intent to destroy a group', the main—if not the only—'open door' for an 'evolutionary interpretation' of the *mens rea* therefore remains at the national level, in those jurisdictions which have either afforded a constant interpretation in favour of a broader understanding of the *mens rea*, in the line of the German case law, or in which genocide is codified in broader terms.[270] Mireille Delmas Marty has thus noted the national legislatures' tendency to renationalize the definition of genocide when transposing it into their domestic criminal codes and tend to either broaden its scope to include the protection of political groups (Latin America) and self-genocide (Cambodia) or restrict it.[271] For instance, the Israeli Nazis and Nazi Collaborators (Punishment) Law, adopted in 1950, and

[267] Schabas, *Genocide in International Law* (n 46) p. 271.

[268] Permanent Forum on Indigenous Issues, 'Study on International Criminal Law and the Judicial Defence of Indigenous Peoples' Rights (submitted by the Special Rapporteur Bartlomé Clavero)' (8 February 2011) UN Doc. E/C.19/2011/4, p. 10.

[269] Ana F. Vrdoljak, 'Cultural Heritage in Human Rights and Humanitarian Law' in Orna Ben-Naftali (ed.), *International Humanitarian Law and International Human Rights Law* (Oxford; New York: Oxford University Press, 2011) p. 299.

[270] See e.g. Elizabeth Santalla Vargas, 'An Overview of the Crime of Genocide in Latin American Jurisdictions' (2010) 10 *I.C.L.R.* 441, pp. 441–52.

[271] Mireille Delmas-Marty, *Le Relatif et l'Universel: Les Forces Imaginantes du Droit* (Paris: Seuil, 2004) p. 82.

which was used to prosecute Adolf Eichmann, paraphrased the 1948 definition of genocide in respect of the crimes perpetrated against the Jewish people. Even though the victim group was more restrictive, the *actus reus* has been broadened to encompass acts such as 'destroying or desecrating Jewish religious or cultural assets or values'.[272] On the other end of the spectrum, Paraguay's criminalization of genocide encompasses the impossibility for a group 'to exercise its cult or practice its customs'.[273] Such practice can bear the risk of infringing the rights of the defence, the scope for which arises in the case that the definition would have been adapted *ex post facto*,[274] as the ECtHR reminded in the *Vasiliauskas* case. Furthermore, from the perspective of general international law, this may create an undesirable fragmentation of international law, especially when the national interpretation conflicts with an international one, as the judicial process of the Former Yugoslavia has displayed.

However, the legal framework of genocide only constitutes a small fraction of the body of international law likely to apply to the concept of cultural genocide. Consequently, shifting the focus to the 'cultural' dimension of the concept may open new perspectives.

[272] Nazis and Nazi Collaborators (Punishment) Law, 5710-1950 (1 August 1950) art. 1(b)(6).

[273] Codigo penal de Paraguay, ley 1.160/97 (1997), art. 319 c) 'El que con la intención de destruir, total o parcialmente, una comunidad o un grupo nacional, étnico, religioso o social: (...) 4. imposibilitara el ejercicio de sus cultos o la práctica de sus costumbres (...)' available at: http://www.oas.org/dil/esp/Codigo_Penal_Paraguay.pdf (last accessed 3 July 2016).

[274] See the issue in Bangladesh and the implication to facts that occurred in 1971: *The International Crimes (Tribunals) Act*, Act No. XIX of 1973 (20 July 1973), modified by *The International Crimes (Tribunals) (Amendment) Act*, 2009 (Act No. LV of 2009).

4

International Law and the Protection of Cultures

After 1948, international law primarily took the protective turn triggered by the Universal Declaration of Human Rights (UDHR) rather than the criminal turn initiated by the Genocide Convention. This is particularly salient when it comes to the protection of cultures as encompassed within the 'cultural genocide' concept. Despite its non-inclusion in the Genocide Convention, the international community did not remain completely passive and gradually acknowledged the importance of cultures in relation to fully realizing human rights and preventing the perpetration of mass atrocities, as argued by Raphael Lemkin in the early 1930s.

However, the process has been quite long and marked by sporadic and diffuse initiatives, which did not follow a single taxonomical approach. The protection of cultures has thus been addressed in a wide range of legal disciplines, though taking two predominant directions, which have intersected to some extent. Firstly, in the wake of the UDHR, international human rights law has dedicated increasing importance to human cultural rights. Secondly, a category of law known as 'international cultural heritage law' has progressively developed, starting from international humanitarian law and the protection of tangible cultural heritage in time of armed conflict, to evolving towards a holistic understanding of cultural heritage. The connection with genocide, and the return to the essence of the concept of cultural genocide came later, with the consolidation of these two branches of cultural protection, converging particularly around the role of cultural protection in preventing genocide.

4.1 The Human Rights Approach

Not only have the norms related to cultural rights multiplied over time, but some groups have also progressively been recognized as the bearers of such rights. After having recalled the main strands of these evolutions, the study then focuses on emerging human rights that tend to revisit the language of cultural genocide.

The Concept of Cultural Genocide: An International Law Perspective. First Edition. Elisa Novic.
Published 2016 by Oxford University Press.

4.1.1 The development of cultural rights

An important body of legal scholarship is already dedicated to the evolution of international human rights law in relation to cultural rights.[1] Only the main evolutions are traced back in this present section. While the draft minority rights project was rejected from the UDHR, Article 27(1) of the same Declaration introduced an early formulation of cultural rights in the following words: 'Everyone has the right freely to participate in the cultural life of the community, to enjoy the arts and to share in scientific advancement and its benefits.'[2] This non-binding provision was later codified in Article 15(1)(a) of the 1966 International Covenant on the Economic, Social and Cultural Rights (ICESCR), which reiterated the same principle of the 'right of everyone to take part in cultural life', though without reference to the notion of 'community'.[3] This is the only provision of the entire Covenant explicitly protecting cultural rights. As every other right stated in the ICESCR, Article 15(1)(a) is conferred a programmatic taint, since Article 2(1) of the same Covenant makes the state obligation to implement these rights contingent upon 'the maximum of its available resources'. In contrast, Article 2 of the 1966 International Covenant on Civil and Political Rights (ICCPR) established clear positive obligations for states with respect to the rights contained in the Covenant, including minority cultural, linguistic, and religious rights, as enshrined in Article 27:

> In those States in which ethnic, religious or linguistic minorities exist, persons belonging to such minorities shall not be denied the right, in community with the other members of their group, to enjoy their own culture, to profess and practise their own religion, or to use their own language.[4]

While this provision tends to be criticized for its negative formulation, it constitutes the first recognition of specific rights that accompany the status of belonging to a minority.

Thematic international human rights treaties have also incorporated cultural concerns in their ambit. For instance, Article 5(d)(e)(vi) of the 1965 International Convention on the Elimination of All Forms of Racial Discrimination (CERD) reiterates the prohibition of racial discrimination in relation to the enjoyment of 'the right to equal participation in cultural activities'.[5] In the context of

[1] See e.g. Elsa Stamatopoulou, *Cultural Rights in International Law: Article 27 of the Universal Declaration of Human Rights and Beyond* (Leiden; Boston: Martinus Nijhoff Publishers, 2007) pp. 11–36; Francesco Francioni and Martin Scheinin (eds.), *Cultural Human Rights* (Leiden; Boston: Martinus Nijhoff Publishers 2008).

[2] Universal Declaration of Human Rights (adopted 10 December 1948) UNGA Res. 217 A(III) (UDHR).

[3] International Covenant on Economic, Social and Cultural Rights (adopted 16 December 1966, entered into force 3 January 1976) 993 UNTS 3 (ICESCR) art. 15(1).

[4] International Covenant on Civil and Political Rights (adopted 16 December 1966, entered into force 23 March 1976) 999 UNTS 171 (ICCPR) art. 27.

[5] Convention on the Elimination of All Forms of Racial Discrimination (adopted 7 March 1966, entered into force 4 January 1969) 660 UNTS 195 (CERD); similar formulation in Convention on the Elimination of All Forms of Discrimination against Women (adopted 18 December 1979, entered into force 3 September 1981) 1249 UNTS 13 (CEDAW) art. 13(c).

anti-discrimination, culture has also become a strong component of the international legal anti-discrimination framework, especially with the falling into disgrace of the concept of 'race' in the 1950s.[6] In a way, 'ethnicism' can be said to have substituted racism,[7] despite the reminiscence of the latter concept in various international legal instruments. Thus, in spite of its title, the CERD addresses a range of discriminatory grounds that go beyond mere racial discrimination:

the term 'racial discrimination' shall mean any distinction, exclusion, restriction or preference *based on race, colour, descent, or national or ethnic origin* which has the purpose or effect of nullifying or impairing the recognition, enjoyment or exercise, on an equal footing, of human rights and fundamental freedoms in the political, economic, social, *cultural* or any other field of public life.[8]

It is worth highlighting the relevance of this instrument in relation to genocide, in respect of which the intent to destroy a national, racial, religious, or ethnic group is often fuelled by a feeling of hatred towards the targeted group.[9] The anti-discrimination framework may thus constitute the human rights counterpart to the prohibition of genocide.

The 1989 Convention on the Rights of the Child (CRC) is also particularly illustrative of the cultural trend in the codification of thematic human rights, especially with regard to the right to education. This right was already stated in general international human rights instruments. For instance, Article 26(3) UDHR states that: 'Parents have a prior right to choose the kind of education that shall be given to their children.'[10] The CRC dedicates two articles to the cultural dimension of the right to education in a more explicit manner. Article 29(1)(c) provides that:

[T]he education of the child shall be directed to (. . .) [t]he development of respect for the child's parents, *his or her own cultural identity*, language and values, for the national values of the country in which the child is living, the country from which he or she may originate, and for civilizations different from his or her own.[11]

Article 30 specifically focuses on the right to education in the particular context of minorities within the state:

In those States in which ethnic, religious or linguistic minorities or persons of indigenous origin exist, a child belonging to such a minority or who is indigenous *shall not be denied the*

[6] Claude Lévi-Strauss, *L'Anthropologie Face aux Problèmes du Monde Moderne* (Paris: Seuil, 2011) pp. 115–23.

[7] Tove Skutnabb-Kangas and Robert Dunbar, 'Indigenous Children's Education as Linguistic Genocide and a Crime Against Humanity? A Global View' (2010) 1 *Gáldu čála: Journal of Indigenous Peoples Rights*, p. 41.

[8] CERD (n 5) art. 1(1) (emphases added). See also art. 5(d);(e)(vi).

[9] See e.g. 'Report of the Secretary-General on the Implementation of the Five Point Action Plan and the Activities of the Special Adviser on the Prevention of Genocide' E/CN.4/2006/84 (9 March 2006) (UNSG Report on the Five Point Action Plan (2006) para. 11.

[10] UDHR (n 2) art. 26. This right is reiterated in art. 13(1) of the ICESCR, which specifies that education shall be 'directed to the full development of the human personality and the sense of its dignity'.

[11] Convention on the Rights of the Child (adopted 20 November 1989, entered into force 2 September 1990) 1577 UNTS 3 (CRC) art. 29 (emphasis added).

right, in community with other members of his or her group, to enjoy his or her own culture, to profess and practise his or her own religion, or to use his or her own language.[12]

The focus of these two provisions is clearly intergenerational, aiming at setting the ground for free transmission of one's culture.

As for the regional systems of human rights protection, the founding instruments of the inter-American system faithfully reflect the international provisions on cultural rights. Article 13 of the American Declaration of the Rights and Duties of Man reproduces almost word-for-word Article 15 ICESCR, while its preamble contains powerful language in relation to culture:

> Since culture is the highest social and historical expression of that spiritual development, it is the duty of man to preserve, practice and foster culture by every means within his power.
>
> And, since moral conduct constitutes the noblest flowering of culture, it is the duty of every man always to hold it in high respect.[13]

The American Convention on Human Rights (ACHR) does not contain a cultural right provision as such, although its preamble reiterates the right to everyone, in accordance with the UDHR, to 'enjoy his economic, social, and cultural rights, as well as his civil and political rights'.[14] The 1988 Protocol of San Salvador, related to economic, social, and economic rights, has remedied this absence, by reintroducing a 'right to the benefits of culture' in its Article 14, which formulation is similar to Article 13 of the American Declaration.[15]

At the European level, no mention of cultural rights is to be found in either the ECHR or its Protocols. The right to participate in cultural life will therefore be included within other provisions, such as Article 8 in relation to the right to respect for private and family life.[16] The prohibition of discrimination is stated at Article 14, but this provision is not autonomous and discrimination can only be found in the enjoyment of other rights, either explicit in the ECHR or 'set forth by law'.[17]

[12] Ibid., art. 30 (emphasis added).

[13] American Declaration of the Rights and Duties of Man, OAS Res. (1948) reprinted in Basic Documents Pertaining to Human Rights in the Inter-American System OEA/Ser L V/II.82 Doc. 6 Rev. 1 at 17 (1992) (ADHR) preamble, paras. 5, 6.

[14] American Convention on Human Rights (adopted 22 November 1969, entered into force 18 July 1978) OAS, Treaty Series, NO. 36, 1144 UNTS 123, reprinted in Basic Documents Pertaining to Human Rights in the Inter-American System OEA/Ser L V/II.82 Doc. 6 Rev. 1 at 25 (1992) (ACHR) preamble, para. 4.

[15] Additional Protocol to the American Convention on Human Rights in the Area of Economic, Social and Cultural Rights (Protocol of San Salvador) (entered into force 16 November 1999) OAS Treaty Series No. 69 (1988) reprinted in Basic Documents Pertaining to Human Rights in the Inter-American System OEA/Ser L V/II.82 Doc. 6 Rev. 1 at 67 (1992).

[16] Convention for the Protection of Human Rights and Fundamental Freedoms (European Convention on Human Rights, as amended) (adopted 4 November 1950, entered into force 3 September 1953) CETS No.: 005 (ECHR). Also relevant are art. 10—freedom of expression; art. 11—freedom of assembly and association; art. 14—prohibition of discrimination.

[17] Ibid., art. 14; Protocol No. 12 to the Convention for the Protection of Human Rights and Fundamental Freedoms (adopted 4 November 2000, entered into force 1 April 2005) CETS No.: 117, art. 1(1).

Finally, at the African level, the African Charter on Human and Peoples' Rights (ACHPR) protects both individual and peoples' rights.[18] Article 17(2) thereof provides that '[e]very individual may freely take part in the cultural life of his community' while paragraph (3) imposes positive obligations upon the state to promote and protect 'morals and traditional values recognised by the community'. Article 22 sets out the right to economic, social, and cultural development. It is noteworthy that the African Court on Human and Peoples' Rights has jurisdiction to review alleged violations of human rights, which are not only stated in the African regional instruments but also in 'any other relevant Human Rights instrument ratified by the States concerned'.[19]

This non-exhaustive list of 'cultural rights' provisions highlights two issues inherent to these rights as such. First, beyond the mere acknowledgement of either the right to take part in cultural life or the right to enjoy one's own culture, there is no definition of either the content of these rights or the word 'culture'. The second issue is rather quantitative and concerns the scarcity of mention of cultural rights in these various instruments, which are almost always the object of one single provision, unlike the other categories of rights. This is quite illustrative of the level of consideration that was first granted to this category of rights. Cultural rights have long been considered as 'secondary' rights, of lesser importance in relation to other rights, especially political and civil rights, leading Symonides to qualify these rights as 'neglected' and 'treated as "poor relatives" '.[20] The implementation of these rights was also considered to drift from the realization of civil and political rights. However, as Louise Arbour puts it: '[t]he full realization of human rights is never achieved as a mere by-product, or fortuitous consequence, of some other developments, no matter how positive'.[21]

Nevertheless, other rights, such as religious or linguistic rights,[22] may as well be considered as part of cultural rights so that the quantitative issue should not be overstated. Furthermore, the situation has evolved towards a greater consideration for these rights. From a formal point of view, cultural rights have been gradually considered as equal to other categories of rights, considering the interdependency and interrelationship between all human rights. This was asserted in the 1993 Vienna Declaration, which was issued as the outcome of the World Summit on Human Rights.[23] One year later, in its General Comment No. 23 on Article 27 ICCPR,

[18] African Charter on Human and Peoples' Rights (adopted 27 June 1981, entered into force 21 October 1986) (1982) 21 ILM 58 (ACHPR).

[19] Protocol to the African Charter on Human and Peoples' Rights on the Establishment of the African Court on Human and Peoples' Rights (adopted 9 June 1998, entered into force 25 January 2004) Doc. OAU/LEG/EXP/AFCHPR/PROT (III) art. 3(1).

[20] Janusz Symonides, 'Cultural Rights: A Neglected Category of Human Rights' (2002) 50 *Int'l Soc. Sci.J.l.* 559, p. 559.

[21] World Conference on Human Rights, 'Status of Preparation of Publications, Studies and Documents for the World Conference' (1993) UN Doc. A/CONF.157/PC/62/Add.5, para. 4. Quoted in Louise Arbour, 'Economic and Social Justice for Societies in Transition' (2007-2008) 40 *N.Y.U.J.Int.L.Pol.* 1, p. 3.

[22] Yvonne Donders, *Towards a Right to Cultural Identity?* (Antwerpen; New York: Intersentia, 2002) p. 3.

[23] UNGA Res. CONF.157/23 (12 July 1993) 'Vienna Declaration and Programme of Action' para. 5.

the Human Rights Committee recognized, among others, that the negative formulation of this provision did not undermine its 'right' nature, therefore requiring states to adopt positive measures of protection.[24] It later consecrated Article 27 as a 'peremptory norm', in its General Comment on Article 40(4) ICCPR:

provisions in the Covenant that represent customary international law (and a fortiori when they have the character of peremptory norms) may not be the subject of reservations. Accordingly, a State may not reserve the right (. . .) to deny to minorities the right to enjoy their own culture, profess their own religion, or use their own language.[25]

From the point of view of the content, cultural rights have also received extensive interpretation thanks to various judicial and human rights bodies involved in the implementation of the above-mentioned international instruments and others. Beyond the equal consideration of the various categories of rights established in the two covenants, the indivisibility of human rights also tends to dismiss the very notion of 'category'. If some rights may be at first sight preponderantly civil, political, economic, social, or cultural, most rights will overlap in practice between different categories. This is especially true in respect of cultural rights. The limited number of provisions in general international human rights instruments is compensated by the increasing recognition of a cultural dimension to most rights. This evolution is directly linked to the legal broadening of the concept of 'culture'. Most instruments that have been quoted so far express a 'narrow' understanding of the word culture, which focuses on 'cultural products, such as arts and literature' and may therefore 'include the protection of such cultural heritage, as well as the right to take part in cultural life and to have access to such products and heritage in museums, theatres and libraries'.[26] The UN human rights treaty bodies have nonetheless interpreted the term 'culture' broadly, so as to become synonymous with 'a way of life', which is understood as matching the 'anthropological conception'.[27] It is stated very clearly in the commentary of the Committee on Economic, Social and Cultural Rights in relation to Article 15(1)(a) ICESCR:

The Committee considers that culture, for the purpose of implementing article 15 (1)(a), encompasses, inter alia, *ways of life*, language, oral and written literature, music and song, non-verbal communication, religion or belief systems, rites and ceremonies, sport and games, methods of production or technology, natural and man-made environments, food, clothing and shelter and the arts, customs and traditions through which individuals, groups of individuals and communities express their humanity and the meaning they give to their existence, and build their world view representing their encounter with the external forces

[24] UNHRC, 'General Comment No. 23: Article 27 (Right of Minorities)' (8 April 1994) UN Doc. CCPR/C/21/Rev. 1/Add.5, para. 6.1.

[25] UNHRC General Comment No. 24: Article 40, para. 4 ICCPR (11 November 1994) UN Doc. CCPR/C/21/Rev. 1/Add.6, para. 8.

[26] Yvonne Donders, 'Do Cultural Diversity and Human Rights Make a Good Match?' (2010) 61 *Int'l Soc.Sci.J.* 15, pp. 18–19.

[27] Stamatopoulou, *Cultural Rights in International Law* (n 1) p. 4; Donders, 'Do Cultural Diversity and Human Rights Make a Good Match?' (n 26) p. 19.

affecting their lives. Culture shapes and mirrors the values of well-being and the economic, social and political life of individuals, groups of individuals and communities.[28]

This long list actually reflects well the existing case law in relation to what is considered as being part of an individual or group culture. While again it is not possible to refer to all of the case law and decisions related to such an understanding, one particularly illustrative example is identifiable in the recognition by the HRC of the notion that economic activities can potentially constitute the expression of a group culture.[29]

While the very category of cultural rights is contested and can be considered—as any other category of human rights—as conceptually flawed, the term 'cultural rights' will nonetheless be used in the present study to describe the set of human rights that possess a cultural component. They can either be contained in the specific so-called 'cultural provisions' that have been mentioned throughout this section or be associated with other human rights, which, in the specific context surrounding their exercise, may display a strong cultural dimension. Already transparent from this description of the status of cultural rights in international human rights law is the significance of their collective dimension. 'Culture' and 'groups' are actually two sides of the same coin: the recognition of cultural rights cannot be made without the acknowledgement of the surrounding community, to which the culture actually relates.

4.1.2 The collectivization of cultural rights

According to the *Stanford Encyclopedia of Philosophy*, '[a] group right is a right held by a group as a group rather than by its members severally', so that they 'should not be confused with rights that people possess in virtue of being members of groups'.[30] As precluded by the negotiations of the draft minority provision in the UDHR, the place groups should be granted in the human rights framework has consequently been a bone of contention since the 1940s. The inter-war minority rights failed framework is clearly one reason; the liberal ideology that has prevailed since then is another. States feared especially that granting rights to groups as such would have repercussions in the political sphere and favour the claims of self-determination, if not secession.[31] Yet, it has not only been states that have expressed reluctance towards granting 'group' or 'collective' rights. Many scholars and civil society

[28] CESCR 'General Comment 21: Right of Everyone to Take Part in Cultural Life (art. 15, para. 1(a), of the International Covenant on Economic, Social and Cultural Rights)', (2–20 November 2009), UN Doc. E/C.12/GC/21, para. 13. See also paras. 11–12 (emphasis added).

[29] *Bernard Ominayak, Chief of the Lubicon Lake Band v. Canada*, Communication 167/1984 (26 March 1990) Report of the Human Rights Committee, GAOR, Thirty-Eighth Session, Suppl. No. 40 (A/38/40) para. 32(2).

[30] Peter Jones, 'Group Rights' in Edward N. Zalta (ed.), *Stanford Encyclopedia of Philosophy* (2008, rev. 2016) available at: http://plato.stanford.edu/entries/rights-group/ (last accessed 3 July 2016).

[31] Elsa Stamatopoulou, 'Taking Cultural Rights Seriously: The Vision of the UN Declaration on the Rights of Indigenous Peoples' in Stephen Allen, Alexandra Xanthaki (eds.), *Reflections on the UN Declaration on the Rights of Indigenous Peoples* (Oxford: Hart Publishing, 2011) p. 389.

organizations are concerned that if entitled with autonomous rights, groups may end up oppressing their own members. Liberal theorists were particularly active in developing the former argument,[32] although their position evolved progressively towards an increased acknowledgement of groups, especially in the context of debates on multiculturalism. Will Kymlicka, for instance, proposed the introduction of 'group-differentiated' rights for ethnic groups, that is rights that are granted on the basis of group membership. He argues that 'societal culture' is essential to individual freedom, 'because of the role it plays in enabling meaningful individual choice and in supporting self-identity'.[33]

In addition to the issue of why groups should be included in the human rights framework, the debate on collective rights has also focused considerably on defining the groups entitled to such rights. For instance, in a seminal piece aiming at the identification of the groups that could be entitled to exercise the right to self-determination, Raz and Margalit considered that such groups should be 'encompassing', which could be identified through six criteria: a 'common culture that encompass many, varied and important aspects of life', the transmission of this culture to newcomers in the group, membership through both mutual recognition and self-identification, which is seen as 'a matter of belonging, not of achievement', and the anonymous character of the group.[34]

Finally, the third dimension of the theoretical debate has concerned the content of such rights. Some authors have considered that collective rights should depend on whether they concern public goods, although the definition of such goods is quite controversial.[35]

This debate is therefore multidimensional and often confused as to its focus.[36] In this regard, international law recognizes group rights, understood in the sense of the *Stanford Encyclopedia of Philosophy*, with parsimony. Only two types of groups are recognized as potential bearers of rights in international human rights law. Firstly, minorities have been increasingly acknowledged in the context of human rights, although the perspective remains highly individual. Secondly, the rising

32 Chandran Kukathas, 'Are There Any Cultural Rights?' (1992) 20 *Pol. Theory* 105; Yael Tamir, 'Against Collective Rights' in Lukas H. Meyer, Stanley Paulson, and Thomas W. Pogge (eds.), *Rights, Culture, and the Law: Themes from the Legal and Political Philosophy of Joseph Raz* (Oxford; New York: Oxford University Press, 2003) pp. 184–5.

33 Will Kymlicka, *Multicultural Citizenship, A Liberal Theory of Minority Rights* (Oxford: Clarendon Press; New York: Oxford University Press, 1995) p. 105.

34 Avishai Margalit, and Joseph Raz, 'National Self-Determination' (1990) 87 *J.Phil.* 439, pp. 444–5. The authors give six criteria, which they find crucial in order to identify groups likely to be entitled to a right to self-determination.

35 James Griffin, 'Group Rights' in Lukas H. Meyer, Stanley Paulson, and Thomas W. Pogge (eds.), *Rights, Culture, and the Law: Themes from the Legal and Political Philosophy of Joseph Raz* (Oxford; New York: Oxford University Press, 2003) pp. 164–8.

36 Tamir (n 32) p. 198: the author proposes to reverse the terms of the perspective adopted, so that the debate 'takes the fact of pluralism as its starting point and asks what is the best way to assure to individuals, rooted in their own cultural, linguistic, and religious communities, their rights'. She draws conclusions as to the irrelevance of the category of 'collective rights' since she considers that individual human rights are sufficient to fulfil this purpose.

internationalization of the indigenous movements has led to the recognition of collective rights therein.

4.1.2.1 The exercise of rights 'in community': minority rights

Following the failure of the UDHR draft 'minority rights' provision, '[m]inority rights were shunted off into an obscure sub-commission which led a twilight and futile existence for the next few decades'.[37] It actually took the Sub-Commission on Prevention of Discrimination and Protection of Minorities more than four decades to complete its reflections on the issue of minority rights. For a long time, Article 27 ICCPR remained the sole provision related to the protection of minorities in international law. While it was formulated as an individual right, it also referred to the exercise of such rights 'in community, with other members of [the] group'. This expression became a common way to acknowledge the collective context in the human rights framework related to members of minorities, as illustrated by Article 30 CRC, for instance.

As a consequence, minority rights have long been addressed through mere individual rights, especially the principle of non-discrimination, which remained, for a long time, the sole way to acknowledge the existence of groups in international law. This comes back to the very need of ensuring minorities' protection in international law, considering that '[s]ince the 1930s this term has been applied to social groups that are oppressed or stigmatized on the basis of racial, ethnic, biological, or other characteristics'.[38] The PCIJ set out this principle and attributed to it its main orientations in the interwar context of minority treaties.[39] In the wake of the Second World War, provisions on non-discrimination were included in all major human rights instruments. If one recalls the negotiations of the minority rights provision, one argument advanced in the rejection of the draft minority right provision was that Article 2 of the final declaration provided the same protection, without giving rise to the controversy on collective rights.[40] Accordingly, non-discrimination has long substituted in the absence of collective and cultural protection in the Inter-American system,[41] even in so far as to be granted the status of a norm of *jus cogens*, as a result of which it is unable to undergo any possible derogation.[42]

[37] Mark Mazower, 'The Strange Triumph of Human Rights, 1933–1950' (2004) 47 *The Historical Journal* 379, p. 390.

[38] Gordon Marshall and John Scott (eds.), 'Minority Group' in *A Dictionary of Sociology* (3rd rev. edn., Oxford: Oxford University Press, 2009).

[39] *Minority Schools in Albania* (Advisory Opinion) 6 April 1935, PCIJ Rep. Series AB No. 64.

[40] William A. Schabas, 'Preventing Genocide and Mass Killing: The Challenge for the United Nations' (London: Minority Rights Group International, 2006) p. 5.

[41] Bernard Duhaime, 'Vers une Amérique plus Égalitaire: l'Interdiction de la Discrimination et le Système Interaméricain de Protection des Droits de la Personne' in Ludovic Hennebel and Hélène Tigroudja (eds.), *Le Particularisme Interaméricain des Droits de l'Homme* (Paris: Pedone, 2006) pp. 166–8; Lucas Lixinski, *Intangible Cultural Heritage in International Law* (Oxford: Oxford University Press, 2013) p. 158.

[42] *Juridical Condition and Rights of the Undocumented Migrants*, Advisory Opinion OC-18, Inter-American Court of Human Rights Series A No. 18 (17 September 2003) para. 97–101.

Eventually, in 1992, the UNGA adopted a 'Declaration on the Rights of Persons Belonging to National or Ethnic, Religious, and Linguistic Minorities'. This instrument is non-binding and reflects a hybrid approach to the protection of minorities. While states bear obligations towards minorities as such,[43] the rights are only conferred on individual members of such minorities, who can exercise them 'individually or in community with other members of their group'.[44] It is interesting to note that during the four decades passing since the adoption of the UDHR, the drafters of the Declaration on the Rights of Minority and *a fortiori* states were unable to agree on a definition of the term 'minority' itself. This indeed remains a delicate question, to which a reply can be given either with reference to objective criteria—such as the numerical inferiority in relation to a given dominant population and the degree of permanency of presence within the state, or subjective criteria—such as the state of vulnerability and the sharing of a common identity, or both types of criteria.[45] The Human Rights Committee, in its General Comment No. 23 related to Article 27 ICCPR, remained quite vague on this issue, considering that minorities must have an objective existence, which dictates that it does not depend on a state recognition, and that such minorities are defined by the share of a common culture, language, or religion.[46] Among the rights granted to minority members, the first is their 'right to enjoy their own culture, to profess and practise their own religion, and to use their own language, in private and in public, freely and without interference or any form of discrimination'.[47] This provision recalls both the draft 'cultural genocide' and 'minority rights' provisions that were rejected in 1948. As a result of the non-binding character of the Declaration, its input is limited to clarify and, to some extent, help in respect of the identification of the *opinio juris* in relation to potential customary international law related to minority rights. Yet, both the justiciability and enforceability of minority rights still depend on the framework of Article 27 ICCPR. The Declaration is not even mentioned in the Human Rights Committee's General Comment No. 23. In any case, it is not clear whether its provisions actually provide for a wider protection than that granted by Article 27 ICCPR, as interpreted by the Human Rights Committee. In his commentary on the Declaration, Asbjørn Eide thus considers that the addition of the term 'national minorities' by the Declaration 'does not extend the overall scope of application beyond the groups already covered by article 27'.[48]

[43] Declaration on the Rights of Persons Belonging to National or Ethnic, Religious, and Linguistic Minorities (adopted of 18 December 1992) UNGA Res. 47/135 (Minority Rights Declaration) art. 1.

[44] Minority Rights Declaration (n 43) art. 3.

[45] Patrick Thornberry, *International Law and the Rights of Minorities* (Oxford: Clarendon Press; New York: Oxford University Press, 1991) p. 3; Sub-Commission on Prevention of Discrimination and Protection of Minorities (53rd Session), 'Commentary to the Declaration on the Rights of Persons Belonging to National or Ethnic, Religious and Linguistic Minorities, by Asbjørn Eide' (2 April 2001), E/CN.4/Sub.2/AC.5/2001/2 (Eide's commentary on the Minority Rights Declaration) paras. 10–12; Kristin Henrard, 'Minorities, International Protection' in *Max Planck Encyclopedia of Public International Law* (Heidelberg and Oxford University Press, article last updated May 2008) paras. 4–9.

[46] UNHRC, 'General Comment No. 23' (n 24) para. 5.2.

[47] Minority Rights Declaration (n 43) art. 2.1.

[48] Eide's Commentary on the Minority Rights Declaration (n 45) para. 3.

Moreover, some regional initiatives exist, such as the European Charter for Regional or Minority Languages (ECRML) and the Framework Convention for the Protection of National Minorities, a treaty adopted by the Council of Europe in 1995.[49] The latter does not provide for any definition of 'national minority' and rather grants rights to persons belonging to minorities, amongst which is included the right 'to maintain and develop their culture, and to preserve the essential elements of their identity, namely their religion, language, traditions and cultural heritage'.[50] Notwithstanding its status as a binding instrument, the monitoring of this Convention does not fall to a judicial body, but rather a political one: the Council of Ministers of the Council of Europe, with the support of an Advisory Committee.[51]

The issue of minority rights has for a long time encompassed that of indigenous peoples' rights. This in itself can be surprising since indigenous peoples are not necessarily minorities, at least from a quantitative perspective. Indigenous peoples have managed to have their status evolve in international law beyond the one granted to minorities, by emphasizing the specificity of their way of life, especially 'their strong, often spiritual relationship with the land',[52] and the 'special concerns'[53] that this may imply in terms of human rights. Their claims have finally been heard, with the adoption of the 2007 United Nations Declaration on the Rights of Indigenous Peoples.

4.1.2.2 Indigenous peoples' rights, cultural genocide and ethnocide

Siegfried Wiessner justifies indigenous peoples' special status in international law on the basis that they are 'organic groups', that is 'collectivities of human beings, commonly designated as a "nation" or a "people", who have made and maintain a conscious decision (. . .) which manifests their will to live together as a community', in contrast to '[n]on-organic groups, such as women, children, even many religious communities, [who]do not have the same interest in sharing all aspects of life'.[54]

In international law, the very concept of indigenous peoples is subject to controversy similar to that of minority. As a result, no international legal definition exists. It is commonly assumed that to be considered as such, indigenous peoples must have developed a 'historical continuity' in relation to the occupancy of their land, that is the first inhabitants of a given land. Yet, this criterion is highly disputed;[55] the

[49] European Charter for Regional or Minority Languages (adopted 5 November 1992, entered into force 1 March 1998) CETS No. 148; Framework Convention for the Protection of National Minorities (adopted 1 February 1992, entered into force 1 February 1998) CETS No.: 157.

[50] Framework Convention for the Protection of National Minorities (n 49) art. 5.

[51] Ibid., Section 4.

[52] Siegfried Wiessner, 'The Cultural Rights of Indigenous Peoples: Achievements and Continuing Challenges' (2011) 22 *E.J.I.L.* 121, p. 127.

[53] Asbjørn Eide's Commentary on the Minority Rights Declaration (n 45) para. 16.

[54] Wiessner (n 52) p. 125.

[55] Benedict Kingsbury, '"Indigenous Peoples" in International Law: A Constructivist Approach to the Asian Controversy' (1998) 92 *A.J.I.L.* 414, p. 419; David Maybury-Lewis, 'Genocide against

Convention 169 on Indigenous and Tribal Peoples, adopted by the International Labour Organisation (ILO) in 1989,[56] which sets out the legal protection of indigenous peoples' rights, includes this criterion in its definition of 'indigenous peoples' at Article 1(2). Only twenty states have ratified this Convention thus far. The major outcome happened almost twenty years later with the adoption of the United Nations Declaration on the Rights of Indigenous Peoples (UNDRIP) by General Assembly Resolution 61/295 on 13 September 2007. At the time, only four countries voted against[57] and, since then, all four have reversed their position and agreed to adhere to the Declaration. It is a non-binding instrument but it can be considered that some of its provisions reflect customary international law. Again, the Declaration contains no definition of 'indigenous people'. The cultural dimension of indigenous rights is transcendent to the declaration and is 'reflected in at least 17 of the 46 articles of the Declaration'.[58]

Earlier drafts of the Declaration even envisioned protection from ethnocide and cultural genocide in draft Article 7:

Indigenous peoples have the collective and individual right not to be subjected to *ethnocide and cultural genocide*, including prevention of and redress for:
(a) Any action which has the aim or effect of depriving them of their integrity as distinct peoples, or of their cultural values or ethnic identities;
(b) Any action which has the aim or effect of dispossessing them of their lands, territories or resources;
(c) Any form of population transfer which has the aim or effect of violating or undermining any of their rights;
(d) Any form of assimilation or integration by other cultures or ways of life imposed on them by legislative, administrative or other measures;
(e) Any form of propaganda directed against them.[59]

It is undeniable that the language of this draft article went far beyond the draft provisions on 'cultural genocide' discussed during the negotiations of the Genocide Convention; this is particularly clear in respect of the introduction of each listed act with the determiner 'any'. The genocide criminal paradigm had somewhat

Indigenous Peoples' in Alexander L. Hinton (ed.), *Annihilating Difference: The Anthropology of Genocide* (Berkeley, CT; London: University of California Press, 2002) p. 43.

[56] ILO Convention (No. 169) concerning Indigenous and Tribal Peoples in Independent Countries (adopted 27 June 1989, entered into force 5 September 1991) 1650 UNTS 383 (ILO Convention No. 169), which completed ILO Convention (No. 107) on Indigenous and Tribal Populations (adopted 26 June 1957, entered into force 2 June 1959) 328 UNTS 247 (ILO Convention No. 107), which is now considered as 'obsolete'. See http://www.ilo.org/indigenous/Conventions/no107/lang--en/index.htm (last accessed 1 February 2015).

[57] Declaration on the Rights of Indigenous Peoples (adopted 13 September 2007) UNGA Res. 61/295 (UNDRIP). Australia, Canada, New Zealand, and the United States voted against the adoption.

[58] Stamatopoulou, 'Taking Cultural Rights Seriously' (n 31) p. 389.

[59] UNCHR, 'Report of the Sub-Commission on Prevention of Discrimination and Protection of Minorities on the Work of its Forty-Sixth Session' E/CN.4/Sub.2/1994/56 (26 August 1994) p. 107 (emphasis added).

disappeared from the conceptualization of 'ethnocide or cultural genocide' since there is no longer mention of the perpetrators' intent to destroy the group, only the word 'aim' appears at subparagraphs (a), (b), and (c) but immediately watered down by the words 'or effect'. This deletion was deliberate, as emphasized during the negotiations by '[i]ndigenous representatives [who] stated that the requirement to prove "intent" had contributed to the ineffectiveness of the Genocide Convention and that it would be unconscionable for States to knowingly introduce similar elements into the declaration'.[60]

The thin line between 'forced assimilation' and ethnocide was also completely erased at subparagraph (d) while subparagraph (e) tended to recall Article III(c) of the Genocide Convention, which criminalizes '[d]irect and public incitement to commit genocide', though with a much broader formulation.

Almost every aspect of draft Article 7 raised questions and, above all, states' opposition. Unlike the *travaux préparatoires* of the Genocide Convention, those of the UNDRIP are less precise in relation to identifying each state's position. With the exception of Chile, few states seem to have supported the initial language of Article 7. The controversy first arose in relation to the meaning of the two terms, which was soon clarified by the Special Rapporteur, Erica-Irene Daes, who 'explained that "cultural genocide" referred to the destruction of the physical aspects of a culture, while "ethnocide" referred to the elimination of an entire "ethnos" and people'.[61] Cultural genocide was thus considered to be synonymous with the destruction of tangible cultural heritage. This understanding was both more restrictive and broader than the original definition of cultural genocide, as coined by Lemkin or as discussed during the negotiations of the Genocide Convention: more restrictive since it excluded intangible cultural heritage from the scope of the concept; broader since the qualification as cultural genocide was not limited to a wider process of genocide. As for ethnocide, the Special Rapporteur referred to the 1981 San Jose Declaration as 'the first official recognition, in the United Nations system, of the evil and continuing danger of ethnocide' and the definition therein. This definitional explanation was nevertheless insufficient to settle the issue, as states further expressed their concern that ethnocide and cultural genocide 'were not clear concepts'.[62]

One strong argument against the inclusion of this provision in the final Declaration was the absence of recognition in customary international law, especially from 'any existing international human rights instruments', notwithstanding

[60] ECOSOC 'Report of the Working Group Established in Accordance with Commission on Human Rights Resolution 1995/32' (6 January 2003) E/CN.4/2003/92, para. 63.

[61] Sub-Commission on Prevention of Discrimination and Protection of Minorities, 'Report of the Working Group on Indigenous Populations on its Eleventh Session', E/CN.4/Sub.2/1993/29 (23 August 1993).

[62] ECOSOC 'Report of the Working Group Established in Accordance with Commission on Human Rights Resolution 1995/32' (6 December 1999) E/CN.4/2000/84, para. 64. See also ECOSOC 'Report of the Working Group Established in Accordance with Commission on Human Rights Resolution 1995/32' (10 December 1996) E/CN.4/1997/102, paras. 186, 188; E/CN.4/2003/92 (n 60) para. 54.

that 'the incidence of ethnocide or cultural genocide may fall within the scope of the International Covenant on Civil and Political Rights (art. 27)'.[63] In response, representatives of civil society 'expressed the view that the Genocide Convention was not constructed in terms of rights, but deals with prohibitions, individual responsibility and group protection'.[64] Indigenous representatives also fully assumed the idea that this provision did not reflect the state of contemporary international law but rather emphasized 'that the specific purpose of article 7 was to address and/or prevent historical and contemporary acts of ethnocide and cultural genocide'.[65] Others highlighted:

> that the individual right to life is enshrined in many international instruments, but that the collective right to life for indigenous peoples had not yet been addressed outside the Convention on the Prevention and Punishment of the Crime of Genocide. Some representatives recalled that international standards for those terms were evolving. Another said that the disappearance of languages was a form of ethnocide.[66]

In respect of the land issue, indigenous delegates emphasized that the way it was addressed in Article 7 simply reflected 'indigenous perspectives of their profound relationship with the environment'.[67] Finally, the defenders of draft Article 7 resorted to a surprising argument when they advanced the notion that 'the Rome Statute of the International Criminal Court which, in their opinion, expanded the crime of genocide beyond physical genocide to include ethnocide and cultural genocide',[68] an assertion which is far from obvious since the definition in the Rome Statute is identical to Article II of the Genocide Convention.

The drafters finally agreed on removing these two terms during the negotiations, following a proposal jointly made by Norway and New Zealand. Canada reintroduced the specific idea of 'elimination of culture'.[69] As a result of the discussions, Article 7, which became final Article 8, reads as follows:

1. Indigenous peoples and individuals have the right not to be subjected to forced assimilation or destruction of their culture.
2. States shall provide effective mechanisms for prevention of, and redress for:
   (a) Any action which has the aim or effect of depriving them of their integrity as distinct peoples, or of their cultural values or ethnic identities;
   (b) Any action which has the aim or effect of dispossessing them of their lands, territories or resources;

[63] Sub-Commission on Prevention of Discrimination and Protection of Minorities, 'Technical Review of the United Nations Draft Declaration on the Rights of Indigenous Peoples. Note by the Secretariat' UN Doc. E/CN 4/Sub 2/1994/2 (5 April 1994), para. 36.

[64] ECOSOC E/CN.4/2000/84 (n 62) para. 64.

[65] ECOSOC 'Report of the Working Group Established in Accordance with Commission on Human Rights Resolution 1995/32' (6 March 2002) E/CN.4/2002/98, para. 74.

[66] E/CN.4/2003/92 (n 60) para. 59.

[67] ECOSOC 'Report of the Working Group Established in Accordance with Commission on Human Rights Resolution 1995/32 of 3 March 1995' (4 January 1996) E/CN.4/1996/84, para. 66.

[68] E/CN.4/2002/98 (n 65) para. 75.

[69] E/CN.4/2003/92 (n 60).

(c) Any form of forced population transfer which has the aim or effect of violating or undermining any of their rights;
(d) Any form of forced assimilation or integration;
(e) Any form of propaganda designed to promote or incite racial or ethnic discrimination directed against them.

Only the first paragraph thus changed, with the clarification of subparagraph (e).

Protection from genocide is also provided by the current Article 7, which attributes special emphasis to acts of forcible transfer of children:

Indigenous peoples have the collective right to live in freedom, peace and security as distinct peoples and shall not be subjected to any act of genocide or any other act of violence, including forcibly removing children of the group to another group.

While the rejection of the cultural genocide provision could be perceived as a 'defeat' for the protection of indigenous peoples' cultures, experts, such as Elsa Stamatopoulou, rather consider that the Declaration 'has indeed covered what some were hoping to include in 1948, and has even gone beyond that'.[70] This outcome can be read as the definitive closure of the debate on cultural genocide, the process leading to which was mainly carried out by indigenous peoples, with the acknowledgement of the concept through other words, namely those of the language of human rights. Nonetheless, this important step should not cause one to overlook the fact that Article 8 is legally non-binding, as part of a Declaration. However, the International Law Association (ILA) Committee on the Rights of Indigenous Peoples has concluded in 2010 that most provisions of the UNDRIP reflected customary international law, especially the key provisions related to 'self-determination, autonomy or self-government, cultural rights and identity, land rights as well as reparation, redress and remedies'.[71] The Committee underlined that while the customary nature of the UNDRIP should be assessed on a provision-by-provision basis, and hence a study of the relevant state practice and *opinio juris* for each right stated in the UNDRIP:

it would be inappropriate to deal with these areas separately, for the reason that—in light of the holistic vision of life of indigenous peoples—the rights just listed are all strictly interrelated with each other as building blocks of the unique Circle of Life representing the heart of indigenous peoples' identity'.[72]

Indeed, most provisions of the UNDRIP reflect rights contained in international instruments, such as the two 1966 Covenants and the ILO Convention No. 169, which have been the subject of an evolutionary interpretation in the context of

[70] Stamatopoulou, 'Taking Cultural Rights Seriously' (n 31) p. 393; See Permanent Forum on Indigenous Issues, 'Study on International Criminal Law and the Judicial Defence of Indigenous Peoples' Rights (submitted by the Special Rapporteur Bartlomé Clavero)' (8 February 2011) UN Doc. E/C.19/2011/4, para. 28.

[71] Committee on Rights of Indigenous Peoples, 'Rights of Indigenous Peoples, Interim Report' in International Law Association Report of the Seventy-Third Conference (The Hague 2010) (International Law Association, London 2010) p. 43.

[72] Ibid.

human rights treaty bodies and human rights courts.[73] In respect of the specific nature of Article 8 UNDRIP, the working group pointed out that '[t]he prohibition of indigenous peoples' forced assimilation and destruction of their culture falls within the scope of a number of provisions included in international human rights treaties': Article 27 ICCPR, Article 1.1 CERD, and Article 15 ICESCR.[74] At the domestic level, increasingly indigenous peoples' rights have been included in legislative and constitutional frameworks.[75] In addition to the wide ratifications of the aforementioned international instruments, it is noteworthy that the Declaration has gradually become universal, with the rallying of the four opposing states, which clearly displays the existence of an *opinio juris*.[76]

On the basis of these numerous convergences between state practice and *opinio juris*, the working group deemed that the following rights were amongst the provisions that could be ranked as norms of customary international law:

> indigenous peoples have the right to recognition and preservation of their cultural identity. This includes not only the right to not be subject to genocide (which amounts to a rule of *jus cogens*), but also the right to be free from ethnocide. The latter right presupposes that all the prerogatives that are essential to preserve the cultural identity of indigenous peoples *according to their own perspective* must be preserved, including, *e.g.*, the right to use ancestral lands and natural resources according to their own tradition, the right to profess and manifest their religion in community with the other members of the group, the right to pursue their traditional medicines and burial traditions, etc.;[77]

While this statement only reflects the ILA's opinion, further study of the field of international human rights law, and especially of judicial practice, tends to confirm the emergence of human rights counterparts to the concept of cultural genocide, especially in respect of indigenous peoples' rights.

4.1.3 The emergence of human rights counterparts to cultural genocide

The protection of cultural rights in general, and especially Article 27 ICCPR, can be said to cover the material element of cultural genocide. The negative formulation, which is the source of concerns in relation to the level of protection, is not an issue *per se* since this formulation actually encompasses the 'blatant denial' of such rights and is understood as preventing 'forced assimilation (. . .) and preservation of the separate identity of the minority'.[78] Cultural genocide involves the idea that groups exist beyond their individual members, and that the description of this additional feature, its culture, would impact on its very existence. Larry May, who

[73] Ibid., pp. 43–9. [74] Ibid., p. 17.

[75] Ibid., p. 50. See also Wiessner (n 52) p. 135.

[76] ILA 'Interim Report' (n 71) p. 5. See also UNDRIP (n 57). In addition to the rallying of the four opposing states, several of the eleven abstentionist states, such as Colombia and Samoa, subsequently reversed their position and endorsed the Declaration.

[77] Ibid., p. 51 (emphasis added).

[78] Yoram Dinstein, 'Collective Human Rights of Peoples and Minorities' (1976) 25 *I.C.L.Q.* 102, p. 118.

has advocated for the reintroduction of cultural genocide in the legal definition of genocide, thus defines the harm of group destruction from genocide as being two-fold: the 'harm to a group itself'[79]and the 'harm to identity and status of a group's members'.[80] These two concepts of harm echo the emerging rights to collective existence on the one hand, and to cultural identity, on the other hand.

4.1.3.1 A right to collective existence

Most legal statements about the concept of 'group existence', and the idea that a collective 'right' to existence would exist, have so far been limited to the scope of legal instruments and interpretation concerning genocide. As early as 1976, Yoram Dinstein had concluded that the Genocide Convention created a right to 'physical existence' for both peoples and minorities.[81] Almost a decade later, Leo Kuper further found that the Genocide Convention was all about the right to life, not only of individuals but also of the 'group's right to life', which would extend beyond 'physical existence'. According to him '[b]ecause the Genocide Convention deals with the group aspect of the right to life, protection of the right to life would extend automatically to genocide. But genocide is also a denial of the cultural and other contributions of human groups'.[82] Patrick Thornberry also dedicated substantial developments to the group right of existence, on the basis of the provisions of the Genocide Convention. Although he acknowledged that international criminal law was not particularly keen on the use of the language of 'rights', he considered that '[n]one the less the context of the criminal prohibition makes it clear that the reason why this particular conduct is regarded as criminal is precisely because it violates a fundamental right'.[83] More recently, Bartolomé Clavero noted in a report addressed to the UN Permanent Forum on Indigenous Issues (UNPFII):

> The Convention on the Prevention and Punishment of the Crime of Genocide does not provide international criminal protection of the rights set forth in the Universal Declaration of Human Rights except, implicitly, through another right that is collective in nature: *the right to existence and, it should be added, to the dignity of any 'national, ethnical, racial or religious group'*.[84]

The engagement of the idea of 'group existence'—or 'group survival', which is also sometimes employed to describe the same idea[85]—is far from consensual amongst

[79] Larry May, *Genocide: A normative account* (Cambridge; New York: Cambridge University Press, 2010) (n 21) pp. 61–77.

[80] Ibid., pp. 78–91.

[81] Dinstein (n 78) pp. 105, 118. A similar argument is developed by Gaetano Pentassuglia, *Minorités en Droit International* (Strasbourg: Editions du Conseil de l'Europe, 2004) p. 84.

[82] Leo Kuper, *The Prevention of Genocide* (New Haven, CT: Yale University Press, 1985) p. 8; see also Natan Lerner, *Group Rights and Discrimination* (2nd edn., The Hague; New York: M. Nijhoff, 2003) pp. 159–63 (the author dedicates a chapter to 'the right group existence: the Genocide Convention', on the basis of Kuper's writings).

[83] Thornberry (n 45) p. 58.

[84] UNPFII, 'Study on International Criminal Law and the Judicial Defence of Indigenous Peoples' Rights' (n 70) para. 2 (emphasis added).

[85] Griffin (n 35) p. 163, fn. 4: the author regrets that a 'right to group survival' is attributed to some groups.

scholars. One reason for opposing the claim is again based on the reluctance to grant collective rights. Furthermore, unlike Dinstein's earlier formulation of the right, a right to group existence would necessarily involve a non-physical dimension, so as to potentially mean a group right to the survival of its culture. For Griffin, for instance, the harm of denying group culture should rather be remedied by granting 'everyone, equal respect: every human life matters and matters equally, regardless of gender, race, or ethnic group',[86] thus drawing the discourse back to the language of anti-discrimination. Other scholars warn against the risk of essentializing cultures by assimilating 'cultural recognition' to 'cultural survival', which would go against the very idea of culture as dynamic and continuously evolving. As Dembour and Cowan point out, the connection can easily be drawn between support for 'cultural recognition' and the claim for 'cultural survival':

> In the stark distinction between mass or majoritarian cultures, on the other, internal homogeneity is too easily assumed and taken as natural. An endangered 'culture' is perceived as a pre-existing given which must be defended, rather than as something creatively reworked during struggles to actualize rights'.[87]

The conceptualization of a right to group existence thus needs to be framed in response to coercive or violent processes, which target a group culture. In his seminal piece on *Race et Histoire*, Claude Lévi-Strauss emphasized the twofold mission of international institutions in relation to dealing with cultures, to both awake humanity to the cultural richness as well as to make as painless as possible the 'resorption of those dead diversities'.[88] As already outlined in the context of the discussion of Lemkin's distinction between assimilation and cultural genocide, it is hard to draw a line between necessary or inevitable cultural adaptation on the one hand and forceful cultural mutation, on the other hand.

The idea of a right to group existence is based on certain legal documents. The first one to which reference can be made is the 1946 UNGA Resolution 96(1), discussed above, which provided that '[g]enocide is a denial of the *right of existence* of entire human groups'.[89] A few years later, in its advisory opinion on reservations to the Genocide Convention, the ICJ identified one of the objects of the convention as the need 'to safeguard the very existence of certain human groups',[90] without relating it to a human right. At the regional level, the African Charter explicitly refers to this right under the right to self-determination:

> All peoples shall have the right to existence. They shall have the unquestionable and inalienable right to self-determination. They shall freely determine their political status and shall

[86] Ibid., p. 176.

[87] Jane K. Cowan, Marie-Bénédicte Dembour, and Richard A. Wilson, 'Introduction' in Jane K. Cowan, Marie-Bénédicte Dembour, and Richard A. Wilson (eds.), *Culture and Rights: Anthropological Perspectives* (Cambridge, UK; New York, NY, USA: Cambridge University Press, 2001) p. 19.

[88] Claude Lévi-Strauss, *Race et Histoire* (first published 1967, Paris: Denoël, 2008) p. 83: '*Car la mission des institutions internationales est double; elle consiste pour une part dans une liquidation, et pour une autre part dans un éveil.*'

[89] UNGA Res. 96(1) (11 December 1948) 'The Crime of Genocide' (emphasis added).

[90] *Reservations to the Convention on the Prevention and Punishment of the Crime of Genocide*, (Advisory Opinion) [1951] ICJ Rep. 15 (*Reservations to the Genocide Convention*) p. 12.

pursue their economic and social development according to the policy they have freely chosen.[91]

The 1992 Declaration on the Rights of Persons Belonging to National or Ethnic, Religious, and Linguistic Minorities refers to the protection of such 'minorities' existence' as a state duty,[92] while the European framework convention refers in its preamble to the state parties' resolution 'to protect within their respective territories the existence of national minorities'.[93] Moreover, in its General Comment No. 23, the Human Rights Committee considered that the protection of the rights by virtue of Article 27 ICCPR 'is directed towards ensuring the *survival* and continued development of the cultural, religious and social *identity* of the minorities concerned, thus enriching the fabric of society as a whole'.[94]

The UNDRIP is noteworthy in respect of its explicit link between genocide and indigenous peoples' rights, as enshrined in Article 7, which 'constitutes an exception to common practice'.[95] Looking more closely at the provision, the collective character of the rights associated with the prohibition of genocide is not so obvious. Article 7(1) limits the right to life to 'indigenous individuals'. Article 7(2) contemplates a more collective approach in relation to genocide, without recognizing a collective right to life in absolute terms but rather a 'collective right to live in freedom, peace and security as distinct peoples'. The Declaration also addresses the issue of 'group survival', but it seems to endure the same fate as the concept of group existence. For instance, Article 43 of the 2007 UNDRIP states that: '[t]he rights recognized herein constitute the minimum standards for the survival, dignity and well-being of the indigenous peoples of the world' but 'survival' is not considered as a right as such. Consequently, in the Declaration, the right to collective existence, if any, is conceptualized in relative terms, that is through the realization of other rights, rather than in absolute terms.

While not formulated as an explicit right, the way in which group existence is conceived in these various provisions already gives a sense of what might be deemed to constitute group foundations, since 'group existence' is often associated with the recognition of the importance of culture for entire groups and their members. This has been demonstrated more clearly in the case law of the Inter-American Court of Human Rights (IACHR) in relation to the rights of indigenous peoples, in particular the right to the property of their land. On several occasions, the Court has been requested to recognize a collective right to property over the community's ancestral or traditional land. The petitioners argued that the land was essential to the group perpetuation, intergenerational transmission and even, in some cases, to the physical survival of the group since the land constituted the basis of the group subsistence. The first case of this kind was the *Awas Tingni* case, in which the Court

[91] ACHPR (n 18) art. 20(1).
[92] Minority Rights Declaration (n 43) art. 1(1).
[93] Framework Convention for the Protection of National Minorities (n 49) Preamble.
[94] UNHRC, 'General Comment No. 23' (n 24) para. 9 (emphasis added).
[95] UNPFII, 'Study on International Criminal Law and the Judicial Defence of Indigenous Peoples' Rights' (n 70) para. 24.

followed an evolutionary interpretation of Article 21 ACHR, related to the right to property. It concluded that this provision 'protects the right to property in a sense which includes, among others, the rights of members of the indigenous communities within the framework of communal property'.[96] The Court later drew conclusions as to the violation of Article 21, taken in its collective dimension,[97] on the basis of the following considerations:

Disregarding the ancestral right of the members of the indigenous communities to their territories could affect other basic rights, such as the *right to cultural identity and to the very survival* of the indigenous communities and their members.[98]

We note here the affirmation of a right to cultural identity and to the very survival of the indigenous communities, notwithstanding the lack of reference to any further legal basis.

The finding of a collective right to property prepared the ground for the establishment of an unprecedented level of group protection, which was also extended to encompass some tribal[99] and Afro-Colombian communities in Colombia.[100] It was reiterated in the case of the *Yakye Axa community*, which concerned the physical survival of the group members. The Court completed its *Awas Tingni* rationale by identifying, as a main criterion for land restitution, whether 'indigenous territorial rights encompass a broader and different concept that relates to the collective right to survival as an organized people',[101] a determination which ought to be assessed on a 'case-by-case basis'. This finding resulted from an examination of the importance of culture for indigenous peoples:

The culture of the members of the indigenous communities directly relates to a specific way of being, seeing, and acting in the world, developed on the basis of their close relationship with their traditional territories and the resources therein, not only because they are their main means of subsistence, but also because they are part of their worldview, their religiosity, and therefore, of their cultural identity. [102]

The court therefore elevated culture to the rank of fundamental feature of indigenous peoples, on the basis of which it more explicitly founded its existence, as well

[96] *Mayagma (Sumo) Awas Tingni Community*, Judgment on Merits, Reparations, and Costs, Inter-American Court of Human Rights Series C No. 79 (31 August 2001) para. 148.

[97] Ibid., para. 149. [98] Ibid., para. 143 (emphasis added).

[99] *Moiwana Community v. Suriname*, Merits, Reparations, and Costs, Inter-American Court of Human Rights Series C No. 124 (15 June 2005) para. 133. Reaffirmed in *Saramaka People v. Suriname*, Preliminary Objections, Merits, Reparations, and Costs, Inter-American Court of Human Rights Series C No. 172 (28 November 2007) para. 82.

[100] *Caso de las comunidades afrodescendientes desplazadas de la cuenca del río cacarica (Operación Génesis) v. Colombia*, Preliminary Objections, Merits, Reparations, and Costs, Inter-American Court of Human Rights Series C No. 270 (20 November 2013) paras. 355–8. In this case, the extension of the protection to Afro-Colombian communities was based on existing Colombian legislation, which provided a special constitutional status to this ethnic group.

[101] *Yakye Axa Indigenous Community v. Paraguay*, Merits, Reparations, and Costs, Inter-American Court of Human Rights Series C No. 125 (17 June 2005) para. 146.

[102] *Mayagma (Sumo) Awas Tingni Community* (n 96) para. 135.

as the 'subsistence' of its members and, as such, is likely to impact on their 'physical existence'.

Collective existence was also sporadically grounded on the right to life, which is enshrined in Article 4 of the American Convention. The IACHR had already given this right an extensive interpretation in the *Street Children* case, whereby the judges considered that the right to life also included 'the right that [every human being] will not be prevented from having access to the conditions that guarantee a decent existence'.[103] This finding was attributed particular resonance in the *Yakye Axa* and *Sawhoyamaxa* cases.[104] In a separate opinion, Judge Garcia Ramirez went further and provided an original conception of the notion of life—without going so far as to take a stance on the related right as such—and the interrelation between the collective life of a particular community and the individual lives of its members. According to him, 'the collective life becomes part of the individual life, and the latter acquires meaning and worth in the framework of the collective existence'.[105]

The African Commission on Human and Peoples' Rights (AComHPR) has adopted a similar approach to that of the IACHR, by consecrating the collective dimension of the right to property. It even went further by recognizing the collective dimension of the right to life, in a case involving Nigeria's involvement in private activities of oil exploitation on the land of the Ogoni people:

> The pollution and environmental degradation to a level humanly unacceptable has made it living in the Ogoni land a nightmare. The survival of the Ogonis depended on their land and farms that were destroyed by the direct involvement of the Government. These and similar brutalities not only persecuted individuals in Ogoniland but also the whole of the Ogoni Community as a whole. They affected the life of the Ogoni Society as a whole.[106]

In the *Endorois* case, it noted in relation to Article 22, on the right to development, 'that the inadequacy of the consultations left the Endorois feeling disenfranchised from a process of utmost importance to their life as a people'.[107] This case involved the forcible 'displacement of the Endorois community, an indigenous community, from their ancestral lands', which the complainants argued 'ha[d] jeopardized the community's pastoral enterprise and imperilled its cultural integrity'.[108]

In the case of indigenous and tribal peoples, we thus clearly see the interdependence between the cultural and physical dimensions of life, where attacks against a group culture can directly threaten the ability of the group to physically survive.

[103] *Villagrán Morales et al. v. Guatemala* Case ('*Street Children*' *case*) Judgment on Merits, Inter-American Court of Human Rights, Series C No. 63 (19 November 1999) para. 144.

[104] *Yakye Axa Indigenous Community* (n 101) para. 176; *Sawhoyamaxa Indigenous Community v. Paraguay*, Merits, Reparations and Costs, Inter-American Court of Human Rights Series C No. 146 (29 March 2006) para. 166.

[105] *Plan de Sánchez Massacre v. Guatemala*, Reparations, Inter-American Court of Human Rights Series C No. 116 (19 November 2004) Separate Opinion of Judge García-Ramírez, para. 5.

[106] *The Social and Economic Rights Action Center and the Center for Economic and Social Rights v. Nigeria*, Comm. No. 155/96, ACom.HPR (2001) para. 67.

[107] *Centre for Minority Rights Development (Kenya) and Minority Rights Group International on behalf of Endorois Welfare Council v. Kenya* Comm. No. 276/03, ACom.HPR (2009) para. 297.

[108] Ibid., paras. 1, 2, 17, 19.

4.1.3.2 A right to cultural identity

The notion of 'cultural genocide' is often associated with the notion of 'group identity'.[109] It is even sometimes used as a synonym of the concept, in opposition to 'crude threats to the physical existence of groups'.[110] The notion of 'identity' is subject to a certain form of tension: on the one hand, it has the tendency of being constructed and exacerbated, as illustrated by the ethnic conflicts of the 1990s; on the other hand, it also reflects the importance of the relationship between an individual and his or her cultural environment, on the other.

The pessimistic dimension of group identity has thus been underlined by a number of scholars and writers,[111] especially in relation to ethnic identity, or 'ethnicity'. Authors like David Wippman or Rogers Brubaker have denounced the tendency to address ethnicity as a given and objective group feature, against the background of its constructed character.[112] The concept has also been criticized for its potential to be manipulated by unscrupulous elites.[113]

In contrast to this pessimistic dimension, Ben Boer and Stefan Gruber have emphasized that:

> Without their cultural identity recognized, kept intact and mutually respected, culturally and/or ethnically distinct groups generally cannot easily survive as constituent parts of diverse human communities. It can even be argued that the survival of a nation is dependent on the conservation of its culture.[114]

International law has started to recognize the positive dimension of group identity in instruments such as the International Declaration on the Rights of Persons Belonging to Minorities[115] or the UNDRIP.[116] In its interpretation of Article 27 ICCPR, the UN Human Rights Committee has even considered that 'positive

[109] ILC (48th Session), 'Draft Code of Crimes against the Peace and Security of Mankind with Commentaries', *Yearbook of the International Law Commission,* 1996, vol. II, Part Two (ILC 1996 Draft Code of Crimes) Commentary on art. 17, para. 12.

[110] Patrick Thornberry (n 45) p. 141: 'The right to an identity must remain a key element in any overall system to protect minorities. While crude threats to the physical existence of groups have provided a melancholy backdrop to contemporary developments in protecting the rights of man and will continue to do so, minorities may be faced with more subtle threats. The effort to assimilate minorities into society may be as effective in eliminating a group as attacks upon the lives of members; if successful, the result is the death of a culture: the carriers of culture are spared, but they pass on a different culture to succeeding generations – not improbably, the culture of the oppressors.'

[111] See e.g. Amin Maalouf, *Les Identités Meurtrières* (Paris: Grasset, 1998).

[112] Rogers Brubaker, *Ethnicity without Groups* (Cambridge, Mass.: Harvard University Press, 2004) pp. 3, 11; David Wippman, 'Introduction: Ethnic Claims and International Law' in David Wippman (ed.), *International Law and Ethnic Conflict* (Ithaca; London: Cornell University Press, 1998) p. 4.

[113] Lorie Fisler Damrosch, 'Genocide and Ethnic Conflict' in David Wippman (ed.), *International Law and Ethnic Conflict* (Ithaca; London: Cornell University Press, 1998) p. 267; Brubaker (n 112) pp. 19–26; Donders, *Towards a Right to Cultural Identity?* (n 22) p. 8.

[114] Ben Boer and Stefan Gruber, 'Heritage Discourses and Intergenerational Justice' in Kim Rubenstein and Brad Jessup (eds.), *Environmental Discourses in International and Public Law* (Cambridge: Cambridge University Press, 2012) p. 382.

[115] See e.g. Minority Rights Declaration (n 43) art. 1; Eide's Commentary on the Minority Rights Declaration (n 45) para. 4(4).

[116] ILO Convention No. 169 (n 56) art. 2(2)(b).

measures by States may also be necessary to protect the identity of a minority and the rights of its members to enjoy and develop their culture and language and to practise their religion, in community with the other members of the group'.[117]

The mention of a 'right to identity' is nevertheless quite rare, limited to a few non-binding instruments. It was first stated in the Declaration on Race and Racial Prejudice, adopted by the United Nations Educational, Scientific, and Cultural Organisation (UNESCO), in 1978, under the following words:

> the right of all groups to their own cultural identity and the development of their distinctive cultural life within the national and international contexts, it being understood that it rests with each group to decide in complete freedom on the maintenance, and, if appropriate, the adaptation or enrichment of the values which it regards as essential to its identity.[118]

Notwithstanding, this provision has been described not 'as a substantive right but rather as a principle or policy goal'.[119] A right to cultural identity is also enshrined in Article 33(1) of the 2007 UNDRIP, which provides that '[i]ndigenous peoples have the right to determine their own identity or membership in accordance with their customs and traditions. This does not impair the right of indigenous individuals to obtain citizenship of the States in which they live'.[120] The ILA considers that a number of other provisions contained in the UNDRIP also have the aim of protecting this feature, including Articles 7 and 8.[121]

It is mainly at the level of the regional case law that the notion has been elevated to the rank of right, especially in the above-mentioned *Awas Tingni* case. The concept of 'identity' has also been referred to in cases involving unpunished genocide against either indigenous or tribal groups. For instance, in the *Plan de Sánchez* case, the judges were called on to grant justice for the Mayan victims of the genocide, which was perpetrated in Guatemala, as recognized by the Commission for Historical Clarification.[122] This case concerned the massacre of 268 inhabitants of a Mayan village that was attacked by the Guatemalan army in 1982. While the genocide qualification escaped the IACHR's material jurisdiction,[123] the judges took care to note that:

> [F]acts such as those stated, which *gravely affected the members of the Maya achí people in their identity and values* and that took place within a pattern of massacres, constitute an aggravated impact that entails international responsibility of the State, which this Court will take into account when it decides on reparations.[124]

[117] UNHRC, 'General Comment No. 23' (n 24) para. 6.2.

[118] Declaration on Race and Racial Prejudice (adopted 27 November 1978) art. 5(1).

[119] Yvonne Donders, 'A Right to Cultural Identity in UNESCO' in Francesco Francioni and Martin Scheinin (eds.), *Cultural Human Rights* (Leiden; Boston: Martinus Nijhoff Publishers, 2008) p. 331.

[120] UNDRIP (n 57) art. 33.

[121] ILA 'Interim Report' (n 71) pp. 16–20.

[122] Comisión para el Esclaracimiento Histórico (CEH), *Guatemala: Memoria del Silencio*, 1999, available at: http://www.centrodememoriahistorica.gov.co/descargas/guatemala-memoria-silencio/guatemala-memoria-del-silencio.pdf (last accessed February 2015) paras. 840–1257.

[123] *Plan de Sánchez Massacre v. Guatemala*, Merits, Inter-American Court of Human Rights Series C No. 105 (29 April 2004) para. 51.

[124] Ibid. (emphasis added).

Indeed, the cultural dimension of genocide was granted particular significance in the judgment on reparation,[125] particularly in relation to the 'cultural vacuum' caused by the impediment to 'the reproduction and transmission of their culture', which was used as a determining criterion to evaluate the compensation for non-pecuniary damage.[126]

In the same line, the *Moiwana* case also dealt with the several decade-old massacre of a tribal community in Suriname and the survivors' quest for justice. Their case involved a different cultural element as the community argued that the absence of the serious investigation of the crime and the lack of guarantees as to the safety of its members to return to their land induced a specific form of mental harm: the inability to perform the community's traditional mourning rites and therefore the impossibility to pay respect to its dead, a fundamental aspect of the Moiwana culture.[127] The court found that the harm also resulted from the 'separation of community members from their traditional lands' in the sense that 'in order for the culture to preserve its very identity and integrity, the Moiwana community members must maintain a fluid and multidimensional relationship with their ancestral lands'.[128] In line with their case law on the recognition of a collective right to property, the judges emphasized that these community members 'possess an "all-encompassing relationship" with their traditional lands, and that their concept of ownership regarding that territory is not centred on the individual, but rather on the community as a whole'.[129] The Court thus concluded as to a violation of Article 5(1) ACHR in relation to Article 1(1) ACHR—which cover the right to humane treatment and the obligation to respect rights, respectively—underlying the significant degree of 'emotional, psychological, spiritual and economic hardship' endured by the Moiwana community.[130] These two cases therefore show that the cultural dimension of genocide does not seem to be such a controversial issue from the human rights perspective.

The human rights dimension of the concept of 'identity' has more especially been the object of developments in the individual opinion of some judges. Judge Abreu Burelli thus attempted to list all of the existing international and Inter-American grounds of such a right, which, he admitted, 'is still undergoing permanent construction and (. . .) is primarily dependent on cultural rights'[131] and is 'subject to the same limitations as the other rights embodied in the American Convention'.[132] Among these legal bases, he listed the provisions of the American Declaration and the San Salvador Protocol that establish cultural rights, as well as a number of other provisions of the American Convention, such as the right to privacy (Article 12 ACHR), the freedom of conscience and religion (Article 12 ACHR), freedom of

[125] *Plan de Sánchez Massacre* (Reparations) (n 105) paras. 49(13), 49(14), 49(16), 49(18).
[126] Ibid., paras. 87(a)–(b).
[127] *Moiwana Community* (n 99) paras. 86(6)–86(8), 86(42), 100.
[128] Ibid., para. 101.
[129] Ibid., para. 133. Reaffirmed in *Saramaka People* (n 99) para. 82.
[130] *Moiwana Community* (n 99) para. 103.
[131] *Yakye Axa Indigenous Community* (n 101) Partially Dissenting Opinion of Judge Abreu-Burelli, paras. 21 et seq.
[132] Ibid., para. 35.

thought and expression (Article 13 ACHR), and the right of assembly and freedom of association (Articles 15 and 16 ACHR). It is noteworthy that all of the Inter-American norms quoted therein either reproduce or are reproduced in equivalent norms at the level of international human rights law. The Inter-American Court's finding of a right to cultural identity could thus be extended to the realm of customary international human rights, on the same legal bases as those listed by Judge Abreu Burelli, since a counterpart to all the quoted Inter-American sources can be found at the international human rights law level. Judge Cançado Trindade also addressed the issue of 'identity' in several of his opinions,[133] which he even considered to be part of the 'right to life':

> An attack against cultural identity, as is the case with the Sawhoyamaxa Community, is an attack against the right of life *lato sensu*, the right to live, with the aggravating circumstances of those who actually died. A State cannot release itself from the due diligence duty to safeguard the right to live.[134]

The way in which this opinion is formulated and the fact that it is separate and thus outside the core of the IACHR judgment shows that such a conception of the right to life is not yet part of customary international law, not even of customary regional law.

The recognition of a legal status of the notion of 'identity' is not limited to indigenous peoples and the Latin-American context. In the context of minority rights to pursue their own lifestyle, the ECtHR has found, in the *Chapman* case, that Article 8 of the Convention, which guarantees the right to respect for private and family life and home, covers the protection of minority lifestyles when it would constitute 'an integral part of [the applicant's] ethnic identity'.[135] Notwithstanding, while it considered that this right entailed positive obligations from states to facilitate its exercise, it ultimately considered that the majority interest—which it identified as the need to safeguard the environment—should prevail in this specific case.[136] While other cases have also touched upon the issue,[137] the *Chapman* judgment may constitute the closest form of recognition of a right to cultural identity at the European human rights level. The criticisms that were formulated in relation to this case illustrate well the difficulty of dealing with the concept of 'identity' from

[133] See e.g. *Mayagma (Sumo) Awas Tingni Community* (n 96) Joint Separate Opinion of Judges Cançado Trindade, Pacheco-Gómez and Abreu-Burelli, para. 4.

[134] *Sawhoyamaxa Indigenous Community* (n 104) Separate Opinion of Judge Cançado Trindade, para. 33. See also similar formulation in *Yakye Axa Indigenous Community* (n 101) Separate Dissenting Opinion of Judges Cançado- Trindade & Ventura-Robles, para. 4. Judge Cançado- Trindade eloquently restated the interminglement of both the right to life and the right to cultural identity in his dissenting opinion in the ICJ case on the *Application of the Convention on the Prevention and Punishment of the Crime of Genocide (Croatia v. Serbia)* (Judgment) [2015] ICJ Rep. 24, para. 419.

[135] *Chapman v. the United Kingdom*, App. No. 27238/95 (ECtHR, Grand Chamber) 18 January 2001, para. 73.

[136] Ibid., para. 96.

[137] For the detailed list of such cases, see European Court of Human Rights, Research Division, *Cultural Rights in the Case-Law of the European Court of Human Rights* (2011) paras. 14–19.

a legal perspective. On the one hand, the Strasbourg judges were criticized for not recognizing the violation of Ms. Chapman's rights in this specific case; on the other hand, the case was criticized for its essentialized and distorted description of the 'Gypsies' identity', by mainly focusing on the applicant's right to live in a caravan.[138]

The delineation of the scope of a potential 'right to identity' therefore remains unclear.[139] The case law of the IACHR is clearly more elaborated than that of the ECtHR in this regard, as it actually deals with cases that can be reflected upon in terms of 'cultural genocide' or 'ethnocide'. Throughout this case law, the mention of identity allows for the acknowledgement of the victims' specific harm in relation to their indigenous or ancestral culture. In this regard, the right to identity emerges as a positive or extended version of the right not to be discriminated against. This would fit into the line of argument developed by Siegfried Wiessner to distinguish indigenous peoples from other ethnic minorities. While the latter 'are primarily concerned about not being discriminated against by the ruling elites', the former 'demand to be treated differentially *ab initio*'.[140] However, the formulation of a human right to cultural identity may not bring any particular added value in comparison with more general cultural rights, as described in the first section of this chapter. Consequently, in addition to all of the above-mentioned issues related to the very concept of identity, Yvonne Donders notes that this concept is 'too broad and vague to be translated into a separate human right' so as to 'prevent such a right from being justiciable'.[141]

While its character as a substantial right is questionable, identity has become an important object of concern in international human rights law, one which is likely to be strengthened and to guide the interpretation of the existing framework of protection of cultural rights.[142] The conceptualization of 'identity' as a guiding principle of international human rights law thus echoes the concept of cultural genocide, by introducing the specificity of the harm caused by certain violations of human rights, especially concerning the collective right to property over indigenous peoples' ancestral land. As it has emerged from this section, cultural rights are necessarily exercised in relation to features, such as the land and language, which constitute cultural heritage. The latter is the object of a separate branch of international law.

138 Doris Farget, 'Defining Roma Identity in the European Court of Human Rights' (2012) 19 *I.J.M.G.R.* 291, pp. 300–4.

139 Marco Odello, 'Indigenous Peoples' Rights and Cultural Identity in the Inter-American Context' (2012) 16 *I.J.H.R.* 25, p. 41.

140 Wiessner (n 52) p. 125.

141 Donders, *Towards a Right to Cultural Identity?* (n 22) p. 337.

142 Ibid., p. 345. Yvonne Donders thus considers that identity should be developed 'as a principle for the interpretation and implementation of cultural rights'.

4.2 The Cultural Heritage Approach

International cultural heritage law has often been accused of being inspired by a rather 'Western State-centred approach',[143] that is overly focused on the protection of the narrow conception of culture. A process of 'recalibration'[144] has been slowly undertaken in the field of international cultural heritage law, in the sense that '[t]he rationale for the protection of cultural heritage is no longer its universal importance to humanity because of the advancement of the arts and sciences (though this important aim remains), rather it is more complex and relates to the significance of the heritage to peoples'.[145] In other words, the scope of the protection of cultural heritage now goes beyond the mere value of cultural items to consecrate instead their 'intrinsic importance to people and individuals, to their identity, and their enjoyment of their human rights'.[146]

4.2.1 The 'recalibration' of international cultural heritage law

Soon after the Genocide Convention, the process of codification of international humanitarian law began with the adoption of the four 1949 Geneva Conventions. Geneva Convention IV relative to the protection of civilian persons in time of war,[147] increased the protection of cultural heritage in times of armed conflict in comparison with that afforded under the 1899 and 1907 Hague Conventions.[148] The major development was achieved with the adoption of the 1954 Hague Convention for the protection of cultural heritage in the event of armed conflicts. As indicated by its title, this Convention, as well as much of international humanitarian law, only applies to the protection of tangible cultural heritage, such as religious sites, libraries, and moveable objects of artistic interest, in times of armed conflict.[149] Protection of cultural heritage is therefore not absolute since it is submitted to some

[143] Federico Lenzerini, 'Intangible Cultural Heritage: The Living Cultures of People' (2011) 22 *E.J.I.L.* 101, p. 109.

[144] Ana F. Vrdoljak, 'Cultural Heritage in Human Rights and Humanitarian Law' in Orna Ben-Naftali (ed.), *International Humanitarian Law and International Human Rights Law* (Oxford; New York: Oxford University Press, 2011) p. 281.

[145] Ibid. [146] Ibid., pp. 250–1.

[147] Geneva Convention relative to the Protection of Civilian Persons in Time of War (adopted 12 August 1949, entered into force 20 October 1950) 75 UNTS 287 (Geneva Convention IV) arts. 27 and 58. See also Protocol Additional to the Geneva Conventions of 12 August 1949, and relating to the Protection of Victims of International Armed Conflicts (adopted 8 June 1977, entered into force 7 December 1978) 1125 UNTS 3 (Protocol I) art. 53; Protocol Additional to the Geneva Conventions of 12 August 1949, and relating to the Protection of Victims of Non-International Armed Conflicts (adopted 8 June 1977, entered into force 7 December 1978) 1125 UNTS 699 (Protocol II) art. 16.

[148] Hague Convention (IV) Respecting the Laws and Customs of War on Land and Its Annex: Regulations Concerning the Laws and Customs of War on Land (adopted 18 October 1907, entered into force 26 January 1910) (Hague Convention IV) inter alia arts. 23(g), 27, 28, 46, 47, and 56.

[149] Convention on the Protection of Cultural Property in the Event of Armed Conflict (adopted 14 May 1954, entered into force 7 August 1956) 249 UNTS 215 (1954 Hague Convention) art. 1.

of the general principles of the laws of the war, such as the principle of military necessity.[150] International cultural heritage has, however, evolved and extended the protection granted to cultural heritage to contexts of peacetime while increasingly acknowledging its 'human dimension'.

4.2.1.1 The protection of cultural heritage in peacetime

The 1954 Hague Convention also provided for preventive measures to be adopted in peacetime. Its preamble echoes early formulations of genocidal harm, by stating 'that damage to cultural property belonging to any people whatsoever means damage to the cultural heritage of all mankind, since each people makes its contribution to the culture of the world'.[151] Its provisions are primarily binding on state parties to the Convention, which would be involved in an international armed conflict. 'Each party to the conflict' is bound by Article 4, related to the 'respect of cultural property', which prohibits a party to endanger the property by either targeting it directly or using it for its protection.[152] While the Convention set out a wide-range of obligations incumbent to state parties in relation to the protection of cultural heritage, it did not provide for mechanisms of enforcement until 1999, with the adoption of the Second Protocol to this Convention (hereinafter 'The Hague Framework').[153] This Protocol strengthened the obligations set out in the Convention and created, among others, a status of 'enhanced protection' for particularly outstanding pieces of cultural heritage.[154] Its fourth chapter also imposed on states a duty to criminalize attacks on cultural heritage perpetrated in times of armed conflict, on the basis of the principle of universal jurisdiction.[155]

The prohibition on destroying tangible cultural heritage in a context of armed conflict has further been elevated to the rank of a norm of customary international law, at the occasion of the partial award ruled in the dispute opposing Eritrea to Ethiopia. One of Eritrea's claims sought the recognition of Ethiopia's responsibility for the destruction of the Stela of Matara, 'an obelisk that is perhaps about 2,500 years old'.[156] Since neither of the two states were parties to the 1954 Hague Convention, the Commission grounded the finding of customary international law on Article 56 of the Hague Regulations, which aligns the status of cultural property in time of armed conflict to that of 'civil property' by providing that '[a]ll seizure of, destruction or wilful damage (. . .) is forbidden and should be made the subject of legal proceedings'.[157] As a result, the Commission found that state responsibility

[150] 1954 Hague Convention (n 149) art. 4(2).

[151] UNGA Res. 96(1) (n 89) preamble.

[152] 1954 Hague Convention (n 149) art. 19.

[153] Second Protocol to the Hague Convention of 1954 for the Protection of Cultural Property in the Event of Armed Conflict (adopted March 1999, entered into force 9 March 2004) 2253 UNTS 172 (1999 Hague Second Protocol).

[154] Ibid., arts. 10–12.

[155] Ibid., art. 16.

[156] *Central Front Eritrea's Claims 2, 4, 6, 7, 8, & 22, between the State of Eritrea and the Federal Democratic Republic of Ethiopia* (Partial Award) The Hague (28 April 2004) Eritrea Ethiopia Claims Commission, para. 107.

[157] Hague Convention IV (n 148) art. 56.

is likely to be entailed for the destruction of cultural heritage that occurred in times of international armed conflict.[158]

The peacetime lacuna was finally filled in 1972, with the adoption of the Convention on the Protection of the World Cultural and Natural Heritage (hereinafter the World Heritage Convention).[159] Article 4 thereof provides that a state has a 'duty of ensuring the identification, protection, conservation, presentation and transmission to future generations of the cultural and natural heritage'. The enforcement of this duty is exclusively a state matter, notwithstanding the establishment of a World Heritage Committee to manage the World Heritage List, as well as a specific list for cultural heritage in danger.[160] Even in this latter case, the prerogative of listing an endangered item belongs to the state on whose territory the asset is located. This Convention does not provide for sanctions in case of the violation of its provisions, not even in respect of intentional damage against a protected asset of cultural heritage. In this regard, the most powerful language is contained in the Preamble of the Convention, which considers 'that deterioration or disappearance of any item of the cultural or natural heritage constitutes a harmful impoverishment of the heritage of all the nations of the world'.[161]

Only in 2003 were attacks against tangible cultural heritage occurring in peacetime explicitly prohibited, although this was provided for in a non-binding instrument, when the General Assembly of UNESCO unanimously adopted the Declaration concerning the Intentional Destruction of Cultural Heritage. This Declaration constituted the international community's response to the destruction of the Buddhas of Bamiyan by the Taleban, in March 2001. Afghanistan was not at the time of destruction—and is still not—a party to the 1954 Hague Convention. Most of the country was then controlled by the Taleban authoritarian regime, although some groups were at the time engaged in military actions against it, such that the 2001 situation could be qualified as an internal armed conflict.[162] However, the Buddhas were not destroyed in connection with the armed conflict, but as a purely gratuitous act. They represented a Buddhist heritage but not a Buddhist group, which does no longer exist in Afghanistan; consequently, the targeted interest was difficult to identify. The Buddhas had not been listed on the World Heritage List by the Afghan government, although Article 12 of the 1972 World Heritage Convention provides that this is not an obstacle to the implementation of the other provisions of the Convention—those not related to the two lists—which tends to confirm the persistence of the state duty provided by Article 4. The Declaration thus aimed at preventing further attacks of a similar nature. It only concerns tangible

158 *Central Front Eritrea's Claims* (n 156) paras. 113–14; Francesco Francioni, 'The Human Dimension of International Cultural Heritage Law: An Introduction' (2011) 22(1) *The European Journal of International Law*, p. 12.

159 Convention concerning the Protection of the World Cultural and Natural Heritage (adopted 16 November 1972, entered into force 17 December 1975) 1037 UNTS 151 (World Heritage Convention).

160 The World Heritage Committee is set up by the World Heritage Convention (n 159) art. 8.

161 World Heritage Convention (n 159) Preamble, para. 2.

162 Francesco Francioni and Federico Lenzerini, 'The Destruction of the Buddhas of Bamiyan and International Law' (2003) 14 *E.J.I.L.* 619, p. 623.

assets of cultural heritage, in spite of its broad title pertaining to 'cultural heritage'. This can be said to make sense in light of the Afghan context surrounding its adoption, as well as the objective of the Declaration, that is to prohibit the 'intentional destruction'. It further establishes a correlation between the harm caused to a group culture and the harm consequently caused to humanity,[163] which attributes new emphasis to the responsibility of the international community as a whole.[164] More specifically, Article VI of the Declaration provides for state responsibility when the destruction results from intentional action or an omission of the state. Article VII deals with individual criminal responsibility, which should be sought and organized at the domestic level. Yet, the Declaration remains silent as to the potential legal bases to enforce either individual or state responsibility, especially when it comes to attacks perpetrated in peacetime. It only states the idea that this heritage should be of 'great importance for humanity'.

Thus far, the analysis has focused on tangible cultural heritage, which is contained in a framework that poorly reflects the human dimension of cultural heritage, whether in respect of the content of this heritage or the relationship between cultural heritage and human groups.[165] The notion of human harm associated with the destruction of cultural property is rarely present in the framework of protection of tangible cultural heritage. The only reference is to be found in Article 1 of the 1954 Hague Convention, which defines cultural property as 'movable or immovable property of great importance to the cultural heritage of every people'. As for the 1972 World Heritage Convention, the sole references to peoples are to be found in its preamble, as well as in Article 27, as national states are expected 'to strengthen appreciation and respect by their peoples of the cultural and natural heritage'. This second lacuna was more recently addressed, predominantly through the development of an international legal framework related to intangible cultural heritage.

4.2.1.2 The opening of the framework to intangible cultural heritage

The second dimension of the process of recalibration, its 'humanisation', has emerged as a response to the growing criticism that items of tangible cultural heritage constitute only one type of cultural expression, and indeed, one rather specific to the Western world.[166] This so-called 'Western ethnocentrism' has only been reversed recently, with the acknowledgement of other forms of cultural expression and their importance in international law, in the aftermath of the process of decolonization and the affirmation of new actors' roles on the international stage. This has

[163] See UNESCO Declaration concerning the Intentional Destruction of Cultural Heritage (adopted 17 October 2003) preamble.

[164] Francesco Francioni, 'Culture, Heritage and Human Rights: An Introduction' in Francesco Francioni and Martin Scheinin (eds.), *Cultural Human Rights* (Leiden: Martinus Nijhoff Publishers, 2008) p. 10.

[165] Federico Lenzerini, 'The Role of International and Mixed Criminal Courts in the Enforcement of International Norms Concerning the Protection of Cultural Heritage' in Francesco Francioni and James Gordley (eds.), *Enforcing International Cultural Heritage Law* (Oxford: Oxford University Press, 2013) p. 55.

[166] Lenzerini, 'Intangible Cultural Heritage' (n 143) p. 109.

led UNESCO to extend its focus to two new features: intangible cultural heritage on the one hand, and cultural diversity on the other.

In respect of the former, concerns relating to the safeguarding of intangible cultural heritage could already be identified in the framework of international humanitarian law, especially in relation to the rules applicable to situations of occupation. It should indeed be noted that the modalities of destruction of tangible cultural heritage in wartime are necessarily different from those of intangible cultural heritage. While the former may only require an episodic attack, potentially attributable to individual perpetrators, the latter must rather be the result of a long-term process, such as in a context of occupation, as underlined by Lemkin. The international norms of the law of occupation thus contain provisions that could be understood as protecting features of intangible cultural heritage, even if they were drafted before the international legal acknowledgement of the term. Geneva Convention IV provides within the 'provisions common to the territories of the parties to the conflict and to occupied territories' that:

> Protected persons are entitled, in all circumstances, to respect for their persons, their honour, their family rights, *their religious convictions and practices, and their manners and customs.* They shall at all times be humanely treated, and shall be protected especially against all acts of violence or threats thereof and against insults and public curiosity.[167]

This provision has been described by the International Red Cross Committee as a response to the practice of 'cultural genocide' that occurred during the Second World War.[168]

Furthermore the ICJ ruled, in its 2004 Advisory Opinion on the *Legal Consequences of the Construction of a Wall in the Occupied Palestinian Territory*, that the ICCPR and ICESCR, and hence their respective Articles 27 and 15(1), remained binding upon state parties beyond their own territory and also applied to occupied territories.[169] Outside the context of armed conflict, human rights have long constituted the only available tool to protect human groups' intangible cultural features, mostly through negative state obligations. The adoption of the 2003 Convention on the Safeguarding of Intangible Cultural Heritage, three decades after the World Heritage Convention, thus constituted a milestone in the process of the recalibration of international cultural heritage law. The former convention would necessarily be more human-oriented than the latter. Ensuring 'respect for the intangible cultural heritage of the communities, groups and individuals concerned' is thus an explicit purpose of the framework.[170] Article 2(1) defines 'intangible

[167] Geneva Convention IV (n 147) art. 27 (emphasis added). See also Hague Convention IV (n 148) art. 46.

[168] Vrdoljak, 'Cultural Heritage in Human Rights and Humanitarian Law' (n 144) p. 259, quoting 'Pictet, Geneva Convention relative to the Protection of Civilian Persons in Time of War, Commentary (1958) at 204'.

[169] *Legal Consequences of the Construction of a Wall in the Occupied Palestinian Territory* (Advisory Opinion) [2004] ICJ Rep. 136, para. 109 (ICCPR); para. 112 (ICESCR).

[170] Convention for the Safeguarding of the Intangible Cultural Heritage (adopted 17 October 2003, entered into force 20 April 2006) 1268 UNTS 1 (Intangible Cultural Heritage Convention) art. 1(b).

cultural heritage' in very broad terms, emphasizing again its human and intergenerational dimension:

> The 'intangible cultural heritage' means the practices, representations, expressions, knowledge, skills—as well as the instruments, objects, artefacts and cultural spaces associated therewith—that communities, groups and, in some cases, individuals recognize as part of their cultural heritage. This intangible cultural heritage, transmitted from generation to generation, is constantly recreated by communities and groups in response to their environment, their interaction with nature and their history, and provides them with a sense of identity and continuity, thus promoting respect for cultural diversity and human creativity.

However, as for the framework on tangible cultural heritage, each aspect of the management and protection of intangible heritage remains in the hands of states; this is true even of its inscription on the Intangible Cultural Heritage List, which is managed by the UNESCO Intergovernmental Committee for the safeguarding of intangible cultural heritage.[171]

In the same perspective, UNESCO has developed a specific branch of law dedicated to cultural diversity, the development of which culminated in the adoption of the 2001 Universal Declaration on Cultural Diversity, followed in 2005 by the adoption of the Convention on the Protection and Promotion of the Diversity of Cultural Expression. 'Cultural diversity' has become an umbrella concept, which is to say that it makes the link between all facets of the legal framework on cultural protection, in particular cultural heritage and human rights.[172] This is very obvious through the provisions of both the UNESCO Declaration and Convention. The Declaration thus defines 'cultural diversity' in Article 1 thereof, as nothing more than the 'common heritage for humankind'. This concept allows for an inter-temporal perspective by encompassing both the past—'heritage',[173] present—'human rights',[174] and future—'development'[175]—dimensions of culture. In the Convention, cultural diversity 'refers to the manifold ways in which the cultures of groups and societies find their expression. These expressions are passed on within and among groups and societies'.[176] The Convention thus reasserts the importance of culture for humanity as a whole, but on the basis of the definition of culture of groups and societies rather than on that of the determination of a few states. Yet, the legal framework on cultural diversity seems to be more programmatic than prescriptive. Most of the Convention establishes objectives and guidelines. It affords a counterweight to some effects of the globalization and

[171] Intergovernmental Committee for the Safeguarding of Intangible Cultural Heritage, set up by the Intangible Cultural Heritage Convention (n 170) art. 5.

[172] Francioni, 'Culture, Heritage and Human Rights' (n 164) p. 13.

[173] UNESCO Universal Declaration on Cultural Diversity (2 November 2001) art. 1.

[174] Ibid., arts. 4, 5; Convention on the Protection and Promotion of the Diversity of Cultural Expressions (adopted 20 October 2005, entered into force 18 March 2007) UNESCO, Records of the General Conference, 33rd Session, Paris, 3–21 October 2005, (2 vols. 2005), vol.I, at 83 art. 2(1).

[175] Declaration on Cultural Diversity (n 173) art. 2; Convention on Cultural Diversity (n 174) art. 2(5)(6).

[176] Convention on Cultural Diversity (n 174) art. 4(1).

liberalization of trade by providing some tools for a state to limit its participation in the former.[177] It nevertheless contains some relevant provisions in relation to 'cultural extinction'; Article 8 provides that:

1. (. . .) a Party may determine the existence of special situations where cultural expressions on its territory are at risk of extinction, under serious threat, or otherwise in need of urgent safeguarding;
2. (. . .) Parties may take all appropriate measures to protect and preserve cultural expressions (. . .).

This provision only provides 'rights' for state parties. Furthermore, the only apparent obligation is enshrined in Article 17, which provides for 'international cooperation in situations of serious threat to cultural expression', though not defining the scope of the word 'threat', nor the details of this obligation of cooperation.[178]

Cultural diversity may however constitute a useful guiding principle in the implementation of international law. It has induced a double shift in the way of thinking about cultures at the international legal level. Firstly, cultures, and especially cultural differences, are no longer seen in negative terms, as a danger for individuals, but rather in positive terms, as enrichment for humanity. Secondly, culture is no longer exclusively protected for its outstanding value, as determined by a limited number of actors, but also for its intrinsic human dimension and the importance it represents for individuals and communities, as well as humanity as a whole.[179] The principle of cultural diversity has even penetrated other spheres, such as international criminal law. The ICC Rome Statute states, in its preamble, that state parties are '[c]onscious that all peoples are united by common bonds, their cultures pieced together in a shared heritage, and concerned that this delicate mosaic may be shattered at any time'. However, it is one of the very few explicit references to the importance of cultural heritage, beyond tangible assets and *a fortiori* beyond contexts of armed conflict.

[177] Convention on Cultural Diversity (n 174) preambular para. 19: '*Noting* that while the processes of globalization, which have been facilitated by the rapid development of information and communication technologies, afford unprecedented conditions for enhanced interaction between cultures, they also represent a challenge for cultural diversity, namely in view of risks of imbalances between rich and poor countries.'

[178] These provisions have been interpreted as constituting a potential tool for the prevention of 'cultural genocide' but the argument again fails to specify the modalities of such tool, if it were to exist. See Germann Avocates et al., 'Implementing the UNESCO Convention of 2005 in the European Union', Study requested by the European Parliament's Committee on Culture and Education, IP/B/CULT/IC/2009_057; PE 438.587 (May 2010) p. 68.

[179] Emmanuelle Jouannet has gone so far as to consider that the consecration of the principle of cultural diversity tends to put an end to centuries of denying the recognition of customs, cultures, and traditions belonging to some peoples who have been for so long dominated and marginalized. See Emmanuelle Jouannet, 'Le Droit International de la Reconnaissance' (2012) 116 *R.G.D.I.P.* 769, p. 780: '*La consécration du principe de diversité culturelle tend en effet à mettre fin à des siècles de déni de reconnaissance des coutumes, des cultures, et des traditions de certains peuples qui ont été si longuement dominés ou marginalisés.*'

4.2.2 The partial criminalization of attacks against cultural heritage

The criminalization of attacks against cultural heritage has been an important component of the development of this branch of law, as reflected in Protocol II to the 1954 Hague Convention on the protection of cultural property in the event of armed conflicts. Almost all Statutes of international criminal tribunals criminalize unlawful attacks against cultural property under the category of war crime, with differences in formulation.[180] The ICTY has been particularly active in relation to enforcing this provision, having considered that the criminalization of attacks against tangible cultural heritage was part of customary international law.[181] It even considered, at the occasion of the conviction of several individuals for the shelling of the Croatian city of Dubrovnik, that the destruction of assets listed on the World Heritage List constituted a factor of aggravated individual responsibility.[182]

Another important development is the ICC's opening of investigations into the situation in Mali[183] and the subsequent issuance of an arrest warrant against Ahmad Al Faqi Al Mahdi, one of the religious leaders of the Ansar Dine group. This group is responsible for most crimes against cultural heritage perpetrated during the Malian internal armed conflict in 2012 and 2013.[184] In the opening of the investigation, the OPT reviewed the damage intended and caused to 'at least 9 mausoleums, 2 mosques and 2 historical monuments in the city of Timbuktu',[185] taking care to add that the latter 'was listed as a World Heritage by the UNESCO Heritage Committee'.[186] The investigation thus far has focused on the war crime of 'intentionally directing attacks against protected objects' pursuant to Article 8(2)(e)(iv) of the ICC Statute. The arrest warrant is even more striking as it focuses on the destruction of cultural heritage only, especially the nine mausoleums and the Sidi Yahia mosque. Like the ICTY, the ICC emphasizes the gravity of the crimes, which were mostly perpetrated against monuments registered on the World Heritage List while the city of Timbuktu itself had been listed as endangered

[180] See e.g. Rome Statute of the International Criminal Court (adopted 17 July 1998, entered into force on 1 July 2002) 2187 UNTS 3 (ICC Rome Statute) art. 8(a)(ix); 8(e)(ic); Statute of the International Tribunal for the Former Yugoslavia (adopted 25 May 1993) UNSC Res. 827 (ICTY Statute) art. 3; Statute of the International Criminal Tribunal for Rwanda (adopted 8 November 1994) UNSC Res. 955 (1994) (ICTR Statute) art. 3; Regulation on the Establishment of Panels with Exclusive Jurisdiction over Serious Criminal Offences in Timor-Leste (6 June 2000) UN Doc. UNTAET/REG/2000/15 (SPTL Statute) art. 6(b)(ii); Law on the Establishment of the Extraordinary Chambers, as amended (27 October 2004) NS/RKM/1004/006 (ECCC Statute) art. 6. On the differences between the statute of the ICTY and that of the ICC, see Michaela Frulli, 'The Criminalization of Offences against Cultural Heritage in Times of Armed Conflict: The Quest for Consistency' (2011) 22 *E.J.I.L.* 203, pp. 203–17.

[181] *Kordić & Čerkez Case* (Trial) IT-95-14/2 (26 February 2001) para. 206.

[182] *Jokić, Miodrag* (Trial) IT-01-42/1 (18 March 2004) paras. 46, 51, 53; *Strugar Case* (Trial) IT-01-42 (31 January 2005) paras. 232, 327.

[183] International Criminal Court, Office of the Prosecutor, 'Situation in Mali: Article 53(1) Report' (16 January 2013) para. 111.

[184] *Prosecutor v. Ahmad Al Faqi Al Mahdi* (Arrest Warrant) ICC-01/12-01/15 (28 September 2015) Pre-Trial Chamber I. The arrest warrant was only available in French at the time of writing.

[185] ICC-OTP, *Situation in Mali* (n 183) para. 111.

[186] Ibid., para. 110.

heritage in June 2012.[187] During the audience on the confirmation of charges, Al Mahdi seemed inclined to plead guilty.[188] This case will most certainly constitute a milestone in the criminalization of attacks against cultural heritage, since such ICC prosecutions epitomize the value now provided to cultural heritage in international law and the gravity of attacks against it.

Notwithstanding, none of the international criminal statutes contain explicit provision in relation to the criminalization of attacks against tangible cultural heritage occurring in peacetime. Nor do the statutes criminalize attacks against intangible cultural heritage. The 2003 Declaration concerning the Intentional Destruction of Cultural Heritage itself is very unlikely to constitute a legal basis for such prosecutions, because of its non-binding character. The question therefore arises as to whether customary international law provides for a general prohibition of intentional attacks against cultural heritage that would be reflected in the provisions of the Declaration. Prior to its adoption, Francesco Francioni and Federico Lenzerini had argued that the Taleban attacks 'constitute[d] a breach of customary international law forbidding the wanton destruction of cultural heritage'.[189] While the argument may raise little doubt in context of armed conflict—the category in which the authors classified the 2001 Afghan context—the conclusion seems less clear when it comes to attacks perpetrated in peacetime. As Roger O'Keefe, considered, '[t]he Declaration does not itself impose obligations on Member States of UNESCO. (. . .) Rather, the *travaux [préparatoires]* and the consistent references in the text to existing conventional and customary international law make it clear that the instrument is a restatement of the *droit acquis*, as well as a statement of political consensus and intent'.[190] If it is undeniable that the Declaration 'provides formal recognition of the ongoing process of internationalization of the concern for preservation and protection of cultural heritage',[191] this process is still in the making, especially for acts perpetrated in 'peacetime'.

Still, the ICTY repeatedly used the crime against humanity of persecution to prosecute acts of destruction of religious and cultural heritage perpetrated on discriminatory grounds in Bosnia and Herzegovina,[192] in addition to the above-cited finding in the *Krstić* case that such destruction could constitute evidence of the intent to commit genocide. Even though these findings were made in relation to the destruction of tangible cultural heritage in the context of armed conflict, both the categories of crimes against humanity and genocide also theoretically apply to crimes perpetrated in peacetime.

[187] *P. v. Ahmad Al Faqi Al Mahdi* (Arrest Warrant) (n 184) para. 6.

[188] *Prosecutor v. Ahmad Al Faqi Al Mahdi* (Decision on the Confirmation of Charges) ICC-01/12-01/15 (24 March 2016) Pre-Trial Chamber I, para. 28.

[189] Francioni and Lenzerini (n 162) p. 638.

[190] Roger O'Keefe, *The Protection of Cultural Property in Armed Conflict* (Cambridge: Cambridge University Press, 2006) p. 359.

[191] Francioni, 'Culture, Heritage and Human Rights' (n 164) p. 9.

[192] See e.g. *Blaškić Case* (Trial) IT-95-14 (3 March 2000) para. 235; *Kordić & Čerkez Case* (Trial) (n 181) para. 207. Further discussed in Chapter 5.

In this regard, the current criminal process in front of the Extraordinary Chambers in the Courts of Cambodia (ECCC) may contribute to filling the gap and help framing the criminal status of intentional attacks perpetrated against cultural heritage in peacetime. The Statute of the ECCC thus constitutes one notable exception as it explicitly criminalizes attacks perpetrated against cultural and religious institutions, although on the basis of a domestic provision, which was contained in the 1954 Criminal Code. As a hybrid international criminal tribunal, the ECCC indeed applies both Cambodian and customary international law applicable at the time of the perpetration of the Khmer Rouge's crimes, between 1975 and 1979. During this period, the Khmer regime launched an extreme and paranoid socialist revolution and 'embarked on a vast experiment in social engineering',[193] which aimed to destroy all bases of Cambodian society and the abolition of 'all ethnic, national, religious, racial, class and cultural differences'.[194] This 'cultural suicide'[195] notably involved forced transfers of the population from urban to rural areas, where people were enslaved for fieldwork and forced to adapt to communalized life. The regime intended to control all aspects of private life, including marriage.[196] Particular victims of this policy were ethnic minorities—in particular the Cham, Vietnamese, and Chinese—as well as the Buddhist monkhood and a wide-range of the Khmer population itself, including former officials of the regime, so-called 'intellectuals' and city dwellers. The death toll is estimated at two million of a population of eleven million. Other patterns of this policy involved the wide destruction of tangible cultural heritage—pagodas, other pieces of Buddhist heritage, libraries, and books in general[197]—and a wide campaign of re-education of elements perceived as subversive.

All of these acts were reviewed in the report of the Group of Experts for Cambodia, which had been appointed to investigate on Khmer crimes,[198] following which the ECCC was created. So far, four main cases have been opened; the second one, which involves four former Khmer Rouge officials, is particularly relevant. In the closing order of investigation of Case 002, the co-investigating judges dedicated particular attention to the offences against Cambodians' culture and its implications:

> Despite the appalling number of dead (. . .), a substantial majority of Cambodians survived this period, although the long-term impact on the country remains incalculable because the educated and skilled were especially targeted and because of the psychological and physical scars left on the survivors.[199]

[193] Frank Chalk and Kurt Jonassohn, *The History and Sociology of Genocide: Analyses and Case Studies* (3rd edn., New Haven, CT; London: Yale University Press, 1990) p. 402.

[194] Group of Experts for Cambodia, 'Report of the Group of Experts for Cambodia Established Pursuant to General Assembly Resolution 52/135' (18 February 1999) para. 207.

[195] Rebecca Knuth, *Burning Books and Levelling Libraries: Extremist Violence and Cultural Destruction* (Westport, CT: Praeger, 2006) p. 122.

[196] Chalk and Jonassohn (n 193) p. 405.

[197] Knuth, *Burning Books and Levelling Libraries* (n 195) p. 127.

[198] Group of Experts for Cambodia (n 194).

[199] *Case 002* (Closing Order) No: 002/19-09-2007-ECCC-OCIJ (15 September 2010) para. 33.

They therefore mentioned on several occasions in the factual findings that many Buddhist 'pagodas and sanctuaries were destroyed, or converted for other purposes such as security centres, pig pens, dining halls, hospitals or warehouses'.[200] Such acts were indicted under the count of 'religious persecution'.[201] The indictment also addresses attacks against the Khmer people and Cham minority's cultures under the count of religious persecution:

> There was a country-wide suppression of Cham culture, traditions and language. The CPK banned the practice of Islam and forbade the Cham from praying, seized and burned Qurans, closed or destroyed mosques, and forced Cham people to eat pork. Religious leaders and learned Islamic scholars were arrested and killed. Cham women were forced to cut their hair and were prohibited from covering their heads. Cham communities were broken up and Cham people were forcibly moved throughout Cambodia and dispersed among other communities.[202]

The upcoming judgment of the ECCC on the charges of genocide against the Cham and the Vietnamese, and persecution, forced marriage and treatment of Buddhists in Case 002/2, assuming that it will ever be held,[203] is likely to contribute considerably to the determination of customary international law in relation to the criminalization of attacks against tangible cultural heritage perpetrated in peacetime, since most crimes under its jurisdiction occurred outside of any context of armed conflict.[204]

The underestimation of intangible cultural heritage and attacks against tangible assets perpetrated in peacetime in positive international criminal law, with the exception of the ECCC Case 002/2, is unsurprising from the perspective of the interconnection between international criminal law on the one hand, and human rights law and humanitarian law on the other. Consequently, considering that the former tends towards the criminalization of the two latter,[205] international criminal law might require some time to adjust to the developments that have recently occurred in the two other fields. The next chapter of the book strives to deconstruct in more depth the current international criminal categories and the

[200] Ibid., para. 555 footnotes omitted, see also inter alia paras. 210, 743, 978.

[201] Ibid., para. 1421.

[202] Ibid., para. 1420. Acts targeting the physical integrity of the Cham group members have rather been indicted under the count of genocide.

[203] Amongst the four accused, Ieng Sary died on 14 March 2013 and Ieng Thirith has been ruled mentally unfitted to stand trial. Considering the age of the two accused remaining on trial, the latter has been split into several stages. See *Case 002* (Decision on Severance of Case 002/01 following Supreme Court Chamber Decision 8 February 2013) No: 002/19-09-2007-ECCC/TC-E-284 (26 April 2013); *Case 002* (Decision on Additional Severance of Case 002 and Scope of Case 002/02) -E 301/9/1 (4 April 2014). The first stage only focused on the evacuation of Phnom Penh for which Non Chea and Khieu Samphan were convicted for crimes against humanity and sentenced to life imprisonment in *Case 002(1)* (Judgment) No: 002/19-09-2007-ECCC/TC-E-313 (7 August 2014).

[204] With the exception of the crimes perpetrated in the case of the armed conflict between Cambodia and Vietnam.

[205] Steven R. Ratner, Jason S. Abrams, and James L. Bischoff, *Accountability for Human Rights Atrocities in International Law: Beyond the Nuremberg Legacy* (3rd edn., Oxford; New York: Oxford University Press, 2009) p. 13.

way in which they have been interpreted, in order to determine whether international criminal law could be recalibrated on the model of international cultural heritage law. This would imply a greater consideration of non-tangible demonstrations of culture and the criminalization of attacks against both assets of tangible and intangible cultural heritage perpetrated in peacetime. In this regard, the legal framework related to the safeguarding of intangible cultural heritage is mainly concerned with situations unrelated to armed conflicts, which might limit the perspectives of its enforcement through international criminal law. However, its content overlaps significantly with the content of human rights, and especially the protection of individual and collective rights related to the enjoyment of one's own culture. Some further developments thus need to be dedicated to the potential enforcement of international cultural heritage law through the field of international human rights.

4.2.3 The emergence of human rights related to cultural heritage

This growing acknowledgement of the human dimension to cultural genocide necessarily calls on the human rights language. If cultural heritage is indeed so closely related to individuals and groups, does any right belong to them with regard to such cultural heritage? In its Comment on Article 15(1) ICESCR, the UN Committee on Economic, Social and Cultural Rights has articulated state parties' obligations to guarantee 'the right of everyone, individually or in association with others or within a community or group (. . .) [t]o have access to their own cultural and linguistic heritage and to that of others'[206] as well as the obligations to '[r]espect and protect cultural heritage in all its forms, in times of war and peace, and natural disasters'[207] and '[r]espect and protect cultural heritage of all groups and communities, in particular the most disadvantaged and marginalized individuals and groups, in economic development and environmental policies and programmes'.[208]

The independent expert in the field of human rights, Farida Shaheed, has reiterated and further detailed this statement in a report drafted in 2011 for the attention of the Human Rights Council.[209] The logic introduced by the recalibration of the international law on cultural heritage in a human perspective was pushed further therein.[210] From the moment such a human dimension is acknowledged, the independent expert considered that it implied 'to connect cultural heritage with its source of production'.[211] Underlining the intertwinement between cultural heritage and human dignity and identity,[212] she drew conclusions as to the existence of a 'right of access to and enjoyment of cultural heritage as part of international human rights law'[213] on the basis of the various provisions protecting cultural rights. The

206 CESCR 'General Comment 21' (n 28) para. 49(d).
207 Ibid., para. 50(a).
208 Ibid., para. 50(b).
209 Human Rights Council (17th Session) 'Report of the Independent Expert in the Field of Cultural Rights, Farida Shaheed' (21 March 2011) A/HRC/17/38.
210 Ibid., para. 6.
211 Ibid., para. 2.
212 Ibid., para. 2.
213 Ibid., para. 78.

Special Rapporteur relied on the definition of cultural heritage provided by the UN Committee on Economic, Social, and Cultural Rights in its Comment No. 21 on the right of everyone to access cultural life, to conclude:

> Therefore, to speak of cultural heritage in the context of human rights entails taking into consideration the multiple heritages through which individuals and communities express their humanity, *give meaning to their existence*, build their worldviews and represent their encounter with the external forces affecting their lives.[214]

The Special Rapporteur also noted that in spite of the lack of acknowledgement granted to 'cultural heritage' in the context of human rights, the content of cultural rights and cultural heritage have converged towards 'a deep-seated interdependence'.[215] This is particularly true in the case of intangible cultural heritage, the features of which can also be the object of specific rights, such as the linguistic rights associated with a group language, which is in itself, an asset of intangible cultural heritage. Again, the case of indigenous peoples is the most illustrative of such an inter-twinement, especially with regard to their relationship with their land. The ILO Convention No. 169 and the UNDRIP also make explicit reference to indigenous peoples' right over their cultural heritage.[216] The manifestation of the right to access cultural heritage can also be found in procedural rights, in particular the right to free and prior informed consent from groups concerned by the implementation of public projects.[217] This right is again highly relevant for indigenous peoples whose land—and the resources it may contain—is often the subject of public and private projects of exploitation.

The report offers fewer legal bases with regard to the human dimension of tangible cultural heritage, although it refers to the case law of the ICTY criminalizing attacks against tangible cultural heritage perpetrated with the intention to harm a specific group.[218] It still remains to be seen to what extent the findings of international criminal law can fuel the idea of a 'right to cultural heritage', the scope of the two categories of international law being different. It is nonetheless interesting to note that progress has been made in this sense in the former Yugoslavian context of post-conflict justice. In addition to the mechanisms of international and internationalized criminal justice, the Dayton Peace Agreement also provided for the implementation of human rights mechanisms, and in particular, the Human Rights Chamber of Bosnia and Herzegovina,[219] an international court mandated with the adjudication of human rights disputes subsequent to the entry into force of the Agreement. This Chamber was confronted with several claims of the Islamic

214 Ibid., para. 6 (emphasis added).
215 Ibid., para. 20.
216 ILO Convention No. 169 (n 56) art. 5(a); UNDRIP (n 57) arts. 11–12.
217 ILO Convention No. 169 (n 56) art. 7; UNDRIP (n 57) art. 32; CESCR 'General Comment 21' (n 28) paras. 36–7.
218 'Report of the Independent Expert in the Field of Cultural Rights' (n 209) para. 18.
219 The General Framework Agreement for Peace in Bosnia and Herzegovina, Dayton (14 December 1995) (Dayton Peace Agreement) Annex VI.

Community in relation to the various obstacles encountered in the process of reconstructing the mosques that were destroyed during the campaign of ethnic cleansing. In this context, it systematically referred to the UN Declaration on the Elimination of All Forms of Intolerance and of Discrimination Based on Religion or Belief[220] to ground the violation of Article 9 ECHR, its main legal basis according to the Dayton Peace Agreement.[221] In particular, the Chamber referred to Article 6(1)(a) of the Declaration, which includes the freedom to 'worship or assemble in connection with a religion or belief, *and to establish and maintain places for these purposes*' under 'the right to freedom of thought, conscience, religion or belief'. Moreover, in the *Endorois* case, referred to above, the AComHPR stated under Article 17 of the ACHPR that 'protecting human rights goes beyond the duty not to destroy or deliberately weaken minority groups, but requires respect for, and protection of, their religious and cultural heritage essential to their group identity, including buildings and sites such as libraries, churches, mosques, temples and synagogues'.[222] The 2004 ICJ Advisory Opinion is also noteworthy as it considered, in relation to the freedom of movement under Article 12 ICCPR, that 'account must also be taken of specific guarantees of access to the Christian, Jewish and Islamic Holy Places'.[223]

This growing interconnection between cultural heritage and human rights should not result in one overlooking the possibility that some assets of cultural heritage might nevertheless escape the human rights framework. Firstly, the recognition of human groups' interest and concern in the safeguarding of cultural heritage does not necessarily make them the owners of such heritage. Secondly, there nevertheless exists a difference of scope between international human rights law and international cultural heritage law. The former mainly relies on individual rights and mechanisms of enforcement whereas the latter rather protects a collective interest, with its enforcement mostly depending on states' goodwill. Of course, as already stated, such a tension is not new and does not limit itself to the issue of cultural genocide. This tension has even been overcome to some extent by the convergence of the two branches, especially in relation to intangible cultural heritage.[224] There may still be cases for which the human dimension of cultural heritage may not be easily identifiable, as illustrated by the destruction of the Buddhas of Bamiyan.

[220] UNGA Res. A/RES/48/128 (20 December 1993) 'Declaration on the Elimination of All Forms of Intolerance and of Discrimination Based on Religion or Belief'.

[221] *The Islamic Community in Bosnia and Herzegovina against the Republika Srpska* (Decision on Admissibility and Merits) No. CH/96/29 (11 June 1999) Human Rights Chamber (*Islamic Community, Banja Luka case*) paras. 178, 182. Further discussed in Section 7.3.1.1.

[222] *Centre for Minority Rights Development (Kenya)* (n 107) para. 241.

[223] *Legal Consequences of the Construction of a Wall in the Occupied Palestinian Territory* (n 169) para. 129.

[224] Lucas Lixinski, *Intangible Cultural Heritage in International Law* (Oxford: Oxford University Press, 2013) pp. 149–52.

4.3 The Emergence of Synergies Between Cultural Rights, Cultural Heritage, and Genocide Prevention

The indigenization of the issue of cultural genocide has entailed the creation of important synergies between international human rights law and international criminal law, as illustrated by the inclusion of the prohibition of genocide in the 2007 UNDRIP, a human rights instrument. In spite of the different scope of international human rights law and international criminal law, such synergies are inevitable since the two fields are likely to consider the same situations and acts, albeit in a different legal language. As such, cases have occurred in which international human rights courts have had to address the cultural dimension of some genocidal processes, and have had to consider the same situations, and the same acts; such occurrences are illustrated in the IACHR judgments in the *Moiwana* and *Plan de Sánchez* cases.

The development of a genocide prevention framework in the aftermath of the 1994 Rwandese genocide has also made explicit the link between culture and genocide, predominantly through a human rights perspective. As a result, fifty years after the Convention, the monitoring body of CERD has explicitly acknowledged the correlation and drafted a *Declaration on the prevention of genocide*, in which it has declared its intention 'to develop a special set of indicators related to genocide, including the cultural and historic roots of genocide and the importance of recognizing the multicultural dimension of most societies (. . .) on contemporary forms of racism, racial discrimination, xenophobia and related intolerance',[225] and '[u]rge[d] the international community to look at the need for a comprehensive understanding of the dimensions of genocide, including in the context of situations of economic globalization adversely affecting disadvantaged communities, in particular indigenous peoples'.[226] This single document displays the evolutionary approach to discrimination, which has been updated in light of both anthropological findings in relation to group existence, and contemporary social and political growing concerns about the factors of structural discrimination. The CERD also drafted 'Indicators of patterns of systematic and massive racial discrimination', as a follow-up to its Declaration.[227] While the cultural dimension is not explicitly emphasized, the indicators encompass '[p]olicies of forced removal of children belonging to ethnic minorities with the purpose of complete assimilation'[228] and

[225] CERD 'Declaration on the Prevention of Genocide' (11 March 2005), UN Doc. CERD/C/66/1, para. 3.

[226] Ibid., para. 12.

[227] CERD 'Decision on Follow Up to the Declaration on the Prevention of Genocide: Indicators of Patterns of Systematic and Massive Racial Discrimination' (14 October 2005) UN Doc. CERD/C/67/1. Other such analysis frameworks exist amongst scholars. See e.g. Gregory Stanton, 'The Eight Stages of Genocide' (1998), available at: http://www.genocidewatch.org/aboutgenocide/8stagesofgenocide.html (last accessed 1 February 2015); Barbara Harff, 'No Lessons Learned from the Holocaust? Assessing Risks of Genocide and Political Mass Murder since 1955' (2003) 97 *Am.Pol.Sc.R.* 57, pp. 61–5.

[228] CERD 'Decision on Follow Up to the Declaration on the Prevention of Genocide' (n 227) para. 6.

'[p]olicies of segregation, direct and indirect, for example separate schools and housing areas'.[229]

These indicators were indeed aimed at framing an exchange of information with the UN Special Adviser on the Prevention of Genocide (UNSAPG),[230] a position created in 2005 by the then-UNSG, Kofi Annan. In his 'five-point action plan', the latter made clear that '[w]e must protect the rights of minorities, since they are genocide's most frequent targets'.[231] This objective constituted the basis of an extended mandate for the UNSG, whose action cannot be bound 'by legalistic arguments about whether a particular atrocity meets the definition of genocide or not'.[232] The creation of this Special Adviser was concomitant with the affirmation of the 'responsibility to protect populations from genocide, war crimes, ethnic cleansing and crimes against humanity',[233] which was therefore included in its mandate. For this purpose, the work of the UN Special Adviser has consisted in, amongst other tasks, the identification of indicators and potential early-warning mechanisms. In a 2006 report, he underlined those 'violations of human rights and humanitarian law, which may become massive or serious', including, for instance:

(b) violations of civil and political right affecting a specific group (e.g. (. . .) destruction of property, looting, lack of freedom of speech, press, assembly or religion);
(c) serious or massive violations of economic, social and cultural rights (e.g. destruction of subsistence food supply, denial of water or medical attention, man-made famine, redirection of aid supplies);
(d) instances of discrimination (e.g. access to work and resources, political marginalization, restricted movement, education).[234]

These provisions highlight the crosscutting character of cultural rights, which is even more visible in the 'analysis framework' used by the office of the UNSAPG (OSAPG). This framework lists 'eight categories of factors that the OSAPG uses to determine whether there may be a risk of genocide in a given situation'.[235] The formal presentation of these indicators differs from the CERD categories, but their content is very much overlapping. A few of these 'factors' are particularly relevant with regard to the issue of cultural genocide. The first factor relates to '[i]nter-group relations, including record of discrimination and/or other human rights violations committed against a group' and encompasses inter alia '[e]xisting and past conflicts over land, power, security and expressions of group identity, such as language, religion and culture'. The sixth factor is entitled 'genocidal acts'. While one would expect to read a faithful reproduction of Article II of the Genocide Convention,

[229] Ibid., para. 7.
[230] CERD 'Declaration on the Prevention of Genocide' (n 225) para. 3.
[231] 'UN Secretary-General Kofi Annan's Action Plan to Prevent Genocide' (Press Release) SG/SM/9197 AFR/893, HR/CN/1077 (7 April 2004).
[232] Ibid.
[233] UNGA Res. 60/1 (24 October 2005) 'World Summit Outcome', paras. 138–9.
[234] UNSG Report on the Five Point Action Plan (2006) (n 9).
[235] OSAPG 'Analysis framework' available at: http://www.un.org/en/preventgenocide/adviser/pdf/osapg_analysis_framework.pdf (last accessed 1 February 2015).

supposedly the 'starting point for an analysis',[236] the analysis framework covers acts with a much stronger socio-cultural flavour, for instance the '[c]reation of circumstances that could lead to a slow death, such as lack of proper housing (. . .); [p]rograms intended to prevent procreation, (. . .) prohibition of marriage and long-term separation of men and women'. Finally, the eighth factor relates to the *mens rea* of genocide, identifying 'evidence of intent to destroy in whole or in part' one of the four potential victim groups. Among the non-exhaustive list of such evidence, we find, in a very *Krstić* line, '[t]he destruction of or attacks on cultural and religious property and symbols of the targeted group that may be designed to annihilate the historic presence of the group or groups', as well as '[o]ther practices designed to complete the exclusion of targeted group from social/political life'.

It is noteworthy that while tangible cultural heritage is an element of the intent to destroy and thus of the very crime of genocide, elements of intangible cultural heritage are rather considered at the level of group discrimination. This differentiation needs to be assessed from a practical perspective, as the destruction of tangible cultural heritage may be more immediate than that of intangible cultural heritage. From an evidentiary perspective, it may be more difficult to prove the destructive intent underlying the non-recognition of specific groups' cultural rights and manifestations than that underpinning material cultural destruction. Nevertheless, the inclusion of acts of cultural destruction at the periphery of the legal concept of genocide raises the question of their legal status, and of whether legal responses should be modulated according to the nature of the targeted heritage, that is whether it is tangible or intangible.

The emergence of a dialogue between the CERD and the UNSAPG, through the establishment of these indicators, illustrates another aspect of the UN genocide prevention framework: the cooperation between the various UN organs and bodies. Working towards a better diffusion of the information on the potentiality of upcoming mass atrocities constitutes another crucial part of the UNSAPG's mandate.[237] Such cooperation has already been translated into concrete terms, with representatives of the OSAPG joining missions organized by other UN organs to investigate alleged mass violations of human rights. This was for instance the case in the framework of a mission to Colombia, which was reported by the UNPFII in a Report on the '[s]ituation of indigenous peoples in danger of extinction in Colombia'.[238] This mission took place after the Colombian Constitutional Court warned against the potential extinction of thirty four indigenous tribes mainly due to their internal displacement, either because of the armed conflict opposing governmental forces to various rebel groups, or the uncontrolled and violent appropriation of their land and natural resources by extractive industries, all these acts occurring in a context of structural socio-economic vulnerability of these groups. Relevant parts of the judgment underlined that the risk of extinction was not only

[236] UNSG Report on the Five Point Action Plan (2006) (n 9). [237] Ibid., para. 22.

[238] Permanent Forum on Indigenous Issues (Tenth Session) 'Situation of Indigenous Peoples in Danger of Extinction in Colombia: Summary of the Report and Recommendations of the Mission by the Permanent Forum to Colombia' (11 February 2011) E/C.19/2011/3, para. 2.

physical, but also cultural.[239] A substantial part of the legal rationale is based on the harm to the special relationship between indigenous communities and their land, such as forced transfers of populations,[240] the corollary appropriation of the groups' means of subsistence[241] and the desecration of the land due to military and industrial activities. The court also emphasized other elements contributing to the 'cultural disintegration' of the group such as the enrolment of children in military and paramilitary forces,[242] the special targeting of community leaders,[243] sexual violence against indigenous women,[244] as well as the 'prevailing socio-ethnic weakening and acculturation',[245] and the general situation of poverty, which pre-existed but were exacerbated by the conflict. After having drawn conclusions on a number of violations of constitutional provisions related to fundamental rights, such as the 'collective fundamental rights to autonomy, identity and territory',[246] the court concluded as to the responsibility of the Colombian State for having both failed to 'prevent the causes of indigenous peoples' forced displacement and to support displaced indigenous peoples with the necessary differential focus'.[247] It finally imposed very detailed positive obligations on the Colombian Government, in particular the adoption of a programme to guarantee the rights of indigenous peoples affected by the displacement, as well as the implementation of existing plans of ethnic safeguarding.[248]

The numerous emphases on the ideas of 'destruction' and 'prevention' throughout the judgment render it difficult to avoid thinking of the word 'genocide' in relation to the situation endured by Indigenous communities in Colombia, although neither the term genocide, nor other criminal language was ever mentioned by the court. Yet, this judgment confirmed the possibility of group cultural destruction, which may result from either direct or indirect attacks against the group culture. In spite of the powerful denunciation of the attack against the cultural integrity of indigenous peoples in Colombia, the 2010 UNPFII report dedicated very little attention to this dimension of the human rights violations. The list of 'human rights abuses' only focuses on physical aspects, such as 'targeted killings of members of indigenous peoples', which may constitute crimes against humanity'.[249]

4.4 Concluding Remarks

This chapter draws several concluding remarks in relation to the recognition of both the conceptual and normative content of cultural genocide. Firstly, international law seems to have conceptually accepted the two meanings of cultural genocide, either as part of a process or as a process of its own. Thus, international

[239] *Auto 004/09* (16 January 2009) Constitutional Court of Colombia, para. 1 p. 4, p. 13.
[240] Ibid., para. 3 p. 11, see also p. 14. [241] Ibid., para. 2.2.9.
[242] Ibid., para. 2.2.8. [243] Ibid., para. 2.2.5. [244] Ibid., para. 2.2.10.
[245] Ibid., para. 2.4.5. [246] Ibid., p. 30.
[247] Ibid., p. 31 (translated from Spanish). [248] Ibid., pp. 31–5.
[249] UNPFII, 'Situation of Indigenous Peoples in Danger of Extinction in Colombia' (n 238) para. 94.

instruments and case law have increasingly evidenced the interconnection between attacks against a group culture and genocide against this same group, whether at the level of perpetration, as a consequence of genocide, or as a step towards genocide.[250] In the meantime, the very possibility of group destruction through the destruction of the group culture no longer seems to be challenged. This is illustrated by Article 8 UNDRIP, the IACHR case law related to the rights to identity and collective existence, and even the Colombian case law, which while relying on domestic law, has triggered international involvement in the field of genocide prevention.

Secondly, the normative content of cultural genocide seems to be covered by international law, through the articulation of several of its branches.[251] Many of the norms that explicitly refer to cultural destruction are included in non-binding instruments (inter alia the 2003 UNESCO Declaration on Intentional Destruction of Cultural Heritage and the 2007 UNDRIP). Still, the articulation of these declaratory provisions with well-anchored principles of international human rights law and international cultural heritage law—for instance, the negative formulation of Article 27 ICCPR—tends to address the minimum common denominator of cultural genocide: that of an international prohibition to intentional attacks against a group culture. The major developments in the field of 'group cultural destruction' thus occurred in the human rights field. This can partly be explained by the structure of the claim of cultural genocide itself, as 'cultural genocide' could indeed be substituted with a wide-range of other terms. For instance, in the Colombian case, the whole situation could equally have been qualified as 'cultural genocide' or 'forcible transfers of population', to quote the most prominent feature of the human rights violations in this case.

The normative evolution gives rise to the question of the consequences of the international prohibition of cultural genocide. The non-binding character of many of the pertinent instruments still raises the issue of enforcing the prohibition, *a fortiori* in a consistent and holistic manner. The field of human rights undeniably offers some responses, although it remains limited in relation to tangible cultural heritage. The latter thus lacks mechanisms of enforcement, especially in peacetime. This gap could be partially remedied by the recognition of human rights to cultural heritage, which could entail state responsibility by reintroducing cultural heritage in the sphere of human rights. In times of armed conflict, both state and individual responsibility for wanton destruction of cultural heritage are now recognized as part of international customary law. This however raises the question of the selectivity of the approach, especially in the field of international criminal law and the rationale underlying the unique concern with regard to attacks against tangible features

[250] Elazar Barkan, 'Genocide of Indigenous Peoples' in Robert Gellately and Ben Kiernan (eds.), *The Specter of Genocide: Mass Murder in Historical Perspective* (Cambridge: Cambridge University Press, 2003) p. 120.

[251] The same conclusion is reached by William A. Schabas, *Genocide in International Law: The Crime of Crimes* (2nd edn., Cambridge: Cambridge University Press, 2009) p. 214; Yvonne Donders, 'Old Cultures Never Die? Cultural Genocide in International Law' in Ineke Boerefijn et al. (eds.), *Human Rights and Conflict, Essays in Honour of Bas de Gaay Fortman* (Cambridge: Intersentia Publishing, 2012) p. 303.

perpetrated in times of armed conflict. This rationale seems to be grounded both on evidentiary and chronological issues. On the one hand, the damage to tangible cultural heritage is self-evident while the damage to intangible heritage will likely result from a longer-term process, which may call on state rather than individual responsibility. Secondly, international criminal law is highly dependent on developments that occur in other fields, especially international human rights law and international humanitarian law. The delay in addressing intangible cultural heritage may thus cause delay in criminalizing attacks against it. These various and partial connections between cultural rights and intangible heritage on the one hand and between tangible heritage and humanitarian law on the other, call for the consolidation of other connections: between cultural rights and tangible heritage on the one hand and intangible heritage and international crimes on the other.

From this seemingly normative mess, one conclusion emerges: no valid argument may support the partial criminalization of attacks against group cultures, which mostly focuses on tangible features. If no doubt subsists as to the existence of a cultural dimension to group destruction and *a fortiori* to genocide, the issue of conferring an adequate criminal status to this dimension remains pending.

5

Beyond Words

From 'Cultural Genocide' to 'Cultural Persecution'

The treatment of the cultural genocide issue through the sole lens of the crime of genocide has illustrated a series of interconnected issues, which all converge towards the same conclusion: that is, the need for an integrated approach of international law to the matter. The genocide-based approach to cultural genocide has reached very limited outcomes. While the *actus reus* of genocide clearly translates into human rights violations, the judicial practice, fostered by the International Law Commission's (ILC) prescriptions, has clustered the crime of genocide into a 'crime of crimes' category, with the result that too great a reliance on other norms is perceived as having the effect of trivializing the crime. As a result, genocide has been very much disconnected from broader international law. Even though international courts have displayed an increasing awareness of the cultural dimension of the crime, it is mainly uneasiness that emerges from the judgments that touch upon the issue. This is not surprising if one considers the reluctance of courts to implement the criminal category of genocide, even in cases involving acts of physical destruction. The factual existence of these acts has led Louise Arbour to urge '[t]he use of statutes of existing international and national courts to adjudicate economic, social and cultural violations as international crimes'.[1] Her concerns seem to have been heard, at least with regard to the issue of cultural genocide, since William Schabas concluded that '[a]ny lacunae have been filled by the new texts covering crimes against humanity and war crimes'.[2] The development of the category of crimes against humanity is especially noteworthy. Unlike the crime of genocide, no 'Convention on the prevention and punishment of crimes against humanity' exists. These crimes have been codified in every statute of international criminal tribunals, the respective provisions of which all include a more or less exhaustive list of crimes against humanity; none of them refers to cultural crimes.

[1] Louise Arbour, 'Economic and Social Justice for Societies in Transition' (2007–2008) 40 *N.Y.U.J.Int.L.Pol.* 1, pp. 15–16.

[2] William A. Schabas, 'Judicial Activism and the Crime of Genocide' in Shane Darcy and Joseph Powderly (eds.), *Judicial Creativity at the International Criminal Tribunals* (Oxford: Oxford University Press, 2010) p. 78; Permanent Forum on Indigenous Issues, 'Study on International Criminal Law and the Judicial Defence of Indigenous Peoples' Rights (submitted by the Special Rapporteur Bartlomé Clavero)' (8 February 2011) UN Doc. E/C.19/2011/4, para. 16.

Two sub-crimes against humanity could at first sight turn out to be of particular interest for addressing intentional attacks against group cultures: persecution and inhuman acts, which are both formulated in broad terms. However, the crime of inhuman acts should be discarded at the outset, since the purpose of this part is to build on existing synergies in international law, and the crime against humanity of inhuman acts has thus far never been used to address the type of cultural crimes that are relevant to our subject-matter—the closest example being the criminalization of forced marriage by the Extraordinary Chambers in the Courts of Cambodia (ECCC) and the Special Court for Sierra Leone.[3] This chapter will therefore only focus on the crime of persecution, the 'non-identical' twin of genocide at Nuremberg, which has been used to prosecute acts of destruction of tangible cultural heritage before the International Criminal Tribunal for the Former Yugoslavia (ICTY)[4] as well as acts of destruction of intangible cultural heritage in front of the ECCC. Only the case law of the ICTY will be analysed below, since no judgment has yet been rendered in Case 002/2.

This chapter will therefore seek to determine whether these ICTY's promising developments could be expanded and systemized in such a way as to legally substitute with the concept of 'cultural genocide'.[5] In other words, has the crime of persecution indeed filled one of the most persistent 'lacunae' of the legal conceptualization of the crime of genocide: the issue of cultural genocide? It should be noted at the outset that the aim of this section is not to develop a new crime, but rather to determine whether, and under which conditions, a crime of 'cultural persecution' could constitute a derivative of the crime against humanity of persecution. The adjunction of 'cultural' is rather more of a rhetorical figure to echo the concept of 'cultural genocide'. The term 'cultural persecution' is actually not new, as it has already been used to describe the 'annihilation of the German intelligentsia' during the Second World War, especially their exclusion from German social life and the

[3] *Brima, Kamara, and Kanu Case* (Trial) SCSL-04-16-T (20 June 2007); *Brima, Kamara, and Kanu Case* (Appeals) SCSL-04-16-T (22 February 2008). For a commentary, see Neha Jain, 'Forced Marriage as a Crime against Humanity: Problems of Definition and Prosecution' (2008) 6 *J.I.C.J.* 1013, pp. 1028–32.

[4] See e.g. *Blaškić Case* (Second Amended Indictment) IT-95-14 (25 April 1997) para. 6.3; *Kordić & Čerkez Case* (Amended Indictment) IT-95-14/2 (30 September 1998) para. 37(k); *Karadžić Case* (Prosecution's Marked-Up Indictment) IT-95-5/18-I (12 October 2009) para. 53; *Stakić Case* (Fourth Amended Indictment) IT-97-24 (10 April 2002) para. 54(b); *Vasiljević Case* (Amended Indictment) IT-98-32 (12 July 2001) para. 40; *Naletilić & Martinović Case* (Second Amended Indictment) IT-98-34 (28 September 2001) para. 34(c); *Brđanin Case* (Sixth Amended Indictment) IT-99-36 (9 December 2003) para. 47(b); *Krajišnik Case* (Consolidated Amended Indictment) IT-00-39 (7 March 2002) [19(k)]; *Milošević, Slobodan Case* (Amended Indictment "Bosnia and Herzegovina") IT-02-54 (22 November 2002) para. 35(j); *Prlić et al. Case* (Second Amended Indictment) IT-04-74 (11 June 2008) inter alia para. 39(c); *Šainović et al. Case* (Third amended joined indictment) IT-05-87 (21 June 2006) para. 76(d); *Mladić Case* (Fourth Amended Indictment) IT-09-92 (16 December 2011) para. 52.

[5] Parts of this chapter have previously appeared in Elisa Novic, 'From "Genocide" to "Persecution": "Cultural Genocide" and Contemporary International Criminal Law', in Andrzej Jakubowski (ed.), *Cultural Rights as Collective Rights: An International Law Perspective* (Leiden, Boston: Brill, 2016) pp. 313–35.

decision imposed on these intellectuals to choose between forced exile and extermination. The scope of this earlier concept is therefore different from the one studied in this chapter, as it focuses on one 'technique' of genocide.[6]

5.1 The Development of the Crime against Humanity of Persecution

The history of the crime of persecution is intertwined with that of the crime of genocide. It was originally used during the Nuremberg Trials to criminalize acts that would have been considered as genocide, had the crime then existed; its contemporary formulation and implementation tend to overlap with the scope of the crime of genocide.

5.1.1 Persecution as a crime against humanity

The judicial processes, which started in the 1990s, have rendered the crime against humanity of persecution a pillar of the repression of mass atrocities. This was made possible thanks to the lack of codification and the broadness of its formulation, which allowed for some form of judicial creativity.[7] This of course does not mean that the judges have completely invented a new crime and tailored it for the purposes of addressing the crimes brought under their review. However, having only the Nuremberg precedent and the successive ILC Draft Codes of Crimes against the Peace and Security of Mankind, the consolidation of the elements of the crime against humanity of persecution has indeed required some judicial innovation. The adoption of the Rome Statute changed the situation, albeit in a limited way. While this statute had either already been adopted or almost been finalized at the time when most international criminal trials took place, it could only have been used as an external source of interpretation, to the extent that it would codify customary criminal international law.[8]

The definition of the Rome Statute of the ICC nevertheless constitutes a useful basis for discussion; the definition of the crime against humanity of persecution is enshrined in Article 7, the relevant paragraphs of which read as follows:

[6] Frederic V. Grunfeld, 'Cultural Persecution: The First Step Towards Genocide' (1985) 38 *The UNESCO Courier: A Window Open on the World* 6, pp. 6–7.

[7] Jonas Nilsson, 'The Crime of Persecution in the ICTY Case-Law' in Bert Swart, Alexander Zahar, and Göran Sluiter (eds.), *The Legacy of the International Criminal Tribunal for the Former Yugoslavia*, (Oxford: Oxford University Press, 2011) p. 220.

[8] It should be noted that its formulation was partly inspired by *Tadić Case* (Trial) IT-94-1 (7 May 1997); Machteld Boot, Rodney Dixon, and Christopher K. Hall, 'Article 7—Crimes Against Humanity' in Otto Triffterer (ed.), *Commentary on The Rome Statute of the International Criminal Court: Observers' Notes, Article by Article* (2nd edn., München: Beck; Portland, OR.: Hart; Baden-Baden: Nomos, 2008) p. 256, para. 115.

1. For the purpose of this Statute, 'crime against humanity' means any of the following acts when committed as part of a widespread or systematic attack directed against any civilian population, with knowledge of the attack:
   (h) Persecution against any identifiable group or collectivity on political, racial, national, ethnic, cultural, religious, gender as defined in paragraph 3, or other grounds that are universally recognized as impermissible under international law, in connection with any act referred to in this paragraph or any crime within the jurisdiction of the Court;
2. For the purpose of paragraph 1:
   (g) 'Persecution' means the intentional and severe deprivation of fundamental rights contrary to international law by reason of the identity of the group or collectivity.

While it is noteworthy that all the statutes of international criminal tribunals criminalize persecution as a crime against humanity, there are no two identical provisions. Some variations are located at the broader level of the *chapeau* of crimes against humanity. Article 3 of the ICTY Statute thus limits the scope of the criminal provision to crimes committed in times of—international—armed conflict. Sometimes, crimes against humanity are also accompanied by a discriminatory element, which, as Christopher K. Hall noted, can lead to some absurd outcomes, 'such as requiring that political persecution must be based on political, racial or religious grounds' in the case of the ICTR.[9] Article 7(2)(a) of the Rome Statute does not contain such a requirement but its formulation is sometimes criticized for being ambiguous in this respect.[10]

Differences can also appear in the formulation of the crime of persecution itself, the list of discriminatory grounds of which may vary. If we look at ethnic and cultural grounds, which are especially relevant for the present study, we note that there is no consistency in their treatment. These grounds are found neither in the ILC Nuremberg principles[11] nor in the statutes of the ICTY, the International Criminal Tribunal for Rwanda (ICTR), or the ECCC, for instance.[12] In its three successive Draft Codes of Crimes against the Peace and Security of Mankind, the ILC has alternated between the use of

[9] Ibid., p. 218, para. 62.

[10] Yann Jurovics, 'Article 7—Crimes Contre l'Humanité' in Julian Fernandez and Xavier Pacreau (eds.), *Statut de Rome de la Cour Pénale Internationale: Commentaire Article par Article* (Paris: Pedone, 2012) p. 249.

[11] ILC (2nd Session) 'Principles of International Law Recognized in the Charter of the Nürnberg Tribunal and in the Judgment of the Tribunal, with Commentaries', *Yearbook of the International Law Commission*, 1950, vol. II: 'political, racial or religious grounds'.

[12] Statute of the International Tribunal for the Former Yugoslavia (adopted 25 May 1993) UNSC Res. 827 (ICTY Statute) art. 5(h); Statute of the International Criminal Tribunal for Rwanda (adopted 8 November 1994) UNSC Res. 955 (1994) (ICTR Statute) art. 3; Law on the Establishment of the Extraordinary Chambers, as amended (27 October 2004) NS/RKM/1004/006 (ECCC Statute) art. 5. All three provisions criminalize 'persecutions on political, racial, and religious grounds'.

'cultural'[13] and 'ethnic'[14] grounds. The drafters of the ICC Rome Statute finally adopted a comprehensive approach on the issue, criminalizing acts of persecution perpetrated 'on political, racial, national, ethnic, cultural, religious, (...) or other grounds that are universally recognized as impermissible under international law'.[15] This formulation therefore marks a shift from that of the Genocide Convention, since 'cultural' is deemed to have a broader sense than 'ethnic' or 'ethnical', somewhat less 'biological'. The latter is often understood as referring to the group traditions and cultural roots[16] while 'cultural' would have a more 'modern'[17] meaning, covering 'customs, arts, social institutions, etc. of a particular group or people'.[18] The two are, however, intrinsically connected, as reflected by the following definition of ethnicity, in the *Encyclopedia of Crimes Against Humanity and Genocide*: 'as a cultural attribute that links individual human beings, such as a common language, social rituals and routines, and a feeling of togetherness'.[19] In any event, the ground should not be confused with the nature of the human rights at stake, although violations of cultural rights may be particularly harmful when it comes to ethnic and cultural groups, since such rights undeniably constitute an essential part of their identity.

[13] ILC (6th Session) 'Draft Code of Offences against the Peace and Security of Mankind with Commentaries', *Yearbook of the International Law Commission*, 1954, vol. II (ILC 1954 Draft Code of Offences) para. 11: 'persecutions, committed against any civilian population on social, political, racial, religious or cultural grounds'; ILC (43rd Session), 'Draft Code of Crimes against the Peace and Security of Mankind with Commentaries', *Yearbook of the International Law Commission*, 1991, vol. II (ILC 1991 Draft Code of Crimes) art. 21: 'persecution on social, political, racial, religious or cultural grounds'.

[14] ILC (48th Session), 'Draft Code of Crimes against the Peace and Security of Mankind with Commentaries', *Yearbook of the International Law Commission*, 1996, vol. II, Part Two (ILC 1996 Draft Code of Crimes) art. 18(e): 'Persecution on political, racial, religious or ethnic grounds'; (f) Institutionalized discrimination on racial, ethnic, or religious grounds involving the violation of fundamental human rights and freedoms and resulting in seriously disadvantaging a part of the population. See also Agreement between the United Nations and the Government of Sierra Leone on the Establishment of a Special Court for Sierra Leone (with Statute) (adopted 16 January 2002, entered into force 12 April 2002) 2178 UNTS 137 (SCLC Statute) art. 2(h): 'Persecution on political, racial, ethnic or religious grounds'.

[15] Rome Statute of the International Criminal Court (adopted 17 July 1998, entered into force 1 July 2002) 2187 UNTS 3 (ICC Rome Statute) art. 71(h), reproduced at Regulation on the Establishment of Panels with Exclusive Jurisdiction over Serious Criminal Offences in Timor-Leste (6 June 2000) UN Doc. UNTAET/REG/2000/15 (SPTL Statute) art. 5(1)(h).

[16] Boot, Dixon, and Hall (n 8) p. 219, para. 67; Thomas Hylland Eriksen, 'Between Universalism and Relativism: A Critique of the UNESCO Concept of Culture' in Jane K. Cowan, Marie-Bénédicte Dembour, and Richard A. Wilson (eds.), *Culture and Rights: Anthropological Perspectives* (Cambridge, UK; New York, NY, USA: Cambridge University Press, 2001) p. 134.

[17] Hylland Eriksen (n 16) p. 135.

[18] Boot, Dixon, and Hall (n 8) p. 219, para. 68 (quoting the definition of the *Oxford Advanced Learner's Dictionary of Current English* (4th edn., 1989)).

[19] Siegfried Wiessner, 'Ethnic Group' in Dinah L. Shelton (ed.), *Encyclopedia of Genocide and Crimes Against Humanity*, vol. 1 (New York: Macmillan Reference USA; Thomson Gale, 2004) p. 304.

5.1.2 Persecution as quasi-genocide

5.1.2.1 The common origin of the two crimes

The idea that acts originally conceived as 'cultural genocide' could fall into the category of persecution is firstly based on a historical rationale. At Nuremberg, the crime of genocide was still in the making such that acts which could now be categorized as genocide were rather criminalized under the category of 'persecution'. Article 6(c) of the Charter of Nuremberg defined crimes against humanity as follows: 'murder, extermination, enslavement, deportation, and other inhumane acts committed against any civilian population, before or during the war; or persecutions on political, racial or religious grounds in execution of or in connection with any crime within the jurisdiction of the Tribunal (. . .)'.[20] The jurisdiction of the International Military Tribunal of Nuremberg was limited *ratione materiae* to crimes related to the War (the war nexus). In the main indictment, crimes against culture were criminalized under the category of war crimes[21] while the charges related to the crime of persecution only covered crimes perpetrated against the Jews, such as the confiscation of property, 'concentration' through deprivation of liberty, and 'extermination' from 1 September 1939 onwards.[22] The core of the judgment contained several points of convergence between crimes against Jews' culture and persecution. For instance, in the *Rosenberg* case, the Tribunal convicted the accused for crimes against peace, war crimes, and crimes against humanity, in particular for having 'organized and directed the "Einsatzstab Rosenberg," which plundered museums and libraries, confiscated art treasures and collections, and pillaged private houses'.[23] It is not clear however which of these acts fell under the category of war crimes and which under the category of persecution.[24] In the *Streicher* case, involving the director of *Der Stümer*, a newspaper conveying propaganda against the Jewish people, the conviction was more straightforward as the accused was only convicted for crimes against humanity, including the destruction of the synagogue of Nuremberg, amongst others.[25]

[20] See Charter of the International Military Tribunal (adopted 8 August 1945) 82 UNTS 280 (IMT Charter) art. 6(c).

[21] *Hermann Goering et al.*, 'Indictment' (6 October 1945) Count 3—War Crimes: (e) 'plunder of public and private property'; (g) 'wanton destruction of cities, towns, and villages and devastation not justified by military necessity'.

[22] Ibid., Count 4 (B).

[23] Judgment of 1 October 1946, in The Trial of German Major War Criminals. *Proceedings of the International Military Tribunal sitting at Nuremberg, Germany*, Part 22 (22 August 1946 to 1 October 1946) (IMT Nuremberg) 'Rosenberg', p. 496.

[24] Some authors consider the acts were convicted as 'war crimes' only; see e.g. Steven R. Ratner, Jason S. Abrams, and James L. Bischoff, *Accountability for Human Rights Atrocities in International Law: Beyond the Nuremberg Legacy* (3rd edn., Oxford; New York: Oxford University Press, 2009) p. 76. Others consider that these acts also fall in the criminal category of persecution; see e.g. Yaron Gottlieb, 'Criminalizing Destruction of Cultural Property: A Proposal for Defining New Crimes under the Rome Statute of the ICC' (2005) 23 *Penn. St. Int'l L. Rev.* 857, p. 873.

[25] IMT Nuremberg (n 23) pp. 501–2.

Control Council Law No. 10, which related to the 'punishment of persons guilty of war crimes, crimes against peace and against humanity' in the German territories under the Allies' control, transposed the same definitions of crimes as in Nuremberg, with one notable change: the renouncement of the war nexus requirement. Several convictions were also secured in relation to crimes against culture, with the Prosecutors sometimes using the term 'genocide' to describe the charged acts.[26] Particularly noteworthy is the above-mentioned *RuSHA* case, tried by the United States International Military Tribunal of Nuremberg, which dealt with, amongst other activities, the 'kidnapping of "racially valuable" alien children', for which the accused were indicted of war crimes and crimes against humanity, notably for the 'elimination and suppression of national characteristics', and convicted on both counts.[27]

Following the Nuremberg trials and the codification of the law on genocide, the category of crimes against humanity, including that of persecution, did not receive much implementation, with the exception of some cases at the domestic level.[28] Since its first reference in the Nuremberg Charter, the crime was reshuffled on various occasions by the ILC, which contemplated three successive definitions in its three successive drafts of its Draft Code of Crimes against the Peace and Security of Mankind. In the 1954 Draft Code, both crimes of genocide and persecution were included within one single criminal category: 'inhumane acts', which reproduced Article II of the Genocide Convention—though without using the word 'genocide'[29]—and the Nuremberg definition of the crime of persecution—without the requirement of a nexus with other crimes.[30] The 1991 Draft Code provided for a more categorical terminological shift as the expression of 'inhumane acts' was substituted with 'systematic or mass violation of human rights', encompassing among others 'persecution on social, political, racial, religious or cultural grounds'.[31] The 1996 Draft Code consecrated the terminology 'crimes against humanity', which had already been used in the statutes of the ad hoc ICTY and ICTR.[32]

In its commentary related to the 1991 provision, the ILC suggested that persecution could take the form of:

> a prohibition on practising certain kinds of religious worship; prolonged and systematic detention of individuals who represent a political, religious or cultural group; a

[26] *Hermann Goering et al.* (n 21): 'Genocide' is mentioned once in relation to Count 3—'War crimes, (a) murder and ill-treatment of civilian populations of or in occupied territory and on the high seas'.

[27] *Ulrich Greifelt et al. (RuSHA case)* Judgment (1949) United Nations War Crimes Commission, XIII Law Reports of Trials of War Criminals 1, United States Military Tribunal, Nuremberg, Indictment, para. 2(ii).

[28] The most notable case is the Eichmann Trial, see *Attorney-General of the Government of Israel v Adolf Eichmann* (Trial Judgment) Case 336/61, District Court of Jerusalem (15 December 1961).

[29] ILC 1954 Draft Code of Offences (n 13) art. 2, para. 9.

[30] Ibid., para. 10: 'Inhuman acts such as murder, extermination, enslavement, deportation or persecutions, committed against any civilian population on social, political, racial, religious or cultural grounds by the authorities of a State or by private individuals acting at the instigation or with the toleration of such authorities.'

[31] ILC 1991 Draft Code of Crimes (n 13) Commentary on art. 21.

[32] ICTY Statute (n 12) art. 5; ICTR Statute (n 12) art. 3.

prohibition on the use of a national language, even in private; systematic destruction of monuments or buildings representative of a particular social, religious, cultural or other group.[33]

This amounted to nothing more than the definition of 'cultural genocide', identical, but for certain wording, to that contained in the first draft of the Genocide Convention.[34] However, it disappeared from the commentary on the 1996 Draft Code. Instead, the ILC reiterated the multifaceted character of this crime of persecution, which it defined as 'the denial of the human rights and fundamental freedoms to which every individual is entitled without distinction as recognized in the Charter of the United Nations (Arts. 1 and 55) and the International Covenant on Civil and Political Rights (art. 2)'.

5.1.2.2 A similar criminal structure

This brief history of the legal evolution of the crime of persecution provides a basis on which we can draw its main characteristics. Firstly, as a crime against humanity, persecution is perpetrated in a context of systematic or massive attack against a civilian population, either in times of armed conflict or in peacetime.[35] Secondly, the material element of the crime, the *actus reus*, constitutes a serious denial of fundamental rights. Thirdly, the intentional element of the crime goes beyond the mere intention to perpetrate the *actus reus*; it requires a specific intent, or *dolus specialis*, that is there is a requirement that the acts are perpetrated on discriminatory grounds, the list of which seems to be inexhaustive.[36] The question as to whether the category of persecution is an autonomous criminal category or whether a crime's qualification as such should depend on the perpetration of other international crimes has remained opened.[37] This structure is therefore very similar to that of genocide, in particular with regard to the existence of a *dolus specialis*.[38]

There are still notable differences between the two crimes, in particular from a formal perspective. In the case of genocide, the international community has taken care to define the crime in a strict and limited manner, through definitive codification. In contrast, the crime of persecution has been defined in a much more open-ended way, leaving the task of defining its precise features to the field of customary international law. As a result, persecution is likely to encompass the same acts as genocide, as well as others; it also encompasses the same victim groups as genocide,

[33] ILC 1991 Draft Code of Crimes (n 13) Commentary on art. 21, para. 9.

[34] United Nations Economic and Social Council (ECOSOC) 'Draft Convention on the Crime of Genocide' E/447 (26 June 1947), in Hirad Abtahi and Philippa Webb, *The Genocide Convention—The Travaux Préparatoires*, 2 vols. (Leiden; Boston: Martinus Nijhoff Publishers, 2008) pp. 234–5.

[35] Art. 5 of the ICTY Statutes established a war nexus (cf. chapeau) while art. 3 of the ICTR Statute did not.

[36] Additional grounds have been added in art. 7(1)(h) of the ICC Rome Statute.

[37] Discussed more at length in Section 5.2.2.

[38] Discussed more at length in Section 5.1.2.3 on 'Escalation'.

as well as others. With regard to the acts, they are defined in terms of fundamental rights in the category of persecution while the acts are described as attacks in the law of genocide. As noted by the ILC in its 1996 Draft Code, '[t]he provision [on persecution] would apply to acts of persecution which lacked the specific intent required for the crime of genocide under article 17'.[39]

Nevertheless, it should be observed that the broad definition of the crime might raise issues in relation to the *nullum crimen sine lege* principle. In practice, the choice of qualifying a given situation as either 'persecution' or 'genocide' has proven to be a very sensitive exercise. In a number of situations, international judges have indeed favoured the crime of 'persecution' to that of genocide, while the acts could *prima facie* fall into either category. For example, the ICTY prosecutor has systematically co-criminalized criminal acts that he would otherwise qualify as genocide, under the count of persecution. The difficulty of identifying the *dolus specialis* of genocide has led judges to resort to 'persecution', which has consequently become a substitute for situations of 'quasi-genocide'. However, the standard of evidence of the intent to discriminate equates to that of the genocidal intent to destroy the group, since '[i]t is not sufficient for the accused to be aware that he is in fact acting in a way that is discriminatory; he must consciously intend to discriminate'.[40] This is therefore the material content of 'the intent to discriminate' that makes it easier to prove than the 'intent to destroy'.

Notwithstanding, international criminal tribunals have been perceived as 'struggl[ing] to identify the requirements to this crime'[41] and as failing 'to convincingly distinguish persecutions from genocide'.[42] As for the term 'ethnic cleansing', the crime of persecution has been criticized for being a 'euphemism of genocide'. The blurred lines between genocide and persecution are particularly noteworthy in the following statement of Schabas, in relation to the issue of 'genocide without murders':

> One of the most vexing issues in the interpretation and application of the Genocide Convention in recent years has been tracing the boundaries of the crime with respect to *acts of persecution* of protected groups falling short of outright physical destruction.[43]

He both implies the interconnection between the acts of persecution and the crime of genocide, as well as the possibility for the former to be constituted of acts targeting non-physical group members' features, two issues that have been addressed by the ICTY.

39 ILC 1996 Draft Code of Crimes (n 14) Commentary on art. 18(e), para. 11.

40 *Krnojelac Case* (Trial) IT-97-25 (15 March 2002) para. 435.

41 Margaret deGuzman, 'Crimes Against Humanity' in William A. Schabas and Nadia B. Bernaz (eds.), *Routledge Handbook of International Criminal Law* (Abingdon: Routledge, 2011) p. 134.

42 Caroline Fournet and Clotilde Pégorier, '"Only One Step Away from Genocide": The Crime of Persecution in International Criminal Law' (2010) 10 *Int.C.L.R.* 713, p. 738—the two authors argue that the list of potential victim groups is the only feature that allows for distinguishing genocide from persecution.

43 Schabas, 'Judicial Activism and the Crime of Genocide' (n 2) p. 74 (emphasis added).

5.1.2.3 The potential for escalation from persecution to genocide

The ICTY did not really lack the legal bases to address the wide cultural destructions, which occurred during the armed conflict. Its Statute conferred jurisdiction on the tribunal to assess grave breaches of the 1949 Geneva Conventions[44] and violations of the laws or customs of war, this latter provision making special mention of the 'seizure of, destruction or wilful damage done to institutions dedicated to religion, charity and education'.[45] These provisions would thus only concern material destruction of tangible cultural heritage, perpetrated in warfare, notwithstanding their importance for any given group, since the harm is reviewed as affecting the broad category of civilians. In line with the conclusions of the Commission of Experts,[46] several individuals were convicted on this sole ground, amongst whom were included those responsible for the shelling of the city of Dubrovnik.[47] The systematic destruction of mosques and churches on the territory of Bosnia was instead reviewed under the category of persecution. This difference in treatment between the different categories of cultural destructions was explained well by Riedlmayer, a specialist in Islamic art and architecture, who testified as an expert of Balkan cultural heritage in front of the ICJ during the *Bosnia v. Serbia* proceedings. The shelling of cities such as Dubrovnik or Sarajevo was indisputably part of the warfare, occurring 'within besieged towns'[48] while the destruction of religious cultural heritage was rather committed 'outside of the context of armed conflict' in the sense that 'these were not buildings caught in cross-fire during military action, but that the destruction happened either in the absence of any fighting or after the fighting was over'.[49]

The ICTY has thus introduced, through judicial practice, a similar connection between the crimes contained in its Statute. In this context, acts of cultural destruction have played a major role in defining the contours of the statutory crimes: from mere war crime to an element of a campaign of persecution; from persecution to evidence of the special intent to commit genocide.

The *Blaškić* and *Kordić & Čerkez* cases are illustrative of the first development. The Prosecutor had addressed the alleged acts of destruction of Muslim cultural heritage under two different counts: war crimes and crimes of persecution.[50] The Trial Chamber confirmed both crimes, first qualifying them as war crimes under

[44] ICTY Statute (n 12) art. 2(d) 'extensive destruction and appropriation of property, not justified by military necessity and carried out unlawfully and wantonly'.

[45] Ibid., art. 3(d).

[46] UNSC 'Final Report of the Commission of Experts Established Pursuant to Security Council Resolution 780 (1992)' (27 May 1994) UN Doc. S/1994/674, paras. 285–97.

[47] *Strugar Case* (Trial) IT-01-42 (31 January 2005) paras. 326–30; 461; *Jokić, Miodrag* (Trial) IT-01-42/1 (18 March 2004) paras. 66–8.

[48] Cf. A. Riedlmayer's testimony, in Public sitting in the case concerning the *Application of the Convention on the Prevention and Punishment of the Crime of Genocide (Bosnia and Herzegovina v. Serbia and Montenegro)*, 17 March 2006, Peace Palace, Verbatim Record, 2006, para. 38.

[49] Ibid., para. 51.

[50] *Blaškić Case* (Indictment) (n 4) paras. 6(3), 11; *Kordić & Čerkez Case* (Indictment) (n 4) paras. 37(k); 39(j); 57–8.

the ICTY Statute[51] and then adding that '[t]his act, when perpetrated with the requisite discriminatory intent, amounts to an attack on the very religious identity of a people'.[52] The intentional element therefore appeared as the pivotal dimension of the crime of persecution. Such escalation from war crime to crime against humanity was justified for acts, 'when perpetrated with the requisite discriminatory intent, which [amount] to an attack on the very religious identity of a people'.[53] With regard to *prima facie* discriminatory destruction of cultural heritage, the Prosecutor of the ICTY has either used a strategy of double indictment for both war crimes and crimes against humanity[54] or indicted the acts within the sole category of persecution.[55]

The same approach was also adopted in relation to the conviction of high-level officials of the Croatian Defence Council (HVO) of the self-proclaimed Croatian Republic of Herceg-Bosna for the destruction of the Mostar Bridge, which occurred during the siege of Mostar. The Trial Chamber first qualified the acts as war crimes under the count of 'extensive destruction of property' and 'wanton destruction',[56] thus rejecting the argument of military necessity, as the accused argued that the Bosnian army's use of the bridge to resupply its troops and send military equipment to the frontlines had made it a military target.[57] The judges notably grounded their rationale on the damage caused to the civilian population[58] and the outstanding cultural, historical, and symbolic value of the Bridge, especially for the Muslim population.[59] By granting the bridge a religious and ethnic dimension, beyond its mere cultural—or multicultural—value, the Trial Chamber shifted towards the language of non-discrimination. The judges thus prepared the ground for the qualification of the destruction of the bridge as part of a campaign of persecution, alongside other war crimes, such as the infliction of terror upon the besieged population, inhumane acts and the destruction of mosques. The Court concluded that:

> the HVO committed all these crimes with the intention of discriminating against the Muslims of the Municipality of Mostar and violating their basic rights to life, human dignity, freedom and property between May 1993 and April 1994, and that these crimes constitute the crime of persecution recognised by Article 5 of the Statute.[60]

In respect of the second type of escalation, from persecution to genocide, the general principle of potential escalation was clearly stated in the *Kupreškić* judgment, in

[51] Under art. 2(d) ICTY Statute in *Blaškić Case* (Trial) IT-95-14 (3 March 2000) para. 234; under art. 3(d) ICTY Statute in *Kordić & Čerkez Case* (Trial) IT-95-14/2 (26 February 2001) para. 206.

[52] *Kordić & Čerkez Case* (Trial) (n 51) para. 207.

[53] *Blaškić Case* (Trial) (n 51) para. 235; *Kordić & Čerkez Case* (Trial) (n 51) para. 207.

[54] See e.g. *Blaškić Case* (Indictment) (n 4); *Kordić & Čerkez Case* (Indictment) (n 4); *Naletilić & Martinović Case* (Indictment) (n 4); *Milošević Case* (Indictment) (n 4); *Prlić et al. Case* (Indictment) (n 4) para. 116 (deals, among other acts, with the destruction of the Mostar Bridge).

[55] *Karadžić Case* (Prosecution's Marked-Up Indictment) (n 4); *Stakić Case* (Indictment) (n 4); *Krajišnik Case* (Indictment) (n 4); *Šainović et al. Case* (Indictment) (n 4).

[56] *Prlić et al. Case* (Trial) IT-04-74 (29 May 2013) Vol. 3, para. 1545 (extensive destruction of property); ibid., paras. 1583–7 (wanton destruction).

[57] Ibid., para. 1582.

[58] Ibid., para. 1584.

[59] Ibid., para. 1585.

[60] Ibid., para. 1713.

the same line as the ILC's commentary on the 1996 Draft Code. Having outlined that 'persecution as a crime against humanity is an offence belonging to the same genus as genocide', the ICTY held that:

from the viewpoint of mens rea, genocide is an extreme and most inhumane form of persecution. To put it differently, when persecution escalates to the extreme form of wilful and deliberate acts designed to destroy a group or part of a group, it can be held that such persecution amounts to genocide.[61]

This statement can be inscribed in the continuation of earlier case law,[62] which can be traced back to Nuremberg and the Eichmann trial, as quoted in the *Tadić* trial judgment.[63] All these sources tend to confirm that persecution is a necessary component of genocide, such that the identification of persecution can be said to have a 'double function: allowing for its specific criminalization and constituting an element of presumption of the existence of a criminal policy against humanity'.[64] This crime could therefore transpire to be a potentially powerful tool for the purposes of providing the concept of genocide prevention with some legal content.

This general principle of escalation was further implied and implemented in a number of other judgments, specifically in relation to acts of cultural destruction. The *Krstić* judgment is particularly emblematic of this trend. The Trial Chamber first reviewed the count on persecution, before analysing the count on genocide. It did not devote much time to identifying the *actus reus* of the latter, as it concluded that the crime of persecution had already materialized as the 'physical and mental harm' of genocide.[65] The Trial Chamber proceeded in the same way in the *Krajišnik* case, in which it defined the *actus reus* of genocide as 'some instances of cruel or inhumane treatment',[66] thus not including the attacks against cultural heritage. Furthermore, as already discussed at length, in the *Krstić* case, one of the main difficulties was the determination of the existence of an intent to destroy the group as such, in the context of which the cultural destruction became crucial evidence. Thus, if acts of physical persecution are likely to constitute the *actus reus* of genocide, acts of socio-cultural persecution may only be taken into account at the level of the *mens rea.*

While there is an undeniable logic in this idea of escalation, its formulation is not immune from flaws. It should be noted that what is hereby described as a scale of gradation only works for crimes, the *actus reus* of which overlaps with the elements of different statutory crimes. This is, for instance, the case of crimes against cultural heritage, for which the difference in the perpetrator's *mens rea* impacts on the ultimate

[61] *Kupreškić et al. Case* (Trial) ICTY-95-16 (14 January 2000) para. 636.
[62] Fournet and Pégorier (n 42), p. 718.
[63] *Tadić Case* (Trial) (n 8) para. 699: it refers to 'the decision of the Israeli District Court in the *Attorney General of Israel v. Eichmann* ("*Eichmann* case") which held that all that the accused did "with the object of exterminating the Jewish People also amounts *ipso facto* to persecution of Jews on national, racial, religious and political grounds"'.
[64] Jurovics (n 10) p. 442.
[65] *Krstić Case* (Trial) ICTY-98-33 (2 August 2001) para. 543.
[66] *Krajišnik Case* (Trial) IT-00-39 (27 September 2006) para. 867.

criminal qualification. It is not clear whether the differentiation on the sole basis of the author's intent is enough to satisfy the criterion of the specificity of crimes, a condition of the principle of legality.[67] However, the crime of persecution allows for the acknowledgement of one particular element, which is not encompassed by the category of war crimes: that is, the intent to 'discriminate' against a group. More problematic is perhaps the interrelationship between the crime of persecution and that of genocide. Some authors thus consider that the only difference lies in the list of groups, the limitation of which in the definition of genocide leads to crimes which could satisfy the *actus reus* and *mens rea* of genocide, but which are perpetrated against victim groups that fall short of the characteristics required by the definition of genocide.[68] Notwithstanding, the issue of 'cultural destruction' may escape the criticism since it was excluded from the scope of the *actus reus* of genocide. So far, the state of conceptualization of the crime of persecution—whether it emerges from the ILC Draft Codes, and in particular its 1991 Draft Code or from its concrete use by some international tribunals—could give rise to the possibility of envisaging the reintroduction of the idea of 'cultural genocide' within its scope.

5.2 Cultural Persecution as an International Crime

At the moment, it remains to be seen whether the crime of 'persecution' could actually be the formulation of a holistic approach to crimes against culture, likely to encompass those which were formerly covered or implied by the concept of cultural genocide, including attacks against intangible cultural heritage, and more broadly, attacks against cultural rights of specific human groups. Considering that a right to cultural heritage, in particular intangible cultural heritage, derives, amongst others, from a right to take part in cultural life, can the crime of persecution be formulated in such a way as to address situations of widespread cultural destruction? In particular, two main challenges need to be addressed. First, to what extent are cultural rights 'fundamental enough' to be encompassed within the *actus reus* of persecution? Second, the autonomy of the crime of persecution is the object of divergences within international criminal law, as reflected in the Rome Statute of the ICC.

5.2.1 The 'fundamental' character of cultural rights in question

At the outset, the semantic choice of 'fundamental rights' needs to be underlined, since it diverges from the more common 'human rights' language of international law and might imply some form of restrictive understanding. Generally speaking, the expression is highlighted for its vagueness, as it is likely to be defined in three different ways, which all tend to be 'incomplete' and 'incoherent'.[69] According to

[67] Fournet and Pégorier (n 42), p. 719. [68] Ibid., pp. 737–8.

[69] Etienne Picard, 'Droits Fondamentaux' in Denys Alland and Stéphane Rials (eds.), *Dictionnaire de la Culture Juridique* (Paris: Presses Universitaires de France, 2003) p. 545.

the 'ordinary conception of fundamental rights', the epithet 'fundamental' would aim at emphasizing the importance of certain human rights, which bears the risk of excessive subjectivity and arbitrariness in the selection of such rights.[70] A second 'positivist conception' would rather define fundamental rights as rights that are constitutionally guaranteed,[71] as is the case in the European Union framework.[72] The last 'objectivist conception' considers that fundamental rights are those rights which are essential both to the legal system which bears them and to the humanity of its holders.[73] In light of these different conceptions, the question therefore arises as to whether the semantic of fundamental rights used in international criminal law implies the restriction of the catalogue of human rights to be covered by the *actus reus* of 'persecution', or whether it should rather be understood as synonymous with international human rights.

5.2.1.1 The fundamental character of cultural rights in international criminal law

The emergence of the 'fundamental rights' language is quite recent in the field of international criminal law. No mention of either fundamental rights or human rights is to be found in the early relevant documents, whether the Charter of Nuremberg or the 1954 ILC Draft Code of Crimes Against the Peace and Security of Mankind. Neither the Statutes of the two ad hoc tribunals, nor that of the hybrid tribunals, define 'persecution'. In the 1991 ILC Draft Code, the notion appears in the commentary on Article 21, related to 'systematic or mass violations of human rights', the equivalent of the current notion of 'crimes against humanity'. The ILC noted that 'the common factor in all the acts constituting crimes under this draft article was a serious violation of certain fundamental human rights', so that the expression is not limited to the crime of persecution.[74] As for the latter, the commentary states that '[persecution] relates to human rights violations other than those covered by the previous paragraphs'.[75] As already mentioned, the ILC 1996 Draft introduced, along with the crime against humanity of 'persecution',[76] a crime against humanity of 'institutionalized discrimination (. . .) involving the violation of fundamental human rights and freedoms'.[77]

There is therefore no evidence of such a formulation preceding the Rome Statute and the reference to 'severe deprivation of fundamental rights contrary to

[70] Ibid. [71] Ibid., p. 546.

[72] See the development of a corpus of fundamental rights by the Court of Justice of the European Union since Case 26/69 *Erich Stauder v. City of Ulm* [1969], ECR 419; as well as its codification in the European Union Charter of Fundamental Rights, Charter of Fundamental Rights of the EU 2000/C 364/01 (adopted 18 December 2000). Against this background, Frédéric Sudre concludes that the European notion of 'fundamental rights' ultimately overlaps with that of 'human rights', in Frédéric Sudre, *Droit Européen et International des Droits de l'Homme* (10ème ed., Paris, Presses Universitaires de France, 2011) para. 97, fn. 1.

[73] Picard (n 69) pp. 548–9.

[74] ILC 1991 Draft Code of Crimes (n 13) Commentary on art. 21, para. 2.

[75] Ibid., para. 9. [76] Ibid., art. 18(e). [77] Ibid., art. 18(f).

international law' made in Article 7(2)(g). The ICC Elements of Crimes are not particularly helpful since they only focus on Article 7(1)(h) and explain that '[t]he perpetrator severely deprived, contrary to international law, one or more persons of fundamental rights'.[78] A footnote adds that '[t]his requirement is without prejudice to paragraph 6 of the General Introduction to the Elements of Crimes'.[79] This paragraph finally provides that: '[t]he requirement of "unlawfulness" found in the Statute or in other parts of international law, in particular international humanitarian law, is generally not specified in the elements of crimes'.[80]

The origins of the 'fundamental rights' expression can actually be traced back to the first international legal decision on the crime of persecution since Nuremberg, the *Tadić* case, which itself relied on the *Barbie* case, a judgment rendered by the French courts in the 1980s. The ICTY thus quoted the conclusions of Rapporteur Le Gunehec, who wrote in relation to the crime of persecution: 'par dessus tout, ces crimes violent les *droits fondamentaux* de l'humanité'. [81] The Trial Chamber thus concluded that:

> it is evident that what is necessary is some form of discrimination that is intended to be and results in an infringement of an individual's fundamental rights. (. . .) It is the violation of the right to equality in some serious fashion that infringes on the enjoyment of a basic or fundamental right that constitutes persecution, although the discrimination must be on one of the listed grounds to constitute persecution under the Statute.[82]

Following the Barbie judgment, the *Tadić* trial judgment was the first to address the issue of defining the *actus reus* of persecution. It emphasized that 'persecution can take numerous forms, so long as the common element of discrimination in regard to the enjoyment of *a basic or fundamental* right is present, and persecution does not necessarily require a physical element'.[83] It added that:

> The notion of persecutory act provides broad coverage, including acts mentioned elsewhere in the Statute as well as acts which, although not in and of themselves inhumane, are considered inhumane because of the discriminatory grounds on which they are taken.[84]

The *Kupreškić* trial judgment built on this first judgment and stated, in relation to the *actus reus,* that 'persecution can also involve a variety of other discriminatory acts, involving attacks on political, social and economic rights'.[85] We note here that among the five categories of acts protected by the two UN Covenants, one has been omitted: cultural rights. The judgment offers further arguments, which would tend to exclude those acts from the scope of the crime of persecution. It considers that:

> restrictions placed on a particular group to curtail their rights to participate in particular aspects of social life (such as visits to public parks, theatres or libraries) constitute

[78] ICC Elements of Crimes, ICC-ASP/1/3(part II-B) (adopted and entered into force 9 September 2002) art. 7.1(h), para. 1.

[79] Ibid., art. 7.1(h), para. 1, fn. 21.

[80] Ibid., General Introduction, para. 6.

[81] *Tadić Case* (Trial) (n 8) para. 696 (French version) (emphasis added).

[82] Ibid., para. 697.

[83] Ibid., para. 707 (emphasis added).

[84] Ibid., para. 715.

[85] *Kupreškić Case* (Trial) (n 61) para. 615 (c).

discrimination, which is in itself a reprehensible act; however, they may not in and of themselves amount to persecution.[86]

Two months after the *Kupreškić* judgment, the ICTY opened the path to the systematic criminalization of attacks against religious and cultural heritage under the category of 'persecution' in the *Blaškić* judgment.[87] This is noteworthy, especially if one considers the debate which occurred a few years later in 2003 at the UNESCO level about how to address the destruction of the Buddhas of Bamiyan in Afghanistan, which confers a progressive taint to the ICTY's case law. While we find evidence of such concerns in the Nuremberg judgment, the negotiations of the Genocide Convention in relation to 'cultural genocide' and the successive ILC Draft Codes, a literal reading of various provisions on persecution does not necessarily call for the inclusion of such attacks within the *actus reus* of persecution. Although the focus on tangible cultural heritage, which is not necessarily the object of customarily recognized human rights, can seem *a priori* surprising, it has to be read in line with the judicial finding that the *actus reus* of persecution can either be constituted as a violation of another international crime contained in the ICTY statute or the violation of a fundamental right recognized in customary international law.[88] Thus, as noted by the Trial Chamber in the *Blaškić* case:

> It is the specific intent to cause injury to a human being because he belongs to a particular community or group, rather than the means employed to achieve it, that bestows on it its individual nature and gravity and which justifies its being able to constitute criminal acts *which might appear in themselves not to infringe directly upon the most elementary rights of a human being*, for example, attacks on property.[89]

The ICTY judges continued in this direction in the *Kordić & Čerkez* judgment:

> This act, when perpetrated with the requisite discriminatory intent, amounts to an attack on the very religious identity of a people. As such, it manifests a nearly pure expression of the notion of 'crimes against humanity', for all of humanity is indeed injured by the destruction of a unique religious culture and its concomitant cultural objects.[90]

The result can therefore seem paradoxical since the ICTY ended up recognizing, under a crime that is defined as a 'serious violation of fundamental rights', the part of cultural genocide that is the furthest away from the scope of human rights protection. As described in Chapter 4, the destruction of cultural heritage in times of armed conflict is mainly addressed under international cultural heritage law, although a right to access and enjoy cultural heritage can be deemed to be emerging. The consolidation of such a right would be more than welcome in order to

[86] Ibid. The Tribunal then adds in the same paragraph that '[t]hese acts must not be considered in isolation but examined in their context and weighed for their cumulative effect'.
[87] *Blaškić Case* (Trial) (n 51) paras. 227, 233.
[88] *Vasiljević Case* (Trial) ICTY-98-32 (29 November 2002) para. 246; *Stakić Case* (Trial Judgment) IT-97-24 (31 July 2003) paras. 735–6.
[89] *Blaškić Case* (Trial) (n 51) para. 235 (emphasis added).
[90] *Kordić & Čerkez Case* (Trial) (n 51) para. 207.

expand the scope of the crime of cultural persecution to situations of destruction of tangible cultural heritage that occur in peacetime.

Hence, the ICTY's case law tends to strengthen the existence of such a right in customary international law, as illustrated by the finding of the Trial Chamber in the *Prlić* case that the crimes perpetrated in Mostar, including the destruction of the Mostar bridge and ten mosques, constituted violations of the Muslim population's rights to life, freedom, and dignity. The recent *Karadžić* judgment has confirmed this approach in an even more explicit manner. In addition to the charge of genocide analysed in Chapter 3, Karadžić was also convicted for the crime against humanity of persecution in several municipalities of Bosnia and Herzegovina, including for the 'wanton destruction of private property and public property including cultural monuments and sacred sites'. Whereas this count was about tangible cultural heritage, the Trial Chamber considered that the religious sites constituted 'indispensable and vital assets of the population', similar to homes. On this basis, it concluded that these acts 'were of equal gravity to the other crimes listed under Article 5 of the Statute'.[91] As such, the ICTY transferred the analysis of the gravity from the destruction itself to its impact on the population, and therefore its human dimension. It may thus be possible to conclude, along with Francesco Francioni, that 'serious violations of international cultural heritage law [are now assimilated] to grave violations of human rights entailing the international criminal responsibility of the offender'.[92]

As for intangible heritage, while it seems to be completely obliterated from the ICTY case law, because of the very facts that were brought under its review, its strong connection with cultural rights could also allow for the introduction, under the scope of cultural persecution, of attacks aimed at group intangible features. In this respect, the ICTY has focused on another element: the notion of the gravity of the violation of such rights. This notion is twofold as it implies both that 'the illicit behaviour is based on the criteria of the "substantial" gravity, that is the importance of the right breached, and the "circumstantial" gravity, ie the intensity of the violation'.[93] Gravity was set as a criterion in the *Kupreškić* trial judgment: 'acts of persecution must be of an equal gravity or severity to the other acts enumerated under Article 5'.[94] Assessing the gravity of such acts implies a certain degree of subjectivity, as illustrated by the *Kupreškić* finding, which tends to consider cultural rights as secondary. In any event, the *Kupreškić* examples of violations of cultural rights that would not amount to persecution—that is 'visits to public parks, theatres or libraries'—were nevertheless of limited gravity as they constitute reversible limits to one's right to access and enjoy cultural life.

[91] *Karadžić Case* (Trial Judgment) IT-95-5/18-I (24 March 2016) para. 2557.

[92] Francesco Francioni, 'Culture, Heritage and Human Rights: An Introduction' in Francesco Francioni and Martin Scheinin (eds.), *Cultural Human Rights* (Leiden: Martinus Nijhoff Publishers, 2008) p. 8.

[93] Ottavio Quirico, 'The Evolving Notion of Persecution in the Law and Jurisprudence of International Criminal Tribunals' (2011) 21 *Ital. YBIL.* 203, p. 206.

[94] *Kupreškić Case* (Trial) (n 61) para. 619; reiterated in *Blaškić Case* (Appeals Judgment) ICTY-95-14 (29 July 2004) para. 138.

The *Kupreškić* seemingly pessimistic perspective of a crime of 'cultural persecution' was somehow watered down in the subsequent *Brđanin* trial judgment, which rejected the idea of constructing a list of 'fundamental rights' and rather considered that:

> it is the context of the individual acts and the necessity that the acts, as well as the violations occasioned by them be examined collectively that determines the gravity of the acts as a whole, and that it is this gravity which determines whether or not the rights violated are therefore 'fundamental' for the purposes of the crime of persecution.[95]

While the *Kupreškić* conceptualization of 'gravity' seemed to be grounded on the nature of rights or items under attack—and preconceptions about them—the *Brđanin* understanding has tended to shift the focus to the context of the crimes and therefore, the chapeau of crimes against humanity. This can be explained by the acts which were indicted in this case and which involved alleged violations of the right to employment, the right to freedom of movement, and the right to proper judicial process.[96] The two conceptions are not antagonistic though, since the *Brđanin* rationale is mostly grounded on the *Kupreškić* test according to which '[i]n order to establish the crime of persecution, underlying acts should not be considered in isolation, but in context, looking at their cumulative effect'.[97] The difference lies rather in the fact that according to the *Brđanin* finding, the general context of crimes against humanity might be enough to assess the gravity of the attack under review, that is whether these violations happen in the broader context of a widespread or systematic attack against an identified group.

5.2.1.2 The fundamental character of cultural rights in international human rights law

In case doubts would subsist as to the 'fundamental' character of cultural rights, it would be sufficient to acknowledge the developments that have occurred in the fields of both international human rights law and international cultural heritage law. While these two branches are only relevant for identifying state responsibility, their material understanding of cultural rights may constitute a relevant source for the interpretation of the *actus reus* of the crime of persecution. In particular, two different sets of issues need to be addressed: firstly, how the concept of persecution is dealt with in this field; secondly, which status is granted to cultural rights.

At the outset, it should be noted that the notion of 'persecution' is strongly entangled with the idea of forced emigration and *a fortiori* status of refugees.[98] Refugee law became the first field in which persecution was addressed in the post-war era. Article 14(1) of the Universal Declaration of Human Rights (UDHR)

[95] *Brđanin Case* (Trial) IT-99-36 (1 September 2004) para. 1031, fn. 285.
[96] *Brđanin Case* (Indictment) (n 4) para. 47(5).
[97] *Brđanin Case* (Trial) (n 95) para. 1031; *Kupreškić Case* (Trial) (n 61) para. 716(e).
[98] Hannah Arendt, *Origins of Totalitarianism* (New York: Schoken Books, 2004); Yoram Dinstein, 'Collective Human Rights of Peoples and Minorities' (1976) 25 *I.C.L.Q* 102, p. 120.

thus provided that: '(1) Everyone has the right to seek and to enjoy in other countries asylum from persecution'.[99] Article 1(A)(2) of the Convention related to the status of refugee grounds the notion of 'refugee' on a 'well-founded fear of being persecuted for reasons of race, religion, nationality, membership of a particular social group or political opinion'.[100] While persecution is not defined as such in any of these instruments, it is commonly understood as the serious denial of human rights.[101] The question has therefore been raised as to the violations of which rights could amount to persecution, especially in relation to cultural rights. As Zimmermann relates, drawing up a list of rights *in abstracto* is 'both unnecessary and unhelpful' since the notion of persecution partly depends on the harm felt by the individual victim.[102] Moreover, it is the discriminatory dimension of the human rights violation, which makes it amount to persecution.[103] Consequently, there is no reason to exclude cultural rights from the scope of persecution. Rather, the situation is quite the contrary since a violation of cultural rights often has a collective and therefore discriminatory dimension.[104] However it has been pointed out that this actual collective dimension could raise a major difficulty in relation to 'the need to individualize the "well-founded fear of persecution"'.[105]

Nevertheless, while the term persecution is identical to the one used in international criminal law and although the notion of discrimination is essential to the concept, it seems hard to ground the interpretation of international criminal law in the interpretation attributed to the term in international refugee law, which is based on a case-by-case analysis and thus depends on national courts or bodies. Above all, the scope of international criminal law and international refugee law are radically different. International refugee law is indeed not concerned about the persecution itself or the perpetrator's intent. Rather it merely focuses on granting a status to an individual or a group of individuals that do have 'well-founded fears'. It does not need to take a stance on whether persecution has actually occurred and whether it is a crime against humanity but rather on whether the individual seeking refuge is legitimate in requesting such a status. The difference in the scope of international criminal law and international refugee law has led the ICTY Trial Chamber in the *Tadić* case to consider that:

[99] Universal Declaration of Human Rights (adopted 10 December 1948) UNGA Res. 217 A(III) (UDHR) art. 14(1).

[100] Convention relating to the Status of Refugees (adopted 28 July 1951, entered into force 22 April 1954) 189 UNTS 137, art. 1(A)(2).

[101] Andreas Zimmermann (ed.), *The 1951 Convention Relating to the Status of Refugees and its 1967 Protocol: A Commentary* (Oxford: Oxford University Press, 2010) p. 345, para. 216.

[102] Ibid., p. 354, para. 248.

[103] Ibid., p. 357, para. 259.

[104] Ibid., p. 358, para. 262.

[105] Nazila Ghanea, 'Repressing Minorities and Getting Away With It: A Consideration of Economic, Social and Cultural Rights' in Nazila Ghanea and Alexandra Xanthaki (eds.), *Minorities, People and Self-Determination: Essays in Honour of Patrick Thornberry* (Leiden; Boston: Martinus Nijhoff Publishers, 2005) p. 195.

Although there has been an attempt to define the concept in the context of asylum and refugee law this is a distinct area of municipal and international law and thus its norms *cannot readily* be applied to customary international criminal law entailing individual criminal responsibility.[106]

It is noteworthy that the judges did not completely reject the possibility of integrating findings of international refugee law. This brief overview of the consideration of cultural rights in this field is useful to the extent that such rights are not excluded from the scope of persecution. It should be noted that Article II(f) of the International Convention on the Suppression and Prevention of the Crime of Apartheid (ICSPCA) also includes under this crime the 'persecution of organizations and persons, by depriving them of fundamental rights and freedoms, because they oppose apartheid'.[107] This provision is however of limited relevance, considering the lack of implementation of this convention, as well as the criminalization of apartheid as a specific count of crime against humanity. Apartheid is therefore a more specific provision than the crime of persecution.

However, international human rights law is relevant from a second perspective: the way in which culture is now considered. As already conveyed in Chapter 3, cultural rights are no longer considered to be secondary. Unlike the ICTY's suggestion in the *Kupreškić* case that cultural rights may not fall within the scope of fundamental rights as such, a study of the state of international human rights law does not allow for the corroboration of such an idea. Again, fundamental rights are not a particularly used expression in international legal instruments. However, the few references that can be found tend not to exclude cultural rights from having the status of fundamental rights. First, we note that cultural rights are also protected in the European Union Charter of Fundamental Rights (EUCFR).[108] Moreover, the 'fundamental character' of cultural rights is undeniable in the case of indigenous peoples, whether from an ordinary, positivist, or objectivist point of view. Such rights have indeed been found to be essential to the survival of indigenous peoples;[109] this was enshrined in various international instruments, in particular the United Nations Declaration on the Rights of Indigenous Peoples (UNDRIP); and the protection of such rights is an objective necessity of the framework of protection of indigenous peoples, which itself derivates from the protection of cultural diversity at the level of humanity as a whole. More important are the provisions of the International Covenant on Civil and Political Rights (ICCPR) and the International Covenant on Economic, Social, and Cultural Rights (ICESCR). The ILC 1996 Draft Code identified Article 2 ICCPR[110] as a source of the fundamental

[106] *Tadić Case* (Trial) (n 8) para. 694 (emphasis added).

[107] International Convention on the Suppression and Punishment of the Crime of Apartheid (adopted 30 November 1973, entered into force 18 July 1976) 1015 UNTS 243, art. II(f).

[108] See e.g. art. 14(3) on 'the right of parents to ensure the education and teaching of their children in conformity with their religious, philosophical and pedagogical convictions', art. 22 related to 'religious, cultural and linguistic diversity'.

[109] See e.g. *Mayagma (Sumo) Awas Tingni Community*, Judgment on Merits, Reparations, and Costs, Inter-American Court of Human Rights Series C No. 79 (31 August 2001), as well as other IACHR case law mentioned in Section 4.1.3.

[110] ILC 1996 Draft Code of Crimes (n 14) Commentary on art. 18, para. 11.

rights likely to be criminalized under the court of participation. This provision provides for states' duties in relation to the rights contained in the Covenant, thus including Article 27 related to the protection of minorities' rights to 'not be denied the right, in community with the other members of their group, to enjoy their own culture, to profess and practise their own religion, or to use their own language',[111] a norm that has been considered as 'peremptory'.[112] Further still, both Articles 5 of the ICESCR and the ICCPR refer to 'fundamental human rights' in relation to rights that would exist in national systems but would not be included in either of the two Covenants.[113]

A further question remains as to whether all cultural rights could be criminalized under the count of 'persecution', in particular collective rights, such as the right to collective property. While nothing in the formulation of the crime in the Rome Statute seems to preclude such a possibility—the crime of persecution being exclusively formulated in collective terms—the ICTY statement in the *Tadić* paragraph cited above rather emphasized the 'individuals' fundamental rights'. However, it might be a non-issue in the context of international criminal law, which is not concerned with recognizing rights of victims, and rather focuses on punishing perpetrators for serious international crimes that often involve targeted collective interests.

In view of these considerations, it seems therefore correct to challenge the *Kupreškić*'s finding, which does not seem to be sufficiently well-grounded, especially in relation to developments that have occurred in the field of international human rights law. Unlike the case of international refugee law, it would seem impossible to ignore these developments under the pretext that the scope of international criminal law and international human rights law is different. These two categories of international law indeed have a different scope, as has been stated on several occasions throughout this work. However, when it comes to the *actus reus* of persecution, the definition of persecution as 'severe violations of fundamental rights' clearly overlaps with the definition of such rights, and therefore with human rights law. Furthermore, international criminal trials have already resorted to human rights law to define the substantive elements of crimes. For instance, it specified the requirements of the *actus reus* of torture on the basis of the European Court of Human Rights (ECtHR) case law.[114]

What is possible in the field of genocide, that is the dismissal of acts of cultural genocide because they do not fit in the definition of genocide, is therefore less likely to happen *per se* with regard to the crime of persecution, since its definition explicitly calls for reference to international human rights law as a legal source of interpretation. This prohibits the drawing of a list of fundamental rights at the outset since

[111] International Covenant on Civil and Political Rights (adopted 16 December 1966, entered into force 23 March 1976) 999 UNTS 171 (ICCPR) art. 27.

[112] UNHRC General Comment No. 24: Article 40, para. 4 ICCPR (11 November 1994) UN Doc. CCPR/ C/ 21/ Rev. 1/ Add.6, para. 8. See Boot, Dixon, and Hall (n 8) p. 262, para. 117.

[113] ICCPR (n 111) art. 5(2); International Covenant on Economic, Social and Cultural Rights (adopted 16 December 1966, entered into force 3 January 1976) 993 UNTS 3 (ICESCR) art. 5(2).

[114] See e.g. *Furundžija Case* (Trial Judgment) IT-95-17/1 (10 December 1998) paras. 148, 160, 163.

it would contradict the increasing tendency, within international human rights law, to dismiss any formal hierarchy between different categories of human rights. In a *Brđanin* approach, cultural rights are likely to be considered as fundamental rights, provided that they are the object of a discriminatory and severe infringement, in the context of a widespread or systematic attack against a civilian population.[115] Discrimination is thus the 'essence'[116] of the crime of persecution in the same way as destruction is the essence of the crime of genocide. This was already asserted in various judgments of the ICTY, in particular in the *Tadić* trial judgment:

> Because the 'persecution type' is separate from the 'murder type' of crimes against humanity it is not necessary to have a separate act of an inhumane nature to constitute persecution; the discrimination itself makes the act inhumane.[117]

In the *Blaškić* judgment, the Appeals Chamber recalled that the discriminatory intent is not sufficient and reiterated that 'acts of persecutions, considered separately or together, should reach the level of gravity of other crimes listed in Article 5 of the Statute'.[118] This was a response to the Trial Chamber's statement that: ' "persecution" (. . .) also acts which appear less serious, such as those targeting property, so long as the victimized persons were especially selected on grounds linked to a particular community'.[119] Rather than rejecting outright the qualification of acts against property as 'serious', the Appeals Chamber rather confirmed the need to determine whether this condition is fulfilled *in concreto*.

If attacks against tangible cultural heritage in times of armed conflict can definitely constitute a crime of persecution under international law, it seems likely that attacks against intangible cultural heritage, if re-qualified as attacks against fundamental rights, should benefit from the same status. This, however, will depend on whether they can be considered to be of equal gravity as other international crimes. It goes without saying that the attacks at stake should also satisfy the general requirements of crimes against humanity. The ECCC will undoubtedly bring their stone to the edifice, at least with regard to attacks against intangible cultural heritage, as no crime against tangible cultural heritage has been the object of an indictment at this stage. Theoretically speaking, there is no substantive obstacle to the criminalization, under the category of persecution, of attacks against culture that target specific groups under the category of persecution as long as these attacks satisfy the main requirements of the crime, as defined by the ILC, the ICTY, the ICC Rome Statute, and ICC Elements of Crimes.[120] The main issue, however, is concerned with ensuring the respect of the *nullum crimen sine lege* principle. The strong reliance of the crime in the field of human rights could actually be the solution to this potential conflict, in which fundamental rights are now well anchored

[115] *Brđanin Case* (Trial) (n 95) para. 1031: 'The Trial Chamber reiterates its view that there is no list of established fundamental rights and that such decisions are best taken on a case by case basis.'

[116] Jurovics (n 10) p. 442.

[117] *Tadić Case* (Trial) (n 8) para. 697. See also para. 715.

[118] *Blaškić Case* (Appeals) (n 94) paras. 138, 139: 'It is not the case that any type of act, if committed with the requisite discriminatory intent, amounts to persecutions as a crime against humanity.'

[119] *Blaškić Case* (Trial) (n 51) para. 233.

[120] ICC Elements of Crimes (n 78).

and identifiable. These synergies might well result in the establishment of a coherent system of both protection of collective rights, in particular cultural rights, and the punishment of gross violations of these same rights when they reach a certain level of gravity. If this seems to be less and less questionable in relation to the idea of cultural genocide as a technique, further reflection might be required in relation to that of cultural genocide as a process of its own.

5.2.2 The autonomy of the crime of 'cultural persecution' in question

This analysis therefore raises a further question, in relation to the autonomy of the potential crime of 'cultural persecution'. Although the *Kupreškić* trial judgment considered that 'persecution is commonly used to describe a series of acts rather than a single one',[121] the ICTY case law has finally settled on the notion that one single discriminatory act is enough to constitute persecution,[122] which should therefore encompass both the destruction of cultural heritage and gross violations of fundamental cultural rights. In the meantime, the judges have also emphasized the notion of 'campaign of persecution' or 'context of a wider discriminatory attack'.[123] The emphasis on such context is not surprising considering the Balkan situation. In the cases submitted to the ICTY, cultural destruction never occurred in isolation but rather in connection with acts of forced transfers of population, detention in camps, or murders. The question remains open as to whether these latter acts are 'key' to the concept of persecution.[124] Notwithstanding, as noted by Bassiouni, 'there has never been a case involving the charge of "persecution" that has not involved other specific criminal acts'.[125]

Acknowledgement of this concurrence as fact is one thing, writing it in law is another. Yet this is what the drafters of the Rome Statute did when they supplemented the crime of persecution with the requirement that the attack should be perpetrated 'in connection with any act referred to in this paragraph or any crime within the jurisdiction of the Court'.[126] This requirement was introduced during the negotiations of the Rome Statute due to some delegations' fear that the crime of persecution would be too broad.[127] The ICTY considered that the connection imposed by the Rome Statute was contrary to customary international law.[128] In times of armed conflict, this should not constitute a significant obstacle to the punishment of unlawful acts of persecution. The same holds true for so-called acts of

[121] *Kupreškić Case* (Trial) (n 61) para. 615(d).

[122] *Vasiljević Case* (Appeals) IT-98-32 (25 February 2004) para. 113.

[123] *Krajišnik Case* (Trial) (n 66) para. 839.

[124] Alexander Zahar and Göran Sluiter, *International Criminal Law: A Critical Introduction* (Oxford; New York: Oxford University Press, 2008) p. 200.

[125] M.C. Bassiouni, *Crimes Against Humanity: Historical Evolution and Contemporary Application* (Cambridge; New York: Cambridge University Press, 2011) p. 405.

[126] ICC Rome Statute (n 15) art. 7(1)(h).

[127] Jurovics (n 10) p. 449.

[128] *Kupreškić Case* (Trial) (n 61) para. 580. See also Antonio Cassese, *Cassese's International Criminal Law* (3rd edn., Paola Gaeta et al. rev. Oxford: Oxford University Press, 2013) p. 107.

'cultural genocide', as conceptualized by Lemkin, which will necessarily involve the implementation of other techniques of genocide—or crimes against humanity in the present case. However, in peacetime, in the context of which the crime of persecution is also supposed to apply, this formulation begs the question of the means of criminalizing gross violations of human rights which do not necessarily harm the physical integrity of the members of a group, but rather attack the symbols of its cohesion.[129]

Firstly, some case law already exists with regard to the distinction between the chapeau requirement of an 'attack' and 'armed conflict'. In the *Kunarac* case, the ICTY has addressed the issue very clearly by stating that:

> The concepts of 'attack' and 'armed conflict' are not identical. (. . .) Under customary international law, the attack could precede, outlast, or continue during the armed conflict, but it need not be part of it. Also, the attack, in the context of a crime against humanity is not limited to the use of armed force; it encompasses any mistreatment of the civilian population.[130]

Beyond the ICTY, the ECCC has already implemented its provision on crimes against humanity, as well as the sub-crime of persecution, for crimes perpetrated in peacetime.[131] In Case 001, the ECCC also reiterated the distinction from 'armed conflict'. It will also be interesting to follow the development in the second case, in relation to which the closing order finds that '[a]s regards the actus reus, this attack consisted of the imposition of dictatorial control over the entire population of Cambodia, in line with the Communist Party of Kampuchea's (CPK) objective to bring about rapid socialist revolution in Cambodia and to eliminate both internal and external enemies'.[132] All these indications thus tend to dismiss the idea that the attack would imply the use of armed force.

Secondly, it is not clear that the ICC requirement would constitute such an obstacle in practice. If we consider more closely some of the cases mentioned throughout this work, it is hard to think of one single case that would involve only violations of cultural rights. Cultural genocide, especially when considered as a process of its own, results from the perpetration of various acts and violations of human rights, which may possess a strong cultural dimension but which might not necessarily fall into the category of cultural rights, for instance. The cultural dimension of the attack rather results from the context of its perpetration, especially the nature and intensity of the bond that unites the group members. In most of the indigenous peoples' cases reviewed by the Inter-American Court of Human Rights (IACHR) or in the Colombian case in particular,[133] the forced transfer of indigenous peoples out of their traditional and ancestral land turns out to be understood as the crucial element of the process. Such acts actually fall within another *actus reus* of crimes

[129] Gottlieb (n 24), pp. 875–7.
[130] *Kunarac et al. Case* (Appeals) ICTY-96-23 & 23/1 (12 June 2002) para. 86.
[131] Case 001 (Trial) No: 001/18-07-2007/ECCC/TC (26 July 2010) paras. 298–9.
[132] Case 002 (Closing Order) No: 002/19-09-2007-ECCC-OCIJ (15 September 2010) para. 1351.
[133] *Auto 004/09* (16 January 2009) Constitutional Court of Colombia.

against humanity and are, for instance, criminalized in Article 7(1)(d) of the ICC Rome Statute.

In this regard, in its Preliminary report of investigation on the situation of Colombia, the ICC Office of the Prosecutor (OTP) reviewed the ICC jurisdiction over the crimes perpetrated in this country, acknowledging the Colombian State's apparent lack of 'willingness' to prosecute such crimes.[134] The OTP focused in particular on the crimes of forcible transfers perpetrated against indigenous peoples and Afro-Colombian communities by both non-state actors and state armed forces. While the report shows the variety of coordinated acts that have targeted indigenous peoples, the OTP rather chose to address the crimes in isolation from each other, reviewing successively the 'targeted killing of community leaders and activists'[135] under Article 7(1)(a) of the ICC Rome Statute (murder), 'forcible transfer of population'[136] under Article 7(1)(d) and so on. The crime of persecution is not mentioned as a possible tool to criminalize the specific—and discriminatory—attacks against these groups. The report also mentions several decisions and opinions of the Supreme Court of Colombia, but no mention is made of Order No. 004/2009. Moreover, the crime against humanity of forcible transfer of population is only attributed to non-governmental groups[137] while Order No. 004 also pointed at the responsibility of the Colombian State armed forces.

The crime of persecution is currently included in indictments in most situations reviewed by the ICC. Nevertheless, the use of this crime so far mainly concerns acts of physical harm.[138] The Mali situation has opened the scope of international criminal prosecutions outside mere physical crimes, by exclusively focusing on attacks against cultural heritage in the city of Timbuktu. In its 2013 Report on the Situation in Mali, the OTP had touched upon the possibility that crimes against humanity had been perpetrated. It concluded however that there was a lack of sufficient evidence while contemplating the possibility of addressing such crimes in the future, in relation to the 'imposition of sentences without a just and fair legal process' and the enforced disappearances of several soldiers.[139] If the specific *Al Mahdi* case, mentioned in Section 4.2.2, confirms that it is unlikely that there will be any cases of 'cultural persecution' in the Malian situation, it still opens, if not deepens, a breach in the assumption that the only acts against physical integrity, as most serious crimes, may fall under the jurisdiction of the ICC.

Further, the system of complementarity, established by the Rome Statute, may open the path for the actual prosecution of 'cultural persecution' at the national

[134] International Criminal Court, Office of the Prosecutor, 'Situation in Colombia: Interim Report' (November 2012).

[135] Ibid., paras. 57–9. [136] Ibid., paras. 60–7.

[137] The crimes against humanity so far attributed to the Colombian governmental forces are limited to 'murder' and 'enforced disappearances'. See ibid., para. 111.

[138] With some exceptions, see e.g. *Prosecutor v. Ahmad Muhammad Harun and Ali Muhammad Ali Abd-Al-Rahman* (Warrant of Arrest) ICC-02/05-01/07 (27 April 2007) Pre-Trial Chamber I, p. 6: Count 1 on Persecution includes attacks against property.

[139] ICC International Criminal Court, Office of the Prosecutor, 'Situation in Mali: Article 53(1) Report' (16 January 2013) paras. 128–32.

level, provided that criminal codes are amended correctly to firstly include crimes against humanity—which was, for a long time, an issue at the German level, for instance—and *a fortiori* to adopt a formulation which allows for the prosecution of 'cultural persecution' on the model of Article 7(1)(h) and 7(2)(g) of the Rome Statute.

5.3 Concluding Remarks

This chapter has thus endeavoured to tackle the alleged failure of international criminal law to address serious violations of economic, social, and cultural rights.[140] The crime of persecution has the potential to apply to most cases studied in this book, which are associated with the 'cultural genocide' label. As such, it can be deemed to constitute a powerful counterpart to the normative human rights framework already identified in relation to cultural genocide. It should be noted that it does not preclude the qualification of some processes as genocidal, especially in the cases of the forcible transfer of children in former settler colonies, which still fit in the *actus reus* of genocide. Nor should 'cultural persecution' be understood as an argument against an evolutionary interpretation of the definition of genocide, especially of its *mens rea*. This crime is intended to fill the gaps currently existing in international criminal law, identified throughout Chapters 3 and 4, in relation to addressing acts targeting the cultural integrity of a given group. Moreover, in case the existence of the *dolus specialis* of genocide would be called into question, it has been explicitly stated that the *actus reus* of the crime against humanity of persecution encompassed the *actus reus* of genocide. There is therefore no objection to including forced transfers of children within the *actus reus* of persecution, provided that this is not a pretext to avoid the genocide label.

Of course, this may not satisfy victims, who may still argue that their experience is that of group destruction, a phenomenon which is not explicitly tackled by the crime of persecution. However, the category of persecution manages to address most of the facets of the concept: a potential step towards genocide, a technique of genocide, and a process of group destruction itself. The destruction of tangible cultural heritage *per se*—as seems to be the case *prima facie* in respect of the destruction of the Buddhas of Bamiyan—would thus be excluded from the scope of such a crime. However, this should not necessarily be seen as a limit of the crime of 'cultural persecution'. Such acts may indeed harm humanity as a whole—understood as an abstract entity—but not a group, which is what is at stake in genocide, what was at stake in cultural genocide, and the concern to which the crime of persecution is intended to reply.

[140] Larissa van den Herik, 'Economic, Social and Cultural Rights—International Criminal Law's Blind Spot?' in Eibe Riedel et al. (eds.), *Economic, Social and Cultural Rights: Contemporary Issues and Challenges* (Oxford: Oxford University Press, forthcoming)/Grotius Centre Working Paper Series 2013/002-ICL.

Beyond the criminal dimension of the concept of cultural genocide, this chapter has underlined the potential for the mutual reinforcement of the fields of international criminal law and international human rights, which are both invoked in the formulation of the crime of persecution. Lenzerini has thus considered that '[t]he ICTY (. . .) epitomizes how—in most recent times—the perception by the international community of the significance of cultural heritage has evolved toward a markedly holistic perspective'.[141] As already underlined in relation to the right to access and enjoy cultural heritage, the criminalization of its violation under persecution may actually strengthen the customary nature of this right. The conceptualization of the crime of persecution has also echoed recent developments of international law, such as the cultural dimension of the frameworks of genocide prevention. Further reflection is therefore needed on the potential repercussions that the several findings made throughout this chapter may have on general international law. Not only is individual criminal responsibility complementary to state responsibility, but this complementarity is also fostered by the common material scope implied by the conceptualization of cultural persecution, which altogether reflects an individual crime, a serious and discriminatory violation of fundamental rights, and a step towards genocide.

[141] Federico Lenzerini, 'The Role of International and Mixed Criminal Courts in the Enforcement of International Norms Concerning the Protection of Cultural Heritage' in Francesco Francioni and James Gordley (eds.), *Enforcing International Cultural Heritage Law* (Oxford: Oxford University Press, 2013) p. 55.

6

State Responsibility for Cultural Crimes

The anchoring of cultural genocide in the field of international human rights law has allowed for the consolidation of its status both in relation to state and individual criminal responsibility. As for state responsibility, there is no doubt as to the state's obligation not to destroy assets of cultural heritage and to prevent a group from enjoying its own culture. The recognition of the importance of cultural rights has thus gone as far as to confer on the state positive obligations in order to promote the flourishing of group cultures. This recalibration of the importance of culture and related cultural rights has allowed for the penetration of culture in the field of international criminal law, through the door of the crime of persecution. The ongoing process of recalibration of international criminal law may in turn open new perspectives—or at least renew the perspective—for studying state responsibility in respect of cultural genocide. At the outset, it should be underlined that the crime of forcibly transferring children from one group to another is likely to trigger state international responsibility for genocide, in light of the 2007 ICJ judgment on the *Application of the Genocide Convention* in the dispute opposing Bosnia and Herzegovina to Serbia and Montenegro. In the case that the *mens rea* of genocide might be reinterpreted in a more socio-cultural understanding and/or parts of its *actus reus*, especially subparagraphs (b) and (c), would be opened up to acts of cultural destruction, state responsibility for genocide could also be further envisioned. However, these latter options remain hypothetical; as such, this chapter rather focuses on the implications that can be drawn from the crime of cultural persecution, as conceptualized in Chapter 5, on general international law and therefore on state responsibility.

The conceptualization of this crime has confirmed earlier findings made in relation to cultural genocide. Firstly, it is clear that the grounding of the crime of persecution on human rights concepts necessarily involves a state dimension, since state responsibility is central to the international human rights legal framework. It remains to be seen how this crime might actually be articulated within wider international law and consequently influence branches other than international criminal law, including, in particular, general international law and international human rights law. Secondly, the crime of persecution—and *a fortiori* cultural persecution—was found to be relevant in the context of genocide prevention, since it is proven and legally acknowledged that it can constitute a step towards genocide through the idea of 'escalation' of criminal intents. It remains to be seen whether this seemingly powerful finding may have any concrete impact on state responsibility, since the state remains the subject obliged to prevent genocide.

6.1 State Aggravated Responsibility for Cultural Crimes

In the current context of the international law of state responsibility, the relationship between state responsibility and the crime of cultural persecution can be analysed through two different lenses: firstly, that of state responsibility for the crime against humanity of cultural persecution as such, and secondly, the acknowledgement of the criminal context for framing state responsibility for violations of cultural-related rights.

6.1.1 State responsibility for cultural persecution

The crime of genocide possesses the advantage of having been included in an international treaty, which sets out *erga omnes* obligations, and which is thus likely to entail state responsibility. In the 2007 International Court of Justice (ICJ) judgment on the *Application of the Genocide Convention*, the ICJ ruled that a state could be held responsible for perpetrating genocide on the basis of Article IX of the Genocide Convention.[1] Yet, no such provision exists in relation to the crime against humanity of persecution, which might at first sight appear as a weakness. The only inter-state convention related to the topic is the 1968 Convention on the Non-Applicability of Statutory Limitations to War Crimes and Crimes against Humanity which does not contain any provision tantamount to Article I of the Genocide Convention, following which state responsibility for crimes against humanity could be interpreted as emanating from the obligation to prevent and punish such crimes.[2] While this Convention has been used in the interpretation of the requirements of crimes against humanity, especially in respect of its application in peacetime,[3] its material scope is limited to ensuring that no statutory limitation applies in cases of war crimes and crimes against humanity—including genocide—even in respect of heads of states.[4] The special status granted to the crime of genocide contributes to fuel the incorrect perception that it is the only crime likely to trigger the international community's intervention.[5]

[1] *Application of the Convention on the Prevention and Punishment of the Crime of Genocide (Bosnia and Herzegovina v. Serbia and Montenegro)* (Judgment) [2007] ICJ Rep. 43 paras. 166–9, 179.

[2] Convention on the Non-Applicability of Statutory Limitations to War Crimes and Crimes against Humanity (adopted 26 November 1968, entered into force 11 November 1970) 754 UNTS 73, art. I(b).

[3] See e.g. 001 (Trial) No: 001/18-07-2007/ECCC/TC (26 July 2010) para. 291.

[4] Convention on the Non-Applicability of Statutory Limitations to War Crimes and Crimes against Humanity (n 2) arts. I–IV.

[5] Gareth Evans, 'Crimes against Humanity: Overcoming Indifference', 8 *J.G.R.* 325, p. 330, UNGA Res. 60/1 (24 October 2005) 'World Summit Outcome', paras. 138–9: the principle of 'responsibility to protect' also applies to crimes against humanity.

In 2013, the International Law Commission (ILC) added to its agenda the possibility of drafting a convention on crimes against humanity, to address inter alia state cooperation related to crimes against humanity, following the model of the Genocide Convention.[6] A group of some of the most eminent scholars in the field had already drafted a similar project, reaffirming the complementarity of both regimes of individual responsibility for crimes against humanity and state responsibility for serious wrongful acts, on the basis that crimes against humanity have already been prohibited under customary international law.[7] The ILC framework would thus supplement the International Criminal Court (ICC) legal framework, which is constrained by the restricted definition of its jurisdiction.[8] In 2015, the ILC provisionally adopted three first draft articles as suggested by Special Rapporteur Sean Murphy.[9] Article 1 relates to the scope of the future convention; Article 2 provides, as a general obligation that 'Crimes against humanity, whether or not committed in time of armed conflict, are crimes under international law, which States undertake to prevent and punish.' The latter's language is very close to Article I of the Genocide Convention and could therefore be considered as open to enshrining state responsibility for crimes against humanity on the model of the principle developed in 2007 by the ICJ in the *Bosnian Genocide* case. However, so far, the ILC only mentions that '[t]hose specific obligations will address steps that States are to take within their national legal systems, as well as their cooperation with other States, with relevant intergovernmental organizations, and with, as appropriate, other organizations'.[10] The rest of the commentary predominantly focuses on the question of the nexus requirement, to eventually conclude that customary international law has now recognized that crimes against humanity could also be perpetrated in peacetime. Draft Article 3 finally reproduces most parts of the definition of crimes against humanity set out in the ICC Rome Statute.[11]

In any event, the question of whether the commission of international crimes can entail state responsibility is not limited to the crime of genocide. At the international level, the issue has long been addressed in broad terms, whether in the general framework of state responsibility or that of international crimes. The debate has long been inspired by the famous statement of Nuremberg, which read

[6] ILC (66th Session), 'Annex B—Crimes against Humanity (Mr. Sean D. Murphy)', in *Report on the Work of its Sixty-Fifth Session* (6 May to 7 June and 8 July to 9 August 2013), UN Doc. A/68/10, available at: http://legal.un.org/ilc/reports/2013/english/annex.pdf (last accessed 1 February 2015) paras. 1, 8, 10.

[7] Washington University School of Law, Whitney R. Harris World Law Institute, Crimes Against Humanity Initiative, *Proposed International Convention on the Prevention and Punishment of Crimes Against Humanity* (2010), available at: http://law.wustl.edu/harris/cah/docs/EnglishTreatyFinal.pdf (last accessed 1 February 2015) Preambular para. 11; the definition of persecution reproduces the definition of the ICC Rome Statute, see arts. 1, 3(1)(h), 3(2)(g).

[8] Ibid.

[9] ILC (67th Session), 'First Report of the Special Rapporteur, Mr. Sean D. Murphy', in (2015), UN Doc. A/CN.4/680.

[10] ILC (67th Session), 'Chapter VII—Crimes against Humanity', UN Doc. A/70/10 (2015) Commentary on draft art. 2, para. 1, p. 53.

[11] Ibid. Commentary on draft art. 3, para. 1, p. 58. The changes are qualified as 'non-substantive'. The crime of persecution remains connected to other international crimes.

as follows: 'Crimes against international law are committed by men, not by abstract entities, and only by punishing individuals who commit such crimes can the provisions of international law be enforced.'[12] The idea that international crimes could only entail individual responsibility was strengthened by the provisions of the Genocide Convention, almost all of which relate in one way or another to individual criminal responsibility.[13] State obligations are limited to 'prevent and punish' the crime of genocide. Article IX of the Genocide Convention provides that:

Disputes between the Contracting Parties relating to the interpretation, application or fulfilment of the present Convention, including those relating to the responsibility of a State for genocide or any of the other acts enumerated in Article 3, shall be submitted to the International Court of Justice at the request of any of the parties to the dispute.

The absence of codified state responsibility for genocide, and more broadly for international crimes, was mainly motivated by the concern of avoiding the infliction of 'collective guilt' and the need to focus instead on those truly responsible.[14] However, the Nuremberg statement was later re-contextualized so as to highlight its true meaning: Nazi officers could be held responsible in spite of the criminal logic set up by the Nazi party. Thus, the International Military Tribunal was primarily concerned with justifying individual responsibility rather than excluding state responsibility per se. Such an exclusion subsequently turned out to be problematic in the face of the involvement of state organs in most contemporary processes of genocide and other international crimes.[15]

Even in its 1954 Draft Code of Offences against the Peace and Security of Mankind, the ILC systematically referred to state authorities in the provisions related to the definition of each crime.[16] In the subsequent 1991 and 1996 Draft Codes, the ILC eventually included the idea of complementarity between state and individual responsibility:

The fact that the present Code provides for the responsibility of individuals for crimes against the peace and security of mankind is without prejudice to any question of the responsibility of States under international law.[17]

[12] Judgment of 1 October 1946, in The Trial of German Major War Criminals *Proceedings of the International Military Tribunal sitting at Nuremberg, Germany*, Part 22 (22 August 1946 to 1 October 1946) (IMT Nuremberg) 'the law of the Charter'.

[13] Convention on the Prevention and Punishment of the Crime of Genocide (adopted 9 December 1948, entered into force 12 January 1951) 78 UNTS 277 (Genocide Convention) arts. IV–VII.

[14] M. Cherif Bassiouni, *Introduction to International Criminal Law: Second Revised Edition* (Leiden; Boston: Martinus Nijhoff Publishers, 2013) pp. 104–5.

[15] William A. Schabas, *Genocide in International Law: The Crime of Crimes* (2nd edn., Cambridge: Cambridge University Press, 2009) p. 512.

[16] ILC (6th Session) 'Draft Code of Offences against the Peace and Security of Mankind with Commentaries', *Yearbook of the International Law Commission*, 1954, vol. II (ILC 1954 Draft Code of Offences) art. 2, pp. 135–7.

[17] ILC (48th Session), 'Draft Code of Crimes against the Peace and Security of Mankind with Commentaries', *Yearbook of the International Law Commission*, 1996, vol. II, Part Two (ILC 1996 Draft Code of Crimes) art. 4. See also Rome Statute of the International Criminal Court (adopted 17 July 1998, entered into force 1 July 2002) 2187 UNTS 3 (ICC Rome Statute) art. 10.

The two commentaries on these Draft Codes also make clear 'that an individual may commit a crime against the peace and security of mankind as an "agent of the State", "on behalf of the State", "in the name of the State" or even in a de facto relationship with the State, without being vested with any legal power'.[18] The 2001 ILC Draft Articles on state responsibility echoed this principle in the following words:

These articles are without prejudice to any question of the individual responsibility under international law of any person acting on behalf of a State.[19]

These latter Draft Articles were the result of a long-lasting discussion on the issue of 'state criminal responsibility'. The issue had constituted a bone of contention for more than two decades, arising initially with Special Rapporteur Roberto Ago's proposal in 1976,[20] and subsisting as such until the final adoption of the 2001 ILC's articles and their acknowledgement by the United Nations General Assembly (UNGA). As is well known, Roberto Ago introduced a distinction between state responsibility for international delicts and international crimes. This proposal was embodied in draft Article 19, which read as follows:

1. An act of a State which constitutes a breach of an international obligation is an internationally wrongful act, regardless of the subject-matter of the obligation breached.
2. An internationally wrongful act which results from the breach by a State of an international obligation so essential for the protection of fundamental interests of the international community that its breach is recognized as a crime by that Community as a whole, constitutes an *international crime*. (...)[21]

It was only in 1996 that the ILC addressed the practical consequences of state crimes. In addition to entailing the same consequences as international delicts,[22] it provided for some aggravated consequences. For instance, the limits of the obligation of restitution would not apply to the commission of an international

[18] ILC 1996 Draft Code of Crimes (n 17) Commentary on art. 5, p. 23, para. 1; Similar formulation in ILC (43rd Session), 'Draft Code of Crimes against the Peace and Security of Mankind with Commentaries', *Yearbook of the International Law Commission*, 1991, vol. II (ILC 1991 Draft Code of Crimes) Commentary on art. 5, p. 99.

[19] ILC (53rd Session), 'Draft Articles on Responsibility of States for Internationally Wrongful Acts, with Commentaries', *Yearbook of the International Law Commission*, 2001, vol. II, Part Two (ILC 2001 Draft Articles on State Responsibility) art. 58.

[20] James Crawford, 'International Crimes of States' in James Crawford, Alain Pellet, and Simon Olleson (eds.), *The Law of International Responsibility* (New York: Oxford University Press, 2010) p. 406: 'The distinction between two categories of internationally wrongful acts had its origins in a proposal from Special Rapporteur García Amador in 1956 to distinguish "merely wrongful" from "punishable" acts. "Punishable" acts were defined as acts done by individuals who were organs of the State and acting as such, with the consequence that they could be pursued and punished by States other than their own'.

[21] ILC (28th Session) 'Report of the International Law Commission on its Twenty-Eighth Session', *Yearbook of the International Law Commission*, 1976, vol. II, Part Two, p. 75. A third paragraph would detail the material grounds of state criminal responsibility, such as '*(c)* a serious breach on a widespread scale of an international obligation of essential importance for safeguarding the human being, such as those prohibiting slavery, genocide and *apartheid*'.

[22] ILC (48th Session), 'State Responsibility', *Yearbook of the International Law Commission*, vol. II, Part Two, 1996 (ILC 1996 State Responsibility), art. 51, p. 70.

crime.[23] Moreover, the perpetration of international crimes would create 'obligations for every other state', as provided by Draft Article 53:

(a) Not to recognize as lawful the situation created by the crime;
(b) Not to render aid or assistance to the State which has committed the crime in maintaining the situation so created;
(c) To cooperate with other States in carrying out the obligations under subparagraphs (*a*) and (*b*); and
(d) To cooperate with other States in the application of measures designed to eliminate the consequences of the crime.[24]

These 'rather limited consequences' were deemed to be insufficient with regard to the gravity of state crimes, as set out in Draft Article 19.[25] The choice was thus made in 2001, following the report of the previous Special Rapporteur James Crawford, to discard Article 19 and substitute the criminal semantic with the language of 'serious breaches of obligations under peremptory norms of general international law', as defined in Article 40 of the 2001 ILC articles:

1. This chapter applies to the international responsibility which is entailed by a serious breach by a State of an obligation arising under a peremptory norm of general international law.
2. A breach of such an obligation is serious if it involves a gross or systematic failure by the responsible State to fulfil the obligation.

The reference to 'peremptory norms of general international law' was meant to echo the Vienna Convention on the Law of Treaties (VCLT) provisions on *jus cogens*,[26] which, in the 2001 Draft Articles, formally became more than a mere treaty rule of normative conflict-settlement. During the negotiations of both former Article 19 and those of current Article 41, the prohibition of genocide was repeatedly presented as an example of such norms.[27] The same holds true in respect of the crimes of torture and aggression, however crimes against humanity were left to the side of the discussion. At the same time, these were only deemed to be examples and no list of imperative norms was formally drafted. With regard to the consequences, the ILC substantially reduced the scope of its 1996 Draft Articles to provide for the following obligations, established in Article 41:

1. States shall cooperate to bring to an end through lawful means any serious breach within the meaning of article 40.

[23] Ibid., art. 52, p. 71. [24] Ibid., p. 72. [25] Crawford (n 20) p. 408.

[26] Vienna Convention on the Law of Treaties (adopted 23 May 1969, entered into force 27 January 1980) 1155 UNTS 331 (VCLT) art. 53: 'A treaty is void if, at the time of its conclusion, it conflicts with a peremptory norm of general international law. For the purposes of the present Convention, a peremptory norm of general international law is a norm accepted and recognized by the international community of States as a whole as a norm from which no derogation is permitted and which can be modified only by a subsequent norm of general international law having the same character.'; art. 64: 'If a new peremptory norm of general international law emerges, any existing treaty which is in conflict with that norm becomes void and terminates.' See ILC 2001 Draft Articles on State Responsibility (n 19) Commentary on art. 40, paras. 2–6, p. 113.

[27] ILC 2001 Draft Articles on State Responsibility (n 19) Commentary on Article 40, para. 4, pp. 112–13.

2. No State shall recognize as lawful a situation created by a serious breach within the meaning of article 40, nor render aid or assistance in maintaining that situation.
3. This article is without prejudice to the other consequences referred to in this Part and to such further consequences that a breach to which this chapter applies may entail under international law.

As is evident from this provision, 'the ILC abandoned [the] idea [of *more serious consequences*] and opted for an *"additional consequence"* approach'.[28] No specific consequence was therefore provided for in relation to the content of the obligation to repair. This was part of the movement of 'depenalisation' undertaken by the ILC and the corollary removal of any potential reference to 'punitive damages'.[29]

While the debates mainly took place within the mandate of the ILC, and therefore outside of the 1948 Genocide Convention legal framework, the 2007 ICJ judgment in the *Application of the Genocide Convention* case allowed for the first articulation of the relationship between the ILC articles on state responsibility and the provisions of the Genocide Convention. In spite of Serbia's strong arguments against the existence of a state obligation not to perpetrate genocide, the ICJ ruled that 'the obligation to prevent genocide necessarily implies the prohibition of the commission of genocide'.[30] As a consequence, the international judges found that the 1948 Genocide Convention created a state obligation not to perpetrate genocide. In this regard, it strongly re-asserted the validity of its own test for identifying state responsibility: the direct control of the state on the organs which perpetrated the breach of international law.[31] The ICJ made very scarce reference to the ILC 2001 Draft Articles on state responsibility but the judgment is clearly enshrined in the spirit of these articles, with a subtle reference to the *jus cogens* character of the prohibition of genocide, a principle that had already been stated in the 2006 judgment in the *Case Concerning Armed Activities On the Territory of the Congo*.[32] Nevertheless in the ILC line, the ICJ took care to distinguish the form of state responsibility deriving from the Genocide Convention from the controversial concept of 'State criminality'. Serbia indeed argued that the recognition of state responsibility for genocide would necessarily entail a form of state criminal responsibility that was incompatible with general international law. The ICJ replied that:

the obligations in question in this case, arising from the terms of the Convention, and the responsibilities of States that would arise from breach of such obligations, are obligations

[28] Paola Gaeta, 'The Character of the Breach' in Crawford, Pellet, and Olleson (eds.), (n 20) p. 427.

[29] Crawford (n 20) p. 410.

[30] *Application of the Genocide Convention (Bosnia and Herzegovina v. Serbia and Montenegro)* (Judgment) (n 1) para. 166.

[31] Reaffirmation of the *Nicaragua* test at ibid., para. 391; rejection of the ICTY *Tadic* test at ibid., paras. 403–7. For a criticism of the ICJ's test in the 2007 ICJ Judgment, see Paola Gaeta, 'On What Conditions Can a State Be Held Responsible for Genocide?' (2007) 18 *E.J.I.L.* 631, p. 635.

[32] *Application of the Genocide Convention (Bosnia and Herzegovina v. Serbia and Montenegro)* (Judgment) (n 1) para. 161. Reference to *Case Concerning Armed Activities on the Territory of the Congo (New Application: 2002) (Democratic Republic of the Congo v. Rwanda)* (Judgment on Jurisdiction and Admissibility) [2006] ICJ Rep. 6, at para. 64.

and responsibilities under international law. They are not of a criminal nature. This argument accordingly cannot be accepted.[33]

The ICJ has thus constructed the principle of state responsibility for genocide according to general principles of state objective responsibility for wrongful acts, even though its further implementation of the principle contained several references to criminal liability, as discussed in Chapter 3.

There is therefore no reason why a state could not be held responsible for crimes of 'cultural persecution' since both violations of fundamental cultural rights and the destruction of cultural heritage constitute 'international wrongful acts' under customary international law.[34] Thus, as it has already been developed in Chapter 4, state responsibility is inherent to the finding of the violation of human rights, *a fortiori* when such a violation is perpetrated on discriminatory grounds, either on the basis of the state's omission to prevent the violation or the active infringement of its international obligations. Accordingly, this gap may not be as problematic as might seem once the analytical scope is broadened beyond the borders of international criminal law.

In this perspective, the dispute brought by Georgia against Russia in front of the ICJ in 2008 may give rise to the possibility of state responsibility for the crime against humanity of persecution—at least indirectly—either within or outwith the context of potential genocide. While the Court ultimately considered that it did not have jurisdiction to find a violation of the provisions of the CERD,[35] it had previously made orders of provisional measures on both countries requiring that any kind of discrimination towards the population of Abkhazia and South Ossetia cease.[36] Reading the claims of the Georgian government, the use of the CERD as a legal basis for the dispute may seem like a disproportionate ground for dismissing the claim in relation to the alleged gravity of the facts revealed.[37] The use of the words 'widespread and systematic' constitute a clear reference to crimes against humanity, when not explicitly invoked as a breach of the CERD:

the sponsoring, defending, and supporting of ethnic discrimination by the *de facto* South Ossetian and Abkhaz separatist authorities and the recognition as lawful of a situation created by a serious breach of Russia's obligations under CERD and of its obligations *erga omnes*, namely recognition in whole or in part of the South Ossetian and Abkhaz separatist entities amounting to recognition of a situation created by *'ethnic cleansing'*

[33] *Application of the Genocide Convention* (*Bosnia and Herzegovina v. Serbia and Montenegro*) (Judgment) (n 1) para. 170.

[34] ILC 2001 Draft Articles on State Responsibility (n 19) art 1.

[35] *Application of the International Convention on the Elimination of All Forms of Racial Discrimination* (*Georgia v. Russia*) (Preliminary Objections) [2011] ICJ Rep. 70, paras.182–4.

[36] *Application of the International Convention on the Elimination of All Forms of Racial Discrimination* (*Georgia v. Russia*) (Request for the Indication of Provisional Measures) [2008] ICJ Rep. 353, para. 149.

[37] Phoebe Okowa, 'The Georgia v. Russia Case: A Commentary', *The Hague Justice Portal*, 2009, available at: http://www.haguejusticeportal.net/Docs/Commentaries%20PDF/Okowa_Georgia_ICJ_EN.pdf (last accessed 1 February 2015) p. 2.

constituting the crime against humanity of persecution and systematic discrimination on ethnic grounds.[38]

Furthermore, Georgia, 'reserve[d] its right to invoke Article IX of the Convention on the Prevention and Punishment of the Crime of Genocide as an additional basis for the jurisdiction of the Court'.[39] Indeed, soon after the application was made, Georgia filed an amended request for the indication of provisional measures:

directed at an immediate cessation of the violent forms of racial discrimination against ethnic Georgians that continue unabated in the areas of Georgian territory under the control of the Russian Federation and for an immediate cessation of the various measures adopted or supported by the Russian Federation to frustrate the right of return of the ethnic Georgians who have either been forcibly expelled or who have fled as a result of this violence.[40]

More precisely, it aimed at securing two human rights: firstly, 'the right to the security of the person and protection against violence or bodily harm', which also covered 'the destruction and pillage of property, and other acts intended to expel them from their homes in South Ossetia',[41] and secondly, the right to return of the internally displaced persons and refugees. The ICJ's order of provisional measures seemed to open the path for the development of a legal tool to address state responsibility for crimes against humanity, especially the sub-crime of persecution, as well as for potentially circumscribing, at a rather early stage, the potential escalation towards genocide. This was made possible through an unusual legal construction, namely, the reliance on the CERD, which indeed constitutes the closest human rights counterpart to the crime against humanity of persecution and possesses the advantage of being widely ratified.[42]

However, in its later judgment on the preliminary matters, the ICJ closed the path it had itself opened, interpreting Article 22 CERD—the compromissory clause grounding its jurisdiction—in a restrictive manner so as to require the parties to have, at a preliminary stage, undertaken the procedure provided by this article, that is either to hold negotiations on the specific CERD-related dispute or to seize the CERD mechanism of dispute-settlement.[43] This article provides that, in case the CERD procedure would fail, the parties could then refer the case to the ICJ. In the present case, the Court did not find sufficient evidence that the two parties had held negotiations on the matter, or that Georgia had used the procedures provided for in the CERD.[44] This raised the question of which authority to grant to its first finding in the order of provisional measures, in which it had found that:

whereas the phrase 'any dispute . . . which is not settled by negotiation or by the procedure expressly provided for in this Convention' does not, in its plain meaning, suggest that formal

[38] *Application of the International Convention on the Elimination of All Forms of Racial Discrimination* (*Georgia v. Russia*) (Application Instituting Proceedings) 13 August 2008, para. 81(e) (emphasis added).

[39] Ibid., para. 20.

[40] *Application of the International Convention on the Elimination of All Forms of Racial Discrimination* (*Georgia v. Russia*) (Amended Request) 25 August 2008, para. 4.

[41] Ibid., para. 16.

[42] Ratified by 176 state parties as of 19 February 2014.

[43] *CERD Case* (Preliminary Objections) (n 35) para. 148.

[44] Ibid., paras. 182–3.

negotiations in the framework of the Convention or recourse to the procedure referred to in Article 22 thereof constitute preconditions to be fulfilled before the seisin of the Court; whereas however Article 22 does suggest that some attempt should have been made by the claimant party to initiate, with the Respondent Party, discussions on issues that would fall under CERD.[45]

After the judgment on the preliminary objections, it seems that a state party to the CERD would no longer be able to use such a procedure to assert the responsibility of another for the violation of those rights enshrined in the CERD. Among the criticisms of this judgment, Judge Cançado Trindade deplored, in a strong dissenting opinion, the order of priorities set by the ICJ, which privileged the notion of inter-state consent over the principles inherent to a human rights treaty such as the CERD.[46] According to the Brazilian judge, the ICJ could have reached a different result, had it considered the CERD as a 'living instrument',[47] thus privileging its purpose and object.[48] Furthermore, he reproached the ICJ for having neglected the victims' interest and the harm they were suffering, and more generally the interest of 'realization of justice'.[49] Interestingly, he relied on the IACHR case law that he himself had contributed to, and reasserted the *jus cogens* character of the principle of non-discrimination,[50] to strengthen the dissenting opinion. The IACHR has indeed adopted a particularly progressive case law when confronted with contexts of gross human rights violations that could also entail international individual responsibility.

6.1.2 Cultural persecution as an aggravating factor of state responsibility

According to the same logic as the ICTY's finding of aggravated individual responsibility for the targeting of assets of cultural heritage that were listed on the UNESCO World Heritage List,[51] human rights violations occurring in a context of international criminality—either genocide or crimes against humanity—could perhaps constitute an aggravating factor of state responsibility. The ILC has enshrined the concept of aggravated responsibility for violations of imperative norms of general international law in its 2001 Articles on State Responsibility. As the *travaux préparatoires* and the Commentary attached to these Draft Articles show, these norms encompass the crime of genocide but do not explicitly mention crimes against humanity. In its Commentary, the ILC thus referred to norms that the ICJ had already elevated to the rank of *jus cogens*: 'the prohibitions against slavery and the slave trade, genocide, and racial discrimination and apartheid',[52] as well as 'the

[45] Ibid., para. 114.
[46] Ibid. Dissenting opinion of Judge Cançado Trindade, paras. 140, 144, 214.
[47] Ibid., paras. 167 et seq. [48] Ibid., paras. 66–78. [49] Ibid., paras. 145–66.
[50] Ibid. Dissenting opinion of Judge Cançado Trindade, para. 87.
[51] Finding of aggravated responsibility for the destruction of the Old City of Dubrovnik in *Jokić, Miodrag* (Trial) IT-01-42/1 (18 March 2004); state aggravated responsibility provided by ILC 2001 Draft Articles on State Responsibility (n 19).
[52] ILC 2001 Draft Articles on State Responsibility (n 19) Commentary on Article 40, para. 4, p. 112.

prohibition against torture, (. . .) the basic rules of international humanitarian law applicable in armed conflict (. . .) [and] the obligation to respect the right of self-determination'.[53] It specified however that this list was not exhaustive.[54] Moreover, Article 40(2) shows that state aggravated responsibility depends on the intensity of the violation, that is a 'gross or systematic failure by the responsible State' and not on the nature of the violated norm itself. The ILC Commentary nevertheless tends to provide for the interpretation of this provision as excluding the aggravation of state responsibility for 'minor' violations of imperative norms of *jus cogens*, rather than extending this responsibility to violations of other types of norms.[55]

While the ILC concept of aggravated responsibility has been overlooked in the 2007 ICJ judgment on the *Application of the Genocide Convention*, the issue has received a much wider reflection within the Inter-American system. The IACHR revived the concept of aggravated state responsibility in relation to situations of gross human rights violations that could otherwise be characterized as genocide or crimes against humanity. Two main factors have contributed to this jurisprudential move. Firstly, the IACHR operates in a very specific context, that of a continent which emerged politically from violence, not to say genocide, which has been perpetuated over time, leading in the worst cases, to the destruction of some indigenous communities.[56] These structural inequalities, together with the dark era of authoritarian and dictatorial regimes, which shook the continent from the 1970s onwards, have underscored the role of the state machinery in the perpetration of crimes against humanity and genocide.[57] Secondly, the case law of the court on aggravated responsibility has been very much initiated by the judicial activism of one of its members, Judge Cançado Trindade, who conceptualized in great detail the grounds and consequences of such a concept in a number of separate opinions. While Judge Cançado Trindade has not hesitated to refer to the controversial label of 'State crime', considering that '[s]ince State crime is a reality, as the facts of the instant case prove conclusively, the *concomitant* determination of the State's international responsibility and the criminal liability of the perpetrators is essential',[58] the court has remained much more cautious and has limited its statements to the acknowledgement of aggravated responsibility under specific circumstances. Although the court did not enter into the 'State crime' rhetoric, it has predominantly applied the concept of aggravated responsibility in contexts of

[53] Ibid., para. 5, p. 113. [54] Ibid., para. 6, p. 113.

[55] Ibid. Commentary on Article 41, para. 7, p. 113.

[56] Laurence Burgorgue-Larsen and Amaya Úbeda de Torres, *The Inter-American Court of Human Rights: Case Law and Commentary* (Oxford: Oxford University Press, 2010) p. 500.

[57] Marcia Esparza, 'Globalizing Latin American Studies of State Violence and Genocide' in M. Esparza, Henry R. Huttenbach, and Daniel Feierstein (eds.), *State Violence and Genocide in Latin America: the Cold War Years*, (London; New York: Routledge, 2010) pp. 4–8.

[58] *Plan de Sánchez Massacre v. Guatemala*, Reparations, Inter-American Court of Human Rights Series C No. 116 (19 November 2004) Separate Opinion of Judge A.A. Cançado Trindade, para. 9. See also *Myrna Mack Chang v. Guatemala*, Merits, Reparations and Costs, Inter-American Court of Human Rights Series C No. 101 (25 November 2003) Reasoned Opinion of Judge A.A. Cançado Trindade, para. 34.

international crimes, which it has assimilated to human rights violations.[59] The use of aggravated responsibility has already been mentioned in the *Plan de Sánchez* and *Moiwana* cases, involving massacres of entire indigenous and tribal villages that could be qualified as genocide. Thus, the Inter-American Court considered that state's responsibility should be aggravated, not only on the basis of the gravity of the massacre, but also on the basis of the spiritual harm suffered by the surviving members of these communities.[60]

The principle of state aggravated responsibility was also asserted in cases that would rather amount to crimes against humanity. While the facts might seem distant from those engaged by the concept of cultural genocide, the findings may turn out to be useful in relation to determining which aspects of the crime against humanity of cultural persecution could entail aggravated responsibility. This jurisprudential move started with the *Myrna Mack Chang* case, in relation to the murder by the military intelligence of an anthropologist who had been conducting research on the internally-displaced population of Guatemala. The Inter-American Court found a violation of the victim's right to life, in respect of which it concluded as to Guatemala's aggravated responsibility, in light of the context surrounding the murder:

> This circumstance was worsened because at the time of the facts there was in Guatemala *a pattern of selective extra-legal executions fostered by the State*, which was directed against those individuals who were considered 'internal enemies'. Furthermore, since then and still today, there have not been effective judicial mechanisms to investigate the human rights violations nor to punish those responsible, all of which gives rise to an aggravated international responsibility of the respondent State.[61]

While the court reviewed the extra-legal execution of one single individual, the emphasis on the existence of a 'pattern' of similar murders tends to paraphrase the contextual element of crimes against humanity.[62] Following this statement, the court emphasized that the victim was 'single[d]-out (. . .) in view of her professional activity'.[63] The emphasis on the victim's professional—and to some extent political—affiliation thus mirrors the criterion of discrimination set out in the definition of the crime against humanity of persecution. In this case, the court underlined the importance of the right to life, which 'plays a fundamental role in the American Convention because it is a prior condition for realization of the other rights'.[64]

The aggravation of a state's international responsibility was also recognized in relation to the crime of enforced disappearance. In the *Goiburú* case, Paraguay's

[59] Mireille Delmas-Marty, *Le Relatif et l'Universel: Les Forces Imaginantes du Droit* (Paris: Seuil, 2004) p. 176.

[60] *Plan de Sánchez Massacre v. Guatemala*, Merits, Inter-American Court of Human Rights Series C No. 105 (29 April 2004) para. 51; *Moiwana Community v. Suriname*, Merits, Reparations, and Costs, Inter-American Court of Human Rights Series C No. 124 (15 June 2005) para. 192.

[61] *Myrna Mack Chang* (n 58) para. 138 (emphasis added).

[62] Ibid., para. 142, which describes the pattern in further details.

[63] Ibid., para. 141.

[64] Ibid., para. 152.

responsibility for its involvement in such crimes, which are prohibited by norms of *jus cogens*,[65] was 'increased' on a double ground: the 'context' of the individual violations of human rights, as constituted by the Operation Condor, in which the 'three branches of the State' were involved;[66] and Paraguay's failure to effectively fight impunity and to criminalize enforced disappearance according to the same level of gravity as that provided for by international law.[67] The same grounds were reiterated in the case of *La Cantuca v. Perú*, in which the court made an explicit reference to the context of the disappearances as being a crime against humanity:

> the international responsibility of the State is aggravated if the disappearance is part of a systematic pattern or a practice applied or tolerated by the State, for it constitutes a crime against humanity involving a flagrant disavowal of the essential principles on which the inter-American system is based.[68]

In the *Maipiripán* case, the responsibility of Colombia was also aggravated for the violation of procedural rights—the right to a fair trial and the right to judicial protection—following the massacre of forty nine individuals by Colombian paramilitary forces, 'as a consequence of non-fulfilment of the duty to provide protection and of the duty to investigate the facts, as a consequence of the lack of effective judicial mechanisms to this end and to punish all those responsible for the Maipiripán Massacre'.[69]

In the *Masacre de Ituango* case, the notion of aggravated responsibility was not recognized in relation to the nature of the right at stake but rather as to the vulnerability of the population targeted. The case related to the massacre and forced displacement of inhabitants of several Colombian villages as perpetrated by paramilitary forces. The Inter-American Court noted the existence of a pattern of similar massacres, but only for the purpose of recognizing the victimhood of the individuals who were not listed in the claim.[70] However, it recognized Colombia's aggravated responsibility for the murder of a minor during the massacre, as well as the damage caused to other children:

> who experienced this violence in a situation of armed conflict, who have been partially orphaned, who have been displaced, and whose physical and psychological integrity has been violated. The special vulnerability, owing to their condition as children, is even more evident in a situation of internal armed conflict, as in this case, because children are less prepared to adapt or respond to this type of situation and suffer its excesses disproportionately.[71]

[65] *Goiburú and others v. Paraguay*, Merits, Reparations, and Costs, Inter-American Court of Human Rights, Series C No. 153 (22 September 2006) para. 84.

[66] Ibid., para. 67. [67] Ibid., para. 93.

[68] *La Cantuca v. Perú*, Merits, Reparations, and Costs, Inter-American Court of Human Rights, Series C No. 162 (29 November 2006) para. 115.

[69] *"Maipiripán Massacre" v. Colombia*, Merits, Reparations, and Costs, Inter-American Court of Human Rights Series C No. 134 (15 September 2005) para. 214.

[70] *The Ituango Massacres v. Colombia*, Preliminary Objections, Merits, Reparations, and Costs, Inter-American Court of Human Rights Series C No. 148 (1 July 2006) para. 278.

[71] Ibid., para. 246.

All of these cases illustrate that the interconnection between international crimes, especially crimes against humanity and genocide, on the one hand, and state responsibility, on the other, is now recognized and articulated, notwithstanding that the case law mainly deals with attacks against the physical integrity of individuals or entire communities. The cultural dimension of some of these attacks does constitute an aggravating factor of responsibility, provided that they are connected to physical attacks. The criterion of 'vulnerability' could still turn out to be particularly relevant in cases in which the persecutions do not necessarily target the physical integrity of the individual group members. It should nonetheless be noted that the IACHR has made less and less use of the concept of aggravated responsibility, even in cases involving a context of massive and widespread attack against a civilian population, and a strong pattern of discrimination against the same group,[72] a trend which might be related to Judge Cançado Trindade's termination of mandate and transfer to the ICJ.

The IACHR case law has been reflected to some extent at the European level. For example, the European Committee on Social Rights (ECSR) has recognized the notion of 'aggravated responsibility', in a case opposing the Centre on Housing Rights and Evictions (COHRE) to Italy. This Committee has the mandate of settling disputes brought by civil society organizations against Member States in relation to the rights contained in the European Social Charter.[73] Even if this Charter does not deal with cultural rights, the *COHRE* case is noteworthy as Italy's aggravated responsibility was found in relation to the violation of social rights: the right to housing and the right of migrant workers and their families to protection and assistance, both in connection with a violation of the principle of non-discrimination. In this case, the Committee on social rights considered that:

> an aggravated violation is constituted when the following criteria are met:
>
> on the one hand, measures violating human rights specifically targeting and affecting vulnerable groups are taken;
>
> on the other, public authorities not only are passive and do not take appropriate action against the perpetrators of these violations, but they also contribute to such violence.[74]

The Committee grounded its own finding on aggravated responsibility on the Inter-American case law,[75] although it ultimately went beyond the IACHR conception. While the IACHR rather tended to increase state responsibility in cases of state's active participation in the violations of human rights with the status of norms of *jus cogens*,[76]

[72] See e.g. *Caso de las comunidades afrodescendientes desplazadas de la cuenca del río cacarica (Operación Génesis) v. Colombia*, Preliminary Objections, Merits, Reparations, and Costs, Inter-American Court of Human Rights Series C No. 270 (20 November 2013).

[73] European Social Charter, (adopted 18 October 1961, entered into force 26 February 1965, revised 3 May 1996) CETS No. 163.

[74] *Centre on Housing Rights and Evictions (COHRE) v. Italy*, No. 58/2009 (ECSR), 25 June 2010, para. 76.

[75] Ibid., para. 75.

[76] Frédéric Mégret, 'Le Renouveau de la Notion de Crime d'Etat devant la Cour Interaméricaine: San José Reprend le Flambeau Abandonné à Genève et Néglige la Haye?' in L. Hennebel and H. Tigroudja (eds.), *Le Particularisme Interaméricain des Droits de l'Homme* (Paris: Pedone, 2006) p. 321.

the ECSR rather admitted aggravated state responsibility based on the state's negligence. This position also contrasts with the ILC's Draft Articles on state responsibility, by shifting the focus from the *ratione materiae* to the *ratione personae* scope of the human rights violation, without restriction based on the nature of the human rights at stake.

This shift of aggravated responsibility outside the realm of attacks against the physical integrity is promising and could have positive consequences on the ECtHR case law. For instance, the ECtHR has been confronted with violations of the rights of Roma people, which could entail the criminal qualification of persecution from the perspective of individual criminal responsibility. In other cases, the violations even matched the *actus reus* of the crime of genocide, especially the forced sterilizations imposed on Roma women in Slovakia without their free and informed consent. The Strasbourg judges have sometimes been reluctant to recognize the discriminatory pattern underlying the violations of human rights induced by these sterilizations.[77] In the *K.H. and Others v. Slovakia* case, the ECtHR thus rejected, at the admissibility stage, the argument grounded on Article 14, limiting its jurisdiction to the human rights violation caused by the impediment for the women to access their medical file.[78] In the judgment on the merits, it only found there to have been violations of the women's right to a private and family life as well as other procedural rights related to the access to the victims' medical files.[79] In the *V.C. v. Slovakia* judgment, in its finding on the merits, the court went further and recognized a violation of the right not to be submitted to inhuman and degrading treatment—Article 3 ECHR—as well as the right to private and family life—Article 8 ECHR[80]—but concluded in relation to Article 14 that it did not possess sufficient evidence: 'the sterilisation without [the applicant's] informed consent calls for serious criticism, the objective evidence is not sufficiently strong in itself to convince the Court that it was part of an organized policy or that the hospital staff's conduct was intentionally racially motivated'.[81] This statement was surprising, especially in light of the judges' reference in the next paragraph to the evidence submitted by the Human Rights Commissioner and the European Commission against Racism and Intolerance. The latter underlined that Roma women had been particularly targeted by the policy of forced sterilization, although they were not the only victims.[82]

77 Sonja Grover, *The European Court of Human Rights as a Pathway to Impunity for International Crimes*, (Heidelberg: Springer, 2010) pp. 93–129; Mathias Möschel, 'Is the European Court of Human Rights' Case Law on Anti-Roma Violence "Beyond Reasonable Doubt"?' (2012) 12 *H.R.L. Rev.* 479, pp. 479–507.

78 *K.H. and others v. Slovakia*, App. No. 32881/04 (ECtHR, decision) 9 October 2007.

79 *K.H. and others v. Slovakia*, App. No. 32881/04 (ECtHR) 28 April 2009.

80 *V.C. v. Slovakia*, App. No. 18968/07 (ECtHR) 8 November 2011, paras. 120, 155.

81 Ibid., para. 177; reiterated in *I.G. and others v. Slovakia*, App. No 15966/04 (ECtHR) 13 November 2012, paras. 165–67; *N.B. v. Slovakia*, App. No. 29518/10 (ECtHR) 12 June 2012, paras. 121–3.

82 *V.C. v. Slovakia* (n 80) para. 178.

This part of the judgment gave rise to Judge Mijovic's dissenting opinion, who expressed his regret that:

> Finding violations of Articles 3 and 8 alone in my opinion reduces this case to the individual level, whereas it is obvious that there was a general State policy of sterilisation of Roma women under the communist regime (governed by the 1972 Sterilisation Regulation), the effects of which continued to be felt up to the time of the facts giving rise to the present case.[83]

This case law could theoretically have a powerful impact on the enforcement of international law dealing with gross and serious violations of human rights. As discussed in Chapter 7, a declaration of aggravated responsibility has thus far mainly had impact on the level of reparation granted to the victims. However, Article 41 of the ILC Draft Articles provides for both a positive obligation for non-injured states 'to cooperate to bring to an end through lawful means any serious breach'[84] and a duty of abstention, that is, an obligation of non-recognition of the 'situation created by a serious breach'.[85]

6.2 State Responsibility for Failing to Prevent Genocide

If the category of 'persecution' is conceptually linked to genocide prevention, the concrete implementation of this dimension remains uncertain. The ICJ case opposing Bosnia and Herzegovina to Serbia and Montenegro has allowed for both content to be attributed to a potential legal/judicial tool of genocide prevention, through the order of provisional measures, and the clarification of the obligation to prevent genocide, with the recognition, in the 2007 judgment, of Serbia's responsibility for failing to prevent genocide.

6.2.1 Cultural destruction as a trigger of provisional measures

The ICJ case opposing Bosnia and Herzegovina to Serbia and Montenegro started in 1993, when Bosnia and Herzegovina requested that the ICJ recognize Yugoslavia's responsibility for having breached the Genocide Convention, as well as to order the respondent state to cease to commit these violations, which included, amongst others, 'the wanton devastation of villages, towns, districts, cities, and religious institutions in Bosnia and Herzegovina'.[86] Bosnia further requested the Court to order provisional measures to Yugoslavia, especially to:

> immediately cease and desist from all acts of genocide and genocidal acts against the People and State of Bosnia and Herzegovina, including but not limited to murder; summary

[83] Ibid. Dissenting opinion Judge Mijovic.
[84] ILC 2001 Draft Articles on State Responsibility (n 19) art. 41(1).
[85] Ibid., art. 41(2).
[86] *Application of the Convention on the Prevention and Punishment of the Crime of Genocide (Bosnia and Herzegovina v. Yugoslavia [Serbia and Montenegro])* (Requests for the Indication of Provisional Measures) [1993] ICJ Rep. 3, p. 6, para. 2(q).

executions; torture; rape; mayhem; so-called 'ethnic cleansing'; the wanton devastation of villages, towns, districts and cities.[87]

Yugoslavia replied and returned the accusation of 'ethnic cleansing' against Bosnia and Herzegovina, requesting that the court order provisional measures as well. Yugoslavia made no explicit reference to the Genocide Convention but rather quoted the Geneva framework of international humanitarian law,[88] asking the court to order the leader of Bosnia and Herzegovina, Alija Izetbegovic, to respect Bosnian Serbs' human rights. Among others, it asked the ICJ:

to instruct the authorities loyal to A. Izetbegovic to cease immediately any further destruction of Orthodox churches and places of worship and of other Serb cultural heritage, and to release and stop further mistreatment of all Orthodox priests being in prison.[89]

This was not the first time that Yugoslavia had formulated accusations close to 'cultural genocide', if one remembers the Memorandum of the Serbian Academy of Arts and Sciences in which one could foresee the roots of the aggressive policy to come, based on the threat of' "physical, political, legal and cultural genocide" which would be perpetrated in Kosovo against the Serbian population of that province'.[90]

The ICJ replied to these concerns in very broad terms, ordering Yugoslavia to 'take all measures within its power to prevent commission of the crime of genocide'[91] and to ensure that no organ under its control commits any act criminalized in Article III of the Genocide Convention.[92] It further ordered both parties not to 'take any action [that] (...) may aggravate or extend the existing dispute'.[93] It reiterated the two first measures in a subsequent order in September 1993.[94] The exact scope of these measures needs to be read in light of the court's earlier statement in relation to the definition of its material jurisdiction, as conferred by Article IX of the Genocide Convention:

the Court (...) ought not to indicate measures for the protection of any disputed rights other than those which might ultimately form the basis of a judgment in the exercise of that jurisdiction; whereas accordingly the Court will confine its examination of the measures requested, and of the grounds asserted for the request for such measures, to those which fall within the scope of the Genocide Convention;[95]

[87] *Application of the Genocide Convention (Bosnia and Herzegovina v. Yugoslavia)* (Requests for the Indication of Provisional Measures) (n 86) p. 8, para. 3(1).

[88] Ibid., p. 10, para. 9: 'the Geneva Conventions for the Protection of Victims of War of 1949 and the 1977 Additional Protocols'.

[89] Ibid.

[90] Cf. Memorandum of Arts 1986, quoted in *Karadžić & Mladić Case* (Review of the Indictments Pursuant to Rule 61 of the Rules of Procedure and Evidence) IT-95-5-R61; IT-95-18-R6I (11 July 1996) para. 44.

[91] *Application of the Genocide Convention (Bosnia and Herzegovina v. Yugoslavia)* (Requests for the Indication of Provisional Measures) (n 86) p. 24, para. 52(A)(1).

[92] Ibid., para. 52(A)(2).

[93] Ibid., para. 52(B).

[94] *Application of the Convention on the Prevention and Punishment of the Crime of Genocide* (*Bosnia and Herzegovina v. Yugoslavia* [*Serbia and Montenegro*]) (Further requests for the Indication of Provisional Measures) [1993] ICJ Rep. 325.

[95] *Application of the Genocide Convention* (*Bosnia and Herzegovina v. Yugoslavia*) (Requests for the Indication of Provisional Measures) (n 86) para. 35.

In 1993, the 'material scope of the Genocide Convention' was not defined in the same thorough terms as it is nowadays, having not yet received judicial implementation. The only document available at this time was the 1991 ILC Draft Code of Crimes against the Peace and Security of Mankind, which already pointed towards the 'material destruction of a group either by physical or by biological means'[96] but was not quoted in the 1993 Order on provisional measures. However, at the time, some authors were already raising the question of whether the definition of the crime of genocide could encompass acts which, without primarily aiming at the physical disappearance of a group, would nevertheless lead to its disappearance or the risk of its disappearance.[97]

Furthermore, in the 1996 decision on preliminary objections, the ICJ rejected Bosnia's arguments aiming at extending the scope of the ICJ's jurisdiction, beyond Article IX of the Genocide Convention. On the one hand, Bosnia argued that other legal bases could be subsumed by Article IX thus:

> enabling the Court to make findings on some of the means used by Yugoslavia to perpetrate the genocide of which it stands accused, and particularly its recourse to a war of aggression during which it seriously violated the 1949 Geneva Conventions and the 1977 Protocols 1 and II.[98]

On the other hand, Bosnia argued that Yugoslavia had expressed unequivocal consent to the extension of the ICJ's jurisdiction, by formulating requests of provisional measures that exceeded the scope of the Genocide Convention, such as Yugoslavia's above-mentioned quasi-allegation of cultural genocide.[99] In response to both arguments, the court repeated both the content of the provisional measures and the rejection of any jurisdictional ground other than Article IX of the Genocide Convention, since Yugoslavia had consistently objected to the ICJ's jurisdiction.[100]

Since then, the 'material understanding' has been confirmed more than once, including in the 2007 ICJ judgment on the merits of the case. Read in light of these contemporary developments, this raises the question of the likeliness for a state to obtain provisional measures aimed at preventing genocide on the basis of acts that are not necessarily listed in subparagraphs (a) to (e) of Article II of the Genocide Convention, but are nevertheless understood to be part of the genocidal process, especially those which have been recognized as potential evidence of the intent to destroy a group, such as acts of destruction of cultural heritage. Accordingly, the later case law on the matter could contribute to ground the jurisdictional basis of the ICJ, provided that the latter adopts a broad understanding of 'the material scope

[96] ILC 1991 Draft Code of Crimes (n 18) Commentary on art. 19, para. 4, p. 102.

[97] Laurence Boisson de Chazournes, 'Les Ordonnances en Indication de Mesures Conservatoires dans l'Affaire Relative à l'Application de la Convention pour la Prévention et la Répression des Crimes de Génocide' (1993) 39 *A.F.D.I.* 514, p. 530. '*La définition du crime de génocide recouvre-t-elle des actes qui, sans avoir pour objectif premier de faire disparaître physiquement un group, n'en entrainent pas moins la disparition ou le risque de disparation, du fait de leur accomplissement?*'

[98] *Application of the Convention on the Prevention and Punishment of the Crime of Genocide (Bosnia and Herzegovina v. Yugoslavia)* (Preliminary Objections) [1996] ICJ Rep. 595, para. 35.

[99] Ibid., para. 40. [100] Ibid., paras. 38, 40.

of the Genocide Convention'. However, considering the United Nations Special Adviser on the Prevention of Genocide (UNSAPG) analysis framework and the *Krstić* finding in relation to the relationship between destruction of cultural assets and the *mens rea* of genocide, this mechanism might only encompass acts of the destruction of tangible cultural heritage. It should also be highlighted that these attacks are so far only 'evidence' of the intent to destroy. They would therefore not constitute in and of themselves a ground for obtaining provisional measures. In respect of other types of attacks on cultural-related rights or assets of intangible cultural heritage, they would, however, be likely to fall under the criminal category of crimes against humanity of cultural persecution, which may open up another perspective of genocide prevention. Of course, the question remains pending as to whether such acts of cultural destruction could stand the *prima facie* test of provisional measures.[101] It might be, however, that this question is purely theoretical since, as it has been argued throughout this book, these destructions rarely occur in isolation, that is in the absence of any other criminal acts. Hence, if the genocide label is called upon, this can be deemed to be rightly so because these destructions occur in a pattern of widespread discrimination and attacks against a given group. The option of provisional measures to circumscribe the risk of genocide remains an interesting option, as it does not amount to the definitive labelling of the crimes, but only the acknowledgement of the likelihood of their occurrence.

In any event, the possibility of using provisional measures as a potential judicial tool of genocide prevention in relation to attacks against a group culture remains quite limited in scope, since this mechanism depends entirely on the obligations set out in the Genocide Convention and therefore falls within the exclusive jurisdiction of the ICJ. Article IX of the Genocide Convention presupposes an inter-state dispute, which de facto excludes genocide perpetrated against groups within the territory of one given state, with the exception of the possibility that third states may seize the ICJ for the violation of imperative norms of international law.[102] This option would surely fall within the range of 'lawful means' that states shall implement to bring an end to serious breaches of obligation under peremptory norms of general international law, as provided for by Article 41(1) of the ILC Draft Articles. Moreover, Article 48 entitles any state to invoke the responsibility of another state, in case 'the obligation breached is owed to the international community as a whole'[103] and to claim, amongst others, the 'cessation of the internationally wrongful act' from the responsible state.[104]

Beyond these inherent limits and uncertainties as to their material scope, the question of provisional measures to prevent the perpetration of genocide at the moment acts of cultural destruction are perpetrated could still constitute a powerful

[101] See e.g. *Application of the Genocide Convention* (*Bosnia and Herzegovina v. Yugoslavia*) (Requests for the Indication of Provisional Measures) (n 86) para. 14.

[102] Marko Milanović, 'State Responsibility for Genocide: A Follow-Up' (2007) 18 *E.J.I.L.* 669, p. 688.

[103] ILC 2001 Draft Articles on State Responsibility (n 19) art. 48 (1)(b).

[104] Ibid., art. 48 (2)(a).

tool of genocide prevention. As Schabas has noted the 1993 Orders of provisional measures 'did alter the political debate, and were cited in Security Council resolutions and a variety of reports, both official and unofficial. The potential impact of such orders in the case of ethnic conflict should not be gainsaid'.[105] This tool has also been strengthened by the ICJ's interpretation of its own Statute so as to render such orders binding[106] and creating 'international legal obligations which both Parties are required to comply with'.[107] Hence, in case genocide would be perpetrated, in spite of an order of provisional measures, not only could a state be held responsible for the breach of the order, but its responsibility for failing to prevent genocide, which was addressed in the 2007 ICJ judgment, could also be contemplated.

6.2.2 Cultural destruction as a trigger of state responsibility for failing to prevent genocide

In the 2007 judgment, the ICJ eventually found Serbia responsible for the violation of its obligation to prevent genocide according to the Genocide Convention. It first reasserted the 'separate legal existence' of the obligation to prevent[108] before stating that it was an obligation 'of conduct and not one of result'.[109] In this regard, it defined the threshold of obligation as an 'obligation of due diligence'[110] which depends on:

> the capacity to influence effectively the action of persons likely to commit, or already committing, genocide. This capacity itself depends, among other things, on the geographical distance of the State concerned from the scene of the events, and on the strength of the political links, as well as links of all other kinds, between the authorities of that State and the main actors in the events.[111]

The distinction between the obligation not to perpetrate genocide and the obligation to prevent genocide is noted here: in the first case, a state may be found responsible on the basis of the effective control it was exercising on the alleged individual perpetrators; in the second case, a state may be found responsible on the basis of its effective influence. In both cases, the evidence, such as the financing of the individuals or organs, might be common.

The judges then considered that 'a State can be held responsible for breaching the obligation to prevent genocide only if genocide was actually committed'.[112] Recognizing that this could render genocide prevention completely ineffective, they identified, as a starting point, the moment at which the state—incarnated in its

[105] William A. Schabas, 'Preventing Genocide and Mass Killing: The Challenge for the United Nations' (London: Minority Rights Group International, 2006) p. 19.

[106] *LaGrand (Germany v. United States of America)* (Judgment) [2001] ICJ Rep. 466, para. 109.

[107] *Armed Activities on the Territory of the Congo* (*Democratic Republic of the Congo v. Uganda*) (Judgment) [2005] ICJ Rep. 258, para. 263; *Certain Activities Carried Out by Nicaragua in the Border Area* (*Costa Rica v. Nicaragua*) (Provisional Measures) [2011] ICJ Rep. 6, para. 86.

[108] *Application of the Genocide Convention* (*Bosnia and Herzegovina v. Serbia and Montenegro*) (Judgment) (n 1) para. 427.

[109] Ibid., para. 430. [110] Ibid. [111] Ibid. [112] Ibid., para. 431.

political and military leaders—would become aware of the imminence of genocide. Considering the facts of the case, that is the massacre of Srebrenica, the ICJ mainly focused on identifying the exact moment at which Slobodan Milosevic had learnt of the imminence of the massacre. State responsibility for genocide prevention, and accordingly, the related international obligation to prevent genocide, may neither encompass the wider process of genocide, nor the failure to prevent and punish gross human rights violations, which leads to physical genocide.[113] The way in which this duty is constructed thus leaves little, if any, space for the inclusion of the prior steps towards genocide, as identified in the various analytical frameworks elaborated by the UNSAPG or the CERD. Again, this may allow for the acknowledgement of the cultural dimension of the process as evidence of the failure to prevent but not to actually determine the state's responsibility for failing to prevent genocide due to the perpetration of acts likely to escalate towards the perpetration of genocide.

A last option is highly hypothetical but worth underlining nonetheless; it emerges from Bosnia's argument before the ICJ that 'Serb forces engaged in the deliberate destruction of historical, religious and cultural property of the protected group in "an *attempt* to wipe out the traces of their very existence"'.[114] This argument was thus not formulated under the obligation to prevent genocide but rather under the prohibition of genocide. 'Attempt' is criminalized as an act of genocide under Article III of the Genocide Convention but has never received any implementation in international criminal law since, as Schabas notes, 'there is hardly a need to prosecute attempt when a tribunal is set up *ex post facto*'.[115] *A contrario*, in the case of existing tribunals, such as the ICC for individual criminal responsibility and the ICJ for state responsibility, the prosecution and adjudication of attempts to perpetrate genocide could turn out to be more than theoretical hypotheses. However, Bosnia's argument was not explicitly formulated under Article III of the Genocide Convention and as a result, the Court did not address the issue in its final judgment.[116] This argument is still interesting in relation to the articulation between attacks against a group culture and the overall process of genocide. It may differ from the step towards genocide envisaged in the context of genocide prevention since the idea of 'attempt' may not necessarily be considered in a chronological perspective. This is the hypothesis that seems to emerge from Bosnia's statement on the destruction of cultural and religious property. However, the two are overlapping to the extent that the concept of 'attempt' is sufficiently ambiguous,[117] that it might potentially be interpreted as an advanced version of 'preparatory acts',[118]

[113] Ibid., paras. 435–8. [114] Ibid., para. 335 (emphasis added).

[115] Schabas, *Genocide in International Law* (n 15) p. 335.

[116] *Application of the Genocide Convention* (*Bosnia and Herzegovina v. Serbia and Montenegro*) (Judgment) (n 1) para. 416; Jens D. Ohlin, 'State Responsibility for Conspiracy, Incitement, and Attempt to Commit Genocide' in Paola Gaeta (ed.), *The UN Genocide Convention: A Commentary*, (Oxford: Oxford University Press, 2009) p. 377.

[117] Ohlin (n 116) p. 378 thus points at the 'conceptual confusion over whether attempt to commit genocide involves an incomplete predicate act or an incomplete genocide'.

[118] Schabas, *Genocide in International Law* (n 15) pp. 589–92: 'Preparatory acts' were rejected from the final draft of the Genocide Convention. However, the line between preparatory acts and 'attempt' is still blurred (ibid. pp. 337–8).

which could then constitute a useful legal basis for engaging state responsibility for genocide in light of preparatory acts such as cultural destruction, as Bosnia argued in 2007. However, the question remains open as to the conditions that would apply to a potential regime of state responsibility in respect of an attempt to perpetrate genocide, especially in relation to the *mens rea* of genocide, and furthermore as to whether it could be set in terms of knowledge of the attempt or shared intent to destroy the group as such. Again, no criminal case law exists on this matter, nor do the ILC Draft Articles on state responsibility mention the concept of attempt, as they only contemplate state responsibility for either the breach of an international obligation or for the aiding and assisting of another state to commit an internationally wrongful act.[119] The lack of legal development in relation to this issue therefore renders the option as one of an interesting theoretical possibility.[120]

The order of provisional measures would therefore constitute the only potential way to attribute content to the cultural dimension of genocide prevention. Such orders fall under the exclusive jurisdiction of the ICJ, on the basis of Article IX of the Genocide Convention. This possibility is contingent upon a broad interpretation of jurisdiction *ratione materiae* of the Court, in such a way as to cover both acts of genocide proper, and acts that are associated with genocide, as evidence of its intent, the latter being more likely to be perpetrated in anticipation of the former.

6.3 Concluding Remarks

This chapter has shown that the issue of articulating findings made in the context of international criminal law within the international regime of state responsibility is twofold and involves: firstly, consolidating state obligations related to cultural genocide; and secondly, the enforcement of these obligations. The dimensions of the issue are sometimes intertwined, as is the case of genocide prevention, since both the interpretation of related state obligations and their enforcement rely on the ICJ, which tends to adopt a narrow understanding of such obligations. Consequently, mechanisms of enforcement remain important for the purposes of determining the capacity of international law to fully address the concept of cultural genocide. In this regard, the ICJ's jurisdiction to order provisional measures has been underlined as a potential tool of genocide prevention. This mechanism could be articulated with the IACHR and European Social Committee's case law on aggravated state responsibility so as to enable non-injured states to request that the ICJ order provisional measures on the basis of serious and discriminatory violations of cultural rights, perpetrated in the context of crimes against humanity. The order would

[119] ILC 2001 Draft Articles on State Responsibility (n 19) art. 16.

[120] Rafaëlle Maison, 'Le Crime de Génocide dans la Jurisprudence Internationale, Débats et Hypothèses' in Tomuschat C., Lagrange E., and Oeter S. (eds.), *The Right to Life* (Leiden; Boston: Martinus Nijhoff Publishers, 2010) p. 100.

be justified by the human rights violations as such, which constitute breaches of imperative norms, rather than their potential escalation towards genocide.

Recent developments of international law have thus induced the emergence of synergies between branches of law that have often been considered separately. It is possible to play on these synergies to push forward the logic of current international law towards recognizing and addressing complex phenomena such as those labelled under cultural genocide. Accordingly, once these phenomena are reconceptualized as serious violations of human rights—and especially, as cultural rights—this opens up the possibility for their criminalization, provided that they occur in a wider context of systematic or widespread attack against civilians. The effects might be reciprocal; that is to say, this criminal context might itself have repercussions in the field of state responsibility by enhancing the level of responsibility, starting with the state responsibility to protect human rights. This logic is not only relevant to cultural rights but the study has also illustrated that there is no reason why this 'category' of rights should be left aside. Meanwhile, 'keeping a foot' in international human rights law allows for the scope to benefit from the advantages of this framework, especially in relation to the right to reparation.

7

Reparation for Intended Cultural Harm

Exploring the way in which international law might address cultural genocide raises the question of the reparation for the harm resulting from the acts encapsulated by the concept. Indeed, according to Federico Lenzerini, 'the moment in which reparations (ie "substantive redress") are materially granted is the moment in which the idea of justice crystallizes, and only at that precise moment justice is effectively realized'.[1] As will be discussed, reparation has become a principle of international law, which is an automatic consequence of a finding of a breach of international law. As mechanical as it may be, framing the idea of reparation in relation to the concept of cultural genocide is not self-evident. In the current state of international law—which has remained impermeable to the concept of cultural genocide as such—intended cultural harm seems to better capture the idea of reparation for cultural genocide. Even though it is borrowed from the criminal law language, the notion of intent is core to the concept of cultural genocide and tends to constitute the dividing line between 'cultural genocide' and 'violations of cultural rights', for instance.

This chapter only focuses on the material dimension of reparation, in contrast with the wider concepts of redress or remedy, which also encompass the procedural aspects of access to legal remedies.[2] This approach accords with the more general scope of the research, which has thus far mainly been concerned with covering the substantive dimension of cultural genocide. In light of these considerations, the specificity of the intended cultural harm is firstly underlined in this chapter, in order to delineate the object of reparation, before undertaking an analysis of the current international legal frameworks of reparation likely to address the various facets of this harm, in light of the potential legal qualifications previously identified. Finally, a more practical perspective is adopted to determine how cultural harm has been tackled in the various cases that have been mentioned throughout the book.

[1] Federico Lenzerini, 'Reparations for Indigenous Peoples in International and Comparative Law: An Introduction' in Federico Lenzerini (ed.), *Reparations for Indigenous Peoples: International and Comparative Perspectives* (Oxford: Oxford University Press, 2008) p. 8.

[2] Ibid., p. 13. It should, however, be noted that these various aspects of remedies might sometimes overlap, as truth might be part of both the substantive and procedural means of redress.

7.1 The Specificities of Intended Cultural Harm

The philosophy underlying the international legal obligation to repair the damage resulting from an international wrongful act was set out in the *Chorzów factory* judgment of the Permanent Court of International Justice (PCIJ), the forerunner of the ICJ, in the following terms: 'reparation, must, as far as possible, wipe out all the consequences of the illegal act and re-establish the situation, which would, in all probability, have existed if that act had not been committed'.[3] This perspective of 'restorative justice' may nevertheless be deemed insufficient in some cases of historical injustice, such as those involving indigenous peoples.[4] In such cases, there might not be much capable of restoration considering their historical status of second-class citizens, whose marginalization has often triggered the violation and/or increased its impact. This is why a 'transformative perspective' will be preferred, as it implies that the reparation constitutes the opportunity to redress structural discrimination or historical injustice, two concepts that are very much associated with that of 'cultural genocide'.

As in many cases of violations of human rights, repairing cultural harm raises the issue of repairing the irreparable.[5] In this specific case of cultural damage, the difficulty results both from its cultural and collective dimensions. As for its cultural dimension, cultural genocide involves some form of destruction of heritage, either considered in its tangible or intangible forms. Reparation for the destruction of tangible cultural heritage would logically induce the reconstruction of the assets. However, the destruction of a monument needs to be seen from the perspective of both its material and spiritual components. Each stone may possess a value of its own, whether historical, aesthetical, technical, or architectural so that the destruction involves the loss of more than mere stones, going as far as to reflect the loss of a past, a history, which is actually reflected in the very name of 'heritage'. This is indeed what is targeted through attacks against such assets. However, as Bevan notes, religious and cultural assets may acquire the status of 'heritage' because of their destruction:

> Rebuilding can be as symbolic as the destruction that necessitates it. (. . .) What were once unintentional monuments—places of worship, libraries and fountains of everyday life—by their rebuilding can become new, intentional monuments to the events that caused their destruction.[6]

[3] *Factory of Chorzów case* (*Germany v. Poland*) (Merits) 13 September 1928, PCIJ Rep. Series A No. 17, p. 47.

[4] Jennifer Llewellyn, 'Bridging the Gap between Truth and Reconciliation: Restorative Justice and the Indian Residential Schools Truth and Reconciliation Commission' in Marlene Brant Castellano, Linda Archibald, and Mike DeGagné (eds.), *From Truth to Reconciliation: Transforming the Legacy of Residential Schools* (Ottawa: Aboriginal Healing Foundation, 2008) p. 189.

[5] Christine Evans, *The Right to Reparation in International Law for Victims of Armed Conflicts* (Cambridge, UK; New York: Cambridge University Press, 2012) p. 29.

[6] Robert Bevan, *The Destruction of Memory: Architecture at War* (London: Reaktion Books, 2006) p. 176.

Reparation of destroyed intangible cultural features turns out to be equally as problematic, considering its inherent human dimension. Intangible heritage, such as a language, a cultural rite, and the relationship with the land, cannot be reconstructed; it can at best be 'revitalized'. The Convention on the safeguarding of intangible cultural heritage makes reference to the possibility for 'revitalization' of this heritage under its definition of 'safeguarding',[7] though outside a legal context of reparation. This feature is also present in two provisions of the United Nations Declaration on the Rights of Indigenous Peoples (UNDRIP), under the right for indigenous peoples 'to revitalize, use, develop and transmit to future generations their histories, languages, oral traditions, philosophies, writing systems and literatures, and to designate and retain their own names for communities, places and persons',[8] as well as:

> to practise and revitalize their cultural traditions and customs. This includes the right to maintain, protect and develop the past, present and future manifestations of their cultures, such as archaeological and historical sites, artefacts, designs, ceremonies, technologies and visual and performing arts and literature.[9]

This latter right is accompanied by a state obligation to 'redress through effective mechanisms (. . .) with respect to their cultural, intellectual, religious and spiritual property taken without their free, prior and informed consent'.[10] However, in this provision, the right to revitalize constitutes a primary norm rather than a means of redress. It might still be possible to understand 'revitalization' as a secondary norm, though not necessarily on the basis of Article 11 UNDRIP. In any event, none of these instruments provide a proper definition of the concept of revitalization.

As for the collective dimension, it has already been stated several times that it is inherent to the notion of culture. Collective reparation may thus turn out to be particularly adequate to address cultural harm. As Frédéric Mégret underlines, such a possibility is to be welcomed, in a context of post-mass atrocities:

> there would be a very real danger of excessive individualization of reparations in a context where, for all the accumulation of individual suffering, the harm inflicted often targeted groups or the civilian population rather than specific individuals.[11]

This dimension involves two levels of analysis: the harm to a group, associated with the targeted cultural asset or feature, as well as the harm resulting from the 'elimination of diversity',[12] which brings to the fore the broader issue of repairing the 'social

[7] Convention for the Safeguarding of the Intangible Cultural Heritage (adopted 17 October 2003, entered into force 20 April 2006) 1268 UNTS 1 (Intangible Cultural Heritage Convention) art. 2(3).

[8] Declaration on the Rights of Indigenous Peoples (adopted 13 September 2007) UNGA Res. 61/295 (UNDRIP) art. 13(1).

[9] Ibid., art. 11(1).

[10] Ibid., art. 11(2).

[11] Frédéric Mégret, 'Of Shrines, Memorials and Museums: Using the International Criminal Court's Victim Reparation and Assistance Regime to Promote Transitional Justice' (2010) 16 *Buff. Hum.Rts.L.Rev.* 1, p. 20.

[12] Ana F. Vrdoljak, 'Genocide and Restitution: Ensuring Each Group's Contribution to Humanity' (2011) 22 *E.J.I.L.* 17, p. 18.

fabric'. Francesco Francioni thus considers that '[e]nsuring that the memory of past injustices does not manifest itself in present and persistent rancour is probably the most important function of reparation for past injustices'.[13] This goal is very much present in frameworks of transitional justice, in which justice, and hence reparation, is a crucial component of transitioning societies, either from an authoritarian regime to a democracy or from an armed conflict to a situation of peace, in order to close the 'circle of impunity'.[14]

With regard to repairing the group harm, the question as to the relevance and the potential forms of collective reparation arises. The International Center for Transitional Justice (ICTJ) considers collective reparation to be especially relevant to address '[m]assive or systematic rights violations [that] affect means of subsistence, or dismantle organizations or destroy public trust among residents', which are indeed the effects of cultural genocide.[15] The ILA considers collective reparation to be best suited for human rights breaches suffered by indigenous peoples, by contrast with the 'Western vision' of reparation:

> First, in the Western world reparation is essentially conceived as compensation to individuals, while with respect to indigenous peoples it has a real sense only to the extent that it assumes a collective significance. Second, according to the Western vision, monetary compensation is commonly considered the only—or at least the paramount—goal to be achieved in order to ensure effectiveness of reparation itself. In the case of indigenous peoples, material reparation—especially when it takes the form of compensation—is usually inappropriate to ensure effective redress for the pain they have suffered.[16]

The concept of 'collective reparations' may, however, give rise to some tension from a practical perspective. The first level of tension concerns the identification and delimitation of the communities that can benefit from the collective reparation. This necessarily involves the consultation of the communities in the process.[17] However, the very process of selection of groups and communities entitled to collective reparations might result in the exclusion of individuals or other communities from the scope of such programmes, which consequently becomes counterproductive by fuelling resentment amongst communities. It is therefore crucial to couple collective reparations with individual reparations.[18] The mere definition of the harm

[13] Francesco Francioni, 'Is International Law Ready to Ensure Redress for Historical Injustices?' in Federico Lenzerini (ed.), *Reparations for Indigenous Peoples: International and Comparative Perspectives* (Oxford: Oxford University Press, 2008) p. 46.

[14] For a definition of transitional justice, see R.G. Teitel, 'Transitional Justice Genealogy' (2003) 16 *Harv.Hum.Rts.J.* 69, p. 69: 'the conception of justice associated with periods of political change, characterized by legal responses to confront wrongdoings of repressive predecessor regimes'.

[15] International Center for Transitional Justice (ICTJ), 'The Rabat Report: The Concept and Challenges of Collective Reparations' (2009) p. 9.

[16] Committee on Rights of Indigenous Peoples, 'Rights of Indigenous Peoples, Interim Report' in International Law Association Report of the Seventy-Third Conference (The Hague 2010) (International Law Association, London 2010) p. 39.

[17] Redress, 'Collective Reparations: Concept and Principles', available at: http://www.redress.org/downloads/events/CollectiveReparationsMG.pdf (last accessed 1 February 2015) p. 1.

[18] Louise Arbour, 'Economic and Social Justice for Societies in Transition' (2007–2008) 40 *N.Y.U.J.Int.L.Pol.* 1, pp. 19–20; ICTJ, 'The Rabat Report' (n 15) p. 40; Redress (n 17) p. 2; Pablo

to be redressed may also be disputed within the community itself, between the victims and the community leaders for instance,[19] especially when the harm inflicted upon a community has arisen hand in hand with the radicalization—or at least exacerbation—of this same community's identity. As the ICTJ highlights, there is a 'need to distinguish communities—such as Indigenous people with a strong communal culture and common identity—from groups of people that have suffered individually but who may have, as a result of the common experience, developed a common identity'.[20] This twofold approach seems like an appropriate answer to the 'groupism' criticism that collective reparation may induce.[21] Indeed, there is a risk that the very notion of 'collective reparations' unduly fixes those identities that have been constructed on the basis of a common experience of gross violations of human rights.

The second tension concerns the content of reparation, and especially the scope for distinguishing reparation from humanitarian aid and assistance as well as development policies, which might be confused in practice.[22] These various undertakings may overlap in terms of focus but 'collective reparations should not substitute the state's obligation to provide basic services to every citizen', such as housing, education, and social services.[23] 'Symbolic' measures, such as 'memorials', may thus constitute an adequate means, though not an exclusive means, of distinguishing reparations from developmental or humanitarian policies.[24] Memorials might also ensure that the difficulties associated both with individualizing victims and in drawing the exact contours of a community can be avoided.[25] The notion of 'measure of reparation' and its definition has been progressively enshrined in the international legal framework.

7.2 Cultural Reparation in International Legal Frameworks of Reparation

In international law, reparation is the consequence of the violation of a primary norm. In the context of cultural genocide, cultural reparation may therefore occur in three different contexts: general international law, which involves state responsibility for breaches of international law; international human rights law, which

De Greiff, 'Justice and Reparations', in Pablo De Greiff (ed.), *The Oxford Handbook of Reparations* (Oxford: Oxford University Press, 2011) p. 470.

[19] Redress (n 17) p. 8; ICTJ, 'The Rabat Report' (n 15) p. 52.

[20] ICTJ, 'The Rabat Report' (n 15) p. 44.

[21] See Rogers Brubaker, *Ethnicity without Groups* (Cambridge, Mass.: Harvard University Press, 2004).

[22] Arbour (n 18) p. 20; ICTJ, 'The Rabat Report' (n 15) pp. 40, 47.

[23] ICTJ, 'The Rabat Report' (n 15) p. 46; Redress (n 17).

[24] ICTJ, 'The Rabat Report' (n 15) p. 41; Mégret, 'Of Shrines, Memorials and Museums' (n 11) p. 49.

[25] Mégret, 'Of Shrines, Memorials and Museums' (n 11) p. 49.

involves state responsibility for the violations of human rights; and international criminal law, which involves individual criminal responsibility. While the material content of the measures of reparation tends to overlap between these different regimes, the context of their implementation differs; accordingly, these three frameworks will be reviewed successively.

7.2.1 The general framework of state responsibility

State responsibility may arise from the violation either of norms of customary international law or of conventional instruments, such as the 1948 Genocide Convention, the 1954 Hague Convention on the Protection of Cultural Property in the Event of Armed Conflict, the 1972 World Heritage Convention, the 2003 Convention on the Safeguarding of Intangible Cultural Heritage. These instruments only create state obligations towards other states, such that the obligation to repair will necessarily occur in an inter-state context.[26] The argument has been made that reparation for indigenous peoples should occur within the inter-state framework, rather than within the human rights framework, on the basis that the indigenous peoples were illegally deprived of their sovereignty.[27] Such a shift of the relevant legal regime may not have a significant impact on the content of the reparation to be granted in relation to the cultural harm suffered, since the measures of reparation consecutive to human rights violations are almost identical to those provided for by the 2001 ILC Articles on State Responsibility. These articles are deemed to codify customary international law in relation to the obligation to repair an international wrongful act, and therefore to substitute the silence of the few above-mentioned international instruments on the matter. Consequently, none of these instruments contain explicit provision in relation to the secondary obligations that would arise from a breach of the primary obligations. In this regard, it is noteworthy that the first draft of the Genocide Convention included a provision on reparation, which was ultimately excluded from the final text:

> When genocide is committed in a country by the government in power and by sections of the population, and if the government fails to resist it successfully, the State shall grant to the survivors of the human group that is a victim of genocide redress of a nature and in an amount to be determined by the United Nations.[28]

The 2001 ILC Draft Articles thus state the 'obligation to make full reparation for the injury caused by the internationally wrongful act',[29] whether the damage is 'material or moral'.[30] According to Article 34, '[f]ull reparation for the injury

[26] Evans, *The Right to Reparation* (n 5) pp. 29–30.

[27] Lenzerini, 'Reparations for Indigenous Peoples in International and Comparative Law' (n 1) pp. 11–12.

[28] ECOSOC 'Draft Convention on the Crime of Genocide' E/447 (26 June 1947), Draft Article XIII, quoted in Evans, *The Right to Reparation* (n 5) p. 88.

[29] ILC (53rd Session), 'Draft Articles on Responsibility of States for Internationally Wrongful Acts, with Commentaries', *Yearbook of the International Law Commission*, 2001, vol. II, Part Two (ILC 2001 Draft Articles on State Responsibility) art. 31(1).

[30] Ibid., art. 31(2).

caused by the internationally wrongful act shall take the form of restitution, compensation and satisfaction, either singly or in combination';[31] each of these measures is further specified in subsequent provisions. Guarantees of non-repetition might also be granted, although these measures are not considered within the chapter on reparation.[32]

Restitution is thus the first measure to be contemplated. An example of the implementation of this measure can be identified in relation to the art looted by the Nazis during the Holocaust, the undertaking of which injured both states and individuals owners. In 1998, forty-four states adopted the Washington Conference Principles on Nazi-Confiscated Art. These non-binding principles state, among others, the need for the identification of looted art that had not yet been restituted to its original owners,[33] as well as the need for the identification of the 'Pre-War owners' themselves.[34] The case of the Holocaust-looted art has given rise to specific issues, considering the context of racial extermination in which such economic-driven looting occurred.[35] Moreover, restitution is only available in cases involving both material and non-destroyed cultural heritage. In the case that one of these two features is missing from any given situation, financial compensation should then be considered, provided that the damage is 'financially assessable'.[36] Compensation might be possible in respect of issues relating to land in those cases in which the land cannot be restituted or the restitution would be disproportionate with regard to the public interest at stake.[37] This issue of balancing various interests is particularly acute in the case of indigenous peoples, who aim 'at obtaining restitution and peaceful enjoyment of land resources rather than compensation or other forms of reparation'.[38] Restitution and financial compensation should not constitute too heavy a burden on the state. In case state responsibility is related to the violation of imperative norms of general international law, as enshrined in Articles 40 and 41 of the ILC Draft Articles, this limitation no longer stands.

In case neither restitution nor compensation is possible, the ILC states that the 'State responsible for an internationally wrongful act is under an obligation to give satisfaction',[39] which 'may consist in an acknowledgement of the breach,

[31] Ibid., art. 34. [32] Ibid., art. 30(2).

[33] U.S. Department of State, Bureau of European and Eurasian Affairs, *Washington Conference Principles on Nazi-Confiscated Art* (adopted 3 December 1998), Principles 1 and 3.

[34] Ibid. Principle 8.

[35] Sarah Gensburger, *Images d'un Pillage: Album de la Spoliation des Juifs à Paris, 1940–1944* (Paris: Textuel, 2010) p. 153.

[36] ILC 2001 Draft Articles on State Responsibility (n 29) art. 36(2).

[37] See e.g. ILO Convention (No. 169) concerning Indigenous and Tribal Peoples in Independent Countries (adopted 27 June 1989, entered into force 5 September 1991) 1650 UNTS 383 (ILO Convention No. 169), which completed ILO Convention (No. 107) on Indigenous and Tribal Populations (adopted 26 June 1957, entered into force 2 June 1959) 328 UNTS 247 (ILO Convention No. 107), which is now considered as 'obsolete'. See http://www.ilo.org/indigenous/Conventions/no107/lang--en/index.htm (last accessed 1 February 2015) art. 16(4); *Saramaka People v. Suriname*, Preliminary Objections, Merits, Reparations, and Costs, Inter-American Court of Human Rights Series C No. 172 (28 November 2007) para. 118.

[38] Francioni, 'Is International Law Ready to Ensure Redress for Historical Injustices?' (n 13) p. 28.

[39] ILC 2001 Draft Articles on State Responsibility (n 29) art. 37(1).

an expression of regret, a formal apology or another appropriate modality'.[40] Considering its open-ended formulation, this latter category may therefore be particularly suitable for repairing the cultural consequences of genocidal processes, as it has been interpreted as encompassing measures such as the construction of memorials, or 'sites of conscience'.[41] The same could be said to apply to the reconstruction of destroyed or damaged tangible cultural assets, although financial compensation may provide for the same result in practice. It should however be noted that in the *Eritrea v. Ethiopia* dispute, mentioned in Section 4.2.1.1, the Claims Commission only granted financial compensation for the destruction of the Stela of Matara, rejecting Eritrea's request for Ethiopia to apologize for the damage, as a measure of satisfaction:

> in principle, the appropriate remedy for valid claims should be monetary compensation, except where other remedies can be shown to be in accordance with international practice and the commission determines that another remedy would be reasonable and appropriate. No such showing was made here.[42]

The ICJ judgment concerning the case on *the Application of the Genocide Convention* has far from significantly contributed to the implementation of the ILC framework on reparation. Bosnia thus requested 'in its own right and as *parens patriae* for its citizens, reparations for damages to persons and property as well as to the Bosnian economy and environment caused by the foregoing violations of international law in a sum to be determined by the Court'.[43] In addition to financial compensation, Bosnia also requested the ICJ to order Serbia to ensure full compliance with the Genocide Convention, transfer the individuals accused of genocide to the ICTY and give guarantees of non-repetition.[44] The Court only reviewed Bosnia's claims under the consequences that should be drawn from Serbia's failure to prevent genocide in Srebrenica. It conditioned reparations to the finding of a 'causal nexus' between this failure and the actual perpetration of the genocide in Srebrenica. The Court concluded that it was impossible to establish 'whether the genocide at Srebrenica would have taken place even if the Respondent had attempted to prevent it by employing all means in its possession'.[45] As a consequence, it limited reparation to a 'declaration that the Respondent ha[d] failed to comply with the Court's Orders indicating provisional measures'.[46] It further ordered Serbia to comply with the obligation to transfer the perpetrators of the genocide, in particular Ratko Mladić, to the ICTY.[47] In relation to its obligation to

[40] Ibid., art. 37(2). [41] Mégret, 'Of Shrines, Memorials and Museums' (n 11) p. 31.

[42] *Central Front Eritrea's Claims 2, 4, 6, 7, 8, & 22, between the State of Eritrea and the Federal Democratic Republic of Ethiopia* (Partial Award) The Hague (28 April 2004) Eritrea Ethiopia Claims Commission, para. 114.

[43] 'Application of the Republic of Bosnia and Herzegovina', *Application of the Convention on the Prevention and Punishment of the Crime of Genocide* (*Bosnia and Herzegovina v. Yugoslavia* (*Serbia and Montenegro*)) (20 March 1993), para. 135(r).

[44] *Application of the Convention on the Prevention and Punishment of the Crime of Genocide (Bosnia and Herzegovina v. Serbia and Montenegro)* (Judgment) [2007] ICJ Rep. 43, para. 459.

[45] Ibid., para. 462. [46] Ibid., paras. 469, 470(9). [47] Ibid., paras. 465, 471(8).

prevent genocide, the ICJ found that there were no 'sufficient grounds for requiring guarantees of non-repetition',[48] nor for granting reparation for Serbia's failure to respect the provisional orders issued in 1993.[49]

Marko Milanović has qualified this part of the judgment as 'indefensible', since not only is it impossible to prove such a connection between the failure to prevent genocide and the actual perpetration of genocide in practice, but such a requirement is also contrary to both the 2001 ILC Draft Articles on State Responsibility—which do not mention any such condition of 'causal nexus'—and the state of customary law. He further referenced regional human rights case law, in which compensation has repeatedly been granted for the state's failure to prevent human rights violations perpetrated by third parties.[50] Moreover, this judgment raises the issue of its ability to contribute to the reparation of the social fabric and the promotion of reconciliation in the Balkans. Milanović thus argues that other measures of satisfaction would have been more efficient for this purpose, such as ordering Serbia to finance the construction of a memorial, on the model of the Bosnian and Herzegovinian Human Rights Chamber's order that Republika Srpska contribute to the establishment of the Potocari-Srebrenica Memorial.[51]

Both the 2007 ICJ judgment and the *Eritrea v. Ethiopia* dispute thus display the limits of reparation in an inter-state context, in relation to intended group destruction and cultural harm respectively. The human dimension will indeed more easily be overlooked by the state legal fiction.

7.2.2 Reparation for human rights violations

The state duty to repair the damage caused by human rights violations is enshrined in most international and regional human rights instruments. Reparation for victims of gross violations of international human rights law and serious violations of international human rights law was finally formally recognized as a right in 2006, with the adoption by the United Nations General Assembly (UNGA) of Basic Principles and Guidelines on the topic.[52] Its preamble inscribes the Basic Principles in the continuity of some of the major international human rights instruments, such as Article 8 of the Universal Declaration of Human Rights (UDHR), which provides that '[e]veryone has the right to an effective remedy by the competent national tribunals for acts violating the fundamental rights granted him by the constitution or by law'. Principle 8 of the Basic Principles also states clearly that '[f]or purposes of the present document, victims are persons who individually or

[48] Ibid., para. 466. [49] Ibid., para. 469.

[50] Marko Milanović, 'State Responsibility for Genocide: A Follow-Up' (2007) 18 *E.J.I.L.* 669, pp. 688–90. The author refers to the ECtHR *Ilascu* case and the IACHR *Rodriguez-Velasquez* case.

[51] *Ferida Selimovic et al. v. the Republika Srpska et al.* (Decision on Admissibility and Merits) No. CH/01/8365 (7 March 2003) Human Rights Chamber, para. 217.

[52] UNGA Res. A/60/147 'Basic Principles and Guidelines on the Right to a Remedy and Reparation for Victims of Gross Violations of International Human Rights Law and Serious Violations of International Humanitarian Law' (21 March 2006).

collectively suffered harm'. The Basic Principles include the obligation to provide for reparation within the more general state duty 'to respect, ensure respect for and implement international human rights law and international humanitarian law'.[53] The material ground for obtaining reparation—'gross violations of human rights'—is specified within Principle 8 and includes 'physical or mental injury, emotional suffering, economic loss or substantial impairment of their fundamental rights'. Cultural harm might fall, at least, under the emotional ground, if not also under the mental one.[54]

Principles 19 to 23 provide an overview of potential measures of reparation; this outline is more detailed than in the ILC Draft Articles on State Responsibility. In addition to 'restitution' (Principle 19), 'compensation' (Principle 20), and 'satisfaction' (Principle 22), 'guarantees of non-repetition' are explicitly considered as a measure of reparation under Principle 23. Another provision, Principle 21, is dedicated to 'rehabilitation', which 'should include medical and psychological care as well as legal and social services'. Revitalization, as formulated under the UNDRIP, could possibly be understood in rehabilitative terms, provided that 'psychological' would be interpreted in a broad way so as to encompass religious and spiritual practices of healing, for instance. The principle on 'satisfaction' is noteworthy since it reiterates the notion of the guarantee of non-repetition,[55] and dedicates subparagraphs to 'public apology'[56] and 'commemorations and tributes to the victims'.[57] Furthermore, its subparagraph (c) provides for:

> The search for the whereabouts of the disappeared, for the *identities of the children abducted*, and for the bodies of those killed, and assistance in the recovery, identification and reburial of the bodies in accordance with the expressed or presumed wish of the victims, *or the cultural practices of the families and communities* (emphases added).

The two emphases added are particularly relevant for our purpose. The search for 'the identities of the children abducted' directly echoes cases of forcible transfers of children such as those that occurred in the Australian and Canadian settler societies. The mention of 'the cultural practices of the families and communities' may involve some form of cultural revival in a context of wider cultural annihilation, although it is limited to the way in which the victims' corpses should be managed.

The formulation of the title of these guidelines, which focus on 'gross violations' calls for a few remarks as to whether it deals with the intensity of the violation—'massive and systematic'—or with the human rights violation at stake—that is, the category of human rights that is targeted. According to van Boven, in his introductory comment on the United Nations Basic Principles, '[t]he authors had in mind the violations constituting international crimes under the Rome Statute of

[53] Ibid. Principle 3(d).

[54] See the discussion on the interpretation of Article II(b) of the Genocide Convention in Section 3.2.1.1.

[55] 'Basic Principles and Guidelines' (n 52) Principle 22(a): 'Effective Measures Aimed at the Cessation of Continuing Violations'.

[56] Ibid. Principle 22(e). [57] Ibid. Principle 22(g).

the International Criminal Court'.[58] Considering the developments related to the crime of 'cultural persecution', serious violations of cultural rights should therefore fall within the ambit of these guidelines. The question arising in relation to reparation for the destruction of tangible cultural heritage remains open. While these guidelines also encompass serious violations of international humanitarian law, the principles involve the identification of victims, which might constitute an obstacle in practice. The possibility for collective reparation might, however, allow for the inclusion of reparation for such destructions within the provisions on 'compensation' or 'satisfaction'. Moreover, Principle 15 provides that a state may grant reparation to the victims and subsequently turn towards the individual non-state perpetrators of gross violations of human rights for reimbursement, so that the obligation to repair is not necessarily linked to a preliminary recognition of state responsibility.

Among the other human rights frameworks, the UNDRIP refers to 'redress' in no less than seven provisions, which necessarily involve a cultural dimension, considering its overall importance in the Declaration.[59] While most rights are formulated in both individual and collective terms, the provisions related to either a right or a State duty to redress predominantly concern the collective dimension of the protection framework. This makes obvious sense when it comes to repatriation of cultural artefacts, the restitution of land, etc., which in the indigenous peoples' context are indeed conceived as collective goods. Article 8, which substituted the draft provision on 'cultural genocide', establishes a State duty to provide redress for acts that would have contributed to 'forced assimilation or destruction of their culture'.[60] The ILA notes that:

> the meaning of the term 'redress' (. . .) is broad enough to consider such a provision as an open-ended rule according to which the specific kind of reparation to be granted is to be decided on a case- by-case basis, through choosing the most appropriate reparatory measure to re-establish the pre-existing situation and/or to grant effective redress to the victims, taking into primary account their own perception of the matter.[61]

Amongst the measures of 'non-material reparations' for the harm to cultural identity, the experts quote a number of measures: 'recognition of wrongs by the State or other perpetrators; guarantee of non-repetition; disclosure of truth; apology; punishment of the perpetrators; various kinds of psychosocial reparations, which allow victims to fully recuperate their place in the society to which they belong'.[62]

[58] Theo van Boven, 'The United Nations Basic Principles and Guidelines on the Right To a Remedy and Reparation for Victims of Gross Violations of International Human Rights Law and Serious Violations of International Humanitarian Law' (2010), available at: http://legal.un.org/avl/ha/ga_60-147/ga_60-147.html (last accessed 1 February 2015) para. 2(c), p. 1.

[59] UNDRIP (n 8) art. 8 (redress for forced assimilation of cultural destruction); art. 10 (compensation in case of consented removal from the land); art. 11(2) (restitution for looting of indigenous peoples' property); art. 12 (repatriation of 'ceremonial objects and human remains'); art. 20 (just and fair redress for indigenous peoples who would be deprived of their means of subsistence and development); art. 28 (restitution and/or just, fair, and equitable compensation in relation to land, territories and resources); art. 32 (just and fair redress in case of exploitation of the indigenous land).

[60] Ibid., art. 8(1).

[61] ILA 'Interim Report' (n 16) p. 40.

[62] Ibid., p. 40.

These measures of satisfaction and rehabilitation have already been granted by the IACHR, the case law of which is discussed further at a later stage of this chapter. The innovative nature of the human rights framework of reparation has more recently penetrated the field of international criminal law through the International Criminal Court (ICC) framework.

7.2.3 Cultural reparation in the context of international criminal law

It should be noted at the outset that reparation is not a natural dimension of criminal law, whether international or not. Again, this discipline is more concerned with the punishment of perpetrators, and less so with the redress of the victim. Yet, in cases of mass atrocities such as those addressed by international criminal tribunals, the transposition of the national doctrine of criminal law has turned out to be problematic with regard to the issue of reparation. Neither the ICTY nor the ICTR has received any mandate to grant reparation to victims. The Statute of the ICTY only provided for the Tribunal's ability to 'order the return of any property and proceeds acquired by criminal conduct, including by means of duress, to their rightful owners'.[63] As a result, the victims would have to file civil claims in front of national courts to obtain reparation,[64] which might not be able to provide effective remedies, considering the likely post-war or post-genocide state of a national judicial system. However these provisions have received very little consideration.[65] More recently, an ICTY Trial Chamber recognized the possibility for discriminatory property laws amounting to the crime against humanity of persecution;[66] in the case itself, no subsequent order of restitution was made and the conviction was ultimately overturned on appeal.[67]

The right to obtain reparation on the basis of a criminal conviction has not resonated widely at the national level. While, having rendered its judgments, the Bosnian War Crimes Chamber systematically took care to refer the victims to the relevant civil jurisdictions in order to obtain reparation, this never occurred. In any event, in the few cases involving the destruction of religious heritage, this Chamber dealt with these crimes at the level of the chapeau of crimes against humanity, and hence as a contextual rather than an actual element of persecution.[68] It therefore seems unlikely that these convictions could provide an adequate legal basis for the

[63] Statute of the International Tribunal for the Former Yugoslavia (adopted 25 May 1993) UNSC Res. 827 (ICTY Statute) art. 24(3); ICTY Rules of Procedure and Evidence, IT/32/Rev. 49 (adopted 11 February 1994, as amended 22 May 2013), Rule 105.

[64] ICTY Rules of Procedure and Evidence (n 63) Rule 106.

[65] Anne-Marie de Brouwer, *Supranational Criminal Prosecutions of Sexual Prosecutions: the ICC and the Practice of the ICTY and the ICTR* (Antwerp; Oxford: Intersentia, 2005) pp. 296–7; Evans, *The Right to Reparation* (n 5) p. 91.

[66] *Gotovina et al.* (Trial) IT-06-90 (15 April 2011) vol. 2, paras. 1806–7.

[67] *Gotovina et al.* (Appeals) IT-06-90 (16 November 2012).

[68] See *Ljublišić* (Verdict) X-KR-06/241 (29 April 2008) Bosnia War Crimes Chamber, pp. 22–4; *Kujundžić* (Verdict) X-KR-07/442 (30 October 2009) Bosnia War Crimes Chamber, para. 184.

individual perpetrators to be ordered to grant reparation for these religious crimes, for which their direct responsibility has not been clearly established.

The reparation gap was remedied by the Statute of the ICC, Article 75(1) of which provides that '[t]he Court shall establish principles relating to reparations to, or in respect of, victims, including restitution, compensation and rehabilitation'. Article 75(2) further establishes that the bearer of the duty to repair is the individual perpetrator. The absence of measures of 'satisfaction' as potential measures of reparation, as well as the limited scope of the provision related to reparation, is noteworthy since it involves the conviction of an individual perpetrator and *a fortiori* a limited number of victims in contrast to the overall number of victims in a given 'situation'. The ICC Rules of Procedure and Evidence detail the content of the claims for restitution, compensation, and rehabilitation.[69] If 'restitution of assets, property or other tangible items' is foreseen, no explicit measures, except for compensation, are envisaged in case of 'destruction'; compensation transpires to be problematic in relation to tangible cultural heritage, the value of which is hardly assessable. The absence of satisfactory measures turns out to be self-contradictory in light of the definition of 'victims', enshrined in Article 85(b) of the rules of procedure and evidence:

> Victims may include organizations or institutions that have sustained direct harm *to any of their property* which is dedicated to religion, education, art or science or charitable purposes, and *to their historic monuments, hospitals and other places and objects for humanitarian purposes* (emphases added).

The harm to cultural property is thus expressly engaged as a basis for defining a collective victim; however, no consequence, beyond the mere conviction of individual perpetrators, is associated with the perpetration of such harm. Yet, Rule 97(2) provides that 'the Court may appoint appropriate experts to assist it in determining the scope, extent of any damage, loss and injury to, or in respect of victims and to suggest various options concerning the appropriate types and modalities of reparations'. The participatory dimension of the ICC reparatory framework could thus foster the opportunity for religious or cultural institutions to claim satisfactory or compensatory measures in relation to the destruction or damage of their assets.[70] Furthermore, the ICC framework also foresees the possibility of 'collective reparations'. Rule 97(1) provides that: 'Taking into account the scope and extent of any damage, loss or injury, the Court may award reparations on an individualized basis or, where it deems it appropriate, on a collective basis or both'.[71]

The ICC Reparation Mandate is complemented by the Trust Fund for Victims of the ICC (TFV). Article 79 of the ICC Rome Statute confers on the TFV an extended scope *ratione personae* to 'benefit of victims of crimes within the jurisdiction of the

[69] ICC Rules of Procedure and Evidence, ICC-ASP/1/3 (Part II-A) (adopted and entered into force 9 September 2002), Rule 94 (1)(d)(e)(f).

[70] Kristina Hon, 'Bringing Cultural Genocide in by the Backdoor: Victim Participation at the ICC' (2006) 43 *Seton Hall L.Rev.* 359, p. 387.

[71] ICC Rules of Procedure and Evidence (n 69) rule 97.

Court, and of the families of such victims', thus disconnecting the beneficiaries from the actual conviction before the Court. Its mandate *ratione materiae* is also wider since it is entitled to 'provide physical or psychological rehabilitation or material support for the benefit of victims and their families'.[72] Moreover, the regulations of the Trust Fund indicate that:

> Subject to the order of the Court, the Trust Fund shall take into account the following factors in determining the nature and/or size of awards, inter alia: *the nature of the crimes,* the particular injuries to the victims and the nature of the evidence to support such injuries, as well as the size and location of the beneficiary group.[73]

The emphasis on the 'nature of the crimes' could constitute the ground for including the reparation of cultural harm, by virtue of connecting the cultural nature of the crime with the nature of the award to be granted, a hypothesis that should be followed very carefully in the Malian *Al Mahdi* case. Predominantly, the regulations are focused on the deposit of 'financial awards' such that it is for the Trust Fund to convert this money into actual programmes of reconstruction, provided that either the ICC itself or the victims formulate such a request.

The whole reparation scheme should not be read, however, as alleviating the state obligation to repair human rights violations.[74] Indeed, the general mandate of the ICC reproduces the problematic dichotomy between perpetrators and victims; as a result, there is a risk that the more general consideration, relating to the reconstitution of the social fabric, is left to the side.[75]

These various questions surrounding the ICC reparation framework emerged in the *Lubanga* case, which constituted the first opportunity for the ICC to comply with its obligation under Article 75(1) of the Rome Statute to establish principles of reparation. Thomas Lubanga was found guilty of crimes of conscripting and enlisting children under the age of fifteen years into the Patriotic Force for the Liberation of the Congo and using them to participate actively in hostilities in the Democratic Republic of Congo. Even though this case may seem quite distant from the topic of 'cultural genocide', the crime of recruiting child soldiers shares a number of characteristics with the cultural crimes addressed throughout this book,[76] by victimizing both individuals (the child soldiers) and collective entities (their family and, depending on their socio-cultural context, their community). As such, it can be deemed to have a highly disruptive effect on the social fabric, with the rupture—at least temporarily—of the intergenerational link. The difficult reintegration of the former child soldiers in their communities, their marginalization, and the discrimination against their community, which may have both

[72] Regulations of the Trust Fund for Victims Resolution ICC-ASP/4/Res.3 (adopted 3 December 2005), para. 50(a)(i).

[73] Ibid., para. 55 (emphasis added).

[74] Evans, *The Right to Reparation* (n 5) p. 86.

[75] Mégret, 'Of Shrines, Memorials and Museums' (n 11) p. 19.

[76] See also Grover's argument in relation to Article II(e) of the Genocide Convention in Section 3.2.1.1.

facilitated and increased the impact of the crime, make transformative reparation all the more compelling.

In its first order of reparation, the ICC Trial Chamber concluded that Mr. Lubanga was indigent and that the TFV should take care of the reparation.[77] The ICC Prosecutor, the victims' legal representatives, and Mr. Lubanga all appealed this order. In its judgment, the Appeals Chamber found that the ICC Trial Chamber had erred in law on several aspects. It both clarified the principles of reparation and amended the order of reparation in the specific *Lubanga* case. As for the former, the Court addressed a number of essential issues, such as the definition of the victims and their participation in the design of measures of reparation. One of the most remarkable principles is the connection between the reparation and the individual conviction, meaning that the order of reparation should stick to the specific harm generated by the accused's specific crimes for which he has been convicted.[78] The Court thus clearly anchored the reparation in a retributive perspective, although it did not overlook the victims' interest. The Appeals Court also adopted a clear transformative approach, stating that '[r]eparations need to address any underlying injustices'.[79]

As for the measures of reparation, the Court acknowledged the complementarity between individual and collective reparations but eventually ordered the TFV to draft a plan of collective reparation, as it was feared that individual reparation might create tensions within the communities.[80] As the TFV recalled, it primarily operates as an implementing agency in relation to Mr. Lubanga's obligations of reparation. Only in case of Thomas Lubanga's declaration of indigency by the ICC would the TFV partially substitute Mr. Lubanga in its obligation to provide reparation to the victims.[81] Against this background, the TFV's implementation plan also stresses the difficulty of granting collective reparation in the case, which involves former child soldiers, since the direct victims do not constitute a homogenous group.[82]

The Appeals Court also clarified the status of measures of satisfaction and decided that measures 'with a symbolic, preventative or transformative value, may also be appropriate'. The TFV followed this path and discarded compensation[83] and restitution[84] as inadequate measures of reparation. It rather ordered a series of collective measures of rehabilitation and satisfaction in order to address the multi-dimensional harm inflicted on child soldiers and their families,[85] which are articulated around the four main remedies:

(i) measures aimed at restoring the physical and psychological health of victims; (ii) their schooling, both through formal and informal education; (iii) measures aimed at

[77] *Prosecutor v. Thomas Lubanga Dyilo* (Decision Establishing the Principles and Procedures to be Applied to Reparations) ICC-01/04-01/06, Trial Chamber I (7 August 2012) para. 266.

[78] *Prosecutor v. Thomas Lubanga Dyilo* (Amended Order for Reparations (Annex A)) ICC-01/04-01/06 A A 2 A 3, Appeals Chamber (3 March 2015) paras. 20, 32.

[79] Ibid., para. 17.

[80] Ibid., para. 33.

[81] *Prosecutor v. Thomas Lubanga Dyilo* (Filing on Reparations and Draft Implementation Plan) ICC-01/04-01/06, Trial Chamber II (3 November 2015) para. 110.

[82] Ibid., para. 184.

[83] Ibid., paras. 194–204.

[84] Ibid., para. 192.

[85] Ibid., paras. 255–9.

socio-economic development and fostering employment (. . .) and (iv) measures aimed at community reconciliation and awareness raising against child soldier recruitment.[86]

Finally, the Court emphasized that reparations should be proportionate and adequate and should, among other outcomes, aim at reconciliation between the victims and both their families and communities. They should also take into account the victim's culture to the extent that it does not lead to the infringement of other human rights.[87] Although both the ICC Appeals Chamber's order and the TFV's plan adopted a strong transformative perspective, very much focusing on the victims' socio-economic and cultural context, it is noteworthy that the ICC Appeals Court discretely expressed some reservations, in a footnote, on the reconciliatory role of reparation in the specific case:

> The limited scope of the charges brought by the Prosecutor against Mr. Lubanga limited the categories of victims who have participated in this case. They come largely from the same ethnic group and they do not necessarily represent all those who suffered from crimes committed during the relevant conflict in Ituri. The situation could give rise to a risk of resentment on the part of other victims and the re-stigmatisation of former child soldiers within their communities.[88]

This comment is very illustrative of the difficulty of balancing the various interests involved in a criminal case, between the rights of the accused and those of the victims. On the one hand, it may seem obvious, although it was not for the ICC Trial Chamber, that Mr. Lubanga may not be obliged to provide reparation for crimes of which he was not convicted. On the other hand, from the perspective of the field, that is the victims' situation in Ituri, it may be difficult to understand why some individuals, families, and communities receive reparation and not others, while they may have all suffered from egregious crimes. This also reflects the difficult articulation of a 'situation' and 'individual cases' at the ICC, where the former may create expectations that are difficult to fulfil.

This tension may be mitigated by the exercise of the TFV's second function of assistance. The TFV is not only responsible for coordinating the reparation measures ordered by the ICC but it may also provide 'assistance' to the victims and more generally to the persons falling within the geographical scope of the given situation, in spite of them not being recognized as victims in specific cases. Such assistance has so far been shaped as project developments for communities impacted by the armed conflict in the situation area. However, the TFV has taken care to distinguish between reparation functions, in which it deals with victims as 'right-bearers' and its assistance function so that the latter cannot substitute the former.[89] Interestingly, this assistance function is itself criticized, in light of the above-mentioned 'development *versus* collective reparation' tension, as it is sometimes feared that the state

[86] Ibid., para. 60.
[87] *P. v. Lubanga* (Amended Order of Reparation) (n 78) paras. 46–7.
[88] Ibid., para. 71 (fn. 44).
[89] *P. v. Lubanga* (Filing on Reparations) (n 81) para. 155.

will see the TFV's assistance role as an opportunity to not assume its development responsibility.[90]

The ICC mechanisms, as well as the other above-mentioned frameworks, thus provide a number of tools that are likely to remedy the hypothesis of cultural damage occurring from serious violations of international human rights law or international crimes, provided that they are interpreted according to this purpose. It is interesting to note that in its judgment on reparations in the *Lubanga* case, the ICC extensively referred to the case law of the IACHR to interpret its mandate.[91] More generally, it emerges from the three frameworks of reparation studied that they would all possess potential mechanisms to address cultural harm but very rarely state it in an explicit manner. The practice of reparation for cultural damage might well contribute to better frame the potential shape that such reparation may take, whether the relevant damage has occurred in international or national contexts and whether such a practice intended to constitute legal reparation or de facto amounted to such a measure.

7.3 Cultural Reparation in Practice

This section returns to some of the cases that have been repeatedly engaged throughout the previous chapters for the purposes of illustrating how the state of cultural genocide had evolved in international law. These include: (i) the case of the post-war reconstruction of cultural and religious heritage in Bosnia and Herzegovina; (ii) the Inter-American experience, which constitutes the closest recognition of the concept of 'ethnocide'; and (iii) the reparation relevant to the Australian and Canadian cases of forcibly transferred children.

7.3.1 Reparation of destroyed cultural heritage: The Bosnian case

The aim of the destructive campaign of religious and cultural heritage in Bosnia and Herzegovina has widely been understood not only as amounting to the elimination of all traces of particular identities on given parts of the Bosnian territory, but also as the erasure of the traces of the very national, religious, and ethnic 'coexistence'[92]

[90] Mégret, 'Of Shrines, Memorials and Museums' (n 11) p. 24.

[91] *Prosecutor v. Thomas Lubanga Dyilo* (Judgment on the Appeals against the 'Decision Establishing the Principles and Procedures to be Applied to Reparations') ICC-01/04-01/06 A A 2 A 3, Appeals Chamber (3 March 2015) paras. 128, 145, 166. See also *P. v. Lubanga* (Filing on Reparations) (n 81) paras. 233–4.

[92] András J. Riedlmayer, 'From the Ashes: The Past and Future of Bosnia's Cultural Heritage' in M. Shatzmiller (ed.) *Islam and Bosnia: Conflict Resolution and Foreign Policy in Multi-Ethnic States.* (Montreal: McGill-Queens University Press, 2002) pp. 98–135 (e-version available at: http://www.alumniconnections.com/harvard/alumni/images/from_the_ashes.pdf, last accessed 1 February 2015); pp. 98–135; Bevan (n 6) pp. 59–60; Donna-Lee Frieze, The Destruction of Sarajevo's *Vijecnica*: A Case of Genocidal Destruction? in Adam Jones (ed.), *New Directions in Genocide Research* (London; New York: Routledge, 2009) pp. 57–74.

within Bosnia and Herzegovina as a whole.[93] These underlying purposes have thus rendered the reconstruction of Bosnian damaged heritage a particularly sensitive matter. In this context, cultural and religious heritage are not watertight categories. Firstly, it would be biased to look at these assets in isolation from each other, if one thinks—to make reference to the most famous—of the coexistence of religions in cities such as Sarajevo or Mostar.[94] Secondly, the aesthetic and historical value of some religious assets, such as the Ferhadija Mosque of Banja Luka, tends to make these buildings 'shared sacred space', of importance for more than one religious group.[95] At the other side of the spectrum, assets that would rather fit within the 'cultural heritage' category have been ethnicized because of their very destruction. For instance, the Vijećnica, the National Library of Sarajevo, which constituted a symbol of coexistence, has now become a symbol of victimization of the Bosnian Muslim population of Sarajevo.[96] Following the same logic, the destruction of the Mostar Bridge was not only motivated by the destruction of a material and spiritual bridge between the various communities of Mostar—recognizing that the spatial division of these communities would not exactly follow the two sides of the river that the bridge crosses[97]—but by the very origin of the bridge, which was constructed under the Ottoman rule.[98] The Mostar Bridge has thus become a symbol of the Muslim population, as illustrated by the ICTY *Prlić* judgment cited in Chapter 5. Such a tendency might be seen as problematic, since it operates to fuel an undesirable rhetoric of ethnicization.[99] As this brief description shows, these assets are both likely to be ethnicized or multiculturalized, depending on the interests at stake. Indeed, this is what has happened in Bosnia and Herzegovina, a result of the narratives that either accompanied their destruction or their reconstruction.

Thus, when it comes to the post-war management of these assets, a number of issues need to be taken into account. The first and foremost may well be the notion of reconciliation, and of bringing back the feeling of coexistence that has been targeted.[100] Secondly, considering the underlying rationale for destroying these assets—which were 'part of a strategy of intimidation aimed at driving out members of the targeted group, it also serves a long-term goal'[101] as well as to 'eliminate the material evidence (. . .) that could remind future generations that people of

[93] Riedlmayer, 'From the Ashes' (e-version) (n 92) p. 3. [94] Ibid., p. 6.

[95] Dinu Bumbaru, 'Religious Heritage and Sacred Places', ICOMOS, available at: http://isceah.icomos.org/index.php?option=com_content&task=view&id=60&Itemid=27 (last accessed 1 February 2015).

[96] András J. Riedlmayer, 'Crimes of War, Crimes of Peace: Destruction of Libraries During and After the Balkan Wars of the 1990s' (2007) 56 *Library Trends* 107, pp. 110–14; Frieze (n 92) pp. 59, 67.

[97] Carl Grodach, 'Reconstituting Identity and History in Post-War Mostar, Bosnia-Herzegovina' (2002) 6 *City* 61; Xavier Bougarel, Elissa Helms, and Ger Duijzings (eds.) *The New Bosnian Mosaic: Identities, Memories and Moral Claims in a Post-War Society* (Aldershot, Burlington: Ashgate, 2007), p. 2; Riedlmayer, 'Crimes of War, Crimes of Peace' (n 96) p. 120.

[98] Ibid., p. 74. In the perpetrators' minds, Ottoman was shortcut and distorted so as to mean 'Bosnian Muslim'.

[99] Ibid., p. 75.

[100] Tonka Kostadinova, *Policies of External Assistance to the Reconstruction of Cultural Heritage as a Peace-Building Model in Southeast Europe* (Paper kindly communicated by the author).

[101] Riedlmayer, 'From the Ashes' (e-version) (n 92) p. 9.

different ethnic and religious traditions once shared a common heritage and common space in Bosnia'[102]—the notions of return and memory may also play a significant role in this process. All of these issues have turned out to be highly intertwined. Processes of return would not occur without the restitution or reconstruction of destroyed property, as well as the securing of human rights.[103] Moreover, considering that the destruction of cultural and religious heritage has reflected the intent to definitively displace these populations—and, at least in the case of Srebrenica, to 'destroy' them—the reconstruction of such heritage will necessarily play a role in the return of this population and the creation of the environment allowing for their 'sustainable' resettlement in their hometowns.

The legal framework set out in the aftermath of the conflict partly addressed some of these issues. This framework derives from the 1995 Dayton Peace Agreement,[104] which put an end to the conflict, through both endorsing the consequences of ethnic cleansing, by reproducing the administrative division of the country into two main entities—the Federation of Bosnia and Herzegovina and the Republika Sprska—and providing for the *status quo ante* and ordering the return of refugees and the restitution of property.[105] This Agreement does not provide for a programme of reparation, beyond the restitution of property. Generally speaking, reparation, and especially financial compensation, has been almost entirely absent from the post-war process of transitional justice.[106] However, the Dayton framework does contain annexes that are particularly relevant in relation to the above-mentioned issues: the return of refugees and internally displaced persons (IDPs) (Annex 7); the principle of property restitution; the rehabilitation of national heritage (Annex 8); and the human rights framework (Annex 6). These legal provisions have provided the bases for a multidimensional approach to the post-war reconstruction of cultural and religious heritage: the human rights approach, the 'National Monument' approach, and the prevention approach. These axes also reflect the various approaches that have been underlined in relation to the components of the concept of cultural genocide as a technique of genocide.

7.3.1.1 The human rights approach

Annex 6 provides for two human rights mechanisms to secure human rights in the aftermath of the conflict: the Ombudsman and the Human Rights Chamber.

[102] Ibid., p. 8. [103] Ibid., p. 18.

[104] The General Framework Agreement for Peace in Bosnia and Herzegovina, Dayton (14 December 1995) (Dayton Peace Agreement).

[105] Bougarel, Helms, and Duijzings (eds.) (n 97) p.6. A third entity has been set out in the Peace Agreement, the Brčko district.

[106] Ernesto Kiza, 'On the Effectiveness of Judicial Accountability Mechanisms in Bosnia and Herzegovina' in Vesselin Popovski and Mónica Serrano (eds.), *After Oppression: Transitional Justice in Latin America and Eastern Europe* (Tokyo; New York: United Nations University, 2012) pp. 259–60; Frederiek de Vlaming and Kate Clark, 'War Reparations in Bosnia and Herzegovina: Individual Stories and Collective Interests' in Dubravka Zarkov and Marlies Glasius (eds.), *Narratives of Justice in and out the Courtroom: Former Yugoslavia and Beyond* (Cham: Springer, 2014).

The latter ran from 1999 to 2003, and was then replaced by the Human Rights Commission. While this Commission concluded its work in 2006, it continues to exist, implicitly, within the Constitutional Court of the Republic of Bosnia and Herzegovina. The Chamber's *ratione materiae* jurisdiction was mainly grounded on the ECHR, as well as other international human rights instruments, such as the International Covenant on Civil and Political Rights (ICCPR), the International Covenant on Economic, Social and Cultural Rights (ICESCR), and the Convention on the Elimination of Racial Discrimination (CERD).[107] This Chamber operated on the model of the European Court of Human Rights (ECtHR), and thus substituted the Strasbourg court at a time when Bosnia was not yet a party to the ECHR.[108] The jurisdiction *ratione temporis* of this mechanism only ran from the entry into force of the Dayton Peace Agreement, and as such, did not cover the human rights violations perpetrated during the armed conflict.

Soon after its establishment, the Chamber began to review cases involving mosques destroyed during the armed conflict on the territory of the Republika Srpska. Four main cases were brought by the Islamic Community on the bases of alleged violations of the right to property and the right to religious freedom, respectively enshrined in Article 1 Protocol 1 ECHR and Article 10 ECHR. The first case concerned the fifteen mosques of Banja Luka that had been destroyed, including the Ferhadija mosque. The Islamic Community complained to the Human Rights Chamber that the municipality's denial of a permit to reconstruct the mosques violated the religious rights of its members, since the municipality of Banja Luka did not provide them with an adequate space of worship in return.[109] The Court was confronted with similar facts in the *Zvornik,*[110] *Bijeljina,*[111] and *Mrkonjić Grad*[112] cases, in which the Islamic Community complained not only about the various municipalities' denial of a permit to reconstruct the destroyed mosques, but also of the *fait accompli* since the mosques, and often the adjacent graveyards, had been replaced with car parks, market stands, and various business facilities. The *Zvornik* case was particularly sensitive, as it involved the construction of an Orthodox Church in the place of the destroyed Divič mosque, a practice that was not isolated in

[107] Dayton Peace Agreement (n 104) Annex 6, art. 1 and Appendix.

[108] Carla Ferstman and Sheri P. Rosenberg, 'Reparations in Dayton's Bosnia and Herzegovina' in Carla Ferstman, Mariana Goetz, and Alan Stephens (eds.), *Reparations for Victims of Genocide, War Crimes and Crimes Against Humanity: Systems in Place and Systems in the Making* (Leiden; Boston: Martinus Nijhoff Publishers, 2009) p. 511.

[109] *The Islamic Community in Bosnia and Herzegovina against the Republika Srpska* (Decision on Admissibility and Merits) No. CH/96/29 (11 June 1999) Human Rights Chamber (*Islamic Community, Banja Luka Case*).

[110] *The Islamic Community in Bosnia and Herzegovina against the Republika Srpska* (Decision on Admissibility and Merits) No. CH/98/1062 (9 November 2000) Human Rights Chamber (*Islamic Community, Zvornik Case*).

[111] *The Islamic Community in Bosnia and Herzegovina against the Republika Srpska* (Decision on Admissibility and Merits) No. CH/99/2656 (6 December 2000) Human Rights Chamber (*Islamic Community, Bijeljina Case*).

[112] *The Islamic Community in Bosnia and Herzegovina (Mrkonjic Grad) against the Republika Srpska* (Decision on Admissibility and Merits) No. CH/01/7701 (22 December 2003) Human Rights Chamber (*Islamic Community, Mrkonjic Grad*).

the context of ethnic cleansing.[113] In a fifth relevant case, the Catholic Archdiocese complained about the municipality of Travnik's partial attribution of a damaged building—deemed too small and thus unsuitable for worship—for the purposes of its carrying out of its religious activities.[114]

These cases led the Court to address a number of obstacles. At the outset, it was necessary to establish the title of property over both the land and the destroyed buildings. This was not an easy task in the Bosnian context since most religious property had been nationalized in the 1960s. The Court found that, unlike the buildings, the land had not been destroyed, which grounded the Islamic Community's interest to act, and *a fortiori*, its title of property.[115] Secondly, while the Court did not have jurisdiction to address the very destruction of the mosques, it took care to note that '[e]vidence relating to such events may, however, be relevant as a background to events which occurred after the Agreement entered into force'.[116] In the *Banja Luka* case, the Human Rights Chamber indeed underlined 'that the mosques were destroyed at night during curfew',[117] on the basis of which it found both a violation of the applicant's right to property and qualified the whole process as 'a pattern of ongoing discrimination against the applicant's members in Banja Luka'.[118] As recalled in the statement of facts:

> There was no war activity in Banja Luka in the 1990s, but all 15 mosques in Banja Luka were destroyed between 9 April 1993 and the end of September 1993. Remains were removed from the sites of Ferhadija, Armaudija, Gazanferija, Sefer's Bey's and Dolacka-Hadzi Omer's. The destruction of the mosques and the removal of remains took place at night during the period when the city was blockaded and a curfew was in force.[119]

The Court used the Republika Srpska's proven responsibility in the destruction of the mosques as evidence of ongoing discrimination,[120] in addition to the favourable treatment granted to the Orthodox Community of Banja Luka, whose religion was the only one to be officially recognized in the Constitution of Republika Srpska at the time. Finally, the Chamber made an innovative finding in relation to the right to religion, which, as mentioned in Section 4.2.3, was deemed to include 'the right to build a space for practising it',[121] so as to imply positive obligations for Republika Srpska to secure its Muslim constituents' freedom of religion.[122]

[113] András J. Riedlmayer, 'Destruction of Cultural Heritage in Bosnia-Herzegovina, 1992–1996: A Post-War Survey of Selected Municipalities' (International Criminal Tribunal for the Former Yugoslavia, Exhibit Number P486, 2002); Kiza (n 106) p. 249.

[114] *Catholic Archdiocese of Vrhbosna against the Federation of Bosnia and Herzegovina* (Decision on Admissibility and Merits) No. CH/02/9628 (6 June 2003) Human Rights Chamber (*Catholic Archdiocese of Vrhbosna*) para. 110.

[115] *Islamic Community, Banja Luka Case* (n 109) paras. 192–3; *Islamic Community, Zvornik Case* (Admissibility and Merits) (n 110) para. 111; *Islamic Community, Bijeljina Case* (n 111) para.107.

[116] *Islamic Community, Banja Luka Case* (n 109) para. 132; *Islamic Community, Zvornik Case* (Admissibility and Merits) (n 110) para. 71.

[117] *Islamic Community, Banja Luka Case* (n 109) para. 194.

[118] Ibid., para. 133.

[119] Ibid., para. 34.

[120] Ibid., para. 162; *Islamic Community, Zvornik Case* (Admissibility and Merits) (n 110) paras. 98–9.

[121] *Islamic Community, Banja Luka Case* (n 109) para. 182; *Islamic Community, Zvornik Case* (Admissibility and Merits) (n 110) para. 87.

[122] *Islamic Community, Banja Luka Case* (n 109) paras. 184–5; *Islamic Community, Bijeljina Case* (n 111) para. 89.

Throughout its judgments, the Court made several references to the imperatives of transitional justice, in particular the return of refugees and internally displaced persons, as well as reconciliation. In the *Banja Luka* case, it underlined issues such as the 'urgency to remove the climate of fear'[123] and the importance of these mosques for both the Muslim Community of Banja Luka and the whole country:

> The Chamber notes that the 15 destroyed mosques and their surrounding graveyards were hundreds of years old and held significant religious and cultural importance not just for the applicants and its members. They formed part of the cultural-historic heritage of Bosnia and Herzegovina as reflected in the general urban plan for Banja Luka adopted in 1975 and which affords ten of the mosques protection of the first degree.[124]

In several cases, the judges did not hesitate to recall the ethnic cleansing that prompted the claims under their review.[125] In another case, related to the desecration of a private graveyard by the local Orthodox congregation, who invoked the scientific archaeological excavation to rationalize their action, the Human Rights Chamber recalled the extent of ethnic cleansing in Foča and its surroundings, referring to the *Kunarac* case of the ICTY[126] to establish a positive obligation on the part of local authorities to 'create conditions conducive to the return of persons expelled during the armed conflict',[127] which amount to guarantees of non-repetition.

In the four judgments involving the Islamic Community, the Chamber almost systematically reiterated its lack of jurisdiction to grant reparation for the destruction of the mosques[128] such that, as a result, the pecuniary reparation was often marginal, deemed to compensate only the moral damage resulting from the obstacles to the reconstruction. In the *Banja Luka* case, the Court did not grant pecuniary compensation but ordered the Republika Srpska to take positive measures, such as the establishment of fences in order to protect the fifteen sites[129] and the delivery of the necessary permits for the reconstruction of seven of the destroyed mosques.[130] In the *Travnik* case, the Chamber ordered the municipality of Travnik to cede the entire contested building to the Catholic community but did not grant pecuniary compensation.[131]

[123] *Islamic Community, Banja Luka Case* (n 109) para. 185. Similar statements were made in other cases. See *Islamic Community, Zvornik Case* (Admissibility and Merits) (n 110) para. 100; *Islamic Community, Bijeljina Case* (n 111) para. 102. See also *Islamic Community, Mrkonjic Grad* (n 112) para. 154; *Catholic Archdiocese of Vrhbosna* (n 114) para. 114; *The Islamic Community in Bosnia and Herzegovina against the Republika Srpska* (Decision on Admissibility and Merits) No. CH/99/2177 (11 February 2000) Human Rights Chamber, para. 105. (This case involved restrictions placed on the access to and use of the cemetery of Prnjavor by the local Muslims.)

[124] *Islamic Community, Banja Luka Case* (n 109) para. 202.

[125] See e.g. *Islamic Community, Mrkonjic Grad* (n 112) para. 155.

[126] *Enes Cengis against the Federation of Bosnia and Herzegovina and the Republika Srpska* (Decision on Admissibility and Merits) No. CH/02/12016 (10 October 2003) Human Rights Chamber, para. 117.

[127] Ibid., para. 118.

[128] See e.g. *Islamic Community, Zvornik Case* (Admissibility and Merits) (n 110) para. 123; *Islamic Community, Bijeljina Case* (n 111) para. 127.

[129] *Islamic Community, Banja Luka Case* (n 109) para. 212.

[130] Ibid., para. 213.

[131] *Catholic Archdiocese of Vrhbosna* (n 114) paras. 119–20.

The Human Rights Chamber did, however, display some discomfort in respect of the scope for the substitution of the destroyed mosques with immoveable objects. In most cases, the Chamber would order the restitution of the land on which no subsequent construction had been made, the delivery of the construction permit, as well as compensation—but not restitution—for the part of the land on which buildings had been illegally constructed,[132] leaving the possibility open for the community to 'seek an order for the demolition of the unlawfully constructed business premises from the competent authorities'.[133] The Chamber would sometimes grant non-pecuniary damage for the 'particularly serious form of discrimination practiced'[134] or the 'insult' made to the applicants[135] as a way to underline the consequences of the obstacles which precluded those who had been expelled during the armed conflict from returning. In the *Zvornik* case it found 'that the construction of the Serb Orthodox church on this site substantially interfered with the enjoyment of the applicant's property right'.[136] However, it refused to order the destruction or the displacement of the Orthodox Church and rather required that the municipality of Zvornik 'allocate, within 6 months (...) in consultation with the Islamic Community, and for its use only, a suitable building site in the vicinity of the former Divič mosque to permit, upon request of the Islamic Community, the construction of a mosque to replace the former Divič mosque'.[137] The Islamic community appealed against this judgment, but the Chamber ultimately reiterated its conclusion with reference to a domestic legal provision that provided for the possible modulation of reparation 'if the destruction of the facility would not be socially justified'. It thus contemplated the possibility of ordering the destruction of the Orthodox Church but concluded that this would not be socially justified:

> However, bearing in mind the prevailing circumstances in the country, and considering that the Serb Orthodox church has already been in use by members of the local community for some time, the Chamber finds that it would not be appropriate to order demolition of the church currently standing on the site of the former Divič mosque.[138]

[132] *Islamic Community, Bijeljina Case* (n 111) para. 122.
[133] *Islamic Community, Mrkonjic Grad* (n 112) para. 168.
[134] Ibid., para. 174.
[135] *Islamic Community, Bijeljina Case* (n 111) para. 127.
[136] *Islamic Community, Zvornik Case* (Admissibility and Merits) (n 110) para. 112.
[137] Ibid., para. 122.
[138] *The Islamic Community in Bosnia and Herzegovina against the Republika Srpska* (Decision on Review) No. CH/98/1062 (12 October 2001) Human Rights Chamber, para. 33. Some Muslim inhabitants of Zvornik introduced a third claim, arguing that the Chamber's decision 'perpetuate[d] the injustice of allowing an Orthodox church, a product of genocide against the Muslims of the area and built illegally, to stand on the site of the destroyed mosque'; the Court declared the request inadmissible on procedural grounds, since it was directed against itself and not one of the two entities, as provided by the Dayton Peace Agreement. *Citizens of Divič against the Republika Srpska* (Decision on Admissibility) No. CH/02/9853 (6 September 2002) Human Rights Chamber, paras. 4–6. A final claim was formulated by the relatives of persons buried in the graveyard of the Divič's mosque, who, as a result of its destruction, could no longer access the graveyard. It was however rejected, inter alia because it concerned facts that had occurred before the entry into force of the Dayton Peace Agreement. See *Nusreta Mulaosmanovic, Halima Aganovic, and Fahrudin Aganovic against the Republika Srpska* (Decision on Admissibility) No. CH/02/11259 Human Rights Chamber, para. 9.

These various measures show the inadequacy of this human rights mechanism to deal with the *fait accompli* of the war. The Human Rights Chamber failed to implement the strong statements it made in relation to the imperatives of return and reconciliation at the level of making reparation. The follow-up to the *Zvornik* case illustrates this well. Ultimately, the Islamic Community managed to negotiate with the municipality to have the Orthodox Church displaced and the former Mosque rebuilt at its own expense, which went far beyond the compensation of 50,000 convertible marks granted by the Human Rights Chamber.[139] It should, however, be noted that a right to claim reparation also exists before civil jurisdictions. The Islamic Community thus filed a complaint against the government of Republika Srpska in 2000, in order to obtain financial compensation for the destruction of its mosques. In February 2009, a local court in Banja Luka ordered the Bosnian Serb authorities to pay around 65 million convertible marks to the Islamic Community, as compensation for the destruction of sixteen mosques. The judgment was subsequently overruled by the District Court of Banja Luka and the Republika Srpska's Supreme Court in turn on the basis that the statute of limitation for these crimes had expired. In 2015, the Constitutional Court of Bosnia and Herzegovina confirmed the Supreme Court of Republika Srpska's decision to overturn the municipal judgment, suggesting that the ordinary statute of limitation should apply, since no criminal convictions had been secured in relation to the destruction of the mosques.[140] It considered that the statute of limitation started to run in 1999, three years after the war ended and martial law was lifted.[141] As such, the Constitutional Court refused to take into consideration the proceedings in front of the Human Rights Chamber, which the Islamic Community had already initiated in 1996. This raises important concerns in relation to the enforcement of the Human Rights Chamber's judgment, which appears as an isolated mechanism in the Bosnian legal landscape.

Generally speaking, notwithstanding the Human Rights Chamber's efforts to modulate its orders of reparation, these judgments have met a number of obstacles in respect of their enforcement. Thus, the order made in the *Travnik* case to restitute part of the building to the Catholic Archdiocese, had still not been implemented as of 2012.[142] Similar issues were noted in the *Banja Luka* case, as the *Ferhadija* mosque has only reopened on 7 May 2016,[143] exactly twenty-three years after its destruction and around eighteen years after the Human Rights Chamber's

[139] Ema Kovac, 'Controversial Church Relocated', *South East European Times*, 8 June 2009, available at http://www.balkantravellers.com/en/read/article/1268 (last accessed 10 July 2016).

[140] *Islamic Community in Bosnia and Herzegovina* (Judgment on Admissibility and Merits) AP-743/12 (21 July 2015) Constitutional Court of Bosnia and Herzegovina. The judgment is only available in Bosnian; infinite thanks to Špela Kunej for kindly translating the relevant parts of the judgment.

[141] Ibid., para. 50.

[142] U.S. Government, 'Bosnia and Herzegovina 2012 International Religious Freedom Report', available at: http://www.state.gov/documents/organization/208508.pdf (last accessed 5 May 2016) p. 8. It was not possible to find more recent information.

[143] Julian Borger, 'Banja Luka Mosque Rises from Rubble, 23 years after it was Destroyed' in *The Guardian* (7 May 2016), available at: http://www.theguardian.com/world/2016/may/06/banja-luka-mosque-bosnia-herzegovina-serbia-reopens-reconstruction (last accessed 8 May 2016).

judgment. The delay was partly due to political and ethnic tensions, as well as financial reasons and the high standard of authenticity that had been required in order for the mosque to be granted the status of 'national monument'.

7.3.1.2 The 'national monument' approach

In contrast with the previous section, the 'national monument' approach is based on the assets of cultural heritage, rather than on the owner or human beneficiary of that heritage. This approach has been endorsed predominantly by the Commission for the Protection of National Monuments (CPNM), which was set up by virtue of Annex 8 of the Dayton Peace Agreement, and established in 2001. The CPNM operates in concomitance with other supra-level and sub-level entities, including UNESCO, in respect of the management and monitoring of the assets that are listed on the World Heritage List[144] and each entity's Institute for the protection of historical monuments.[145] As is the case with many post-Dayton institutions, the composition of this commission is aimed at ensuring the fair representation of the State of Bosnia, its sub-entities (Republika Srpska and the Federation of Bosnia and Herzegovina), as well as the international community. The CPNM's mandate is defined as follows: 'The Commission shall receive and decide on petitions for the designation of property having cultural, historic, religious or ethnic importance as National Monuments'.[146] The High Representative for Bosnia and Herzegovina has described the Commission's missions as being 'of utmost importance for the reconciliation process throughout Bosnia and Herzegovina as well as for the return of displaced persons and refugees into their pre-war places of residence'.[147]

While based on the model of the UNESCO World Heritage Committee and its eponymous list, its mandate is wider than its international counterpart since the right to petition the Commission in order to have a piece of heritage recognized as a 'national monument' is granted not only to the state and its sub-entities, but also to 'any concerned person in Bosnia and Herzegovina'.[148] The designation of an asset as a 'national monument' entails the obligations, for the entity in whose territory the property is situated, to:

> (a) (...) make every effort to take appropriate legal, scientific, technical, administrative and financial measures necessary for the protection, conservation, presentation and

[144] So far, only two assets are listed: the old town of Mostar—including the Mostar Bridge—and the Mehmed Pacha Sokolović Bridge of Višegrad—Ivo Andric's *Bridge on the Drina*. See http://whc.unesco.org/en/statesparties/ba (last accessed 1 February 2015).

[145] At the sub-level, each canton also has its own office dedicated to the protection of cantonal monuments.

[146] Dayton Peace Agreement (n 104) Annex 8, art. IX.

[147] Decision imposing the RS Law on Implementation of Decisions of the Commission to Preserve National Monuments established under Annex 8 of the Dayton Peace Agreement.

[148] Dayton Peace Agreement (n 104) Annex 8, art. V. Unlike the UNESCO, the CPNM does not draw a list, although it initiated its mandate by consolidating a provisional list elaborated by its predecessor.

rehabilitation of the property, and (b) (. . .) refrain from taking any deliberate measures that might damage the property.

'Rehabilitation' has thus become the most adequate word to designate the works to be undertaken on a damaged or destroyed piece of cultural heritage. It is defined as follows in the law of the Republika Srpska:

'Rehabilitation' shall mean the restoring of damaged or destroyed property to the condition in which it was prior to such damage or destruction, to the extent reasonably possible, including construction of a National Monument, at the same location, in the same shape and form, of the same dimensions and made of the same materials as it was before the destruction, by applying the same construction technology whenever reasonably possible.[149]

Thus, rehabilitation does not necessarily entail the complete reconstruction of the asset, since the latter is bound to the condition of 'authenticity'. [150] This criterion has been engaged as a factor of the exclusion of assets that were quickly reconstructed in the aftermath of the conflict with little consideration of the original 'form and design', 'materials and substance', 'use and function', 'traditions and techniques', 'location and setting', 'spirit and feeling', etc.[151] However the criterion of 'authenticity' reflects certain tensions, notably those between the heritage approach, exclusively focused on the asset to be rehabilitated, and a more human-orientated approach, concerned with the use of the asset such as its direct use or its transformation into some form of memorial. The dilemma is expressed well by Robert Bevan:

The pitfalls of reconstruction in circumstances where there has been an attempt at forced forgetting by the destruction of material culture are particularly treacherous. Not to rebuild, though, would be a counsel for despair. In addition to pragmatic reconstruction necessary for the resumption of life there remains a need to remember, a need to call to account, and a need to prevent destruction from being repeated. Above all, there is a need for truth to be expressed in the raising of buildings. But whose truths are being constructed? Are false memories being erected?[152]

The former approach is embodied by UNESCO in its 1994 Nara Document on Authenticity, which Bevan qualifies as a 'call for truth in architecture'.[153] As it is defined in this document, authenticity seems to be a particularly relevant principle for Bosnia, as a means to transcend identitarian struggles:

In a world that is increasingly subject to the forces of globalization and homogenization, and in a world in which the search for cultural identity is sometimes pursued through aggressive nationalism and the suppression of the cultures of minorities, the essential contribution made by the consideration of authenticity in conservation practice is to clarify and illuminate the collective memory of humanity.[154]

[149] Decision imposing the RS Law (n 147) art. 2.

[150] CPNM Criteria for Designation of the Property as National Monuments, Doc. 01-203/02, Sarajevo (September 2002), art. II(G).

[151] Ibid., art. II(G)(i)–(v) of art. II(G).

[152] Bevan (n 6) pp. 176–7.

[153] Ibid., p. 189.

[154] Nara Document on Authenticity, Experts Meeting (adopted 1–6 November 1994) preambular para. 4.

This approach, however, has been criticized in a number of famous cases, including those concerning the Mostar Bridge and the Ferhadija Mosque in Banja Luka.[155] In both cases, the huge financial cost has been highlighted, since adherence to the principle of authenticity requires the engagement of the techniques that were used at the time of the original construction. This cost might be perceived as indecent in the post-war context in which it might not be possible to cover the costs of essential needs, such as those relating to housing, in respect of which private owners would have to bear the costs of reconstruction.

However, the 'authenticity' criterion is one amongst many; indeed, the adherence to other criteria has turned out to be lax. In contrast to the criteria of UNESCO, the basis is not the 'outstanding universal value of the piece' but rather 'movable or immovable property *of great importance to a group of people with common* cultural, historic, religious or ethnic heritage, such as monuments of architecture, art or history; archaeological sites; groups of buildings; as well as cemeteries'.[156] This idea of 'value' has been further detailed in the 'criteria for designation of the property as national monuments', which take into account, the 'time frame', the 'historic value', the 'artistic and aesthetic value', the 'clarity (documentary, scientific, and educational or pedagogic value)', the 'symbolic value', the 'townscape/landscape value', the 'authenticity', the 'uniqueness/rarity', the 'integrity'. No indication is given in relation to the way these criteria are to be articulated, that is to say, whether they are deemed to be cumulative—undoubtedly, it will not be necessary that an asset of cultural heritage satisfies all criteria—or whether satisfaction of one criterion is sufficient. Thus a simple mosque may satisfy the 'symbolic value' criterion, to the extent that it has 'significance for the identity of a group of people'[157] but it is unlikely that it will also satisfy the 'uniqueness/rarity' criterion. The only indication given is that 'property and political criterions are not of special importance' and that the heritage at stake shall not be posterior to 1960. This latter condition was introduced through an amendment to the Criteria, in order to filter the large numbers of requests that were being received by the Commissioners; notwithstanding, they took care to provide that this condition should not be understood as absolute but would be implemented on a case-by-case basis.[158] This criterion de facto excluded most local religious buildings, which may have contributed the turning of the religious communities to alternative funding, such as that available from the states of the Middle East. In some cases, mosques have thus re-emerged

155 Kathleen Walker Kemezis, *Not What Meets the Eye: Re-examining Reconstruction in Postwar Bosnia and Herzegovina* (Masters thesis, University of Washington, 2012), available at: https://digital.lib.washington.edu/dspace/handle/1773/20226?show=full (last accessed 1 February 2015).

156 Dayton Peace Agreement (n 104) Annex 8, art. VI (emphasis added).

157 CPNM Criteria for Designation of the Property as National Monuments (n 150) art. II(E)(5). The UNESCO criteria also refer to cultural heritage that is 'direct or tangibly associated with (...) *beliefs*' but the 'Committee considers that this criterion should preferably be used in conjunction with other criteria'. See UNESCO Operational Guidelines for the Implementation of the World Heritage Convention, WHC 13/01 (July 2013) para. 77, Criterion (vi).

158 Decision on Amendments to the Criteria for Designating Properties as National Monuments, No: 01.2-6-792/03, Sarajevo (6 May 2003).

in completely different shapes, the Ottoman architecture having sometimes been substituted with Wahhabi architecture.[159] However, the fear that this would allow for the radicalization of Islam in Bosnia and Herzegovina[160] seems to have been overstated.[161] This architectural mutation has rather underlined the absence of a uniform policy, which could have been fulfilled by systemizing reparation for damage made to religious heritage.

Like the decisions of the Human Rights Chambers, the CPNM is also confronted with issues in relation to the implementation of its decisions. Only the Law for Republika Srpska provides for financial penalties in the case that '[t]he responsible person in an administrative body or institution' violates the provisions of the law related to the obligations of the body or the institution concerned. These obligations include the duties: to examine the request for issuance of permits for rehabilitation; not to take decisions in violation of the law; to co-operate with the Commission.[162] In some cases, the decisions of the CPNM have been rejected[163] or have given rise to tension,[164] to the extent that the designation of property as a national monument may result in the freezing of the asset, so as to prevent the owner (whose consent is not required for the designation as national property) from undertaking work or investment activities in relation to his or her asset.[165]

7.3.1.3 The preventive approach

The 'preventive' approach consists of monitoring attacks against relevant cultural and religious heritage in order to prevent forms of violent escalation and to circumscribe the perpetration of hate crimes. It is to say that the reasons underpinning the targeting of cultural and religious heritage during the period of armed conflict have not simply evaporated following the end of the conflict. Cultural, and especially religious, heritage has come to catalyse resentment, intolerance, and ethnic hatred so as to constitute an indicator of the level of *vivre ensemble*. As the Organization for Security and Co-operation in Europe (OSCE) notes:

> Unless the appropriate action is taken, there is a risk that these types of crimes will continue to increase in number and gravity, particularly given the historical context of this country.

[159] Riedlmayer, 'From the Ashes' (e-version) (n 92) p. 18; Bevan (n 6) p. 180.

[160] Riedlmayer, 'From the Ashes' (e-version) (n 92) p. 18.

[161] International Crisis Group, 'Bosnia's Dangerous Tango: Islam and Nationalism', *Europe Briefing N°70* (2013) p. 19.

[162] Decision imposing the RS Law (n 147) art. 15.

[163] U.S. Government (n 142) p. 7.

[164] Institutional tensions were noted by Farida Shaheed during a visit to the country. See UN Special Rapporteur in the Field of Cultural Rights, 'Preliminary conclusions and observations by the Special Rapporteur in the field of cultural rights at the end of her visit to Bosnia and Herzegovina' (24 May 2013), available at: http://www.ohchr.org/EN/NewsEvents/Pages/DisplayNews.aspx?NewsID=13350&LangID=E (last accessed 1 February 2015).

[165] See e.g. the recognition as national monument of properties in a historical area of Sarajevo: the CPNM's decision has had the effect to freeze the asset, and thus to prevent the owner, a Bank, from completing a commercial project for the purpose of which it had already invested some funds. The matter will be settled in Court.

These ostensibly minor crimes have the potential to lead to more serious ones, which could trigger further retaliations and violence within the community.

The public outburst that occurred at the time of the first inauguration of the Ferhadija Mosque, in 2001, is particularly illustrative of the potential for escalation, and the need to adopt a responsive stance in the face of such attacks. Following the Human Rights Chamber's decision, the municipality of Banja Luka granted the construction permit to rebuild the Ferhadija Mosque in March 2001.[166] A ceremony was organized to commemoratethe eighth anniversary of the destruction of the mosque and to lay the first stone of the reconstruction. A mob violently disturbed the ceremony, perpetrating acts of desecration and molesting the attendees—including the High Representative for Bosnia and Herzegovina—who were trapped for several hours in the Islamic Community Centre.[167] This event led to the High Representative's decision to remove the mayor of Banja Luka, as well as several other officials, from office. A second ceremony was organized on 18 June 2001 and passed with no notable incident. The mosque of Banja Luka is now reconstructed, as are a few other mosques within the city. It is worth noting that these mosques no longer need exceptional measures of protection, which tends to attest the suggestion as to the appeasement of the climate in Banja Luka.[168]

Notwithstanding, several reports, mainly deriving from the OSCE mission in Bosnia and Herzegovina and the Inter-Religious Council in Bosnia and Herzegovina, a non-governmental organization consisting of representatives of the four main religious communities, have illustrated that while attacks against religious heritage have decreased over recent years, they continue to occur on a regular basis.[169] Moreover, they are very likely to go unreported and unpunished. The OSCE had thus encouraged the entities of Bosnia and Herzegovina to amend their criminal code in order to better reflect the gravity of 'hate-motivated crimes' through the more thorough criminalization of these offences and the setting of more serious—and thus deterrent—sentences. Amendments of such a nature were made in 2010[170] such that their concrete consequences remain to be assessed. Notwithstanding, both the OSCE and the Inter-Religious Council continue to highlight the lack of enforcement at multiple levels, whether at the level of the investigation of these crimes, the explicit inclusion of a hate count in indictments,[171] or

[166] Riedlmayer, 'From the Ashes' (e-version) (n 92) p. 17.

[167] Office of the High Representative, Sarajevo, 'High Representative Appalled at Outbreak of Violence in Banja Luka' (Press Release) 7 May 2001; Riedlmayer, 'From the Ashes' (e-version) (n 92) p. 17.

[168] András J. Riedlmayer, 'Banja Luka's Ferhadija Mosque Rises Again', 3 March 2008, available at: http://www.bosnia.org.uk/news/news_body.cfm?newsid=2373 (last accessed 1 February 2015).

[169] OSCE-Mission to Bosnia and Herzegovina, 'Tackling Hate Crimes: An Analysis of Bias-Motivated Incidents in Bosnia and Herzegovina with Recommendations' (Sarajevo, 2012) p. 13; Interreligious Council in Bosnia-Herzegovina (ICBH), 'Monitoring and Responses to Attacks on Religious Buildings and Other Holy Sites in BiH—Protection of Holy Sites: Annual Report' (Sarajevo, 2012) p. 3; U.S. Government (n 142) p. 5.

[170] OSCE (n 169) p. 17.

[171] Ibid., pp. 29–32.

the actual conviction and adequate sentencing at the adjudicating phase.[172] As a result, the lack of adequate compensation is also regrettable.[173]

Not only have these two organizations recommended adequate training for relevant staff, but they have also the generalization of the use of video surveillance.[174] Indeed, in those areas in which cameras have been set up, the number of offences has dropped drastically.[175] However, this encouraging sign should not lead to an over-optimistic reaction as to the situation as a whole. Indeed, if it reflects well the efficiency of this deterrence mechanism, it does not necessarily mean or amount to the actual reconciliation of the local populations that are concerned.

The treatment of cultural and religious heritage in the post-war context thus confirms the function of such heritage both for social cohesion purposes and for the prevention of further conflicts, with which international law has become increasingly concerned. However, the case of Bosnia and Herzegovina has underlined two main challenges that might arise in the rehabilitative process. Firstly, it brings to the fore the question of its wider inclusion in the post-conflict process of transitional justice. If the interdependency between rehabilitation of heritage and return is now widely acknowledged, the criticism rather bears on the risk of focusing to too great an extent on restitution and reconstruction—not only of heritage but also of housing—while at the same time overlooking the need for the creation of the adequate socio-economic conditions for return. Secondly, the reconstruction of cultural heritage does not necessarily equate to the creation of an ambitious cultural policy, which can also be seen as a pillar of the reconstruction of the socio-cultural fabric.[176] This consideration brings to the fore again the importance of also focusing on the more immaterial aspects of culture. As the UN Special Rapporteur in the Field of Cultural Rights has deplored, following a visit to Bosnia and Herzegovina: 'too often culture and education are hijacked by the rhetoric of differences, with an immense detrimental impact on the artistic, cultural, scientific and academic life in the country, and on the right of all persons, without discrimination, to enjoy their cultural rights and to access their cultural heritage'.[177]

It should, however, be highlighted that this mixed record has emerged outside of an institutionalized framework of reparation, which has necessarily, and from the outset, hampered a holistic approach. The next section will therefore focus on cases in which such a framework exists.

[172] Ibid., pp. 36–40. [173] Ibid., p. 40. [174] ICBH (n 169) p. 10.

[175] Information provided by the OSCE Office in Srebrenica on 6 August 2013.

[176] Riedlmayer, 'Crimes of War, Crimes of Peace' (n 96) p. 121: at the federal level, there is no minister in charge of cultural affairs; rather, the matter is left to the entities' exclusive jurisdiction and a number of museums have recently shut down due to a lack of budget.

[177] UN Special Rapporteur in the Field of Cultural Rights, 'Visit to Bosnia and Herzegovina' (n 164).

7.3.2 Reparation for 'ethnocide': The Inter-American experience

Granting reparation is an inherent function of human rights courts. The Inter-American case law related to reparation has, from the outset, displayed a progressive approach in relation to addressing the cultural component of the relevant harm. The Court is entitled to grant reparation on the basis of Article 63(1) of the American Convention:

> If the Court finds that there has been a violation of a right or freedom protected by this Convention, the Court shall rule that the injured party be ensured the enjoyment of his right or freedom that was violated. It shall also rule, if appropriate, that the consequences of the measure or situation that constituted the breach of such right or freedom be remedied and that fair compensation be paid to the injured party.

In the Inter-American cases that have been studied in the previous chapters, the cultural characteristics of given indigenous and tribal communities contributed to the shaping of the contours of the affected human rights and relevant measures of reparation. The cultural dimension of reparation had already been set out in the *Aloeboetoe* case, which involved the killing of six male individuals by the Surinamese armed forces, who were members of a community that 'display[ed] a strongly matriarchal familial configuration where polygamy occurs frequently'.[178] The Court ultimately took into account the community's practices, especially polygamy, to identify the victims to whom reparation should be granted.[179]

The reparation ordered by the Court is examined in this section according to the following distinction: firstly, in relation to cases likely to be labelled genocide from an international criminal point of view, and thus involving group destruction; and secondly, in relation to cases in which the Court has found that the cultural integrity of the group was endangered by state policies, especially those infringing some indigenous and tribal peoples' collective right to property. The aim of this section is to determine the impact of the innovative case law in relation to the recognition of the cultural dimension of both group destruction and group existence at the level of the award of reparation.

7.3.2.1 The consequences of aggravated responsibility for cultural harm

As considered in Section 6.1.2, in both the *Plan de Sánchez* and in the *Moiwana* cases, the Court relied on the cultural dimension of the massacres, of which the two communities were victims, in order to determine an aggravated form of responsibility. The few available studies on the issue of aggravated responsibility within the IACHR case law all point towards the idea that such a statement of increased responsibility mainly produces effects at the level of reparation,[180] in addition to

[178] *Aloeboetoe v. Suriname*, Reparations and Costs, Inter-American Court of Human Rights, Series C No. 15 (10 September 1993) para. 58. Fn.: 'Probably a more precise anthropological term would be matrilineal.'

[179] Ibid., para. 66.

[180] Frédéric Mégret, 'Le Renouveau de la Notion de Crime d'Etat devant la Cour Interaméricaine: San José Reprend le Flambeau Abandonné à Genève et Néglige la Haye?' in L. Hennebel and H.

possessing a strong symbolic weight in terms of the condemnation of the state practice. In most cases related to enforced disappearances and violation of the right to life,[181] these consequences are visible at the level of compensation for non-pecuniary damage. In addition, the Court has ordered measures of satisfaction and guarantees of non-repetition such as the obligation 'to investigate the facts that gave rise to the violations in the instant case, and identify, prosecute and punish those responsible',[182] to uncover the whereabouts of the forcefully disappeared victims,[183] to grant 'medical and psychological treatment for the next of kin of executed or forcefully disappeared victims',[184] the state's public acknowledgement of international responsibility,[185] human rights training to the armed forces,[186] to transpose relevant pieces of international human rights law,[187] and the commemoration of the victims through the erection of a monument.[188]

This is also true in the *Moiwana* and *Plan de Sánchez* cases. The cultural harm, which constituted the basis for aggravating state responsibility, has mostly been taken into account at the level of compensation for non-pecuniary damage[189] granted to the community as a whole.[190] Thus, in the *Moiwana* case, the Court took into account the cultural harm in respect of the award of non-pecuniary damage, which amounted to 10,000 U.S. Dollars, to be granted to each of the victims; 20,000 in the *Plan de Sánchez* case.[191] These non-pecuniary damages were made on the findings as to the merits. In the *Moiwana* case, the Court therefore took into

Tigroudja (eds.), *Le Particularisme Interaméricain des Droits de l'Homme* (Paris: Pedone, 2006) p. 340; Elise Hansbury, 'Le Juge Interaméricain et le "Jus Cogens"' No. 11 (2011) *eCahiers*, available at: http://iheid.revues.org/391 (last accessed 1 February 2015) para. 4.1.1(4).

[181] *Myrna Mack Chang v. Guatemala,* Merits, Reparations, and Costs, Inter-American Court of Human Rights Series C No. 101 (25 November 2003) para. 264(a); *Goiburú and others v. Paraguay*, Merits, Reparations, and Costs, Inter-American Court of Human Rights, Series C No. 153 (22 September 2006) para. 160; *La Cantuca v. Perú*, Merits, Reparations, and Costs, Inter-American Court of Human Rights, Series C No. 162 (29 November 2006) para. 219(II); *The Ituango Massacres v. Colombia*, Preliminary Objections, Merits, Reparations, and Costs, Inter-American Court of Human Rights Series C No. 148 (1 July 2006) paras. 385, 390(b)(c); *"Maipiripán Massacre" v. Colombia*, Merits, Reparations, and Costs, Inter-American Court of Human Rights Series C No. 134 (15 September 2005) para. 285.

[182] *Myrna Mack Chang* (n 181) para. 275; *Goiburú and others* (n 181) paras. 163–70; *La Cantuca* (n 181) para. 225; *The Ituango Massacres* (n 181) para. 400.

[183] *Goiburú and others* (n 181) paras. 171–2; *La Cantuca* (n 181) paras. 219–32.

[184] *La Cantuca* (n 181) para. 238.

[185] *Myrna Mack Chang* (n 181) para. 278; *Goiburú and others* (n 181) para. 173; *La Cantuca* (n 181) para. 235; *The Ituango Massacres* (n 181) para. 406.

[186] *Myrna Mack Chang* (n 181) para. 282; *Goiburú and others* (n 181) para. 178; *La Cantuca* (n 181) paras. 239–42; *The Ituango Massacres* (n 181) para. 409.

[187] *Goiburú and others* (n 181) para. 178(g).

[188] *Myrna Mack Chang* (n 181) para. 286; *Goiburú and others* (n 181) para. 178; *The Ituango Massacres* (n 181) para. 408.

[189] *Plan de Sánchez Massacre v. Guatemala*, Reparations, Inter-American Court of Human Rights Series C No. 116 (19 November 2004) para. 81.

[190] *Moiwana Community v. Suriname*, Merits, Reparations, and Costs, Inter-American Court of Human Rights Series C No. 124 (15 June 2005) para. 194; *Plan de Sánchez Massacre* (Reparations) (n 189) para. 86.

[191] *Moiwana Community* (n 190) para. 196.

account how 'long-standing impunity (. . .) fills [the N'djuka] with dread that that offended spirits will seek revenge upon them',[192] the anguish and despair provoked both by the Community's ignorance as to their next of kin's remains and as to the impossibility of practising the death rituals,[193] the forcible transfer from the community's ancestral territory, and how it consequently 'devastated them emotionally, spiritually, culturally, and economically'.[194] In the *Plan de Sánchez* case, the Court also took into account the interruption in the intergenerational transmission of the culture consequent to the events, as 'the death of the women and the elders, oral transmitters of the Maya-Achí culture, caused a cultural vacuum'.[195] The following statement made in this same case is illustrative of the cultural sensitivity of the San Jose judges in these types of cases:

> The Court observes that, in the instant case, the victims belonging to the Mayan indigenous people, of the Achí linguistic community, possess their own traditional authorities and forms of community organization, centered on consensus and respect. They have their own social, economic and cultural structures. For the members of these communities, harmony with the environment is expressed by their spiritual relationship with the land, the way they manage their resources and a profound respect for nature. Traditions, rites and customs have an essential place in their community life. Their spirituality is reflected in the close relationship between the living and the dead, and is expressed, based on burial rites, as a form of permanent contact and solidarity with their ancestors. The transmission of culture and knowledge is one of the roles assigned to the elders and the women.[196]

The measures of satisfaction and non-repetition guarantees were similar to those formulated in the other cases of aggravated responsibility[197] but have also been adapted to the specificity of the relevant cultural harm, underlying which is a strong collective dimension. Thus, in the *Moiwana* case, the Court also ordered Suriname to provide 'guarantees of safety for those community members who decide to return to Moiwana village',[198] to establish a developmental fund aimed at 'providing basic social services to the community members upon their return',[199] and above all to recognize the Moiwana community's collective title to its traditional territories.[200] In the *Plan de Sánchez* case, the Court ordered Guatemala 'to commemorate those executed in the massacre', adding that the 'State must take into account the traditions and customs of the members of the affected communities in this act'.[201] In

[192] Ibid., para. 195(a).

[193] Ibid., para. 195(b); similar finding in *Plan de Sánchez Massacre* (Reparations) (n 189) para. 87(a).

[194] *Moiwana Community* (n 190) para. 195(b).

[195] *Plan de Sánchez Massacre* (Reparations) (n 189) para. 87(b).

[196] Ibid., para. 85.

[197] Obligation to investigate the facts, identify, prosecute, and punish the responsible parties, as well as recover the remains of the Moiwanan community members killed during the 1986 attack in *Moiwana Community* (n 190) paras. 202–8; Obligation to investigate the facts, identify, prosecute and punish the responsible parties in *Plan de Sánchez Massacre* (Reparations) (n 189) para. 98; Public Apology and Acknowledgment of International Responsibility, in *Moiwana Community* (n 190) paras. 216–17; *Plan de Sánchez Massacre* (Reparations) (n 189) para. 100; Establishment of a Memorial in *Moiwana Community* (n 190) para. 218.

[198] *Moiwana Community* (n 190) para. 212.

[199] Ibid., paras. 213–15.

[200] Ibid., paras. 209–11.

[201] *Plan de Sánchez Massacre* (Reparations) (n 189) para. 101.

this case, the victims already had their memorial so the Court rather ordered the state to provide the equivalent of 25,000 U.S. Dollars for the maintenance of the chapel.[202] It also ordered the state to translate the judgment of the Court into the Maya-Achí language.[203] Finally, the Court provided that the state should establish both housing and developmental programmes,[204] as well as adequate psychological support.[205]

Some of these measures actually echo some of the provisions of the Agreement on identity and rights of indigenous peoples, which is part of the General Peace Agreement that was signed in 1995, under the supervision of the United Nations Secretary General (UNSG), between the different parties involved in the Guatemalan conflict. Thus, acknowledging the importance of the Mayan identity for the group members, as well as for the Guatemalan diversity as a whole, the agreement provides for a set of legislative and constitutional measures to be adopted in order to fight discrimination against the Mayan people, and to secure their rights, especially their cultural rights[206]—namely: language; names, surnames, and place names; spirituality; temples, ceremonial centres and holy places; use of indigenous dress; science and technology; education reform—and their land rights,[207] as well as an increased autonomy within the administrative structure of Guatemala.[208] Beyond the issue of its concrete implementation, this agreement is noteworthy for its integrated approach to cultural rehabilitation; notwithstanding, it has been criticized for fixing essentialized and idealized identities[209] and shaping the claims within 'the language of international human rights and multiculturalist discourses'.[210] While the negotiations of peace agreements, as well as the formulation of collective claims in front of a human rights body such as the IACHR, necessarily involve the filtering of the claims through the victims' representatives, the question remains as to the weight that should be accorded to such criticisms. Nevertheless, it is worth mentioning, as it tends to underline the risk for the reparation process to pursue the process of cultural destruction that it attempts to remedy, by granting measures that rather match the dominant group's vision of the needs, to the detriment of the indigenous victims' own perceptions.

While the IACHR measures of reparation of the non-pecuniary damage are not explicitly formulated as a response to the cultural harm, in contrast to the measures of pecuniary compensation, they illustrate the holistic approach that the IACHR has adopted in its judgments on reparation. It acknowledges and remedies both the individual and communal harms, and both physical and cultural harm. The approach is clearly relativist in its essence, 'taking into account cultural diversity in the

[202] Ibid., para. 104. [203] Ibid., para. 102. [204] Ibid., paras. 105, 109–11.
[205] Ibid., paras. 106–8.
[206] Agreement on Identity and Rights of Indigenous Peoples (13 March 1995), art. III.
[207] Ibid., art. IV(F). [208] Ibid., art. IV(C).
[209] Rachel Sieder and Jessica Witchell, 'Advancing Indigenous Claims through the Law: Reflections on the Guatemalan Peace Process' in Cowan, Dembour, and Wilson (eds.) in Jane K. Cowan, Marie-Bénédicte Dembour, and Richard A. Wilson (eds.), *Culture and Rights: Anthropological Perspectives* (Cambridge, UK; New York, NY, USA: Cambridge University Press, 2001) pp. 201, 210, 213.
[210] Ibid., p. 201.

implementation of an international human rights instrument'.[211] In doing so, it does not hesitate to confront some of the challenges that were outlined earlier in this chapter, such as granting development and social services for these structurally vulnerable communities, while taking care to integrate these policy measures in a wider framework of reparation. The *Moiwana* case has also contributed to the conceptualization of a new form of damage, one which Judge Cançado Trindade calls 'spiritual damage':

> an aggravated form of moral damage, which has a direct bearing on what is most intimate to the human person, namely, her inner self, her beliefs in human destiny, her relations with their dead. This *spiritual damage* would of course not give rise to pecuniary reparations, but rather to other forms of reparation. The idea is launched herein, for the first time ever, to the best of my knowledge.[212]

According to him, 'spiritual damage' can be contrasted to the category of 'moral damage', which brings an 'undue emphasis on pecuniary reparations'.[213]

The implementation mechanisms of these measures are also worth outlining, as they demonstrate an interesting and protracted dialogue between the victims and the state authorities, in respect of the implementation of these measures. This was particularly true in the *Plan de Sánchez* case, where the Court's orders on monitoring compliance with the judgments have displayed a progressive evolution towards the implementation of measures tending to the long-term restoration of the victims, such as 'the development of cultural, infrastructure, educational and health programs' or the 'dissemination of the Maya-Achí culture in the communities affected by the massacre', with which Guatemala complied through the establishment of an Academy of Mayan Languages.[214] However, this positive picture should be placed in the wider framework of transitional justice, within which accountability remains a crucially lacking feature, with the delayed trial of General Ríos-Montt, who ruled over Guatemala at the time the genocide was perpetrated.[215] As for the *Moiwana* case, the implementation of the measures of reparation is far less positive, with the IACHR judges declaring, in their third Order of monitoring compliance: 'It is lamentable that twenty-four years after the attack, and five years after service of the Judgment, the State has not been able to provide the Tribunal with any details on advances in either one of these investigations';[216] the obligation to investigate the facts of the case was an essential remedy to the group cultural harm in this case. Generally speaking, states have proved to be more inclined to comply with orders of pecuniary remedies than non-pecuniary ones, such as those involved by cultural harm.[217]

[211] Ludovic Hennebel, 'La Protection de l'"Intégrité Spirituelle" des Indigènes: Réflexions sur l'Arrêt de la Cour Interaméricaine des Droits de l'Homme dans l'Affaire *Comunidad Moiwana c. Suriname* du 15 Juin 2005' (2006) No. 66 *R.T.D.H.* 253, p. 274, para. 22.

[212] *Moiwana Community* (n 190) Separate Opinion of Judge Cançado Trindade; Concurring Opinion Judge Medina-Quiroga, para. 71 (emphasis added).

[213] Ibid., para. 76.

[214] *Plan de Sánchez Massacre v. Guatemala*, Order of Monitoring Compliance with Judgment (28 November 2007), paras. 37, 41; *Plan de Sánchez Massacre v. Guatemala*, Order of Monitoring Compliance with Judgment (21 February 2011), paras. 26–30.

[215] Evans, *The Right to Reparation* (n 5) p. 163.

[216] *Moiwana Community v. Suriname*, Order of Monitoring Compliance with Judgment (22 November 2010), para. 11.

[217] Magnus J. Langer and Elise Hansbury, 'Monitoring Compliance with the Decisions of Human Rights Courts: The Inter-American Particularism' in Laurence Boisson de Chazournes, Marcelo

7.3.2.2 Repairing the damage to group cultural existence

In the three cases referred to above, in which the Court has recognized the violation of the right to communal property under Article 21 of the American Convention, the judges quite logically ordered the various States involved to return their traditional lands to the tribal and indigenous communities. In *Awas Tingni*, the Court ordered Nicaragua to 'create an effective mechanism for delimitation, demarcation, and titling of the property of indigenous communities, in accordance with their customary law, values, customs and mores'.[218] In the case of 'objective and well-founded' reasons that would make the restitution impossible, an alternative land must be found and granted to the community. This land must be 'chosen by means of a consensus with the community, in accordance with its own manner of consultation and decision-making, practices and customs'.[219] However, the implementation of the judgment has been hampered by inter-community disputes over the land. In its third Order of Monitoring compliance with judgment, the Court finally announced:

> That the Inter-American Court sets much store by the fact that the State has fully complied with the reparation measures ordered by this Tribunal in the Judgment on the Merits, Reparations and Costs of August 31, 2001, something which establishes an important legal precedent in International Human Rights Law, since this one is a leading case on the matter of recognition of the property rights vested in the indigenous peoples, as well as of their ancestral values, usages and customs.[220]

In the *Yakye Axa* case, the IACHR also took into account, as part of the non-pecuniary damages, 'the special significance of the land for indigenous peoples in general, and for the Yakye Axa Community in particular', which:

> entails that any denial of the enjoyment or exercise of their territorial rights is detrimental to values that are very representative for the members of said peoples, who are *at risk of losing or suffering irreparable damage to their cultural identity and life and to the cultural heritage to be passed on to future generations.*[221]

In addressing the extent of Paraguay's obligation to hand over its traditional territory to the community, the court again noted the cultural specificity of this sedentarized community to emphasize 'the certain risk of an irreparable ethnic and cultural loss, with the ensuing loss of diversity'.[222]

Kohen, and Jorge E. Viñuales (eds.), *Diplomatic and Judicial Means of Dispute Settlement* (Leiden; Boston: Martinus Nijhoff Publishers, 2013) p. 218.

218 *Mayagma (Sumo) Awas Tingni Community*, Judgment on Merits, Reparations, and Costs, Inter-American Court of Human Rights Series C No. 79 (31 August 2001) para. 164. See also *Saramaka People* (n 37) para. 214(5).

219 *Yakye Axa Indigenous Community v. Paraguay*, Merits, Reparations, and Costs, Inter-American Court of Human Rights Series C No. 125 (17 June 2005) para. 217.

220 *Mayagma (Sumo) Awas Tingni Community*, Order of Monitoring Compliance with Judgment (3 April 2009), para. 15.

221 *Yakye Axa Indigenous Community* (n 219) para. 203 (emphasis added).

222 Ibid., para. 216.

The 'cultural survival' of the group also constituted a determinative consideration in the *Saramaka* case, on which the Court based Suriname's obligation to adopt:

> legislative, administrative, and other measures as may be required to recognize, protect, guarantee and give legal effect to the right of the members of the Saramaka people to hold collective title of the territory they have traditionally used and occupied, which includes the lands and natural resources necessary for their social, cultural and economic survival.[223]

The IACHR sometimes also granted pecuniary reparation,[224] for both material and immaterial damage, sometimes under the form of a development fund.[225] As the organization Redress notes, 'given the inter-ethnic dimension of the conflicts under the jurisdiction of the Court, which often involved land or conflict over other resources, awarding economic damage to one group and not another may simply reignite violence and thwart possibilities of lasting peace'.[226]

The issue of the relevance of pecuniary compensation for the purposes of both remedying cultural or spiritual harm and contributing to the goal of reconciliation has also been addressed in the attempts to deal with the aftermath of forcibly transferred children in Canada and Australia, in the context of which, unlike the Latin American countries, the two states were far less concerned with the scarcity of financial resources.

7.3.3 Reparation for forcibly transferred children in Australia and Canada

Cases of forcible transfer of children outside their families and communities are particularly relevant from the perspective of reparation. So far, these cases have gathered some form of consensus around labelling the process as 'cultural genocide', especially in the Canadian case. Beyond the words, they constitute particularly long-lasting processes, extended over several decades. Their consequences are still visible nowadays, and may still be visible in the future in case no action is taken. The question of dealing with the intergenerational and societal harm is therefore particularly acute in these two countries.

7.3.3.1 Canadian and Australian approaches to reparation

Canada and Australia have dealt with the historical injustice associated with the widespread transfer of indigenous children in different orders. The Australian State institutions—whether the judiciary, the successive governments, or the Parliament—initially displayed great reluctance to recognize the extent of the damage caused to the aboriginal community since the early days of settler colonialism,

[223] *Saramaka People* (n 37) para. 214(7).
[224] Only costs and expenses in *Mayagma (Sumo) Awas Tingni Community* (n 218) paras. 168–9.
[225] *Saramaka People* (n 37) paras. 198–202; *Yakye Axa Indigenous Community* (n 219) paras. 198–202.
[226] Redress (n 17) p. 6.

in contrast to the victim-oriented approach embodied in the conclusions of the *Bringing Them Home Report*. The latter dedicated lengthy consideration to the issue of reparation, which it mainly grounded in international law, due to the absence of Australian law in this respect. It referred amongst others to the *Van Boven principles*, a first version of the 2006 guidelines, as well as the findings of the IACHR in the *Aloeboetoe* case.[227] The conclusions could constitute a case study of the holistic implementation of every available remedy, as reflected in the seventeen recommendations dedicated to the specific issue of reparation. The right to reparation was granted to a wide range of entities: the former child victims of the forced transfers, their family members, their broader communities, and their descendants.[228]

'Acknowledgement and apology' took an important place amongst the range of satisfactory measures. The Australian Human Rights Commission thus recommended the Australian Parliament, the police forces, the churches as well as other non-governmental institutions involved in the transfers, to adopt such measures.[229] However, the Commission did not elaborate in detail on the content of such apologies, and especially as to whether these various authorities should publicly and explicitly engage responsibility for 'genocide'. It rather simply considered that the victims and their communities should be involved in the process of drafting the wording of such declarations. In relation to genocide, the Commission only recommended that the Australian Parliament should implement the provisions of the Genocide Convention,[230] the lack of implementation being one of the reasons why, in some cases, the Australian courts had rejected the victims' claims.[231] On the basis of the report, the Australian Government established a 'sorry day' commemorating 'the history of forcible removal and its effects'.[232] An entire part of the report was dedicated to guarantees of non-repetition, which were mainly directed towards the rest of the Australian population in order to increase the Australians' sensitivity to the fate of their aboriginal fellow citizens. For example, school curricula were expected to address the history and the effects of the forced removals.[233] The Commission also recommended that professional training should be provided to all of the actors likely to be involved in dealing with this historical process and its effects.[234] In addition to these measures, the Australian Commission addressed the issue of land restitution and the revitalization of the Indigenous language and culture,[235] in a broader context of the rehabilitation of the victims of the forced transfer, in order for them to catch up as much as possible with the years of having been isolated from their culture and history.[236] Yet the core of the recommendations was dedicated to financial compensation, through the establishment of a

[227] Australian Human Rights Commission, *Bringing Them Home, Report of the National Inquiry into the Separation of Aboriginal and Torres Strait Islander Children from Their Families* (April 1997) p. 243.

[228] Ibid. Recommendation 4.

[229] Ibid. Recommendations 5, 5a, 6.

[230] Ibid. Recommendation 10.

[231] *Nulyarimma v. Thompson* (1999); *Buzzacott v. Hill* (1999), FCA 1192 (1 September 1999) Federal Court of Australia (Justice Wilcox) paras. 18–30.

[232] Australian Human Rights Commission (n 227) Recommendation 7a.

[233] Ibid. Recommendation 8a.

[234] Ibid. Recommendations 9a, 9b.

[235] Ibid. Recommendations 12, 12b.

[236] Ibid. Recommendation 11.

'National Compensation Fund'.[237] The report specified the amount of money to be granted to each victim and the criteria a victim should satisfy to be entitled to financial compensation.[238] A 'minimum lump sum' was also established in order to avoid the dismissal of claims on the ground that the policy was conducted 'in the best interest of the child'.[239]

As mentioned above, there is a significant contrast to be drawn between the content of these recommendations and their enforcement. After years of governmental resistance, supported by the majority of the population,[240] the Prime Minister finally expressed a public apology in 2007; even then, his speech was criticized for failing to acknowledge state responsibility for genocide. The first Sorry Day was held in 1998. Financial compensation was only granted in one case, in which the reparation granted was mainly made in respect of the sexual abuse that the victim had endured as a board student.[241] All other claims formulated before civil, common law, and constitutional courts were rejected. Furthermore no Fund was ever established, except in the state of Tasmania, which established a Fund of five million Australian Dollars to deliver *ex-gratia* compensation.[242]

The Canadian process has overlapped temporally with that in Australia. While the claims were also similar, they have been tackled in a slightly different way since the current process of truth and reconciliation has actually been triggered by the multiplication of cases brought before the Canadian civil and criminal courts.[243] In 1996, the Royal Commission on Aboriginal Peoples released an official report which highlighted the multifaceted harm caused by the forced transfers of children to residential schools.[244] It also underlined the failure of these schools, which not only relied on the shocking rationale of assimilating children, but also when it failed to do so, sent the children back to their communities, where they were confronted with a culture they no longer knew. Following the report, individual claims and class actions multiplied, some of which—especially those involving sexual assault—were successfully settled by judges.[245] While the claims aiming at the recognition of genocide were dismissed, it is noteworthy that in the *Raubach*

[237] Ibid. Recommendations 15, 16a, 16b, 17.

[238] Ibid. Recommendation 14.

[239] Ibid. Recommendation 18.

[240] B.A. Hocking and M. Stephenson, 'Why the Persistent Absence of a Foundational Principle? Indigenous Australians, Proprietary and Family Reparations' in Federico Lenzerini (ed.), *Reparations for Indigenous Peoples: International and Comparative Perspectives* (Oxford: Oxford University Press, 2008) pp. 487–8.

[241] *Trevorrow v. South Australia*, quoted in Hocking and Stephenson (n 240) p. 492.

[242] Ana F. Vrdoljak, 'Reparations for Cultural Loss' in Federico Lenzerini (ed.), *Reparations for Indigenous Peoples: International and Comparative Perspectives* (Oxford: Oxford University Press, 2008) pp. 221–2.

[243] Bradford W. Morse, 'Indigenous Peoples of Canada and their Efforts to Achieve True Reparations' in Federico Lenzerini (ed.), *Reparations for Indigenous Peoples: International and Comparative Perspectives* (Oxford: Oxford University Press, 2008) p. 282.

[244] Royal Commission on Aboriginal Peoples, *Report of the Royal Commission on Aboriginal Peoples* (1996); Vinodh Jaichand, 'Residential Schools' in Dinah L. Shelton (ed.), *Encyclopedia of Genocide and Crimes Against Humanity*, vol. 2 (New York: Macmillan Reference USA; Thomson Gale, 2004) p. 901.

[245] Morse (n 243) p. 283; Zia Akhtar, 'Canadian Genocide and Official Responsibility' (2010) 10 *Int.C.L.R.* 111, pp. 120–1.

case, the judge, whose jurisdiction was limited to the filtering of the various claims at a preliminary stage, ruled that '[a]ssuming that the plaintiffs [could] prove that some of the assaults they allege were part of a program of cultural genocide, a trial judge might consider the Convention to be relevant to the question of punitive or aggravated damages'.[246] This hypothesis could have constituted an interesting domestic echo to the IACHR and ECSR case law, had the case been adjudicated on its merits.

In 2006, confronted with the rise of individual claims since the early 1990s, the Canadian government undertook to engage in the systematic settlement of these claims, by concluding an agreement with representatives of the First Nations and the Churches that had administered the residential schools. The 2006 Agreement eventually provided for several measures of reparation and for funds to deal with the ongoing consequences of the human rights violations. Each victim became entitled to a minimum of 10,000 Canadian dollars; the more time the victim had spent in residential schools, the higher the financial compensation to be awarded.[247] In addition to this basic and general measure, it was provided that victims of specific crimes, such as sexual violence, would receive additional financial compensation.[248] The Agreement also established a healing fund,[249] a commemoration fund,[250] and a truth and reconciliation commission fund.[251] The three funds were to be dedicated to the provision of collective measures of satisfaction and rehabilitation.

The latter fund allowed for the establishment of a Truth and Reconciliation Commission, which began its work in 2009. Its mandate was criticized, as the Commission did not have any investigative power, nor did it have jurisdiction to qualify the acts or to name potential culprits.[252] However, the Canadian Truth and Reconciliation Commission managed to accommodate both its mandate constraints and the imperative for truth. When it comes to reparation, the report is very critical of the 2006 Agreement and how the government followed it up. In its interim report, the Commission had already outlined the main features of the process endured by Native children in Canada, as well as their claims. Not only do the victims want justice in the form of financial compensation,[253] they also want:

> support to allow them to improve parental skills, (. . .) control over the way their children and grandchildren are educated, (. . .) respect, (. . .) their languages and their traditions (. . .)

[246] *Raubach et al. v. The Attorney General of Canada et al.*, [2005] 1 WWR 334 (6 July 2004) Manitoba Court of Queen's Bench, para. 12.

[247] Indian Residential Schools Settlement Agreement (8 May 2006) (IRS Canada) art. 5, see especially 5.02 ('Common Experience Payment').

[248] Ibid. Schedule D, art. 6.03 ('Independent Assessment Process').

[249] Ibid., arts. 3.02, 8. [250] Ibid., art. 7.02. [251] Ibid., art. 7.01, pp. 53–4.

[252] For a criticism of the mandate of the Canadian TRC, see Matt James, 'Uncomfortable Comparisons: The Canadian Truth and Reconciliation Commission in International Context' (2010) 5 *Les Ateliers de l'Éthique / The Ethics Forum* 23, pp. 23–35.

[253] Truth and Reconciliation Commission of Canada, *Interim Report* (2012); some schools were not included in the Agreement; in some cases, the records and thus evidence of the children's presence in the schools, were lost.

They want the full history of residential schools and Aboriginal peoples taught to all students in Canada at all levels of study and to all teachers, and given prominence in Canadian history texts.[254]

As reported by the Commission in its final report, the government has tended to consider the reparation of residential schools' survivors in a punctual manner, having already decreased the funds to many of the rehabilitation programmes and centres. The Commission's report is thus already a first step in complementing the individual compensation scheme that was granted by virtue of the Settlement Agreement, which has been deemed 'insufficient to repair the harms of residential schools and does not address the harms to communities and future generations'.[255]

The Commission's call for action is formulated in a holistic manner, so as to address both the experience of the residential schools and their overall legacy. The report opens the scope of its analysis to Canada's historical treatment of Aboriginal people, through wide-ranging socio-economic reforms. Overall, the report calls for a radical socio-cultural shift within the Canadian society, to revise its historical understanding of Canada's relationship with Indigenous peoples. As such, the Commission sees reconciliation as a 'way of life',[256] which should legally be framed by the provision of the UNDRIP, thus challenging directly Canada's adherence to the Declaration to the extent that it is a non-binding document.[257] As such, self-determination arises as a core element of the recommended framework of reconciliation. The report suggests the revitalization of indigenous law, as a way to alleviate problems associated with the civil law system, which has shown limited receptivity in relation to indigenous peoples' claims.[258] This report also provides some concrete content to the concept of revitalization set out in Article 11 UNDRIP by identifying Canada's obligation 'to assist Indigenous communities to restore their own spiritual belief systems and faith practices'.[259]

All in all, the reparation rhetoric is however quite limited in the report, which rather focuses on reconciliation (a full volume is dedicated to the topic). While recommending a wide range of measures of satisfaction—memorialization, commemoration, role of museums, access to archives—the report clearly calls for moving 'from apology to action': 'The words of the apologies will ring hollow if Canada's actions fail to produce the necessary social, cultural, political and economic change that benefits Aboriginal peoples and Canadians.'[260]

[254] Ibid., pp. 6–7.

[255] Llewellyn (n 4) p. 199. See also Marlene Brant Castellano, 'A Holistic Approach to Reconciliation: Insights from Research of the Aboriginal Healing Foundation' in Brant Castellano, Archibald, and DeGagné (eds.) (n 4) p. 396.

[256] Truth and Reconciliation Commission of Canada (TRC), *Honouring the Truth, Reconciling for the Future—Summary of the Final Report of the Truth and Reconciliation of Canada* (2015) p. 238.

[257] Ibid., pp. 241–2. [258] Ibid., pp. 255, 266. [259] Ibid., p. 278.

[260] Ibid., p. 263.

7.3.3.2 The recognition of genocide as a measure of satisfaction?

A final and cross-cutting issue: if a judgment constitutes a measure of 'satisfaction' in itself, would *a fortiori* the use of a label other than genocide amount to a failure to make adequate reparation? This question arises as a particularly acute one in relation to the processes of the forcible transfers of children. While the other cases studied throughout this book are likely to be criminally qualified as 'persecution' because the *actus reus* does not fall within the material element of the definition of genocide, forcible transfers of children are explicitly mentioned at Article II (e) of the definition of genocide. This does not mean that all cases, in which children would have been forcibly removed from their family, could entail the qualification as genocide and that some might not be qualified as persecution. For instance, the forced removal of five hundred children from their family under the dictatorship of the Argentinean military junta, from 1979 to 1983, hardly satisfies the definition of the victim group set out in the definition of genocide; as a result, persecution rather constitutes the adequate criminal category in this case.

However, in the Canadian and Australian processes, the request for an official recognition of genocide, whether formulated before national courts or addressed to the respective governments, has been ongoing in the process of truth, reconciliation, and reparation.[261] The Canadian Truth and Reconciliation Commission's report does not particularly address the issue, as it relies on the premise that the process of transferring Canadian Aboriginal children to residential schools was cultural genocide. However, it touches upon the controversy that surrounded the opening of the Human Rights Museum in Manitoba, which was criticized by the indigenous communities for not mentioning the word 'genocide'. In response, its director had justified the Museum's approach and argued that the Museum was a tool to drive Canadian citizens to draw their own conclusions.[262] The Truth and Reconciliation Commission does not take a clear stance on whether the Human Rights Museum should use the word 'genocide' or not. It simply highlights the role of museums:

> Museums have an ethical responsibility to foster national reconciliation and not simply tell one party's version of the past. This can be accomplished by representing the history of residential schools and of Aboriginal peoples in ways that invite multiple, sometimes conflicting perspectives, yet ultimately facilitate empathy, mutual respect, and a desire for reconciliation that is rooted in justice.

As such, the Canadian Truth and Reconciliation Commission seems to accept the Human Rights Museum's argumentation from the moment that the narrative reflects a plurality of ideas and conceptions, and ultimately targets reconciliation.

[261] Rosemary L. Nagy, 'The Scope and Bounds of Transitional Justice and the Canadian Truth and Reconciliation Commission' (2013) 7 *I.J.T.J.* 52, p. 67.

[262] TRC Canada, Summary of the Final Report (n 256) p. 301, which refers to Canadian Museum for Human Rights, 'Statement from the President and CEO: Use of "Genocide" in Relation to Treatment of Indigenous Peoples in Canada' (26 July 2013) available at: https://humanrights.ca/about-museum/news/statement-president-and-ceo-use-genocide-relation-treatment-indigenous-peoples (last accessed 1 May 2016).

In this regard, it is noteworthy that the Canadian Commission chose to refer to 'cultural genocide' rather than genocide, the legal status of which allegedly confers greater resonance on the gravity of the process, and possibly re-opens the scope for judicial claims of genocide. The Canadian context displays the added value of the concept of cultural genocide, since it allows for the analysis to be refocused—particularly in terms of its legacy and reconciliation—on the wider societal and cultural dimension, that is, beyond the mere Aboriginal culture. It is from this premise that the range of policies and measures of reconciliation are spelled out; most of them fall within the social, economic, and cultural field rather than the judicial and political one.

From a judicial perspective, the characterization as genocide of acts of forcibly transferring children, and more broadly of cultural genocide, firstly needs to meet two pre-requisites which were discussed in the previous chapters: that the *mens rea* is understood in socio-cultural terms, and that motives and intent are not confused. To settle the question of the recognition of genocide as a measure of satisfaction, a first track would be to focus on the conditions in which the judgment would be rendered, especially if the tribunal has operated according to the rule of law. The implementation of such a principle is nonetheless not exempt of difficulty, especially in the Australian and Canadian cases, which implied acts that had sometimes preceded the coining of the word 'genocide', the adoption of the Genocide Convention, and its transposition in international law. The response to these claims therefore inherently extends beyond the borders of criminal justice to cross those of historical justice. As for the acts that fall within the jurisdiction *ratione temporis* of the Genocide Convention, they were opposed to formalist arguments of non-transposition of the Genocide Convention. As many authors have argued, the status of *jus cogens* that has long been associated with the Genocide Convention should have allowed for the striking down of this argument, with the result that the conformity of the formalist arguments with customary international law is more than dubious.[263]

As a result of the political opposition to the genocide label, some Canadian First Nations members have set up their own 'Indigenous Human Rights Tribunal', with the explicit mandate:

> to gather the proof that genocide of indigenous people occurred and is occurring across Canada. Under traditional law jurisdiction to establish a public, non-governmental, international Tribunal of Inquiry into the evidence of Genocide in Canadian Indian Residential Schools and hospitals.[264]

However, one can wonder about the relevance of such an initiative, the future findings of which are already anticipated in its mandate, and which operates in

[263] See e.g. Robert van Krieken, 'Rethinking Cultural Genocide: Aboriginal Child Removal and Settler-Colonial State Formation' (2004) 75 *Oceania* 125, p. 127; David B. MacDonald and Gordon Hudson, 'The Genocide Question and Indian Residential Schools in Canada' (2012) 45 *Can.J.Pol.Sc.* 427, pp. 437–8.

[264] Quoted in Akhtar (n 245) p. 124.

complete discordance with other entities involved in the process of reconciliation. While the criteria to qualify genocide are now thoroughly framed in international criminal law, the use of genocide for the purposes of recognizing or denying state responsibility for historical undertakings such as those relevant in the Australian and Canadian processes nevertheless continues to rely on political subjectivity. The question of whether the recognition of genocide should be recognized as a measure of satisfaction thus remains an open one, since it implies the transcending of the closed relationship between the perpetrators and victims and the involvement of the whole society.

7.4 Concluding Remarks

In spite of the variety of situations addressed in this chapter, it is possible to draw some common conclusions. The first conclusion implies the need for an integrated approach to cultural harm, which requires the differentiation of situations and consequently, the individualization of programmes of reparation, in the sense that while best practices may exist, each situation will call for a specific set of measures, depending on what the victims need and claim. All the cases thus tend towards another conclusion, which is already underlined in specialized literature on the topic: the interdependency between collective and individual reparation, and *a fortiori* between compensation and other forms of reparation. The emphasis on individual reparation may to some extent remedy the potential loopholes of general settlements; the emphasis on symbolic reparation may also remedy the risk for an exclusively pecuniary approach, which is unlikely to redress victims in a long-term perspective. This brings the discussion to the need to involve victims, as well as the need to set up an actual programme of transitional justice, or a similar programme where political transition is not at stake. For instance, the cases of forcibly transferred children may be the most impressive acts of a wider genocidal or assimilationist campaign towards indigenous peoples. Much attention has been dedicated to these acts in the context of 'cultural genocide' because of their *sui generis* reference in Article II of the Genocide Convention. Yet, the processes of dealing with the cultural consequences of such acts should be done in association with those dealing with the other features of these populations' experiences of discrimination and stigmatization, such as the restitution of the land and the organization of some vocational training for certain parts of the population which have systematically been considered fit for low-skilled jobs only.

The Former Yugoslavian case has also illustrated the difficulty of dealing with cultural harm in a consistent manner, in the absence of a more general framework of transitional justice. Meanwhile, it has also underlined the potential of including 'culture' in a peace framework, as confirmed by the Guatemalan example. This conclusion can actually be extended to cases in which the process occurs outside a post-war framework, since claims can also be settled by an agreement between the victims and the state in peacetime contexts. This approach may nevertheless also present loopholes, even when negotiations involve victim representatives, which was not the case in the Former Yugoslavia. This 'elite' may not necessarily fully represent the entirety of the victims' claims and needs. However, such agreements set the settlement in stone, which contrasts with the need for a flexible approach to cultural harm, especially when addressed in the long-term perspective of an ongoing violation of human rights.

Finally, the problem of the exclusive 'State or individual perpetrators *versus* victims' approach has constantly arisen, thus leaving the rest of the population completely outside the equation of reparations. Yet, cultural harm often results from a long-term process of general and widespread feelings of discrimination and intolerance, in which the rest of the population may not have actively participated, but which they may have at least passively accepted. Focusing exclusively on victims in the absence of any effort to raise the majority or dominant group's awareness may then hamper the actual effects of reparation—when they actually occur—especially in their dimension of preventing the repetition of past abuses. It may even reach the opposite result, by fostering the idea that the victims constitute a financial burden on the wider society, a rhetoric that is often echoed in societies where indigenous peoples have endured long-lasting discrimination and obtained reparation in the form of financial compensation and rehabilitation.

8
Conclusions

Throughout this book three main axes of research have been used to address the question of whether international law possesses adequate or potential tools to exhaustively address the concept of cultural genocide (taking into account its conceptual evolution and related complexities): (i) the concept of cultural genocide itself; (ii) its relationship with the concept of genocide—both from a legal and interdisciplinary perspective—and, (iii) the relevance of an international legal perspective. The conclusions will therefore be articulated around these three axes, so as to refine them and determine to what extent international law can overcome the conceptual complexity of cultural genocide. This complexity is both due to the concept itself and its intertwinement with the legal concept of genocide.

8.1 The Concept of Cultural Genocide

The most significant conclusion concerns the complexity of cultural genocide, as underlined in the introduction and developed throughout the successive chapters. This complexity derives from the multifaceted character of the cultural genocide concept. It is firstly due to the nature of its main component, the notion of 'culture', whose dynamic and fluid character has already been emphasized several times. It further emerges from its evolution on the contingency of claims, especially indigenous peoples' claims. Seen from this perspective, it must be concluded that it is not possible to overcome the fundamental distinction between cultural genocide as a technique and cultural genocide as a process of group destruction. However, the dichotomy might be reformulated more accurately, especially from an international legal perspective: the destruction of tangible cultural heritage on the one hand, and the destruction of intangible cultural heritage on the other. While the two should be placed on an equal footing since they reflect equally important aspects of human cultures, their modalities of destruction differ greatly. Accordingly, cultural genocide can be the product of a single act, such as the destruction of a mosque or a church, as much as it can result from a long-term process, which may be unveiled over several centuries, as most cases involving structurally vulnerable indigenous communities have shown. The destruction of intangible cultural features might result from direct attacks against these same features, including for instance, the prohibition on a group to practise the group language, as well as indirect attacks,

The Concept of Cultural Genocide: An International Law Perspective. First Edition. Elisa Novic. © Elisa Novic 2016.
Published 2016 by Oxford University Press.

such as the persecution of the group elite, or the dispersion of the group members. Ethnocide must thus have been rethought as the result of a long-term process, in contrast to the early formulation of cultural genocide, which was rather focused on the means of the group destruction. This is what makes the concept so similar to that of genocide, in relation to which Lemkin's definition of a coordinated plan of action aiming at the group destruction is still very accurate. The intent to destroy the group is thus a very crucial element of the conceptualization of ethnocide, in order to distinguish the notion from smoother processes of group acculturation. However, what attributes to the concept its strength, by calling so vividly the attention of the international community, also constitutes its weakness, in light of the developments that have occurred in the context of the genocide framework itself.

8.2 Cultural Genocide and Genocide

In light of the emphasis on 'group destruction', it seems inevitable that cultural genocide, if it were to become a legal concept, especially an international crime, would end up reproducing some of the difficulties that have been underlined in relation to the legal definition of genocide and which has led it to be deemed an 'essentially contested legal concept'. The debate on the meaning of the word 'destroy' would undoubtedly be solved, but several questions would remain especially acute: the definition of the group—especially outside indigenous contexts—, the identification of the perpetrators' intent and, *a fortiori* the identification of the individual perpetrators. The idea of a long-term and state-induced process of group destruction indeed antithesizes the core idea of international criminal law, the latter nevertheless being the field in which the concept of genocide has predominantly evolved.

In this context, as demonstrated in Chapter 3 and extensively supported by legal sources and scholarship, there has been an evolution in the opposite direction between the concept of cultural genocide and that of genocide, even though it is now widely acknowledged that the destruction of tangible cultural heritage can constitute evidence of the intent to destroy the group and further, that cultural concerns have been instrumental in determining the genocidal dimension of certain crimes. However, the evolution of the legal understanding of the crime of genocide has only allowed for the partial coverage of the early formulation of cultural genocide, as a technique of genocide. When it comes to the concept of ethnocide, and thus to the evolution of the concept of cultural genocide, it is undeniable that the enclosing of genocide as a crime of physical-biological destruction goes in a diametrically opposed direction. It must again be emphasized that it is very unlikely that the consecration of a socio-cultural understanding of group destruction would have constituted a legal recognition of ethnocide as genocide as such. Most focus has been on the *mens rea* of genocide, with the risk of omitting the restrictive *actus reus* of the crime. Certainly, there is ground to provide an extensive interpretation of the 'mental harm' of subparagraph (b) and the 'conditions of life' of subparagraph (c). Such developments tend to converge with the findings made in non-criminal settings, such as the Guatemalan Truth and Reconciliation Commission and the

Inter-American Court of Human Rights (IACHR). The former has recognized that the destruction of cultural heritage could cause mental harm while the latter has shed some light on the threat to which forceful displacement and unlawful appropriation of the ancestral land might give rise in relation to some indigenous and tribal communities' physical and spiritual existence. Without stepping into either the ethnocide or genocide rhetoric, the IACHR tends to paraphrase these concepts when it describes the cultural consequences of some human rights violations. Furthermore, the issue of the intent to destroy arises, along with the open question of whether knowledge of the inevitable harm entailed by a state policy or a private practice could satisfy this criterion.

Schabas has noted in relation to the socio-cultural interpretation of the word 'destroy' that 'the words of the Convention could certainly bear such an interpretation'; we have argued that such an interpretation would be desirable and would ensure multilevel coherence: within the definition of genocide, by providing subparagraph (e) with an *effet utile*; within the Genocide Convention, by reflecting the object and purpose of the Convention, as well as echoing the development of a framework of genocide prevention; within international criminal law, by making a clear distinction between the crime of extermination and that of genocide—although the issue of distinguishing genocide from persecution would certainly arise—and finally, at the level of international law, by closing the circle of international law's intervention to safeguard group cultures from intentional destruction. Yet, while desirable, this move is unlikely to happen, mostly because of the criminal nature of the provision of genocide and the constraints that it, rightly or wrongly, entails. As for the 'right' constraints, international criminal law is primarily concerned with prosecuting and convicting individual perpetrators of international crimes. To do so, the system needs to respect the rights of the accused, and thus bar any potential element of arbitrariness that would damage its legitimacy. As such, the illicit character of the acts and the subsequent conviction for such crimes need to be foreseeable. The *nullum crimen sine lege* therefore constitutes one of the pillars of the system and one should refrain from any attempt to downplay the significance of this principle. The 'wrong' constraints, however, concern the conditions of this implementation, as criticized in relation to the *Krstić* case, as well as the application of this principle outside the international criminal legal sphere. The double legal nature of genocide, which can be either an individual crime or a wrongful act of a state, is still very much overlooked, as is clear from the 2007 International Court of Justice (ICJ) judgment in the *Application of the Genocide Convention* case. By endorsing most International Criminal Tribunal for the Former Yugoslavia (ICTY) findings, and especially the finding on the meaning of the word 'destroy' in the definition of genocide, it reproduced an interpretation that was almost exclusively based on principles of international criminal law, since no other legal source converges towards the physical–biological understanding. Even though an even stronger case could have been made in favour of the socio-cultural understanding before the ICJ, one cannot deny that the result might nevertheless have been problematic, especially in the context of the feared fragmentation of international law. However, it still remains to be determined whether this would have amounted to such a fragmented approach, considering that the mechanisms of implementation of state responsibility radically diverge from those of individual criminal responsibility, as well as the context in which such responsibility is sought. State responsibility indeed allows for the introduction of a macro-perspective of the process of mass criminality, unlike individual criminal responsibility, which intends to link one perpetrator's individual intent to a specific context. It is arguable that in the former case, the genocide label would derivate from the factual observance of criminal acts that would display an intent to destroy the group, whether those acts match the *actus reus* of genocide, or are perpetrated in connection with such an *actus reus*. In the latter case, the genocide label can only be confirmed by the existence of individual intent.

The way in which the Genocide Convention has been treated, and the manner in which it has subsequently evolved thus displays the predominance of the perpetrators' approach, to the detriment of a victim-oriented approach, which raises the question of the possibility for international law to ever grasp the whole process of genocide. The 'reality' of the crime thus remains an open issue: does such a reality exist, and is the legal definition even meant to address it? This shows the limits inherent to the genocide concept; as a legal fiction, the concept of genocide has been constructed in legal terms. The reality of genocide did not exist before Lemkin coined the term. Of course, only 'the name was new, the crime was not'. However, the codification of the crime under this precise name has had the effect of distorting the reality that it was aimed to cover, by only focusing on the physical-biological dimension of processes of genocide. This selectivity inherent to the international legal approach to genocide has increased with the 'crime of crimes' rhetoric, according to which the definition of genocide should be interpreted restrictively. Allegedly, the physical destruction of a group, commonly called 'extermination', is the most serious crime that could ever be committed. In the context of cultural genocide, this idea tends to reproduce the general bias of 'Western-ethnocentrism' that has long affected international law, since it implies that the harm resulting from attacks against the individuals' physical integrity is more serious than other types of harm, which would rather affect non-Western communities. This interpretation has been challenged, however, with the rise of indigenous peoples' movements, which have argued that the social cohesion could be destroyed by other means, and that the consequences of the group disintegration could be considered as serious as processes of extermination. The ethnocide version of the concept of cultural genocide hardly fits in contexts other than those of 'organic' communities. Such an idea is still hard to take seriously from a Western perspective. The reply to this perceived watering-down of the physical dimension of the crime of crimes will therefore often take the form of an accusation of 'romanticism'. Cutting through these different conceptions of what is most harmful goes far beyond the scope of this book, which can only limit itself to acknowledge this inherent tension between different visions of group existence.

Beyond the mere exclusion of cultural harm as being as potentially serious as physical harm, the idea of 'crime of crimes' contributes to fuel an undesirable competition of victimization, tending towards the wrong idea that labelling certain crimes as crimes against humanity would result in the downgrading of the victims' experience. It should nonetheless be noted that as desirable as it might be to consider genocide on an equal footing of gravity with crimes against humanity, the historical and legal stigma that adheres to this crime is difficult to conceal.

The focus on the crime of genocide may be useful from a political perspective but is counter-productive as it ultimately encloses the concept in the criminal category, which indeed is the most difficult to prove. Meanwhile, it omits the developments that have occurred within other international legal categories, such as crimes against humanity, which can yet be considered as equally harmful.

8.3 Cultural Genocide and International Law

The complexity inherent to the cultural genocide concept immediately raises the question of the suitability of a single conceptual category to address the various aspects of the concept, even before the issue of the legal categorization is engaged. This lack of conceptual uniformity is not specific to the concept of cultural genocide; the same could be said about many international crimes, and above all, the crime of genocide. Indeed, the material content of international criminal law is set out in very few words in comparison with the variety of situations that it aims to address. Therefore, the lack of conceptual uniformity cannot be opposed as an obstacle per se to the inclusion of cultural genocide within the international legal framework. It nevertheless renders doubtful the possibility for international law to ever exhaust the concept in a satisfactory manner, that is to say, in a way that respects the structural principles of international law and its various branches, such as the principle of legality in the context of international criminal law.

While the difficulty would turn out to be a major one at first sight, the legal perspective might actually allow for this difficulty to be played down. Firstly, international law offers an empirical tool of analysis, which has confirmed the legitimacy of the claims contained in the concept of cultural genocide, whether in respect of the reality of group cultural destruction or the seriousness of its impact on individuals, communities, and humanity as a whole. Without necessarily using the words 'cultural genocide' or 'ethnocide', diplomats, international judges, UN Special Rapporteurs, and various experts have continuously warned against the various threats that a culture may face. The IACHR and the ICTY have certainly adopted a leading role in this campaign, the steps of which remain to be followed in a systematic way. Accordingly, the ICTY, which has so far contributed most to the development of the cultural dimension of international crimes, and especially the crime against humanity of persecution, has gradually given a basis to the idea that the serious violation of fundamental rights could not be anticipated, but rather observed, such that the analysis of the severity of cultural destruction should be assessed on a case-by-case basis. As for the IACHR, it has fully endorsed the possibility of group destruction through the destruction of the culture, and has thus drawn noteworthy conclusions in terms of state responsibility and obligations. However, such a mechanism does not exist in other parts of the world, even where the issue of cultural genocide is particularly acute, if one thinks of situations of cultural oppression such as those endured by the Tibetans in the People's Republic of China and the Rohingyas in Myanmar. Thus, the question remains as to the scope for extending these findings to the realm of general customary international law in contrast to the sphere of regional customary international law. As it has been argued, the methodology of the IACHR relies significantly on international sources. On the one hand, its statutory instruments do not necessarily go further than international instruments in terms of the recognition of cultural rights and collective rights. On the other hand, as it transpires from the separate opinions of some of its judges, it does indeed rely on international sources, with the result that the reasoning could *a fortiori* be transplanted to the realm of international law.

While the ICTY and IACHR constitute radically different international legal tools, they have proven to be complementary for the purposes of addressing the various facets of cultural genocide. Their case law can thus be understood to constitute a solid basis for a more systematic approach to cultural genocide, which brings the discussion to the second advantage that an integrated international legal approach to cultural genocide may offer. International law offers a set of tools, which can be articulated and modulated according to the specific manifestation of cultural genocide: the destruction of tangible cultural heritage, a technique of genocide; the forced transfer of indigenous peoples away from their ancestral land, which is likely to produce a situation of ethnocide; and acts of forced transfers of children intended at annihilating a group culture from an intergenerational perspective, which are potential acts of genocide. It should be underlined that either individuals or states can perpetrate these acts, either in times of armed conflict or in peacetime. These latter contextual variations also determine the legal tools that might be mobilized.

One tool has emerged as pivotal in addressing cultural genocide: international human rights law. The consecration of the indivisibility of international human rights has allowed for a better grasp of the importance of safeguarding cultures as a way to ensure the respect of most other human rights. Thus, cultural genocide goes beyond culture: it does not describe the violation of cultural rights as much as the cultural harm that might result from the gross violation of individual and collective rights, likely to threaten the existence of the group as such. Still, the recalibration of international law is a necessary first step before the criminalization of cultural genocide is even contemplated. This idea of recalibration has been used in the context of international cultural heritage law but, considering the various interconnections that have been underlined throughout this book, it could be applied to other branches of law, including, in particular, international human rights law and international criminal law. Indeed, the tendency to overlook economic, social, and cultural rights and the need to overcome this tendency have repeatedly been underscored in relation to international human rights law, international criminal law, or international legal remedies. This triptych of recalibration should therefore constitute the guiding principle of the pursuit for an international legal answer to cultural genocide. This concept can indeed contribute to the fostering of the recalibration of international law as a whole, as well as benefit from already emerging trends, especially the idea that a prohibition to intentionally destroy group cultures can now be considered as part of customary international law. If this phrase seems at first sight to only be reflected by instruments of soft law, and especially the 2003 UNESCO Declaration on Intentional Destruction of Cultural Heritage and the 2007 United Nations Declaration on the Rights of Indigenous Peoples (UNDRIP), these two major instruments must be read in light of more general principles that have been codified in international law since 1948, as described in Chapter 4. These vague provisions have given rise to a consistent progressive interpretation on the part of human rights bodies and courts, with which states have complied. While the use of customary international law for the purposes of solving the legal status of given issues should be considered with caution, it turns out that the components of cultural genocide are actually addressed by customary international law, though through neither one legal concept nor one legal tool.

Thus the evolution of international law in relation to the main elements of cultural genocide renders the search for one legal category, and allegedly one legal concept, irrelevant. The progressive evolution of the various branches of international law has illustrated the scope for convergence, even though this convergence has occurred through diachronic movements.

8.4 Prospective Routes: Cultural Genocide as a Paralegal Concept?

For the purpose of exhausting the topic of cultural genocide, the choice has thus been made to keep the cultural genocide rhetoric throughout the book. The closest legal transposition of cultural genocide would certainly be the crime of cultural persecution. Yet, cultural persecution can only partially substitute cultural genocide, because of the strict borders of international criminal law within which it is enclosed. Using cultural persecution as a legal substitute for cultural genocide would blur the conceptual borders that we have striven to draw between the various responses that international law might provide to the issue of cultural genocide. The relevance of the rhetoric of cultural genocide is particularly acute in cases that have thus far been labelled 'ethnocide'. Indeed, the destruction of tangible aspects of cultural genocide occurring in a wider context of attacks against a given group, the former a technique of genocide, may not necessarily deserve this label, since their qualification should depend on that of the wider process in which they occur. However, it is now established in international law that they might influence the general qualification, by providing the intent to destroy the group as such.

There thus exists a ground upon which one can argue against the reintroduction of cultural genocide as a legal concept; yet cultural genocide remains a useful concept to qualify specific situations of intentional destruction of cultures. While this concept has been distorted and misused since its early conceptualization, it remains an unparalleled warning tool in respect of the actual or potential cultural harm that state policies or individual actors' practices may cause. From this perspective, it could remain a paralegal concept, in the same way as other concepts are engaged, including those of cultural identity or group existence. While the latter two are often presented as human rights, their substantive content is not sufficiently solid to support such an assertion. However, their reference in some of the judgments of regional courts allows for a more refined approach to the legal characterization of the facts of a given case. It helps for the purposes of drawing the contours of the damage that may result from the violation of human rights, by highlighting their underlying cultural dimension, beyond the letter of the relevant legal provisions. There is no reason why cultural genocide could not fulfil this same function when needed, that is to add an element of seriousness to the determination of violation of human rights, international crimes, or international wrongful acts. This method is already used at the national level, as observed in the report of the Canadian Truth and Reconciliation Commission, where the words fulfil a reconciliatory purpose and have even been preferred to the genocide label. At the international legal level, the concept could be used as a means of establishing aggravating circumstances, especially in the framework of state responsibility, which would materially be reflected at the level of reparation. There is already a fertile ground in international law for such an approach to flourish. It would reflect one potential way of attributing a legal echo to the many non-binding statements that have legitimated the concept of cultural genocide, it would fit in the general framework of international law, without entering into the debate on state criminality, and it would constitute a means of preventing cultural genocide itself, with the possibility in some cases of preventing processes of genocide, understood in the legal physical-biological term.

Finally, it emerges from this book that the merit of cultural genocide lies in its universal dimension, as it is a concept likely to apply to any culture. This finding is not without paradox since its rejection in the late 1940s was partly due to its incompatibility with the universal character of the international legal system.

Bibliography

TEXTS AND MONOGRAPHS

Abtahi H. and Webb P., *The Genocide Convention—The Travaux Préparatoires*, 2 vols. (Leiden; Boston: Martinus Nijhoff Publishers, 2008).

Akhavan P., *Reducing Genocide to Law: Definition, Meaning, and the Ultimate Crime* (Cambridge; New York: Cambridge University Press, 2012).

Alland D. and Rials S. (eds.), *Dictionnaire de la Culture Juridique* (Paris: Presses Universitaires de France, 2003).

Anderson B.R., *Imagined Communities: Reflections on the Origin and Spread of Nationalism* (Rev. edn., London; New York: Verso, 2006).

Arendt H., *Eichmann in Jerusalem: A Report on the Banality of Evil* (first published 1951, New York: Penguin Books, 1994).

Arendt H., *Origins of Totalitarianism* (New York: Schoken Books, 2004).

Barnard A. and Spencer J., *The Routledge Encyclopedia of Social and Cultural Anthropology* (2nd edn., London; New York: Routledge, 2010).

Bassiouni M.C., *Crimes Against Humanity: Historical Evolution and Contemporary Application* (Cambridge; New York: Cambridge University Press, 2011).

Bassiouni M.C., *Introduction to International Criminal Law: Second Revised Edition* (Leiden; Boston: Martinus Nijhoff Publishers, 2013).

Bevan R., *The Destruction of Memory: Architecture at War* (London: Reaktion Books, 2006).

Bloxham D. and Moses A.D. (eds.), *The Oxford Handbook of Genocide Studies* (Oxford: Oxford University Press, 2010).

Bougarel X., Helms E., and Duijzings G. (eds.), *The New Bosnian Mosaic: Identities, Memories and Moral Claims in a Post-War Society* (Aldershot, Burlington: Ashgate, 2007).

Boustany K. and Dormoy D. (eds.), *Génocide(s)* (Bruxelles: Bruylant; Editions de l'Université de Bruxelles, 1999).

Brant Castellano M., Archibald L., and DeGagné M. (eds.), *From Truth to Reconciliation: Transforming the Legacy of Residential Schools* (Ottawa: Aboriginal Healing Foundation, 2008).

de Brouwer A.-M., *Supranational Criminal Prosecutions of Sexual Prosecutions: The ICC and the Practice of the ICTY and the ICTR* (Antwerp; Oxford: Intersentia, 2005).

Brown D., *Bury My Heart at Wounded Knee: An Indian History of the American West* (London: Vintage, 1991).

Brubaker R., *Ethnicity without Groups* (Cambridge, MA: Harvard University Press, 2004).

Burgorgue-Larsen L. and Úbeda de Torres A., *The Inter-American Court of Human Rights: Case Law and Commentary* (Oxford: Oxford University Press, 2010).

Cassese A., *International Criminal Law* (2nd edn., Oxford: Oxford University Press, 2008).

Cassese A., *Cassese's International Criminal Law* (3rd edn., Paola Gaeta et al. rev. Oxford: Oxford University Press, 2013).

Cassese A. et al. (eds.), *International Criminal Law: Cases and Commentary* (Oxford: Oxford University Press, 2011).

Chalk F. and Jonassohn K., *The History and Sociology of Genocide: Analyses and Case Studies* (3rd edn., New Haven, CT; London: Yale University Press, 1990).

Charny I.W. (ed.), *Encyclopedia of Genocide*, 2 vols. (Toulouse; Santa Barbara, CA: ABC-Clio, 1999).
Clavero B., *Genocide or Ethnocide, 1933–2007* (Milano: Giuffré Editore, 2008).
Corten O., *Méthodologie du Droit International Public* (Bruxelles: Editions de l'Université Libre de Bruxelles, 2009).
Cowan J.K., Dembour M.-B., and Wilson R.A. (eds.), *Culture and Rights: Anthropological Perspectives* (Cambridge, UK; New York: Cambridge University Press, 2001).
Cuche D., *La Notion de Culture dans les Sciences Sociales* (4ème éd., Paris: La Découverte, 2010).
Crawford J., Pellet A., and Olleson S. (eds.), *The Law of International Responsibility* (New York: Oxford University Press, 2010).
De Greiff P. (ed.), *The Oxford Handbook of Reparations* (Oxford: Oxford University Press, 2011).
Delmas-Marty M., *Le Relatif et l'Universel: Les Forces Imaginantes du Droit* (Paris: Seuil, 2004).
Donders Y., *Towards a Right to Cultural Identity?* (Antwerpen; New York: Intersentia, 2002).
Dupuy P.-M. and Kerbrat Y., *Droit International Public* (11th edn., Paris: Dalloz, 2012).
Esparza M., Huttenbach H.R., and Feierstein D. (eds.), *State Violence and Genocide in Latin America: The Cold War Years* (London; New York: Routledge, 2010).
Evans C., *The Right to Reparation in International Law for Victims of Armed Conflicts* (Cambridge, UK; New York: Cambridge University Press, 2012).
Fernandez J. and Pacreau X. (eds.), *Statut de Rome de la Cour Pénale Internationale: Commentaire Article par Article* (Paris: Pedone, 2012).
Francioni F. and Scheinin M. (eds.), *Cultural Human Rights* (Leiden; Boston: Martinus Nijhoff Publishers 2008).
Gaeta P. (ed.), *The UN Genocide Convention: A Commentary* (Oxford: Oxford University Press, 2009).
Geertz C., *The Interpretation of Cultures, Selected Essays* (New York: Basic Books, 1973).
Gensburger S., *Images d'un Pillage: Album de la Spoliation des Juifs à Paris, 1940–1944* (Paris: Textuel, 2010).
Grover S., *The European Court of Human Rights as a Pathway to Impunity for International Crimes* (Heidelberg: Springer, 2010).
Hagège C., *Halte à la Mort des Langues* (Paris: Odile Jacob, 2000).
Henham R. and Behrens P. (eds.), *The Criminal Law of Genocide: International, Comparative, and Contextual Aspects* (Burlington, VT: Ashgate Pub. Company, 2007).
Hennebel L. and Tigroudja H. (eds.), *Le Particularisme Interaméricain des Droits de l'Homme* (Paris: Pedone, 2006).
Hinton A.L. (ed.), *Annihilating Difference: The Anthropology of Genocide* (Berkeley, CT; London: University of California Press, 2002).
Jaulin R., *La Paix Blanche. Introduction à l'Ethnocide* (Paris: Seuil, 1970).
Knuth R., *Libricide: The Regime-Sponsored Destruction of Books and Libraries in the Twentieth Century* (Westport, CT: Praeger, 2003).
Knuth R., *Burning Books and Levelling Libraries: Extremist Violence and Cultural Destruction* (Westport, CT: Praeger, 2006).
Kuper L., *The Prevention of Genocide* (New Haven, CT: Yale University Press, 1985).
Kymlicka W., *Multicultural Citizenship, A Liberal Theory of Minority Rights* (Oxford: Clarendon Press; New York: Oxford University Press, 1995).
Lamb C., *The Sewing Circles of Herat* (New York: Perennial, 2004).
Lemkin R., *Axis Rule in Occupied Europe: Laws of Occupation - Analysis of Government - Proposals for Redress* (2nd edn., first published 1944, Clark, NJ: Lawbook Exchange, Ltd. 2008).

Lenzerini F. (ed.), *Reparations for Indigenous Peoples: International and Comparative Perspectives* (Oxford: Oxford University Press, 2008).
Lerner N., *Group Rights and Discrimination* (2nd edn., The Hague; New York: M. Nijhoff, 2003).
Lévi-Strauss C., *Race et Histoire* (first published 1967, Paris: Denoël, 2008).
Lévi-Strauss C., *L'Anthropologie Face aux Problèmes du Monde Moderne* (Paris: Seuil, 2011).
Lixinski L., *Intangible Cultural Heritage in International Law* (Oxford: Oxford University Press, 2013).
Maalouf A., *Les Identités Meurtrières* (Paris: Grasset, 1998).
May L., *Genocide: A Normative Account* (Cambridge; New York: Cambridge University Press, 2010).
Mazower M., *No Enchanted Palace: The End of Empire and the Ideological Origins of the United Nations* (Princeton: Princeton University Press, 2009).
Meron T., *The Making of International Criminal Justice: The View from the Bench: Selected Speeches* (Oxford: Oxford University Press, 2011).
Meyer L.H., Paulson S., and Pogge T.W. (eds.), *Rights, Culture, and the Law: Themes from the Legal and Political Philosophy of Joseph Raz* (Oxford; New York: Oxford University Press, 2003).
Morsink J., *The Universal Declaration of Human Rights, Origins, Drafting and Intent* (Philadelphia: University of Pennsylvania Press, 2000).
Moses A.D. (ed.), *Empire, Colony, Genocide: Conquest, Occupation, and Subaltern Resistance in World History* (1st pbk. edn., New York: Berghahn Books, 2010).
Nolte G. (ed.), *Treaties and Subsequent Practice* (Oxford: Oxford University Press, 2013).
O'Keefe R., *The Protection of Cultural Property in Armed Conflict* (Cambridge: Cambridge University Press, 2006).
Pentassuglia G., *Minorités en Droit International* (Strasbourg: Editions du Conseil de l'Europe, 2004).
Peters B., Meyer L.H., Paulson S., and Pogge T.W. (eds.), *Rights, Culture, and the Law: Themes from the Legal and Political Philosophy of Joseph Raz* (Oxford; New York: Oxford University Press, 2003).
Powell C., *Barbaric Civilization: A Critical Sociology of Genocide* (Montreal: Mc Gill-Queen's University Press, 2011).
Quigley J., *The Genocide Convention: An International Law Analysis* (Aldershot, England; Burlington, VT: Ashgate Pub., 2006).
Ratner S.R., Abrams J.S., and Bischoff J.L., *Accountability for Human Rights Atrocities in International Law: Beyond the Nuremberg Legacy* (3rd edn., Oxford; New York: Oxford University Press, 2009).
Roth J.K. (ed.), *Genocide and Human Rights: A Philosophical Guide* (Houndmills, Basingstoke, Hampshire; New York: Palgrave Macmillan, 2005).
Salmon J. (ed.), *Dictionnaire du Droit International Public* (Bruxelles: Bruylant, 2001).

Schabas W.A., *Genocide in International Law: The Crime of Crimes* (2nd edn., Cambridge: Cambridge University Press, 2009).
Schabas W.A., *The International Criminal Court: A Commentary on the Rome Statute* (Oxford; New York: Oxford University Press, 2010).
Shaw M., *What is Genocide?* (Cambridge: Polity Press, 2007).
Shelton D.L. (ed.), *Encyclopedia of Genocide and Crimes Against Humanity*, 3 vols. (New York: Macmillan Reference USA; Thomson Gale, 2004).

Stamatopoulou E., *Cultural Rights in International Law: Article 27 of the Universal Declaration of Human Rights and Beyond* (Leiden; Boston: Martinus Nijhoff Publishers, 2007).

Sudre F., *Droit Européen et International des Droits de l'Homme* (10th edn., Paris: Presses Universitaires de France, 2011).

Thornberry, P., *International Law and the Rights of Minorities* (Oxford: Clarendon Press; New York: Oxford University Press, 1991).

Totten S. and Bartrop P.R., *Dictionary of Genocide*, 2 vols. (Westport, Conn.: Greenwood Press, 2008).

Triffterer O. (ed.), *Commentary on the Rome Statute of the International Criminal Court: Observers' Notes, Article by Article* (2nd edn., München: Beck; Portland, OR: Hart; Baden-Baden: Nomos, 2008).

Victor J.-C., Raisson V., and Tétart F., *Le Dessous des Cartes: Atlas Géopolitique* (Paris: Arte Editions; Taillandier, 2005).

Villiger M.E., *Commentary on the 1969 Vienna Convention on the Law of Treaties* (Leiden, Boston: Martinus Nijhoff Publishers, 2009).

Vrdoljak A.F., *International Law, Museums and the Return of Cultural Objects* (Cambridge, UK; New York: Cambridge University Press, 2006).

Wippman D. (ed.), *International Law and Ethnic Conflict* (Ithaca; London: Cornell University Press, 1998).

Zahar A. and Sluiter G., *International Criminal Law: A Critical Introduction* (Oxford; New York: Oxford University Press, 2008).

Zimmermann A. (ed.), *The 1951 Convention Relating to the Status of Refugees and its 1967 Protocol: A Commentary* (Oxford: Oxford University Press, 2010).

CHAPTERS IN TEXTS

Andreopoulos G.J., 'Ethnic Cleansing' in *Encyclopædia Britannica Online Academic Edition.* Encyclopædia Britannica Inc., 2013.

Barkan E., 'Genocide of Indigenous Peoples' in Gellately R. and Kiernan B. (eds.), *The Specter of Genocide: Mass Murder in Historical Perspective* (Cambridge: Cambridge University Press, 2003) pp. 117–39.

Bianchi A., 'State Responsibility and Criminal Liability of Individuals' in Cassese A. (ed.), *The Oxford Companion to International Criminal Justice* (Oxford: Oxford University Press, 2009) pp. 16–24.

Boer B. and Gruber S., 'Heritage Discourses and Intergenerational Justice' in Rubenstein K. and Jessup B. (eds.), *Environmental Discourses in International and Public Law* (Cambridge: Cambridge University Press, 2012) pp. 375–98.

Boot M., Dixon R., and Hall C.K., 'Article 7—Crimes against Humanity' in Triffterer O. (ed.), *Commentary on the Rome Statute of the International Criminal Court: Observers' Notes, Article by Article* (2nd edn., München: Beck; Portland, OR: Hart; Baden-Baden: Nomos, 2008) pp. 159–274.

Brant Castellano M., 'A Holistic Approach to Reconciliation: Insights from Research of the Aboriginal Healing Foundation' in Brant Castellano M., Archibald L., and DeGagné M. (eds.), *From Truth to Reconciliation: Transforming the Legacy of Residential Schools* (Ottawa: Aboriginal Healing Foundation, 2008) pp. 383–403.

Burgorgue-Larsen L., 'Le Génocide Oublié du Timor Oriental' in Boustany K. and Dormoy D. (eds.), *Génocide(s)* (Bruxelles: Bruylant; Editions de l'Université de Bruxelles, 1999) pp. 213–50.

Card C., 'Genocide and Social Death' in Roth J.K. (ed.), *Genocide and Human Rights: A Philosophical Guide* (Houndmills, Basingstoke, Hampshire; New York: Palgrave Macmillan, 2005) pp. 238–54.

Chaumont J.-M., 'Génocide et Ethnocide' in Boustany K. and Dormoy D. (eds.), *Génocide(s)* (Bruxelles: Bruylant; Editions de l'Université de Bruxelles, 1999) pp. 251–64.

Conversi D., 'Cultural Homogenization, Ethnic Cleansing and Genocide' in Denemark R.A. (ed.), *The International Studies Encyclopedia*, vol. 1 (Oxford; Boston, MA: Wiley-Blackwell/ ISA, 2010) pp. 719–42.

Cowan J.K., Dembour M.-B., and Wilson R.A., 'Introduction' in Cowan J.K., Dembour M.-B., and Wilson R.A. (eds.), *Culture and Rights: Anthropological Perspectives* (Cambridge, UK; New York, NY, USA: Cambridge University Press, 2001) pp. 1–26.

Crawford J., 'International Crimes of States' in Crawford J., Pellet A., and Olleson S. (eds.), *The Law of International Responsibility* (New York: Oxford University Press, 2010) pp. 405–15.

De Greiff P., 'Justice and Reparations' in De Greiff P. (ed.), *The Oxford Handbook of Reparations* (Oxford: Oxford University Press, 2011) pp. 452–77.

Dembour M.-B., 'Following the Movement of a Pendulum: Between Universalism and Relativism' in Cowan J.K., Dembour M.-B., and Wilson R.A. (eds.), *Culture and Rights: Anthropological Perspectives* (Cambridge, UK; New York, NY, USA: Cambridge University Press, 2001) pp. 56–79.

Donders Y., 'A Right to Cultural Identity in UNESCO' in Francioni F. and Scheinin M. (eds.), *Cultural Human Rights* (Leiden; Boston: Martinus Nijhoff Publishers, 2008) pp. 317–40.

Donders Y., 'Old Cultures Never Die? Cultural Genocide in International Law' in Boerefijn I. et al. (eds.), *Human Rights: Pre-Conflict, In Conflict, and Post-Conflict, Essays in Honour of Bas de Gaay Fortman* (Cambridge; Intersentia Publishing, 2012) pp. 287–303.

Duhaime B., 'Vers une Amérique plus Égalitaire: l'interdiction de la discrimination et le système interaméricain de protection des droits de la personne' in Hennebel L. and Tigroudja H. (eds.), *Le particularisme interaméricain des droits de l'homme* (Paris: Pedone, 2006) pp. 151–82.

Dundes Renteln A., 'Ethnicity' in *Max Planck Encyclopedia of Public International Law* (Heidelberg and Oxford University Press. This article was last updated May 2011).

Esparza M., 'Globalizing Latin American Studies of State Violence and Genocide' in Esparza M., Huttenbach H.R., and Feierstein D. (eds.), *State Violence and Genocide in Latin America: The Cold War Years,* (London; New York: Routledge, 2010) pp. 1–20.

Evans R., '"Crime without a Name": Colonialism and the Case for "Indigenocide"' in Moses A.D. (ed.), *Empire, Colony, Genocide: Conquest, Occupation, and Subaltern Resistance in World History* (1st pbk. edn., New York: Berghahn Books, 2010) pp. 133–47.

Feierstein D., 'National Security Doctrine in Latin America, The Genocide Question' in Bloxham D. and Moses A.D. (eds.), *The Oxford Handbook of Genocide Studies* (Oxford: Oxford University Press, 2010) pp. 489–508.

Fertsman C. and Rosenberg S.P., 'Reparations in Dayton's Bosnia and Herzegovina' in Ferstman C., Goetz M., and Stephens A. (eds.), *Reparations for Victims of Genocide, War Crimes and Crimes Against Humanity: Systems in Place and Systems in the Making* (Leiden; Boston: Martinus Nijhoff Publishers, 2009) pp. 483–513.

Fisler Damrosch L., 'Genocide and Ethnic Conflict' in Wippman D. (ed.), *International Law and Ethnic Conflict* (Ithaca; London: Cornell University Press, 1998) pp. 256–79.

Francioni F., 'Culture, Heritage and Human Rights: An Introduction' in Francioni F. and Scheinin M. (eds.), *Cultural Human Rights* (Leiden: Martinus Nijhoff Publishers, 2008) pp. 1–16.

Francioni F., 'Is International Law Ready to Ensure Redress for Historical Injustices?' in Lenzerini F. (ed.), *Reparations for Indigenous Peoples: International and Comparative Perspectives* (Oxford: Oxford University Press, 2008) pp. 27–46.

Frieze D., 'The Destruction of Sarajevo's *Vijecnica*: A Case of Genocidal Destruction?' in Jones A. (ed.), *New Directions in Genocide Research* (London; New York: Routledge, 2009) pp. 57–74.

Gaeta P., 'The Character of the Breach' in Crawford J., Pellet A., and Olleson S. (eds.), *The Law of International Responsibility* (New York: Oxford University Press, 2010) pp. 421–6.

Gaita R., 'Refocusing Genocide: A Philosophical Responsibility' in Roth J.K. (ed.), *Genocide and Human Rights: A Philosophical Guide* (Houndmills, Basingstoke, Hampshire; New York: Palgrave Macmillan, 2005) pp. 153–66.

Ghanea N., 'Repressing Minorities and Getting Away With It: A Consideration of Economic, Social and Cultural Rights' in Ghanea N. and Xanthaki A. (eds.), *Minorities, People and Self-Determination: Essays in Honour of Patrick Thornberry* (Leiden; Boston: Martinus Nijhoff Publishers, 2005) pp. 193–209.

Griffin J., 'Group Rights', in Meyer L.H., Paulson S., and Pogge T.W. (eds.), *Rights, Culture, and the Law: Themes from the Legal and Political Philosophy of Joseph Raz* (Oxford; New York: Oxford University Press, 2003) pp. 161–83.

deGuzman M., 'Crimes Against Humanity' in Schabas W.A. and Bernaz N.B. (eds.), *Routledge Handbook of International Criminal Law* (Abingdon: Routledge, 2011) pp. 121–37.

Hancock I., 'Romanis', in Shelton D.L. (ed.), *Encyclopedia of Genocide and Crimes Against Humanity*, vol. 2 (New York: Macmillan Reference USA; Thomson Gale, 2004) pp. 919–22.

von Hebel H. and Robinson D., 'Crimes within the Jurisdiction of the Court' in Lee R.S. (ed.), *The International Criminal Court: The Making of the Rome Statute* (The Hague; London; Boston: Kluwer Law International) pp. 79–126.

Henrard K., 'Minorities, International Protection' in *Max Planck Encyclopedia of Public International Law* (Heidelberg and Oxford University Press. This article was last updated May 2008).

van den Herik L., 'The Meaning of the Word "Destroy" and its Implications for the Wider Understanding of the Concept of Genocide' in van der Wilt H.G. (ed.), *The Genocide Convention: The Legacy of 60 years* (Leiden; Boston: Martinus Nijhoff Publishers, 2012) pp. 51–8.

van den Herik L., 'Economic, Social and Cultural Rights—International Criminal Law's Blind Spot?' in Riedel E., Golay C., Mahon C., and Giacca G. (eds.), *Economic, Social and Cultural Rights: Contemporary Issues and Challenges* (Oxford: Oxford University Press, forthcoming) / Grotius Centre Working Paper Series 2013/002-ICL.

Hinton A.L., 'Towards an Anthropology of Genocide' in Hinton A.L. (ed.), *Annihilating Difference: The Anthropology of Genocide* (Berkeley, CT; London: University of California Press, 2002) pp. 1–40.

Hitchkock R.K., 'Indigenous Populations, Genocide of' in Charny I.W. (ed.), *Encyclopedia of Genocide*, vol. 1 (Toulouse; Santa Barbara, CA: ABC-Clio, 1999) pp. 349–54.

Hocking B.A. and Stephenson M., 'Why the Persistent Absence of a Foundational Principle? Indigenous Australians, Proprietary and Family Reparations' in Lenzerini

F. (ed.), *Reparations for Indigenous Peoples: International and Comparative Perspectives* (Oxford: Oxford University Press, 2008) pp. 477–522.

Hylland Eriksen T., 'Between Universalism and Relativism: A Critique of the UNESCO Concept of Culture' in Cowan J.K., Dembour M.-B., and Wilson R.A. (eds.), *Culture and Rights: Anthropological Perspectives* (Cambridge, UK; New York, NY, USA: Cambridge University Press, 2001) pp. 127–48.

Jacobs D., 'International Criminal Law: The Principle of Legality as a Rule of Conflict of Theories', in Jean d'Aspremont and Jörg Kammerhofer (eds.), *International Legal Positivism in a Post-Modern World* (Cambridge: Cambridge University Press, 2014) pp. 451–74.

Jaichand V., 'Residential Schools' in Shelton D.L. (ed.), *Encyclopedia of Genocide and Crimes Against Humanity*, vol. 2 (New York: Macmillan Reference USA; Thomson Gale, 2004) pp. 899–902.

Jones P., 'Group Rights' in Zalta E.N. (ed.), *Stanford Encyclopedia of Philosophy* (2008, rev. 2016) available at: http://plato.stanford.edu/entries/rights-group/.

Jurovics Y., 'Article 7—Crimes Contre l'Humanité' in Fernandez J. and Pacreau X. (eds.), *Statut de Rome de la Cour Pénale Internationale: Commentaire Article par Article* (Paris: Pedone, 2012), pp. 417–78.

Kälin W., 'Assimilation, Forced' in *Max Planck Encyclopedia of Public International Law* (Heidelberg and Oxford University Press. This article was last updated October 2010).

Kiernan B., 'The Cambodian Genocide: Issues and Responses' in Andreopoulos G. (ed.), *Genocide: Conceptual and Historical Dimensions* (Philadelphia: University Of Pennsylvania Press, 1994) pp. 191–228.

Kiza E., 'On the Effectiveness of Judicial Accountability Mechanisms in Bosnia and Herzegovina' in Popovski V. and Serrano M. (eds.), *After Oppression: Transitional Justice in Latin America and Eastern Europe* (Tokyo; New York: United Nations University, 2012) pp. 245–72.

Lalèyê I.P., 'Comment Meurent les Cultures? Interrogations Philosophico-Anthropologiques sur le Concept de Génocide Culturel' in Boustany K. and Dormoy D. (eds.), *Génocide(s)* (Bruxelles: Bruylant; Editions de l'Université de Bruxelles, 1999) pp. 265–93.

Langer M.J. and Hansbury E., 'Monitoring Compliance with the Decisions of Human Rights Courts: The Inter-American Particularism' in Boisson de Chazournes L., Kohen M., and Viñuales J.E. (eds.), *Diplomatic and Judicial Means of Dispute Settlement* (Leiden; Boston: Martinus Nijhoff Publishers, 2013) pp. 213–45.

Lemkin R., 'Le Crime de Génocide' (Paris: La Documentation Française, Notes Documentaires et Etudes No. 417, 1946) in Lemkin R., *Qu'est-ce qu'un Génocide*, Préface de Panné J.-L. (Monaco: Editions du Rocher, 2008).

Lenzerini F., 'Reparations for Indigenous Peoples in International and Comparative Law: An Introduction' in Lenzerini F. (ed.), *Reparations for Indigenous Peoples: International and Comparative Perspectives* (Oxford: Oxford University Press, 2008) pp. 3–26.

Lenzerini F., 'The Trail of Broken Dreams: The Status of Indigenous Peoples in International Law' in Lenzerini F. (ed.), *Reparations for Indigenous Peoples: International and Comparative Perspectives* (Oxford: Oxford University Press, 2008) pp. 73–116.

Lenzerini F., 'The Role of International and Mixed Criminal Courts in the Enforcement of International Norms Concerning the Protection of Cultural Heritage' in Francioni F. and Gordley J. (eds.), *Enforcing International Cultural Heritage Law* (Oxford: Oxford University Press, 2013) pp. 41–64.

Llewellyn J., 'Bridging the Gap between Truth and Reconciliation: Restorative Justice and the Indian Residential Schools Truth and Reconciliation Commission' in Brant Castellano

M., Archibald L., and DeGagné M. (eds.), *From Truth to Reconciliation: Transforming the Legacy of Residential Schools* (Ottawa: Aboriginal Healing Foundation, 2008) pp. 183–204.

Maison R., 'Le Crime de Génocide dans la Jurisprudence Internationale, Débats et Hypothèses' in Tomuschat C., Lagrange E., and Oeter S. (eds.), *The Right to Life* (Leiden; Boston: Martinus Nijhoff Publishers, 2010) pp. 95–119.

Margolin J.L., 'Le "Génocide" Cambodgien: Des Particularités Irréductibles?' in Boustany K. and Dormoy D. (eds.), *Génocide(s)* (Bruxelles: Bruylant; Editions de l'Université de Bruxelles, 1999) pp. 178–212.

Margueritte T., 'International Criminal Law and Human Rights' in W.A. Schabas and N.B. Bernaz (eds.), *Routledge Handbook of International Criminal Law* (Abingdon: Routledge, 2011) pp. 435–52.

Markens E., 'Ethnic Cleansing and Genocide' in Charny I.W. (ed.), *Encyclopedia of Genocide*, vol. 1 (Toulouse; Santa Barbara, CA: ABC-Clio, 1999) p. 215.

Marshall G. and Scott J. (eds.), 'Culture' in *A Dictionary of Sociology* (3rd rev. ed., Oxford: Oxford University Press, 2009).

Marshall G. and Scott J. (eds.), 'Group (Social Group)' in *A Dictionary of Sociology* (3rd rev. ed., Oxford: Oxford University Press, 2009).

Marshall G. and Scott J. (eds.), 'Minority Group' in *A Dictionary of Sociology* (3rd rev. ed. Oxford: Oxford University Press, 2009).

May L., 'Identifying Groups in Genocide Cases' in May L. and Hoskins Z. (eds.), *International Criminal Law and Philosophy* (Cambridge; New York: Cambridge University Press, 2010) pp. 91–107.

May R. and Wierda M., 'Is There a Hierarchy of Crimes in International Law?' in Vohrar L.C. et al. (eds.), *Man's Inhumanity to Man—Essays in International Law in Honour of Antonio Cassese* (The Hague; London; New York: Kluwer Law International, 2003) pp. 511–32.

Maybury-Lewis D., 'Genocide against Indigenous Peoples' in Hinton A.L. (ed.), *Annihilating Difference: The Anthropology of Genocide* (Berkeley, CT; London: University of California Press, 2002) pp. 43–53.

Mégret F., 'Le Renouveau de la Notion de Crime d'Etat devant la Cour Interaméricaine: San José Reprend le Flambeau Abandonné à Genève et Néglige la Haye?' in Hennebel L. and Tigroudja H. (eds.), *Le Particularisme Interaméricain des Droits de l'Homme* (Paris: Pedone, 2006) pp. 313–45.

Meron T., 'Human Rights Law Marches into Next Territory: The Enforcement of International Human Rights in International Criminal Tribunals (Marek Nowicki Memorial Lecture)' in Meron T., *The Making of International Criminal Justice: The View from the Bench: Selected Speeches* (Oxford: Oxford University Press, 2011) pp. 181–98.

Meron T., 'The ICJ's Opinion in Bosnia and Herzegovina v. Serbia and Montenegro' in Meron T., *The Making of International Criminal Justice: The View from the Bench: Selected Speeches* (Oxford: Oxford University Press, 2011) pp. 231–5.

Morse B.W., 'Indigenous Peoples of Canada and their Efforts to Achieve True Reparations' in Lenzerini F. (ed.), *Reparations for Indigenous Peoples: International and Comparative Perspectives* (Oxford: Oxford University Press, 2008) pp. 271–316.

Moses A.D., 'Empire, Colony, Genocide: Keywords and the Philosophy of History' in Moses A.D. (ed.), *Empire, Colony, Genocide: Conquest, Occupation, and Subaltern Resistance in World History* (1st pbk. edn., New York: Berghahn Books, 2010) pp. 3–54.

Moses A.D., 'Lemkin, Culture and the Concept of Genocide' in Bloxham D. and Moses A.D. (eds.), *The Oxford Handbook of Genocide Studies* (Oxford: Oxford University Press, 2010) pp. 19–41.

Nilsson J., 'The Crime of Persecution in the ICTY Case-Law' in Swart B., Zahar A., and Sluiter G. (eds.), *The Legacy of the International Criminal Tribunal for the Former Yugoslavia* (Oxford: Oxford University Press, 2011) pp. 219–46.

Novic E., 'From "Genocide" to "Persecution": "Cultural Genocide" and Contemporary International Criminal Law' in Jakubowski A. (ed.), *Cultural Rights as Collective Rights: An International Law Perspective* (Leiden, Boston: Brill, 2016) pp. 313–35.

Ohlin J.D., 'State Responsibility for Conspiracy, Incitement, and Attempt to Commit Genocide' in Gaeta P. (ed.), *The UN Genocide Convention: A Commentary* (Oxford: Oxford University Press, 2009) pp. 375–80.

Ojeda A.E., 'What is Psychological Torture?' in Ojeda A.E. (ed.), *The Trauma of Psychological Torture* (Westport, Conn.; Praeger, 2008).

Picard E., 'Droits Fondamentaux' in Alland D. and Rials S. (eds.), *Dictionnaire de la Culture Juridique* (Paris: Presses Universitaires de France, 2003) pp. 544–9.

Poscher R., 'The Hands of Midas: When Concepts Turn Legal or Deflating the Hart-Dworkin Debate' in Hage J.C. and von der Pfordten D. (eds.), *Concepts in Law* (Oxford: Hart Publishing, 2009) pp. 99–116.

Prott L.V., 'Ethnocide' in Shelton D.L. (ed.), *Encyclopedia of Genocide and Crimes Against Humanity*, vol. 1 (New York: Macmillan Reference USA; Thomson Gale, 2004) pp. 309–14.

Riedlmayer A.J., 'From the Ashes: The Past and Future of Bosnia's Cultural Heritage' in Shatzmiller M. (ed.), *Islam and Bosnia: Conflict Resolution and Foreign Policy in Multi-Ethnic States* (Montreal: McGill-Queens University Press, 2002) pp. 98–135 (e-version available at: http://www.alumniconnections.com/harvard/alumni/images/from_the_ashes.pdf).

Schabas W.A., 'Judicial Activism and the Crime of Genocide' in Darcy S. and Powderly J. (eds.), *Judicial Creativity at the International Criminal Tribunals* (Oxford: Oxford University Press, 2010) pp. 63–79.

Seibert-Fohr A., 'State Responsibility for Genocide under the Genocide Convention' in Gaeta P. (ed.), *The UN Genocide Convention: A Commentary* (Oxford: Oxford University Press, 2009) pp. 349–74.

Sieder R. and Witchell J., 'Advancing Indigenous Claims Through the Law: Reflections on the Guatemalan Peace Process' in Cowan J.K., Dembour M.-B., and Wilson R.A. (eds.), *Culture and Rights: Anthropological Perspectives* (Cambridge, UK; New York, NY, USA: Cambridge University Press, 2001) pp. 201–25.

Stamatopoulou E., 'Taking Cultural Rights Seriously: The Vision of the UN Declaration on the Rights of Indigenous Peoples' in Allen S. and Xanthaki A. (eds.), *Reflections on the UN Declaration on the Rights of Indigenous Peoples* (Oxford: Hart Publishing, 2011) pp. 387–412.

Tamir Y., 'Against Collective Rights' in Meyer L.H., Paulson S., and Pogge T.W. (eds.), *Rights, Culture, and the Law: Themes from the Legal and Political Philosophy of Joseph Raz*, (Oxford; New York: Oxford University Press, 2003) pp. 183–205.

Tatz C., 'Australian Aborigines, Genocide of' in Charny I.W. (ed.), *Encyclopedia of Genocide*, vol. 1 (Toulouse; Santa Barbara, CA: ABC-Clio, 1999) pp. 111–13.

Totten S., Parsons W.S., and Hitchcock R.K., 'Genocide against Indigenous Peoples' in Hinton A.L. (ed.), *Annihilating Difference: The Anthropology of Genocide* (Berkeley, CT; London: University of California Press, 2002) pp. 54–81.

de Vlaming F. and Clark K., 'War Reparations in Bosnia and Herzegovina: Individual Stories and Collective Interests' in Zarkov D. and Glasius M. (eds.), *Narratives of Justice in and out the Courtroom: Former Yugoslavia and Beyond* (Cham: Springer, 2014).

Vrdoljak A.F., 'Reparations for Cultural Loss' in Lenzerini F. (ed.), *Reparations for Indigenous Peoples: International and Comparative Perspectives* (Oxford: Oxford University Press, 2008) pp. 197–219.

Vrdoljak A.F., 'Cultural Heritage in Human Rights and Humanitarian Law' in Ben-Naftali O. (ed.), *International Humanitarian Law and International Human Rights Law* (Oxford; New York: Oxford University Press, 2011) pp. 250–302.

Wicker G., 'Fiction' in Alland D. and Rials S. (eds.), *Dictionnaire de la Culture Juridique* (Paris: Presses Universitaires de France, 2003) pp. 716–20.

Wiessner S., 'Ethnic Group' in Shelton D.L. (ed.), *Encyclopedia of Genocide and Crimes Against Humanity*, vol. 1 (New York: Macmillan Reference USA; Thomson Gale, 2004) pp. 304–6.

Wippman D., 'Introduction: Ethnic Claims and International Law' in Wippman D. (ed.), *International Law and Ethnic Conflict* (Ithaca; London: Cornell University Press, 1998) pp. 1–21.

Zahar A. and Sluiter G., 'Genocide Law: An Education in Sentimentalism' in Moses A.D. (ed.), *Genocide* (Abingdon; New York, NY: Routledge, 2010, Vol. 6) pp. 116–17.

JOURNAL ARTICLES

Abed M., 'Clarifying the Concept of Genocide', *Metaphilosophy*, Vol. 37, Nos. 3–4, 2006, pp. 308–30.

Akhavan P., 'Preventing Genocide: Measuring Success By What Does Not Happen', *Criminal Law Forum*, Vol. 22, Nos. 1–2, 2011, pp. 1–33.

Akhtar Z., 'Canadian Genocide and Official Responsibility', *International Criminal Law Review*, Vol. 10, No. 1, 2010, pp. 111–35.

Akman W., 'Atrocities Against Humanity during the Liberation War in Bangladesh: A Case of Genocide', *Journal of Genocide Research*, Vol. 4, No. 4, 2002, pp. 543–59.

Ambos K., 'What Does 'Intent to Destroy' in Genocide Mean?', *International Review of the Red Cross*, Vol. 91, No. 876, 2009, pp. 833–58.

American Anthropological Association, the Executive Board, 'Statement on Human Rights', *American Anthropologist*, New Series, Vol. 49, No. 4, 1947, pp. 539–43.

Anayiotos D., 'The Cultural Genocide Debate: Should the UN Genocide Convention Include a Provision on Cultural Genocide, or Should the Phenomenon Be Encompassed in a Separate International Treaty?', *New York International Law Review*, Vol. 22, No. 2, 2009, pp. 99–129.

Arbour L., 'Economic and Social Justice for Societies in Transition', *New York University Journal of International Law and Politics*, Vol. 40, No. 1, 2007–2008, pp. 1–27.

Avery L., 'A Return to Life: The Right to Identity and the Right to Identify Argentina's "Living Disappeared"', *Harvard Women's Law Journal*, Vol. 27, 2004, pp. 235–72.

Boisson de Chazournes L., 'Les Ordonnances en Indication de Mesures Conservatoires dans l'Affaire Relative à l'Application de la Convention pour la Prévention et la Répression des Crimes de Génocide', *Annuaire Français de Droit International*, Vol. 39, pp. 514–39.

Cassese A., 'On the Use of Criminal Law Notions in Determining State Responsibility for Genocide', *Journal of International Criminal Justice*, Vol. 5, 2007, pp. 875–87.
Churchill W., 'Defining the Unthinkable: Towards a Viable Understanding of Genocide', *Oregon Review of International Law*, Vol. 2, 2000, pp. 3–36.
Clastres P., 'De l'Ethnocide', *L'Homme*, Vol. 14, Nos. 3–4, 1974, pp. 101–10. English translation by J. Pefanis and B. Maher in *Art & Text*, Vol. 28, 1988, pp. 51–8.
Dinstein Y., 'Collective Human Rights of Peoples and Minorities', *International Comparative Law Quarterly*, Vol. 25, No. 1, 1976, pp. 102–20.
Donders Y., 'Do Cultural Diversity and Human Rights Make a Good Match?', *International Social Science Journal*, Vol. 61, No. 199, 2010, pp. 15–35.
Engle Merry S., 'Human Rights Law and the Demonization of Culture (and Anthropology Along the Way)', *American Anthropological Association*, Vol. 26, No. 1, 2003, pp. 55–76.
Evans G., 'Crimes Against Humanity: Overcoming Indifference', *Journal of Genocide Research*, Vol. 8, No. 3, pp. 325–39.
Farget D., 'Defining Roma Identity in the European Court of Human Rights', *International Journal on Minority and Group Rights*, Vol. 19, No. 3, 2012, pp. 291–316.
Fournet C. and Pégorier C., '"Only One Step Away from Genocide": The Crime of Persecution in International Criminal Law', *International Criminal Law Review*, Vol. 10, No. 5, 2010, pp. 713–38.
Francioni F., 'Beyond State Sovereignty: The Protection of Cultural Heritage as a Shared Interest of Humanity', *Michigan Journal of International Law*, Vol. 25, No. 4, 2004, pp. 1209–28.
Francioni F., 'The Human Dimension of International Cultural Heritage Law: An Introduction', *The European Journal of International Law*, Vol. 22 No. 1, 2011, pp. 9–16.
Francioni F. and Lenzerini F., 'The Destruction of the Buddhas of Bamiyan and International Law', *European Journal of International Law*, Vol. 14, No. 4, 2003, pp. 619–51.
Frulli M., 'The Criminalization of Offences against Cultural Heritage in Times of Armed Conflict: The Quest for Consistency', *European Journal of International Law*, Vol. 22, No. 1, 2011, pp. 203–17.
Gaeta P., 'On What Conditions Can a State Be Held Responsible for Genocide?', *European Journal of International Law*, Vol. 18, No. 4, pp. 631–48.
Gallie W.B., 'Essentially Contest Concepts', *Proceedings of the Aristotelian Society*, 1955–1956, Vol. 56, pp. 167–98.
Goldsmith K., 'The Issue of Intent in the Genocide Convention and its Effect on the Prevention and Punishment of the Crime of Genocide: Toward a Knowledge-Based Approach', *Genocide Studies and Prevention*, Vol. 5, No. 3, 2010, pp. 238–57.
Gottlieb Y., 'Criminalizing Destruction of Cultural Property: A Proposal for Defining New Crimes under the Rome Statute of the ICC', *Penn State International Law Review*, Vol. 23, No. 4, 2005, pp. 857–96.
Graham L.M., 'Reparations, Self-Determination, and the Seventh Generation', *Harvard Human Rights Journal*, Vol. 21, No. 1, 2008, pp. 47–103.
Grodach C., 'Reconstituting Identity and History in Post-War Mostar, Bosnia-Herzegovina', *City*, Vol. 6, No. 1, 2002, pp. 61–82.
Grover S., 'Child Soldiers as Victims of "Genocidal Forcible Transfer": Darfur and Syria as Case Examples', in *The International Journal of Human Rights*, Vol. 17, No. 3, 2013, pp. 411–27.
Grunfeld F.V., 'Cultural Persecution: The First Step Towards Genocide', *The UNESCO Courier: A Window Open on the World*, Vol. 38, No. 5, 1985, pp. 6–7.

Hansbury E., 'Le Juge Interaméricain et le "Jus Cogens" ', *eCahiers*, No. 11, 2011, available at: http://iheid.revues.org/391.
Harff B., 'No Lessons Learned from the Holocaust? Assessing Risks of Genocide and Political Mass Murder since 1955', *The American Political Science Review*, Vol. 97, No. 1, 2003, pp. 57–73.
Hennebel L., 'La Protection de l'"intégrité spirituelle" des indigènes: Réflexions sur l'Arrêt de la Cour Interaméricaine des Droits de l'Homme dans l'Affaire *Comunidad Moiwana c. Suriname* du 15 Juin 2005', *Revue Trimestrielle des Droits de l'Homme*, Vol. 2006, No. 66, 2006, pp. 253–76.
van den Herik L., 'The Schism between the Legal and the Social Concept of Genocide in Light of the Responsibility to Protect', available at: http://ssrn.com/abstract=1989847.
Hon K., 'Bringing Cultural Genocide in by the Backdoor: Victim Participation at the ICC', *Seton Hall Law Review*, Vol. 43, No. 1, 2013, pp. 359–407.
Jain N., 'Forced Marriage as a Crime Against Humanity: Problems of Definition and Prosecution', *Journal of International Criminal Justice*, Vol. 6, No. 5, 2008, pp. 1013–32.
James M., 'Uncomfortable Comparisons: The Canadian Truth and Reconciliation Commission in International Context', *Les Ateliers de l'Éthique / The Ethics Forum*, Vol. 5, No. 2, 2010, pp. 23–35.
Jones A., 'Gendercide and Genocide', *Journal of Genocide Research*, Vol. 2, No. 2, 2000, pp. 185–211.
Jouannet E., 'Le Droit International de la Reconnaissance', *Revue Générale de Droit International Public*, Vol. 116, No. 4, 2012, pp. 769–800.
Kingsbury B., ' "Indigenous Peoples" in International Law: A Constructivist Approach to the Asian Controversy', *The American Journal of International Law*, Vol. 92, No. 3, 1998, pp. 414–57.
Kletnicki A., 'Disappeared Children in Argentina: Genocidal Logic and Illegal Appropriation', *Journal of Genocide Research*, Vol. 8, No. 2, 2006, pp. 181–90.
van Krieken R., 'Rethinking Cultural Genocide: Aboriginal Child Removal and Settler-Colonial State Formation', *Oceania*, Vol. 75, No. 2, 2004, pp. 125–51.
Kukathas C., 'Are There Any Cultural Rights?', *Political Theory*, Vol. 20, No. 1, 1992, pp. 105–39.
Lemkin R., 'Genocide' *The American Scholar*, Vol. 15, No. 2, 1946, pp. 227–30.
Lenzerini F., 'Intangible Cultural Heritage: The Living Cultures of People', *The European Journal of International Law*, Vol. 22, No. 1, 2011, pp. 101–20.
Luban D., 'Hannah Arendt as a Theorist of International Criminal Law', *International Criminal Law Review*, Vol. 11, 2011, pp. 621–41.
Luban D. and Shue H., 'Mental Torture: A Critique of Erasures in U.S. Law', *The Georgetown Law Journal*, Vol. 100, No. 3, 2012, pp. 823–63.
MacDonald D.B. and Hudson G., 'The Genocide Question and Indian Residential Schools in Canada', *Canadian Journal of Political Science*, Vol. 45, No. 2, 2012, pp. 427–49.
Mako S., 'Cultural Genocide and Key International Instruments: Framing the Indigenous Experience', *International Journal on Minority and Group Rights*, Vol. 19, 2012, pp. 175–94.
Margalit A. and Raz J., 'National Self-Determination', *The Journal of Philosophy*, Vol. 87, No. 9, 1990, pp. 439–61.
May L., 'How Is Humanity Harmed by Genocide?', *International Legal Theory*, Vol. 10, 2004, pp. 1–25.
Mazower M., 'The Strange Triumph of Human Rights, 1993–1950', *The Historical Journal*, Vol. 47, No. 2, 2004, pp. 379–98.

Mégret F., 'Of Shrines, Memorials and Museums: Using the International Criminal Court's Victim Reparation and Assistance Regime to Promote Transitional Justice', *Buffalo Human Rights Law Review*, Vol. 16, 2010, pp. 1–56.

Milanović M., 'State Responsibility for Genocide: A Follow-Up', *European Journal of International Law*, Vol. 18, No. 4, 2007, pp. 669–94.

Morsink J., 'Cultural Genocide, the Universal Declaration and Minority Rights', *Human Rights Quarterly*, Vol. 21, No. 4, 1999, pp. 1009–60.

Mosby I., 'Administering Colonial Science: Nutrition Research and Human Biomedical Experimentation in Aboriginal Communities and Residential Schools, 1942–1952', *Histoire Sociale/Social History*, Vol. 46, No. 91, 2013, pp. 145–72.

Möschel M., 'Is the European Court of Human Rights' Case Law on Anti-Roma Violence "Beyond Reasonable Doubt"?', *Human Rights Law Review*, Vol. 12, No. 3, 2012, pp. 479–507.

Moses A.D., 'Conceptual Blockages and Definitional Dilemmas in the "Racial Century": Genocides of Indigenous Peoples and the Holocaust', *Patterns of Prejudice*, Vol. 36, No. 4, 2002, pp. 7–36.

Moses A.D., 'Genocide', *Australian Humanities Review*, No. 55, 2013, pp. 23–44.

Mundorff, K., 'Other Peoples' Children: A Textual and Contextual Interpretation of the Genocide Convention, Article 2 (e)', *Harvard International Law Journal*, Vol. 50, No. 1, 2009, pp. 61–127.

Nagy R.L., 'The Scope and Bounds of Transitional Justice and the Canadian Truth and Reconciliation Commission', *The International Journal of Transitional Justice*, Vol. 7, No. 1, 2013, pp. 52–73.

Negri S., 'Cultural Genocide in International Law: Is the Time Ripe for a Change?', *Transnational Dispute Management*, Vol. 10, No. 5, 2013, p. 9.

Odello M., 'Indigenous Peoples' Rights and Cultural Identity in the Inter-American Context', *The International Journal of Human Rights*, Vol. 16, No. 1, 2012, pp. 25–50.

Perry B., 'From Ethnocide to Ethnoviolence: Layers of Native American Victimization', *Contemporary Justice Review: Issues in Criminal, Social, and Restorative Justice*, Vol. 5, No. 3, 2002, pp. 231–47.

Pinzauti G., 'The European Court of Human Rights' Incidental Application of International Criminal Law and Humanitarian Law. A Critical Discussion of Kononov v. Latvia', *Journal of International Criminal Justice*, Vol. 6, No. 5, 2008, pp. 1043–60.

Powell C., 'What Do Genocides Kill? A Relational Conception of Genocide', *Journal of Genocide Research*, Vol. 9, No. 4, 2007, pp. 527–47.

Quirico O., 'The Evolving Notion of Persecution in the Law and Jurisprudence of International Criminal Tribunals', *The Italian Yearbook of International Law*, Vol. 21, 2011, pp. 203–18.

Riedlmayer A.J., 'Crimes of War, Crimes of Peace: Destruction of Libraries During and After the Balkan Wars of the 1990s', *Library Trends*, Vol. 56, No. 1, 2007, pp. 107–32.

Rosenberg S., 'Genocide Is a Process, Not an Event', *Genocide Studies and Prevention*, Vol. 7, No. 1, 2012, pp. 16–23.

Santalla Vargas E., 'An Overview of the Crime of Genocide in Latin American Jurisdictions', *International Criminal Law Review*, Vol. 10, No. 4, 2010, pp. 441–52.

Sautman B., '"Cultural Genocide" and Tibet', *Texas International Law Journal*, Vol. 38, No. 2, 2003, pp. 173–247.

Schabas W.A., 'State Policy as an Element of International Crimes', *The Journal of Criminal Law & Criminology*, Vol. 98, No. 3, 2008, pp. 953–82.

Shahabuddeen M., 'Does the Principle of Legality Stand in the Way of Progressive Development of Law?', *Journal of International Criminal Justice*, Vol. 2, No. 4, 2004, pp. 1007–17.

Short D., 'Australia: A Continuing Genocide?', *Journal of Genocide Research*, Vol. 12, Nos. 1/2, 2010, pp. 45–68.

Short D., 'Cultural Genocide and Indigenous Peoples: A Sociological Approach', *The International Journal of Human Rights*, Vol. 14, No. 6, 2010, pp. 833–48.

Simma B. and Alston B., 'The Sources of Human Rights Law: Custom, Jus Cogens, and General Principles', *Australian Yearbook of International Law*, Vol. 82, 1988–89, pp. 82–108.

Singleterry D., '"Ethnic Cleansing" and Genocidal Intent: A Failure of Judicial Interpretation?', *Genocide Studies and Prevention*, Vol. 5, No. 1, 2010, pp. 39–67.

Sirkin M., 'Expanding the Crime of Genocide to Include Ethnic Cleansing: A Return to Established Principles in Light of Contemporary Interpretations', *Seattle University Law Review*, Vol. 33, No. 2, 2010, pp. 489–526.

Skutnabb-Kangas T. and Dunbar R., 'Indigenous Children's Education as Linguistic Genocide and a Crime Against Humanity? A Global View', *Gáldu Čála: Journal of Indigenous Peoples Rights*, Vol. 1, 2010.

Starr S. and Brilmayer L., 'Family Separation as a Violation of International Law', *Berkeley, CT Journal of International Law*, Vol. 21, pp. 213–87.

Symonides J., 'Cultural Rights: A Neglected Category of Human Rights', *International Social Science Journal*, Vol. 50, No. 158, 2002, pp. 559–72.

Teitel R.G., 'Transitional Justice Genealogy', *Harvard Human Rights Journal*, Vol. 16, 2003, pp. 69–94.

Tournaye C., 'Genocidal Intent before the ICTY', *International and Comparative Law Quarterly*, Vol. 52, No. 2, 2003, pp. 447–62.

Triffterer O., 'Genocide: Its Particular Intent to Destroy in Whole or in Part the Group as Such', *Leiden Journal of International Law*, Vol. 14, No. 2, 2001, pp. 399–408.

Vrdoljak A.F., 'Genocide and Restitution: Ensuring Each Group's Contribution to Humanity', *European Journal of International Law*, Vol. 22, No. 1, 2011, pp. 17–47.

Vrdoljak A.F., 'Human Rights and Genocide: The Work of Lauterpacht and Lemkin in Modern International Law', *European Journal of International Law*, Vol. 20, No. 4, 2009, pp. 1163–94.

Wiessner S., 'The Cultural Rights of Indigenous Peoples: Achievements and Continuing Challenges', *European Journal of International Law*, Vol. 22, No. 1, pp. 121–40.

Wolfe P., 'Settler Colonialism and the Elimination of the Native', *Journal of Genocide Research*, Vol. 8, No. 4, 2006, pp. 387–409.

Zahar A., 'Commentary on the Judgment of the ICTY Appeals Chamber in the Case of Prosecutor v. Radislav Krstić', *Annotated Leading Cases of International Criminal Tribunals*, Vol. 19, 2004, pp. 629–38.

REPORTS

Australian Human Rights Commission, 'Bringing Them Home, Report of the National Inquiry into the Separation of Aboriginal and Torres Strait Islander Children from Their Families' (April 1997).

Comisión para el Esclaracimiento Histórico (CEH), Guatemala: Memoria del Silencio, 1999, available at: http://www.centrodememoriahistorica.gov.co/descargas/guatemala-memoria-silencio/guatemala-memoria-del-silencio.pdf.

Committee on Rights of Indigenous Peoples, 'Rights of Indigenous Peoples, Interim Report', in International Law Association Report of the Seventy-Third Conference (The Hague 2010) (International Law Association, London 2010).

Committee on Rights of Indigenous Peoples, 'Rights of Indigenous Peoples, Final Report', in International Law Association Report of the Seventy-Fifth Conference (Sofia 2012) (International Law Association, London 2012).

Germann Avocates et al., 'Implementing the UNESCO Convention of 2005 in the European Union', Study Requested by the European Parliament's Committee on Culture and Education, IP/B/CULT/IC/2009_057; PE 438.587 (2010).

Group of Experts for Cambodia, 'Report of the Group of Experts for Cambodia Established Pursuant to General Assembly Resolution 52/135' (1999).

Human Rights Council (17th session) 'Report of the Independent Expert in the Field of Cultural Rights, Farida Shaheed' (21 March 2011) A/HRC/17/38.

International Center for Transitional Justice, 'The Rabat Report: The Concept and Challenges of Collective Reparations' (2009).

International Commission of Inquiry on Darfur, 'Report of the International Commission of Inquiry on Darfur to the United Nations Secretary-General, Pursuant to Security Council Resolution 1564 of 18 September 2004' (2005).

International Commission of Jurists, 'Tibet and the Chinese People's Republic' (Geneva: International Commission of Jurists, 1960).

International Criminal Court, Office of the Prosecutor, 'Situation in Colombia: Interim Report' (2012).

International Criminal Court, Office of the Prosecutor 'Situation in Mali: Article 53(1) Report' (2013).

International Crisis Group, 'Bosnia's Dangerous Tango: Islam and Nationalism', Europe Briefing N°70 (2013).

International Law Association, 'Rights of Indigenous Peoples, Final Report', Sofia Conference (2012).

Interreligious Council in Bosnia-Herzegovina, 'Monitoring and Responses to Attacks on Religious Buildings and Other Holy Sites in BiH—Protection of Holy Sites: Annual Report' (Sarajevo, 2012).

Nolte G., Introductory Report for the Study Group on Treaties over Time: Jurisprudence of the International Court of Justice and Arbitral Tribunals of ad hoc Jurisdiction Relating to Subsequent Agreements and Subsequent Practice (2010).

Nolte G., Second Report for the ILC Study Group on Treaties over Time: Jurisprudence under Special Regimes Relating to Subsequent Agreements and Subsequent Practice (2011).

OSCE-Mission to Bosnia and Herzegovina, 'Tackling Hate Crimes: An Analysis of Bias-Motivated Incidents in Bosnia and Herzegovina with Recommendations' (Sarajevo, 2012).

Permanent Forum on Indigenous Issues, 'Indigenous Peoples and Boarding Schools: A Comparative Study (Prepared by Andrea Smith)' (2009) UN Doc. E/C.19/2009/CRP.1.

Permanent Forum on Indigenous Issues, 'Study on International Criminal Law and the Judicial Defence of Indigenous Peoples' Rights (Submitted by the Special Rapporteur Bartlomé Clavero)' (2011) UN Doc. E/C.19/2011/4.

Permanent Forum on Indigenous Issues (10th Session) 'Situation of Indigenous Peoples in Danger of Extinction in Colombia: Summary of the Report and Recommendations of the Mission by the Permanent Forum to Colombia' (2011) E/C.19/2011/3.

Redress, 'Collective Reparations: Concept and Principles', available at: http://www.redress.org/downloads/events/CollectiveReparationsMG.pdf.

Riedlmayer A.J., 'Destruction of Cultural Heritage in Bosnia-Herzegovina, 1992–1996: A Post-War Survey of Selected Municipalities' (International Criminal Tribunal for the Former Yugoslavia, Exhibit Number P486, 2002).

Schabas W.A., 'Preventing Genocide and Mass Killing: The Challenge for the United Nations' (London: Minority Rights Group International, 2006).

Sub-Commission on Prevention of Discrimination and Protection of Minorities (31st Session), 'Study on the Question of the Prevention and Punishment of the Crime of Genocide Submitted by the Special Rapporteur Nicodème Rushashyankiko' (1978) E/CN.4/Sub.2/416.

Sub-Commission on Prevention of Discrimination and Protection of Minorities (38th Session), 'Revised and Updated Report on the Question of the Prevention and Punishment of the Crime of Genocide Prepared by Mr. Benjamin Whitaker' (2 July 1985), UN Doc. E/CN.4/Sub.2/1985/6.

Truth and Reconciliation Commission of Canada, Canada, Aboriginal Peoples and Residential Schools: They Came for the Children (2012).

Truth and Reconciliation Commission of Canada, Interim Report (2012).

Truth and Reconciliation Commission (TRC) of Canada, 'Canada's Residential Schools: The Legacy', in The Final Report of the Truth and Reconciliation Commission of Canada, vol. 5 (2015).

Truth and Reconciliation Commission (TRC) of Canada, Honouring the Truth, Reconciling for the Future—Summary of the Final Report of the Truth and Reconciliation of Canada (2015).

United Nations Security Council, 'Final Report of the Commission of Experts Established Pursuant to Security Council Resolution 780 (1992)' (1994) UN Doc. S/1994/674.

United States Government, 'Bosnia and Herzegovina 2012 International Religious Freedom Report', available at: http://www.state.gov/documents/organization/208508.pdf.

OTHER SOURCES

American Anthropological Association, 'Declaration on Anthropology and Human Rights Committee' (1999).

van Boven T., The United Nations Basic Principles and Guidelines on the Right To a Remedy and Reparation for Victims of Gross Violations of International Human Rights Law and Serious Violations of International Humanitarian Law' (2010), available at: http://legal.un.org/avl/ha/ga_60-147/ga_60-147.html.

Broadcast Speech of Prime Minister Winston Churchill, (24 August 1941). Transcription available at: http://www.ibiblio.org/pha/timeline/410824awp.html.

Bumbaru D., 'Religious Heritage and Sacred Places', ICOMOS, available at: http://isceah.icomos.org/index.php?option=com_content&task=view&id=60&Itemid=27.

Eide A., 'Commentary to the Declaration on the Rights of Persons Belonging to National or Ethnic, Religious and Linguistic Minorities' (2001) (53rd Session) E/CN.4/Sub.2/AC.5/2001/2.

European Court of Human Rights, Research Division, *Cultural Rights in the Case-Law of the European Court of Human Rights* (2011).

Jung C., 'Transitional Justice for Indigenous People in a Non-Transitional Society' in *International Center for Transitional Justice Research Brief* (2009).

Lemkin R., 'Les Actes Constituant un Danger Général (Interétatique) Considères comme Délits des Droit des Gens', *Explications Additionnelles au Rapport Spécial Présenté à la Vème Conférence pour l'Unification du Droit Pénal à Madrid* (Paris: Pédone, 1933), English version available at: http://www.preventgenocide.org/lemkin/madrid1933-english.htm.

Nersessian D., 'Rethinking Cultural Genocide under International Law', *Human Rights Dialogue: "Cultural Rights"* (2005).

Okowa P., 'The Georgia v. Russia Case: A Commentary', *The Hague Justice Portal* (2009).

Prime Minister Kevin Rudd, MP - Apology to Australia's Indigenous Peoples (13 February 2008), available at: http://australia.gov.au/about-australia/our-country/our-people/apology-to-australias-indigenous-peoples.

Prime Minister Stephen Harper, 'Statement of Apology to Former Students of Indian Residential Schools' (8 June 2008).

Sartre, J-P. Statement *'On Genocide'*, Second Session of the Bertrand Russell International War Crimes Tribunal on Vietnam, Denmark (1967).

Stanton G., 'The Eight Stages of Genocide' (1998), available at: http://www.genocidewatch.org/aboutgenocide/8stagesofgenocide.html.

UNESCO, *Human Rights: Comments and Interpretations* (Paris: Unesco, 1948), UNESCO/PHS/3 (Rev.).

US Department of State, Bureau of European and Eurasian Affairs, *Washington Conference Principles on Nazi-Confiscated Art* (adopted 3 December 1998), available at http://www.lootedartcommission.com/Washington-principles.

Walker Kemezis K., *Not What Meets the Eye: Re-Examining Reconstruction in Postwar Bosnia and Herzegovina* (Masters Thesis, University of Washington, 2012).

Washington University School of Law, Whitney R. Harris World Law Institute, Crimes Against Humanity Initiative, *Proposed International Convention on the Prevention and Punishment of Crimes Against Humanity* (2010).

World Council of Churches and Programme to Combat Racism PCR 1/71 (E), 'Declaration of Barbados' (1971).

Index